Innovative Redesign and Reorganization
of Library Technical Services

Innovative Redesign and Reorganization of Library Technical Services

Paths for the Future and Case Studies

Edited by Bradford Lee Eden

LIBRARIES UNLIMITED

A Member of the Greenwood Publishing Group

Westport, Connecticut • London

Library of Congress Cataloging-in-Publication Data
Innovative redesign and reorganization of library technical services : paths for the future and case studies / edited by Bradford Lee Eden.
   p. cm.
  Includes index.
  ISBN 1–59158–092–7
   1. Technical services (Libraries)—Management. 2. Technical services (Libraries)—Case studies. 3. Academic libraries—United States—Administration—Case studies. I. Eden, Bradford Lee.
  Z688.5I56 2004
  025'.02—dc22   2003065948

British Library Cataloguing in Publication Data is available.

Library of Congress Catalog Card Number: 2003065948
ISBN: 1–59158–092–7

First published in 2004

Libraries Unlimited, 88 Post Road West, Westport, CT 06881
A member of the Greenwood Publishing Group, Inc.
www.lu.com

Printed in the United States of America

The paper used in this book complies with the Permanent Paper Standard issued by the National Information Standards Organization (Z39.48–1984).

10 9 8 7 6 5 4 3 2 1

Contents

Part 2: Case Studies

Introduction

This book explores the topic of innovative redesign and reorganization of library technical services departments by examining the past (literature reviews, staffing trends, change and adaptation), the present (case studies, surveys), and the future (name changes, roles, and metadata). It is a topic that has generated considerable discussion within the library profession, both theoretical and practical. On the theoretical side, the issues are numerous: use and abuse of professional or support staff and appropriate compensation and career ladders, decline of positions within and downsizing of library technical services departments, the abandonment of cataloging as a core course or curriculum in many ALA-accredited library schools, the mass retirement of professional librarians in the next five to ten years and loss of professional and institutional memory, quality versus quantity and access versus "following the rules" in cataloging production, and the option of outsourcing redundant activities as an increasingly viable and cost-effective alternative to staffing technical services departments. On the practical side, the issues are no less important: training and retraining (continuing education) for new and current professional and support staff, the proliferation of formats within which information is found and archived, the drastic reduction of qualified applicants and applications in the current job pool for open positions in library technical services, accomplishing more difficult and complex work with less staff, metadata and its incorporation and standardization along with the MARC format and AACR standards, and dealing with change or new service models on a more rapid and frequent basis.

These issues have been compounded by the "McDonaldization" of the library profession, a focus on providing service and customer satisfaction both in library schools and in libraries rather than on the building of collections or the organization and description of information, as in previous decades. With almost all state governments dealing with massive budget crises due to the fall of the stock market and the aftereffects of the terrorist attacks of September 11, 2001, libraries are challenged more than ever to do more with less. Library technical services departments have borne the brunt of staff reductions for the past two decades, and most are either operating at a minimal level of staff or are extremely understaffed. Despite the odds, many library technical services departments continue to maintain and even increase productivity of current staff through innovative workflow and design changes. For many, however, these are temporary measures that work only if there are no more cuts in staff and budget.

This book attempts to provide both theoretical and practical information, both research and case studies, on how library technical services departments are dealing with challenges in staffing, workflow, identity, and future in the current environment. Part 1, "Theory," focuses on the theoretical aspects of the dilemma by providing a review of the literature, some definitions of what library technical services is and does, surveys of trends and changes in the field, a discussion of quality cataloging for less, and a look at the future of cataloging in the twenty-first century. Part 2, "Case Studies," contains 15 examples of how library technical services departments have redesigned and reorganized themselves to deal with the many and varied challenges within the field and in their own local environments. These challenges range from database maintenance to new integrated library systems, from vision statements to mergers of departments, from career paths for support staff to workflow analysis, and from personnel turnover to budget situations. The majority of these library technical services departments are located in academic institutions; reorganization and challenges at an academic law library, the U.S. Government Printing Office, and an academic geospatial information repository provide some contrast and variety.

Each chapter is preceded by a short commentary by the editor that both summarizes and encapsulates the content of the chapter. It is hoped that this book will provide research and practical support for library technical services department heads and staff in their efforts to remain viable, functional, and important working units in today's libraries and larger organizational institutions.

Bradford Lee Eden, Ph.D.
Editor
Head, Web and Digitization Services
University Libraries, University of Nevada, Las Vegas

Part 1

Theory

1

Review of the Literature:
Technical Services Redesign and Reorganization

Laurie Lopatin

Editor's note: The author provides an extensive review of the literature regarding technical services redesign and reorganization. From changing roles of both professional librarians and support staff, to outsourcing and various types of reorganizational structures, to current and future issues in technical services, the author provides a thorough list of published research and case studies as an appropriate first chapter for this book.

Academic libraries have undergone many changes since the late 1980s. The implementation of integrated library systems, the prolific growth of information available in electronic form, the outsourcing of some aspects of technical services, the cutbacks in budgets, and the evolving roles of professional librarians and support staff are some of the major developments that have occurred. All of these changes amount to a veritable reorganization of the very structure of the academic library. This chapter presents a selective review of the literature from 1987 to 2002 on reorganization in academic libraries, focusing on trends and changes in technical services.

Academic Library Organization and Reorganization

Several factors have contributed to reorganization in academic libraries since the late 1980s, including the implementation of new library systems, automation, declining budgets, downsizing, and digital technology. However, this reorganization has been more of an evolution than a revolution. The traditional organizational structure of academic libraries has been hierarchical, where decision making is done at the top of the organization, and there are several layers of management. Gorman (1987) confirms that the organization of the majority of academic libraries in the United States is hierarchical, with an organizational division between technical and public services. He asserts that hierarchical structures are rigid and resistant to change, and he recommends a more decentralized organizational structure to increase efficiency. Townley maintains that "most academic libraries continue to be organized as bureaucracies . . . [which] concentrate authority and responsibility in a hierarchy" (1995, p. 155). He concurs that bureaucracies resist innovation. According to Worrell, "traditional management practices and organizational structures are no longer effective in today's changing environment" (1995, p. 351).

A survey of the literature shows a trend of academic libraries toward adopting flatter organizational structures with team management and the empowerment of support staff, although the rate of change has not been rapid. Larsen (1991), reporting on library organizational structures from 1985 to 1990, states that libraries have been slow to make major organizational changes. In Larsen's survey of academic library administrators, 79 percent report that their libraries continue to have public service divisions, and 81 percent have technical service divisions (1991, p. 83). Similar results were found by De Klerk and Euster (1989). Although it had been expected that the new technologies in libraries would lead to major reorganizations, their report on their survey of library directors in the late 1980s states that organizational change tends to be incremental. The authors report a continuing decline in the number of professional librarians in technical services, while public services departments are taking on more responsibilities. Their survey showed that paraprofessionals are doing work once reserved for professionals, such as bibliographic instruction and other reference responsibilities. In studying the changing roles of support staff in libraries in the 1990s, Younger found that they have performed a range of duties throughout libraries, in reference, circulation, cataloging, and selection. She states that "there is much evidence in libraries that considerable rethinking of responsibilities is taking place . . . that cataloging responsibilities previously handled by librarians are in fact being transferred, albeit slowly, to staff" (1996, p. 40).

In 1995, Eustis and Kenney (1996) surveyed ARL libraries about reorganization. They report that 17 out of 53 respondents were engaging or had engaged in library-wide reorganization, and 34 were engaged in the reorganization of specific units. They state that change in the mid-1990s was incremental, not dramatic. Factors influencing change were information technology (51 percent), declining resources (46 percent), and availability of networked information (40 percent) (1996, flyer p. 1). Almost half of the research libraries surveyed have reallocated personnel, mostly from technical services to public services. According to the authors, some outcomes of library reorganizations "have been the combining of units within the libraries . . . , elimination of some services, and a decreased emphasis on catalog maintenance and on the collection of print materials" (1996, flyer p. 2).

The case studies in the literature of academic libraries that reorganized in the late 1980s and the 1990s primarily involved moving from a hierarchical organizational structure to a flattened, team-based structure. For example, Diaz and Pintozzi (1999) describe the reorganization of the University of Arizona Library into a team-based organization, with a focus on customers. The authors state that the decentralized structure is flexible and is committed to continuous change. Britton describes the reorganization of the library faculty at California State University, Long Beach into a matrix organization, "a cross-functional, collegial group structure" (1987, p. 187). Davenport (1991) reports that at the State University of New York at Oswego there is a blurring of the division between technical services and public services, as all librarians provide reference service and are involved in aspects of technical services. Cook and Farthing (1995) outline the reorganization at the Appalachian State University Library. The new organizational structure there features a flattened organization, with faculty and staff in work groups. As at SUNY Oswego, most library faculty at Appalachian State have public service and technical service responsibilities. Shaughnessy (1996) describes restructuring of the library at the University of Minnesota. To streamline library services, the organization was flattened into a team-based structure and several senior administrative and middle management positions were eliminated. The author discusses the issue of support staff playing a greater role and taking on some responsibilities that were formerly performed by professional librarians.

Changes and Trends in Technical Services in the 1990s

Automation, shrinking budgets, and increased demand for library services have had profound impacts on academic library technical services during the past 15 years. "The search for savings and changes in the computer and telecommunications industries are still among the triggers for change in technical services" (Allen and Williams 1995, p. 164). Diedrichs states that the speed of technological change, and "changing patron expectations, demand a new approach to technical services" (1998, p. 113). Several themes emerge from a review of the literature, including blurring of the lines between public and technical services, outsourcing, and larger roles for support staff.

Technical Services and Public Services

Several authors discuss the emergence of new organizational structures in the 1990s that have less rigid divisions between public and technical services. Younger and Gapen discuss advantages and disadvantages of the separation of public and technical services departments, which, although allowing for efficient processing of materials, "has created a structure that is not as responsive as it could be to user needs or technological innovations especially under conditions of restricted budgets" (1998, p. 171). Hirshon states that "libraries must abandon the conventional library organization chart, which neatly divides public and technical services" (1991, p. 50). He recommends "a flatter organizational pattern with managers close to their operations [which] will increase the information flow" (1991, p. 52). Dumont (1989) and Fiste and Thornton (1993) assert that the implementation of online library systems enhances collaboration between public services and technical services departments and leads to less hierarchical organizational structures. McCombs (1992) also believes that libraries are becoming more integrated due to automation. Technical service librarians are becoming more involved in public services and collection development. She predicts that "as collection development, user services, and technical services functions begin to converge . . . organization charts will undoubtedly begin to change" (1992, p. 143).

In fact, there has been a movement of technical service librarians to public services. Williams (1991) maintains that technology has allowed libraries to increase productivity in technical services, while creating demands for new services in public services. He sees the reallocation of librarians from technical to public services to fill those needs. He states that, "whatever else happens, the professional presence in technical services is likely to be diminished, and the roles that librarians play in these departments will change" (1991, p. 37). Echoing this theme, Diedrichs (1998) writes that patrons expect quick access to materials, often in electronic form, causing pressure on public service librarians. "In many libraries, that pressure has been translated into the need to transfer positions from technical services to public services to meet the demand for services" (1998, p. 113).

Changing Roles of Professional Librarians and Support Staff

Another trend over the past 15 years has been the evolving roles of professional librarians and support staff in technical services. While support staff have taken on much of the routine work, and even some of the more complex tasks once the sole purview of professionals, technical services librarians have assumed wider roles, both within and outside of technical services. Shrinking resources and rising user expectations of library services are factors in this trend. Gorman asserts that a positive change is "the movement away from professional involvement in many areas. . . . We can see . . . [this] in the turning over of copy cataloguing, most aspects of acquisitions, and almost all circulation activities to paraprofessionals and clerical staff" (1994, p. 40). This allows librarians to concentrate on more professional responsibilities.

Technical Services Librarians

Technical services librarians are becoming more involved in managerial activities. Sellberg states that "the line between cataloger and cataloging manager is blurring. . . . In addition to producing cataloging records, new cataloging librarians are being asked to prepare budgets, deal with vendors, manage projects, and work with other kinds of specialists to solve library-wide problems" (1995, p. 36). Mohr and Schuneman write that paraprofessionals assuming responsibilities that were formerly professional "reflected emerging thought about the proper role of the professional librarian in technical services—and in the profession in general—as managers, leaders, and innovators, less involved than previously in day-to-day operations" (1997, p. 206). Eskoz (1990) reports the results of a survey of academic library catalog departments in 1986–1987. Besides being involved in cataloging activities, 45 percent of the respondents reported that professionals had a supervisory role in the department (1990, p. 385).

Buttlar and Garcha (1998) surveyed academic library catalog librarians in 1997 to determine how their job responsibilities had changed in the past 10 years. More than 70 percent of the catalogers surveyed said that their primary role was creating bibliographic records (1998, p. 314), and more than 90 percent were routinely involved in descriptive cataloging, assigning call numbers and subject headings (p. 318). However, many were also involved in managerial responsibilities. Approximately 78 percent of catalog librarians reported that they designed cataloging policies and procedures, and 78.1 percent supervised support staff (1998, p. 315), which is 73 percent higher than in the survey reported by Eskoz (1990) 10 years earlier. In addition, the more recent survey showed that catalogers were becoming more involved in activities formerly performed by systems librarians, such as "developing specifications for microcomputer applications" and managing network interfaces (Buttlar and Garcha 1998, p. 315). Buttlar and Garcha conclude that besides their traditional responsibilities of original cataloging and authority work, catalog librarians "are viewed as managers, policymakers, upgraders of the database, bibliographic instructors, collection development librarians, automation librarians, and more" (1998, p. 320).

Support Staff in Technical Services

What specific tasks are support staff performing in technical service departments? Several surveys asked that question. Eskoz's survey of academic library catalog departments found a modest trend toward support staff being involved in complex cataloging. In the 1986–1987 survey, 77.5 percent of the responding libraries reported that support staff were solely responsible for copy cataloging (1990, p. 388). Thirty-five percent had both professionals and support staff engaged in original cataloging and assigning call numbers and subject headings (1990, p. 388).

Oberg et al. (1992) targeted the role of paraprofessionals in academic libraries in their survey in 1990. Twenty-five percent of the libraries reported more paraprofessionals and fewer professional librarians than in the past (1992, p. 221). Eighty-eight percent of the ARL libraries responding schedule paraprofessionals at the reference or information desk (1992, p. 222). As for cataloging responsibilities, 92 percent of the ARL libraries surveyed have paraprofessionals perform copy cataloging, and 51 percent have paraprofessionals do original descriptive cataloging (1992, p. 224). Thirty-six percent had paraprofessionals assign subject headings and classification numbers (1992, p. 224), which is similar to the findings of Eskoz (1990). Also, 20 percent of the libraries surveyed assign collection development responsibilities to paraprofessionals (Oberg et al. 1992, p. 233). "In both technical and public services, paraprofessionals are routinely assigned tasks that in the past they were rarely if ever allowed to perform" (1992, p. 232).

Mohr and Schuneman (1997) surveyed catalog departments in ARL libraries in 1995 to determine the role played by paraprofessionals in original cataloging. They found that 74.7 percent of the responding libraries had paraprofessionals do original descriptive cataloging (1997, p. 209), which is 50 percent higher than the findings by Oberg et al. (1992) only five years earlier. Approximately 50 percent of the respondents in Mohr and Schuneman's study had paraprofessionals assign call numbers for nonfiction works (1997, p. 209). Also, 49 percent of the responding libraries had paraprofessionals assign subject headings (1997, p. 210), which is approximately 43 percent higher than in the surveys of Eskoz (1990) and Oberg et al. (1992). In a survey of ARL libraries in 1998, Bordeianu and Seiser found that 67 percent of the respondents used paraprofessionals in original cataloging activities (1999, p. 539). The results of these surveys indicate that support staff were increasingly becoming involved in original cataloging in the 1990s. Mohr and Schuneman conclude that the trend of paraprofessionals engaged in aspects of original cataloging "will no doubt continue as economic pressures require that libraries become ever more cost-effective" (1997, p. 217).

With support staff handling more complex responsibilities, several authors discuss the importance of the training and education of paraprofessionals (Younger 1996; Rider 1996; Chervinko 1992; Bordeianu and Seiser 1999). Chervinko (1992) outlines a training program to teach original cataloging to experienced paraprofessionals. Bordeianu and Seiser (1999) surveyed ARL libraries to determine the educational requirements of paraprofessional catalogers. Nineteen percent of the responding libraries had postsecondary educational requirements for paraprofessional copy catalogers, ranging from two to four years, while 44.8 percent of the responding libraries had no postsecondary requirements (1999, p. 536). Thirty-one percent of the responding libraries required postsecondary education for paraprofessionals engaged in original cataloging, the majority requiring four years of college and/or a bachelor's degree (1999, p. 538). The results of the survey demonstrate that while some libraries have postsecondary educational requirements for paraprofessionals, most do not. Bordeianu and Seiser conclude that "the higher-level paraprofessional catalogers usually reach their position by promotion from within, presumably after learning the necessary skills and advancing to the next stage of cataloging complexity" (1999, p. 540).

Outsourcing

Another trend discussed in the literature is outsourcing of some or all of technical services operations. Hirshon and Winters define outsourcing as "a method employed by an organization to hire or contract with an outside individual, vendor, or agency to perform an operation or process rather than using in-house staff to accomplish the task" (1996, p. 15). Two main reasons for outsourcing are to reduce costs and to increase productivity. Wilson (1995) presents a detailed literature review of outsourcing projects from the 1960s to the 1990s. Baker (1998) provides a brief history of outsourcing aspects of technical services and an overview of outsourcing in the late 1990s. He states that "outsourcing has the potential to reduce costs, increase customer satisfaction and provide effective and efficient improvements" (1998, p. 38).

The Extent of Outsourcing

Dunkle (1996) discusses various issues involved in outsourcing, including reasons for outsourcing, managing outsourcing projects, and working with vendors. Dunkle maintains that selective outsourcing is a viable option for many institutions, but total outsourcing is not. "Most libraries will find that the risks [of total outsourcing] outweigh the advantages" (1996, p. 41). Scheschy (1999) describes outsourcing as a strategic partnership among the library, the vendor, and the bibliographic utility, and she outlines ways to make the partnership successful. She states that libraries generally outsource retrospective conversion and special materials such as foreign language materials. "What is relatively new is the outsourcing of selected, or even all, routine copy cataloging by libraries where this function had traditionally been done in-house" (1999, p. 32).

Libby and Caudle report on a 1997 survey of outsourcing in academic libraries. Twenty-eight percent of the responding libraries were currently outsourcing or had in the past, and 19 percent were currently considering outsourcing (1997, p. 556). Seventy percent of the libraries that outsource gave the reason of insufficient staff to complete the work in a timely manner, 21 percent lacked in-house expertise, and 30 percent outsourced as a cost savings measure (1997, p. 557). Only 18 percent outsource all cataloging operations, including physical processing, while 45 percent outsource retrospective conversion (1997, p. 558). Slightly more than half (52 percent) of the libraries responded that the outsourcing project "provided the desired result" (1997, p. 558), indicating that outsourcing was not deemed entirely successful in almost half of the libraries surveyed. Libby and Caudle conclude that, "outsourcing does not seem to be a strong trend in academic libraries," with only 33 libraries out of 117 employing outsourcing (1997, p. 559).

Sweetland (2001) presents an overview of outsourcing library technical services, including issues such as cataloging costs and benefits, the potential for increasing productivity, and quality issues. He reviews several surveys of outsourcing, including the one by Libby and Caudle (1997), and concludes that although in some institutions outsourcing has achieved its goals, "the evidence suggests that contracting out library work is not a panacea, and in fact it may not reduce costs while it may reduce quality" (2001, p. 173). Even though outsourcing technical services has received mixed reviews, it is a viable option for cost savings and increasing productivity. Scheschy maintains that "despite the apprehension of catalogers that libraries are compromising their standards and losing control of the tool that has been at the heart of information retrieval, the outsourcing of cataloging is here to stay" (1999, p. 32).

Outsourcing: Case Studies

The most famous case study of outsourcing in academic libraries is that of Wright State University. In 1993 Wright State University reported that they had outsourced their entire catalog department to OCLC Techpro, the first academic library to outsource its entire catalog department. The reasons given for this drastic measure were to increase production, improve quality, and cut costs. Eleven full-time positions in the department were abolished, and the university saved $200,000–$250,000 per year, with the savings redirected to other library services (Hirshon 1994, pp. 17–18). One professional librarian and one support staff member were retained to manage the project.

The participants at Wright State University wrote about the reasons for outsourcing and the issues involved. Winters, the Associate University Librarian, explained that WSU had a large backlog of uncataloged titles and low staff productivity, and the quality of the cataloging at WSU was problematic. After exploring other alternatives, it was felt that complete outsourcing would be the best alternative for the university. Winters believes that "mundane cataloging will be relegated to outsourcing while professionals will be freed up to give the attention that must be given to writing true description of new electronic resources. . . . They will also manage cataloging contracts" (1994, p. 370). Wilhoit (1994), the head of the Bibliographic Control Department, describes the outsourcing procedures used with OCLC Techpro, including procedures for serials, title changes, and quality control. Wilhoit concludes "if we use the . . . measures . . . , cutting costs and improving services, then outsourcing has been an unqualified success for us" (1994, p. 73). Hirshon (1994), the university librarian, discusses reengineering as an organizational change theory and outsourcing as a reengineering strategy. He discusses outsourcing at Wright State, stating that unlike other academic libraries that outsource "add-on" projects, Wright State outsourced all cataloging of new titles. However, he maintains that "while complete cataloging outsourcing was an effective option for Wright State University, other institutions may wish to pursue variations on this option" (1994, p. 18).

There are many other case studies of outsourcing aspects of technical services in the literature. For example, El-Sherbini (1995) discusses outsourcing the cataloging of Slavic language books at Ohio State University, Horenstein (1999) describes outsourcing of copy cataloging at Adelphi University, Hyslop (1995) discusses outsourcing of copy cataloging at Michigan State University, Hill (1998) describes a project to outsource the cataloging of Special Collections monographs at the University of Alabama, and Wilson (1995) describes the outsourcing of copy cataloging at Stanford University.

Technical Services Reorganizations in the 1990s: Case Studies

Case studies of technical services reorganizations in the 1990s show a general trend of technical services departments to reorganize into teams, merge units within technical services, and engage in joint projects with public services departments. The goals of many of the reorganizations were to increase productivity and flexibility and to streamline operations.

Team-Based Structures

There are several case studies of academic library technical services departments that reorganized in the 1990s from hierarchical structures to more flattened, team-based structures. Crooker, Killheffer, and Mandour state that "the technical services departments at Yale were reorganized to adapt to the introduction of a NOTIS integrated online system and to take advantage of a new managerial philosophy which was revolutionizing the business world – the self-managing team" (1991, p. 27). Goals of the reorganization at Yale included greater productivity and flexibility. In the new structure, the acquisitions and catalog departments merged into the Processing Services Department, which consisted of 13 self-managed teams, based on subject, language, and geographic area, or constituency (Rare Books). "Each team is responsible for the total processing of all forms of material falling within its purview" (1991, p. 31). The authors explain how self-managed teams work, and they conclude that, "the concept of self-management has improved the job satisfaction of staff and given the organization added flexibility and creativity" (1991, p. 41).

The Catalog Department of Harvard University's Widener Library was reorganized into teams in 1993. Parallel language and area divisions were established in the Catalog Department and the Collection Development Department in a team-based model, with the goal of "improving communication, coordination, and balance between the two departments" (Clack 1995, p. 439).

In the mid-1990s the technical services department at the Pennsylvania State University Library, which had been highly hierarchical, was reorganized into self-managed teams, "after the adoption of Continuous Quality Improvement (CQI is a version of Total Quality Management) at Penn State" (Bazirjian and Stanley 2001, p. 132). The goals of the reorganization were to streamline processes, increase efficiency, and be more customer-oriented. Several articles were written about the reorganization. Stanley and Branche-Brown (1995) describe the reorganization of the Acquisitions Department into self-managed teams, using CQI decision-making models for evaluating workflow. The authors discuss advantages of the new structure, such as having staff involved in decision making, "improved efficiencies, and employees who creatively contribute to the success of the organization" (1995, p. 424). The main disadvantage mentioned is the amount of time it takes for department members to learn about working in teams, which is "a complete cultural reorientation" (1995, p. 424). Bednar, Brisson, and Hewes (2000) describe the reorganization of the Catalog Department at Penn State into five self-managed teams based on cataloging formats, or type of material, including the Maps Team, Serials Team, and Monographs Team. The organization of the department became flatter, from five levels of hierarchy to two, and there was a reduction in staff from 45 to 36 full-time employees. Catalog librarians assumed additional responsibilities, such as collection development. The authors report that by flattening the organization, service was improved and there was a significant increase in productivity.

In 1999, four years after technical services reorganized into teams at Penn State, there was a formal assessment of the teams to determine their effectiveness. Bazirjian and Stanley (2001) discuss several issues regarding the functioning of the self-managed teams, including leadership, performance, morale, and personnel issues. A performance management tool was developed, which helped to more clearly define "the role of the department head versus the team . . . and [to] provide the teams with a clear understanding of their roles and responsibilities" (2001, pp. 142–143). Freeborn and Mugridge (2002) describe a task force established in 1999 to examine the monographic cataloging workflow after the reorganization of the Catalog Department at Penn State into teams. The task force was charged with making recommendations to increase efficiency in the cataloging process. The authors outline the recommendations of the task force, including training of acquisitions staff in some cataloging activities to streamline operations and to "promote an integrated workflow" (2002, p. 40).

Centralized Structure

The team-based organization was not successful in all libraries. After trying a team-based structure for several years, the Catalog Department at the University of Iowa Libraries was reorganized into a more centralized structure. Dewey (1998) describes several reorganizations of the Catalog Department. In

1988 the department, which had been hierarchical, was organized into teams, including the Humanities and Art Unit, Area Studies, and the Special Materials Unit. In 1990, during a library-wide reorganization, the cataloging teams became part of the newly created Science, Social Science, and Humanities Divisions. The divisions consisted of catalogers, collection development librarians, and public service librarians. Then, to streamline cataloging and increase productivity, cataloging was reorganized again in 1993. Cataloging activities were centralized under one manager. Catalog librarians were removed from copy cataloging and became more involved in management activities, collection development, and user services.

Acquisitions Services

In an effort to streamline operations and increase efficiency, several academic libraries have either merged the acquisitions department with another technical services department or disbanded the acquisitions department altogether. Bazirjian (1993) describes the reorganization of technical services at Syracuse University in 1991. Prior to reorganization, there were separate catalog and acquisitions departments, each having their own department head. With the implementation of the NOTIS library system and with a goal of streamlining and eliminating duplication of effort, the acquisitions and catalog departments were merged into Bibliographic Services. Serials functions, including serials cataloging, were combined in the Serials Unit, primarily to eliminate duplication of effort.

Courtney and Jenkins (1998)describe the reorganization of collection development and acquisitions at the University of Dayton in 1995–1996. This was part of a library-wide restructuring "intended to flatten the organization, establish a participative, team based management system, and ensure that all library functions were responsive to the needs of the library's primary clientele" (1998, p. 288). Before the reorganization, with the exception of the reference collection, faculty in the academic departments selected books for the library. After the reorganization, all librarians participated in collection development in collaboration with teaching faculty and were assigned subject areas. The authors state that the procedures of the acquisitions unit were streamlined.

Niles (1992) outlines the establishment of a Collection Management Office and the disbanding of the Acquisitions Department at the University of Louisville in 1991. Personnel from the Acquisitions Department were reassigned to the monographs department, the serials department, or the new collection management office, which handled functions such as collection development, vendor selection for acquisitions, and fund management. This reorganization occurred in conjunction with the implementation of the NOTIS library system, and it was "built upon earlier efforts to distribute more efficiently the responsibilities for acquisitions, collection management and development, and cataloging" (1992, p. 379).

Joint Projects

Several authors describe joint projects between technical services and public services departments. Alexander and DeForest (1999) describe the close working relationship between public and technical services brought about by a project to catalog government documents at the University of Alabama, using MARCIVE as the vendor. The authors outline the planning and implementation of the project. Thompson discusses the Cataloging Advisory Group (CAG) at the University of Alabama Libraries. CAG is a discussion group that includes personnel from public services and technical services, and it "actively provides assistance in establishing catalog department policies for cataloging and processing materials" (1999, p. 125). This group was established to facilitate communication between public services and technical services, and it "has become an integral and important part of the management of the cataloging process" at the University of Alabama (1999, p. 131).

Flexible Management Approach

A different approach to increasing the productivity of a catalog department is described by Benaud, Steinhagen, and Moynahan (2000), with the introduction of flexible management at the University of New Mexico General Library Catalog Department in 1997. Due to a reduction of staff in the Catalog Department and concern about being marginalized, "cataloging managers decided to become more proactive" (2000, p. 282). Focusing on "delivering the products needed by public service in a more efficient and timely manner" (2000, p. 282), they introduced a flexible scheduling option, telecommuting, and a point system. Under the point system, catalog department staff (not faculty) were assigned points to measure production, with "different point values . . . assigned depending on the complexity of the cataloging required" (2000, p. 285). A minimum of 240 points per month was established. Once a staff cataloger reached 240 points, he or she was finished with work for the month. "Under the point system, the most efficient catalogers became even more efficient. They fully embraced the point system and were able to radically reduce their work hours" (2000, p. 294). The authors discuss positive and negative outcomes of flexible management, and they write that flextime helped increase efficiency in the department.

Current and Future Issues in Technical Services

What are some of the current issues facing technical service departments, and what will these departments look like in the future?

Ahronheim and Marko (2000) envision that technical services for the first decade of the twenty-first century will have a flatter organizational structure and collaborative relationships within the department and with other departments.

Flexibility of staff and management skills will be important. Younger and Gapen (1998) predict continued redesigns of technical services, including reductions in staff, streamlined workflows, and the use of outsourcing to increase efficiency and cut costs. In addition, "team-based structures and cross-functional assignments will be employed" (1998, p. 177). While the role of support staff will continue to grow, professional catalog librarians will be involved not only in cataloging activities but also in such activities as collection development and public services.

The explosion of online resources will be a significant factor in changes in technical services in the future. In fact, Younger and Gapen assert, "The library profession and technical services staff, in particular, must assume an aggressive role in providing effective intellectual access to these [digital] resources" (1998, p. 176). The authors see a new role for technical service librarians in providing access to online resources through development of metadata standards.

Metadata

Several authors discuss metadata and how libraries and technical service departments are and will be working with it in the future. What is metadata? "Simply defined, 'metadata' means data about data . . . "the term 'metadata' commonly refers to any data that aids in the identification, description, and location of networked electronic resources" (Hudgins, Agnew, and Brown 1999, p. 1). Metadata can be imbedded in a document or exist separately.

Different communities inside and outside of the library field have created various metadata standards for resource description. The MARC format widely used in libraries is a metadata standard developed in the 1960s. Hudgins, Agnew, and Brown (1999) describe metadata standards such as Text Encoding Initiative (TEI), Dublin Core, MPEG-4 and MPEG-7 for Audio and Video, Government Information Locator Service (GILS), and FGDC Content Standard for Digital Geospatial Metadata (CSDGM), and outline their potential for libraries. Smits (1999) provides an overview of types of metadata, concentrating on metadata used for describing cartographic and spatial data. Eden (2002b) outlines different metadata standards, their purpose and goals, and key projects. He also discusses issues such as the interoperability of metadata standards, using metadata to build an enriched library catalog (including natural language recognition technology), and the use of metadata in search engines.

Calhoun states that " today library technical services departments have a new imperative: to carry forward their role to organize the world's information and apply it in the digital age" (2002, p. 195). She asserts that with the proliferation of online resources, "it is therefore a future with metadata in it" (2002, p. 195). According to El-Sherbini, metadata "is now generally acknowledged as being vital in order to enable effective retrieval of information in our increasingly complex, digitally-networked information environment" (2000, p. 181).

Fietzer (1998) addresses how technical service librarians will cope with issues that the growth of metadata has generated. He discusses such topics as rights management and data integrity. Librarians can be involved in developing metadata dictionaries, "identifying and defining metadata schemes, [and] analyzing and mapping across various systems" (1998, p. 9). Fietzer advises that librarians will have to acquire new skills to work with various metadata standards. Eden (1999) discusses issues involved in the integration of metadata standards other than MARC into the library online catalog. A goal is to emerge with a uniform method of search that will access information contained in diverse metadata records. Fietzer (1998), Eden (1999), and Ahronheim (1999) advocate that librarians collaborate with constituencies inside and outside the library field in the development of metadata standards. Ahronheim states that, "metadata opportunities for technical service units are limitless as are the decisions needed to take advantage of them" (1999, p. 6).

Ahronheim and Marko, in describing the catalog department of the future, state that catalog librarians will "combine traditional cataloging skills with new tasks, expertise and relationships" (2000, p. 219). They suggest that a metadata specialist, who could be a cataloger or other technical services staff member, "will work collaboratively, as a member of a project team, either integrating existing resources into the library system or helping in the resource's creation" (2000, p. 220). They further forecast that the metadata specialist will move away from MARC and AACR2 and develop and work with other metadata standards. McCue (1997) also discusses the role of a metadata specialist. She states that catalog librarians have concentrated on one type of metadata, the MARC record. It is important for catalogers to keep up with other metadata structures and "to see themselves as metadata specialists, just as comfortable exploring the FGDC standards for spatial data as they are navigating the maze of MARC tags" (1997, p. 228).

Metadata Projects

Several libraries have been involved in digitization projects that entail developing and working with different metadata standards. Hudgins, Agnew, and Brown (1999) present guidelines for a library metadata project. They discuss the role of metadata, staffing of the project, choosing the appropriate metadata standard, metadata record design, and planning workflow. They assert that "catalog librarians should be involved, and in most cases manage, the design and implementation of metadata cataloging projects . . . [which are] usually critical components of a digitization or electronic publishing project" (1999, pp. 41–42).

Hudgins and Macklin (2000) describe two metadata projects at the Georgia Institute of Technology Library involving the digitization of special collections materials. One project involved multiple subjects and formats; the other was a collection of photographs. Encoded Archival Description (EAD) was chosen as the metadata standard for both projects, and catalog librarians and archives staff created the EAD records. The authors describe how the digitization projects were integrated into the regular workflow of technical services and archives. Woodley describes a project at the California State University, Northridge, Library to "create a digital archive documenting the history and growth of the San Fernando Valley" (2002, p. 200). Two part-time catalog librarians were hired to create and work with a metadata standard, which was based on Dublin Core, to provide efficient access to the archive. The author outlines issues of staffing, software, and hardware used in the project.

Glogoff and Forger (2001) describe digital projects at the University of Arizona Library, including a collection of community-based World Wide Web exhibits. Other campus units also had digital resource collections, and there was a desire to manage all these resources. The authors describe the use of such metadata structures as Dublin Core, Gateway to Educational Media (GEM), IMS Metadata, and the Multimedia Educational Resource for Learning and Online Teaching (MERLOT) to manage these digital resources. They conclude, "the ability to manage the vast arrays of digital resources on the Internet is a reality" (2001, p. 13).

Several digitization projects are described in *Cataloging the Web: Metadata, AACR, and MARC 21*, edited by Jones, Ahronheim, and Crawford (2002). In this book, Boehr (2002) describes the development of metadata by the National Library of Medicine for use with online resources issued by NLM. Garrison (2002) outlines the Colorado Digitization Project, a virtual collection of government documents, manuscripts, diaries, and maps. Eden discusses the Instructional Management System (IMS) standard, which was developed to assist "the developers and creators of educational products in the production of interactive, Internet-based 'courseware' that is platform independent" (2002a, p. 123). Mayer describes VARIATIONS, a digital music library at Indiana University, which "provides access to over 6,000 titles of near-CD-quality audio to users . . . " (2002, p. 149).

Recent Reorganizations in Technical Services: Case Studies

Swanekamp (2000) discusses changes and trends in the Catalog Department at Yale University. She reports that the Catalog Department teams—consisting of professionals, support staff, and students—work efficiently. Yale is implementing a new library management system in the early 2000s, and the author sees this "as offering an opportunity to increase our use of technology to do our work more efficiently and effectively" (2000, p. 382). She discusses issues of cataloging digital resources. Two new positions were created to handle online resources. The electronic resources catalog librarian develops strategies for cataloging digital resources, and the art imaging cataloger does cataloging work in the art image database using the VRA (Visual Resources Association) core metadata standard.

Eden and Bierman (2002) describe the reorganization of Technical Services at the University of Nevada, Las Vegas Libraries Library in 1999 with the opening of a new library building. The Acquisitions Department was moved to the Collection Development and Management Division. The Catalog Department (later renamed Bibliographic and Metadata Services Department) and the Library Systems Department were grouped in a new division named KAM (Knowledge Access Management). Routine cataloging of print materials is outsourced "in order to free cataloging staff for future digital directions" (2002, p. 93). In fact, there is an emphasis on Web initiatives and digital projects. The professional and support staff are trained in HTML coding and are responsible for maintaining the library Web site. On average, cataloging staff spend 60 percent of their time on cataloging responsibilities and 40 percent on Web site responsibilities (2002, p. 92). A digitization center was established in the library, and a new position was created—a digital projects librarian. Future directions of the Catalog Department include having cataloging personnel take "an active role in the scanning and digitization of library resources" (2002, p. 102) and training cataloging staff in various metadata formats. The authors state, "The possibilities for the future in the emerging digital information world are limited only by our imagination and initiative" (2002, p. 100).

Martin (2000) discusses changes in the Catalog Department at McMaster University. In the 1990s, as professional catalogers retired or moved into public services, library assistants assumed their responsibilities. Now, original cataloging and database maintenance are performed by library assistants working in teams. The author states that staff members have to take on the responsibility of keeping up with cataloging issues and trends. Martin also discusses cataloging Internet resources, stating that there is a task force looking into technical and public service issues of providing access to electronic resources.

Condron (2001) describes changes in the Technical Services Department at Tufts University. In 1999 the Acquisitions and Cataloging Departments were reorganized into two different departments—Current Processes (CP) and Information Management Initiatives (IMI). Tasks of CP staff include ordering and receiving materials and routine cataloging. IMI staff perform complex cataloging and new work, such as cataloging Internet resources. Condron asserts that the reorganization has helped to "streamline work and eliminate many redundancies, ensure appropriate levels of work, reduce total staff, and build in time for new work (specifically that having to do with digital libraries)" (2001, p. 141). Approximately 25 percent of time is allowed for each IMI team member to participate in such activities as digitization projects and focus groups. Catalog librarians are encouraged to educate themselves about other metadata standards. Condron states that "catalogers must learn new skills to empower us to catalog in the new millennium" (2001, p. 133).

Lee-Smeltzer (2000) outlines changes in cataloging in three academic libraries: Oregon State University, the University of Houston, and Colorado State University. Besides original cataloging responsibilities, professional catalog librarians in the three libraries are involved in formulating policies and procedures. In addition, the catalog librarians at the University of Houston work at the reference desk and have collection development responsibilities. Support staff are taking on more complex work that was previously the responsibility of professional catalog librarians. The author discusses issues concerning cataloging Internet resources, digitization projects at the libraries, and the involvement of catalog librarians in metadata creation. The author concludes that managing online resources will remain a challenge for technical services, and "the need for designing more streamlined and cost-effective cataloging operations by using technology, creating flexible organizational structures, and employing and developing a staff with skills and capability for performing more complex work will continue to be critical in cataloging management in academic libraries" (2000, p. 329).

Conclusion

Academic libraries and technical service departments have been reorganizing from rigid hierarchical and departmental structures to more flexible, flattened, team-based structures. Technical service operations are becoming more efficient and cost effective, with reductions in staff, outsourcing, and the increased use of support staff to handle more complex responsibilities. Technical service professionals are taking on managerial and public service responsibilities. A new and important role for technical services departments is that of providing access to the vast array of online resources, either through cataloging Internet resources with the MARC format or by becoming involved in digitization projects using other metadata standards for resource description. "Managing digital information will be the greatest new challenge for libraries in the new century, and technical services will play a major role in providing intellectual access and preservation of data" (Younger and Gapen 1998, p. 174).

References

Ahronheim, Judith R. 1999. "Technical services management issues in the metadata environment." *Technicalities* 19 (6): 4–6.

Ahronheim, Judith, and Lynn Marko. 2000. "Exploding out of the MARC box: Building new roles for cataloging departments." *Cataloging & Classification Quarterly* 30 (2/3): 217–225.

Alexander, Mary S., and Janet DeForest. 1999. "Dismantling the wall between technical and public services." *Journal of Library Administration* 29 (2): 75–84.

Allen, Nancy H., and James F. Williams II. 1995. "The future of technical services: an administrative perspective." In *Advances in librarianship*. San Diego: Academic Press.

Baker, Barry B. 1998. "Resource sharing: Outsourcing and technical services." *Technical Services Quarterly* 16 (2): 35–45.

Bazirjian, Rosann. 1993. "Automation and technical services organization." *Library Acquisitions: Practice & Theory* 17 (1): 73–77.

Bazirjian, Rosann, and Nancy M. Stanley. 2001. "Assessing the effectiveness of team-based structures in libraries." *Library Collections, Acquisitions, & Technical Services* 25 (2): 131–157.

Bednar, Marie, Roger Brisson, and Judy Hewes. 2000. "Pursuing the three Ts: How total quality management, technology, and teams transformed the cataloging department at Penn State." *Cataloging & Classification Quarterly* 30 (2/3): 241–279.

Benaud, Claire-Lise, Elizabeth N. Steinhagen, and Sharon A. Moynahan. 2000. "Flexibility in the management of cataloging." *Cataloging & Classification Quarterly* 30 (2/3): 281–298.

Boehr, Diane. 2002. "Developing the use of metadata at the National Library of Medicine: from decision-making to implementation." In *Cataloging the Web: Metadata, AACR, and MARC 21,* edited by W. Jones, J. R. Ahronheim, and J. Crawford. Lanham, Md.: Scarecrow Press.

Bordeianu, Sever, and Virginia Seiser. 1999. "Paraprofessional catalogers in ARL libraries." *College and Research Libraries* 60 (6): 532–540.

Britton, Helen H. 1987. "Interactions: a library faculty matrix organization and a public policy and administration program." *The Reference Librarian* 20: 187–204.

Buttlar, Lois, and Rajinder Garcha. 1998. "Catalogers in academic libraries: their evolving and expanding roles." *College & Research Libraries* 59 (4): 311–321.

Calhoun, Karen. 2002. "Special section: Metadata." *Library Collections, Acquisitions, & Technical Services* 26 (3): 195–197.

Chervinko, James S. 1992. "The changing state of original cataloging: Who's going to do it now?" *Illinois Libraries* 74 (6): 493–495.

Clack, Mary E. 1995. "The role of training in the reorganization of cataloging services." *Library Acquisitions: Practice & Theory* 19 (4): 439–444.

Condron, Lyn. 2001. "Management by action: How we're embracing new cataloging work at Tufts." *Cataloging & Classification Quarterly* 32 (2): 127–151.

Cook, Eleanor I., and Pat Farthing. 1995. "A technical services perspective of implementing an organizational review while simultaneously installing an integrated library system." *Library Acquisitions: Practice & Theory* 19 (4): 445–461.

Courtney, Nancy, and Fred W. Jenkins. 1998. "Reorganizing collection development and acquisitions in a medium-sized academic library." *Library Acquisitions: Practice & Theory* 22 (3): 287–293.

Crooker, Cynthia, Robert Killheffer, and Cecile Mandour. 1991. "The reorganization of technical services at Yale." *Technical Services Quarterly* 9 (1): 27–41.

Davenport, Sara E. 1991. "The blurring of divisional lines between technical and public services: an emphasis on access." *The Reference Librarian* 34: 47–53.

De Klerk, Ann, and Joanne R. Euster. 1989. "Technology and organizational metamorphoses." *Library Trends* 37 (4): 457–468.

Dewey, Barbara I. 1998. "Transforming cataloging: the University of Iowa experience." *Collection Management* 23 (1/2): 57–80.

Diaz, Joseph R., and Chestalene Pintozzi. 1999. "Helping teams work: Lessons learned from the University of Arizona Library reorganization." *Library Administration & Management* 13(1): 27–36.

Diedrichs, Carol P. 1998. "Using automation in technical services to foster innovation." *The Journal of Academic Librarianship* 24 (2): 113–120.

Dumont, Paul E. 1989. "Creativity, innovation, and entrepreneurship in technical services." *Journal of Library Administration* 10 (2/3): 57–68.

Dunkle, Clare B. 1996. "Outsourcing the catalog department: a meditation inspired by the business and library literature." *Journal of Academic Librarianship* 22 (1): 33–43.

Eden, Brad. 1999. "Technical services: a vision for the future." *Library Computing* 18 (4): 289–294.

———. 2002a. "The Instructional Management System (IMS) Standard: solutions for interactive instructional software and dynamic learning." In *Cataloging the Web: Metadata, AACR, and MARC 21*, edited by W. Jones, J. R. Ahronheim, and J. Crawford. Lanham, Md.: Scarecrow Press.

———. 2002b. *Metadata and its applications.* Chicago: ALA TechSource.

Eden, Brad, and Kenneth J. Bierman. 2002. "Knowledge access management at Lied Library: cataloging and Web site reengineering." *Library Hi Tech* 20 (1): 90–103.

El-Sherbini, Magda. 1995. "Contract cataloging: A pilot project for outsourcing Slavic books." *Cataloging & Classification Quarterly* 20 (3): 57–73.

———. 2000. "Metadata and the future of cataloging." *Library Computing* 19 (3/4): 180–191.

Eskoz, Patricia A. 1990. "The catalog librarian—change or status quo? Results of a survey of academic libraries." *Library Resources & Technical Services* 34 (3): 380–392.

Eustis, Joanne D., and Donald J. Kenney. 1996. *Library reorganization & restructuring: A SPEC kit.* Washington, D.C.: Association of Research Libraries, Office of Management Services.

Fietzer, William. 1998. "Technical services librarians and metadata: reigning in the new frontier." *Technicalities* 18 (7): 7–10.

Fiste, David A., and Christopher P. Thornton. 1993. "Bibliographic services of the future." *Technical Services Quarterly* 10 (3): 27–43.

Freeborn, Robert B., and Rebecca L. Mugridge. 2002. "The reorganization of monographic cataloging processes at Penn State University Libraries." *Library Collections, Acquisitions, & Technical Services* 26 (1): 35–45.

Garrison, William. 2002. "The Colorado digitization project: An overview." In *Cataloging the Web: Metadata, AACR, and MARC 21*, edited by W. Jones, J. R. Ahronheim, and J. Crawford. Lanham, Md.: Scarecrow Press.

Glogoff, Stuart J., and Garry J. Forger. 2001. "Metadata protocols and standards: bringing order to our digital objects." *Internet Reference Services Quarterly* 5 (4): 5–14.

Gorman, Michael. 1987. "The organization of academic libraries in the light of automation." In *Advances in library automation and networking*, edited by J. A. Hewitt. Greenwich, Conn.: JAI Press.

———. 1994. "Innocent pleasures." In *The future is now: The changing face of technical services.* Dublin, Ohio: OCLC.

Hill, Debra W. 1998. "To outsource or not: University of Alabama Libraries engage in pilot project with OCLC's TechPro." *Cataloging & Classification Quarterly* 26 (1): 63–73.

Hirshon, Arnold. 1991. "Beyond our walls: academic libraries, technical services and the information world." *Journal of Library Administration* 15 (1/2): 43–59.

————. 1994. "The lobster quadrille: the future of technical services in a re-engineering world." In *The future is now: The changing face of technical services*. Dublin, Ohio: OCLC.

Hirshon, Arnold, and Barbara A. Winters. 1996. *Outsourcing library technical services: A how-to-do it manual for librarians*. New York: Neal Schuman.

Horenstein, Bonnie. 1999. "Outsourcing copy cataloging at Adelphi University Libraries." *Cataloging & Classification Quarterly* 28 (4): 105–116.

Hudgins, Jean, Grace Agnew, and Elizabeth Brown. 1999. *Getting mileage out of metadata: applications for the library*. Chicago: American Library Association.

Hudgins, Jean, and Lisa A. Macklin. 2000. "New materials, new processes: implementing digital imaging projects into existing workflow." *Library Collections, Acquisitions, & Technical Services* 24 (2): 189–204.

Hyslop, Colleen F. 1995. "Using PromptCat to eliminate work: MSU's experience." *Library Acquisitions: Practice & Theory* 19 (3): 359–362.

Jones, Wayne, Judith Ahronheim, and Josephine Crawford, eds. 2002. *Cataloging the Web: Metadata, AACR, and MARC 21*. Lanham, Md.: Scarecrow Press.

Larsen, Patricia M. 1991. "The climate of change: library organizational structures, 1985–1990." *The Reference Librarian* 34: 79–93.

Lee-Smeltzer, Kuang-Hwei. 2000. "Cataloging in three academic libraries: Operations, trends and perspectives." *Cataloging & Classification Quarterly* 30 (2/3): 315–330.

Libby, Katherine A., and Dana M. Caudle. 1997. "A survey on the outsourcing of cataloging in academic libraries." *College & Research Libraries* 58 (6): 550–560.

Martin, Cheryl. 2000. "The organization of the cataloguing function at McMaster University." *Cataloging & Classification Quarterly* 30 (1): 111–121.

Mayer, Constance. 2002. "VARIATIONS: Creating a digital music library at Indiana University." In *Cataloging the Web: Metadata, AACR, and MARC 21*, edited by W. Jones, J. R. Ahroheim, and J. Crawford. Lanham, Md.: Scarecrow Press.

McCombs, Gillian M. 1992. "Technical services in the 1990s: A process of convergent evolution." *Library Resources & Technical Services* 36 (2): 135–148.

McCue, Janet A. 1997. "Why should a cataloging department hire a metadata specialist? and, are there any out there?" *Quarterly Bulletin of the International Association of Agricultural Information Specialists* 42 (3/4): 226–229.

Mohr, Deborah A., and Anita Schuneman. 1997. "Changing roles: Original cataloging by paraprofessionals in ARL libraries." *Library Resources & Technical Services* 41 (3): 205–218.

Niles, Judith. 1992. "Acquisitions and collection management reorganization: An exercise in crisis management." *Library Acquisitions: Practice & Theory* 16 (4): 379–382.

Oberg, Larry R., Mark E. Mentges, P. N. McDermott, and Vitoon Harusadangkul. 1992. "The role, status, and working conditions of paraprofessionals: A national survey of academic libraries." *College & Research Libraries* 53 (3): 215–238.

Rider, Mary M. 1996. "Developing new roles for paraprofessionals in cataloging." *Journal of Academic Librarianship* 22 (1): 26–32.

Scheschy, Virginia M. 1999. "Outsourcing: a strategic partnership." *Technical Services Quarterly* 16 (3): 31–41.

Sellberg, Roxanne. 1995. "Managing the cataloging enterprise in an academic library: an introduction." *Wilson Library Bulletin* 69 (7): 33–36.

Shaughnessy, Thomas W. 1996. "Lessons from restructuring the library." *Journal of Academic Librarianship* 22 (4): 251–256.

Smits, Jan. 1999. "Metadata: An introduction." *Cataloging & Classification Quarterly* 27 (3/4): 303–319.

Stanley, Nancy M., and Lynne Branche-Brown. 1995. "Reorganizing acquisitions at the Pennsylvania State University Libraries: From work units to teams." *Library Acquisitions: Practice & Theory* 19 (4): 417–425.

Swanekamp, Joan. 2000. "Cataloging at Yale University in 2000: Challenges and strategies." *Cataloging & Classification Quarterly* 30 (2/3): 373–385.

Sweetland, James H. 2001. "Outsourcing library technical services—what we think we know, and don't know." *The Bottom Line: Managing Library Finances* 14 (3): 164–175.

Thompson, Christine E. 1999. "The cataloging advisory group: A public/technical services forum." *Journal of Library Administration* 29 (2): 123–131.

Townley, Charles T. 1995. "Designing effective library organizations." In *Academic libraries: Their rationale and role in American higher education*, edited by G. B. McCabe and R. J. Person. Westport, Conn.: Greenwood Press.

Wilhoit, Karen. 1994. "Outsourcing cataloging at Wright State University." *Serials Review*. 20 (3): 70–73.

Williams, Delmus E. 1991. "Managing technical services in the 1990s: The ruminations of a library director." *Journal of Library Administration* 15 (1/2): 25–41.

Wilson, Karen A. 1995. "Outsourcing copy cataloging and physical processing: A review of Blackwell's outsourcing services for the J. Hugh Jackson Library at Stanford University." *Library Resources and Technical Services* 39 (October): 359–383.

Winters, Barbara A. 1994. "Catalog outsourcing at Wright State University: Implications for acquisitions managers." *Library Acquisitions: Practice & Theory* 18 (4): 367–373.

Woodley, Mary S. 2002. "A digital library project on a shoestring." *Library Collections, Acquisitions, & Technical Services* 26 (3): 199–206.

Worrell, Diane. 1995. "The learning organization: Management theory for the information age or new age fad?" *Journal of Academic Librarianship* 21 (5): 351–357.

Younger, Jennifer A. 1996. "Support staff and librarians in cataloging." *Cataloging & Classification Quarterly* 23 (1): 27–47.

Younger, Jennifer A., and D. Kay Gapen. 1998. "Technical services organization." In *Technical services today and tomorrow*, edited by M. Gorman. Englewood, Colo.: Libraries Unlimited.

2

What Is Technical Services?: Perspectives from the Field and from LIS Education

Pat Lawton
Deborah Rose-Lefmann

Editor's note: The authors examine the concept of technical services in the literature, particularly in regard to its future, from the perspectives of both practicing technical services librarians and library and information science educators. Examination of both perspectives, and the challenges involved in meeting the needs of practitioners on the one hand and the overall education of librarians by educators on the other, illustrates the challenges that need to be addressed in the field. The authors conclude that technical services librarians will be challenged in the future to find their place in librarianship, but that their roles and duties will still need to be accomplished, in whatever emanation or direction libraries may move toward.

"Technical services," in the thesaurus for the LISA (Library and Information Science Abstracts) database, is synonymous with ("Used for") "Library housekeeping." Narrower terms include Acquisitions, Binding, Cataloguing, Circulation control, Computerized technical services, and Periodicals control. Perhaps "Library housekeeping" is odd only to the non-Anglo ear, but some might agree that the word "housekeeping" in this context is loaded with suggestions of gender and relegation of a matter to relative unimportance. It suggests that technical services comprises the dirty work that, well, someone has to do. It might involve laundry and cleaning and dusting, ordinary day-to-day but essential tasks for the efficient management of the home, and in this case, library. For this chapter, technical services is not defined as housekeeping, but follows Gorman's definition as that which includes bibliographic control and acquisitions (Gorman 1998, p. xv) or, as broadly and well-defined nearly 50 years ago by Tauber and Associates, "services involving the operations and techniques for acquiring, recording, and preserving materials" (Tauber and Associates 1954, p. 4).

This chapter examines literature from approximately the last decade that defines and describes technical services and, in particular, its future. What are the challenges to technical services, and how might future technical services professionals be prepared for this future, as articulated by soothsayers in the recent decade? Of these soothsayers, some are practitioners and some are educators from LIS education. How do the two groups agree or disagree on a vision of the future for technical services and preparation for that future? Is there agreement; is it necessary that there be agreement?

Technology

Two decades ago, Freedman explored the future of technical services through a series of questions (1984, pp. 1197–1203). His questions are astoundingly relevant today, if one simply substitutes the word "technology" for "automation." The questions address the change in professional and paraprofessional staffing, the type of work that technical services workers will engage in, quality control, and the relationship of technical services to other areas of the library. Freedman predicts that workflows will change, paraprofessional and professional duties may alter a bit, and automation will be costly. His final question, though, is particularly provocative and sits at the center of this chapter: Is technical services' future inextricably tied to technology? Can we, in fact, conceive of a future of technical services or any aspect of library and information work that is not tied to technology? Or is it possible that the uproar over technology has subsided and reached an even keel of acceptance? The technological uproar in the last decade has refocused LIS's attention on the distinction between the work and the document. E-resources have been a challenge largely due to the profession's emphasis on the form of the information. If form were not such a focal point, this latest migration to new forms of information may not have been so traumatic. Has LIS moved beyond an emphasis on the document to the intellectual content of a resource? Has the bibliographic control community surmounted this dichotomy? Would Lubetzky be proud to see that the profession has shifted from a document to a work-centered position? The AACR 2002 edition has changed its focus from the document as the primary concern to content, with a significant conceptual shift in its cardinal rule 0.24, which now reads: "It is important to bring out *all* [italics added] aspects of the item being described, including its content, its carrier, it type of publication, its *bibliographic relationships*, and whether it is published or unpublished" (*AACR2R* 2002, Part I-3, emphasis added). Compare this with the AACR 1998 edition's emphasis on description: "It is a cardinal principle of the use of part I that the description of a physical item should be based in the first instance on the chapter dealing with the class of materials to which that item belongs . . . In short, the starting point for description is the physical *form* [italics added] of the item in hand, not the original or any previous form in which the work has been published" (*AACR2R* 1998, p. 8). Has the profession similarly evolved, no longer centered on the thing itself but on the content? Can we now or possibly at any time respond in the negative to Freedman's question, "Is the future of technical services inextricably tied to technology?" What is the view of the present and the future, as articulated by educators and practitioners?

A Conflict of Objectives

In 1982, Blaise Cronin conducted a content analysis and comparison of United Kingdom (UK) library school prospectuses and job announcements and concluded that there is a "conflict of objectives" between educators and practitioners (Cronin 1982, p. 13). The job announcements and LIS curricula did not match; in the eyes of the practitioners, library schools were not preparing graduates properly for the workplace. Ten years prior to Cronin's study, Conant had come to similar conclusions in the United States ; he found that practitioners in the United States did not trust LIS educators to provide the education that professionals needed (Conant 1980, p. 113). (Although the study was done in 1970, the results were not published until 1980.) The practitioners' charge in 1970 was that graduates could not do the job, that there was too much emphasis in library school on theory and too little on practice. Gorman echoes this sentiment in 1998 and focuses the charge on technical services in particular: "Students graduate from library schools . . . without knowing much about some of the important facets of being a librarian . . . they are ignorant of most of the processes that go on in technical service areas and of many of the theories and policies that underlie those processes" (p. 6). In 2001 Barbara Moran noted that

> Positions are hardening in the growing rift between the educators and practitioners in the library field. Many practitioners are convinced that the library and information science (LIS) schools have either abandoned educating librarians or that they are not educating them well (or both). Library educators are persuaded that many practitioners are out of touch with what goes on both in the programs and in present-day higher education. (p. 52)

Also in 2001, Lawton found further evidence of this conflict, but the charge was not that educators were not practical enough but rather that they were not *theoretical* enough (2002, p. 46). Eleven interviews with LIS consultants specializing in the organization of information were conducted to determine participants' views on how catalogers and indexers need to retool for future challenges. Respondents, who were also part-time trainers or educators, indicated almost unanimously (and unprovoked) that LIS education, particularly bibliographic control, was failing to teach graduates the principles of bibliographic control, and that this was a problem for them as trainers in new technologies. They were training people who did not understand the basics of description, vocabulary control, and classification, and this was problematic when they gave workshops on topics such as building thesauri or assigning metadata to digital objects shared over local intranets. Whether consensus about the future and LIS education will be reached any time soon is unlikely, as the roots of this tension are as deep as the history of higher education is long.

Thorstein Veblen's 1918 critique of professional education characterized professional education as inferior education, and claimed that professional education had no real place in higher education (Veblen 1962, p. 23). Veblen's sentiment pervades higher education even in the twenty-first century. Embedded within this argument is the theory and practice issue with which LIS is quite familiar (McKechnie and Pettigrew 2002, p. 407). The thinking goes something like this: A professional school teaches practical skills, as did Melville Dewey's School of Library Economy, begun in 1887. The "real" disciplines, such as the sciences and arts, teach theory and are housed within higher education. It was not until after the 1923 Williamson Report that library education was moved to the universities. Shortly after, theory took center stage. According to Clack, "Theory was introduced into library science programs in 1926 when the first graduate program was opened at the University of Chicago" (1993, p. 28). From this early history to the present day, the LIS literature is rife with practitioners and educators weighing in on what should be taught in the LIS schools, what is necessary in the profession, and whether future professionals are or are not adequately prepared for the future.

Practitioners' Responses to Changes in LIS

Rapid changes in the nature of information and of libraries, especially although not exclusively related to technology, have necessitated changes in the LIS curriculum. The curriculum has to cover many new areas without neglecting the old ones, and there is no general consensus on what constitutes a "core body of knowledge for the profession" (Holley 2003, p. 173). Even within the area of technical services, there is no general agreement on the value and necessity of cataloging education and what, specifically, should be taught. In fact, some library educators are giving students the impression that cataloging is "a dry, picky, boring, non-professional activity" (Hill, 2000 p. 41), hardly worth studying, and certainly not worth pursuing as a career. Cataloging and other technical services topics once occupied about half the library school curriculum, but now cataloging represents only a small portion of course offerings, and other areas of technical services, such as acquisitions, serials, and catalog management, are rarely taught at all.

A number of articles have been written about the perceptions of technical services practitioners of the adequacy of education in the field. Most of these have focused on cataloging, and most have surveyed, or been written by, supervisors who hire and train new catalogers. One study that focused on catalogers themselves was done by Callahan and MacLeod, who in 1992 surveyed entry-level catalogers (with less than four years of experience) in academic libraries regarding their job satisfaction and how well their education had prepared them for the job. Almost two-thirds (63 percent) felt inadequately prepared for their first cataloging job. And, while 85 percent of respondents planned to make their career in cataloging, of those who did not, 100 percent reported feeling that library school did not prepare them well for the work (Callahan and MacLeod 1994, pp. 34–35). One wonders whether at least some of them might have remained in cataloging if they had felt better prepared. When asked how their preparation could have been improved, the respondents overwhelmingly demanded "more in-depth and practical 'hands-on' experience," particularly with cataloging tools such as OCLC, MARC, LCRIs, and subject cataloging (1994, pp. 35–36).

More has been written about the views of those who hire and supervise catalogers regarding the preparation those catalogers receive in library school. In a 1994 survey of practitioners and educators, MacLeod and Callahan found that 67 percent of practitioners thought that entry-level catalogers were not adequately prepared for their first professional positions: "[T]hey indicated that the new cataloger needed much more practical experience in actual cataloging procedures. Without it, they said, the entry-level job became their practicum" (MacLeod and Callahan 1995, p. 158). This is not to say, however, that the practitioners surveyed found theory unnecessary. Fifty-one percent did not find that educators place too much emphasis on theory (MacLeod and Callahan 1995, p. 156) and, when asked what they believed to be the objectives of a cataloging education, over half included "a thorough grounding in theory", along with "knowledge of specific tools, orientation to standards and rules, understanding of procedures and practices, and some kind of hands-on practice or a practicum" (MacLeod and Callahan 1995, pp. 163–164).

Supervisors may expect many different kinds of skills of entry-level catalogers. Debra W. Hill (1997) discusses both general skills, which are not part of the library school curriculum, and specific job-related skills. Some of the general skills she describes are generally desirable traits such as good judgment and problem-solving skills, time management skills, computer literacy, supervisory skills, communication skills, and proficiency in a foreign language (1997, pp. 78–80). Others are more specific to the library setting, and include adaptability to new ideas and concepts in bibliographic control (1997, p. 77) and the ability to appreciate user needs to enhance catalog access. These latter two make a good argument for the importance of theory in cataloging education, since an under-standing of the theory of bibliographic control is necessary to adapt it to new cir-cumstances, and an understanding of user behavior is necessary to user-focused cataloging. Specific skills that should be learned in library school include use of OCLC or RLIN, AACR2R and the LCRIs, LCSH or Sears subject headings, LC or Dewey classification, MARC bibliographic formats, the Subject Cataloging Man-ual, and, ideally, some familiarity with nonbook materials and authority control (Hill 1997, pp. 81–82). If students do not learn these skills in library school or through a practicum, it greatly lengthens their training period on the job.

Anaclare Evans, who is both a manager of catalogers and an educator, of-fers a list of skills desired in an entry-level cataloger that is very similar to Debra Hill's. The syllabus for her cataloging course, however, does not cover all of them due to lack of time (Evans 1993, p. 50). Several areas that she feels need more coverage than time allows "include MARC tagging, authority work and an in-depth knowledge of the rules for determining and structuring access points" (1993, p. 53). Evans would like to see a cataloging curriculum consisting of two courses plus a required laboratory. The first course would consist of basic de-scription, classification, and subject analysis, while the second course would cover nonbook formats, access point construction, and authority work. A labora-tory would allow the students to learn to use OCLC and practice their cataloging skills (1993, p. 54). This is a far cry from reality in most library schools. At the least, more opportunities to practice cataloging skills are needed, whether in the form of a laboratory, a hands-on component to a cataloging course, or an internship.

If Evans would like to see improvements in cataloging education, Janet Swan Hill goes so far as to say that "library schools have abrogated their respon-sibility to educate catalogers and technical services managers," which she attrib-utes to "a mistaken belief that technical services activities are now, or soon will be, automated, clerical, and passé" (2002, p. 249). Not all libraries have the re-sources or personnel to provide extensive on-the-job training for entry-level cat-alogers if they do not acquire the necessary skills during their education, so they are left to fill in the gaps as best they can.

Debra Hill mentioned supervisory skills as desirable for entry-level cata-logers, and the new catalogers surveyed by Callahan and MacLeod also reported that they would have benefited from management coursework (Callahan and MacLeod 1996, p. 18). One effect of the increase in technology in technical ser-vices departments has been that many tasks that were once done by professionals are being done by support staff, and tasks that were once the province of man-agement are being done by catalogers. Supervision and training of support staff, developing departmental policies, and workflow management are tasks fre-quently expected even of entry-level catalogers. Jennifer Younger also observes that, "although many positions may have working titles that don't include the word 'manager,' management responsibilities do occur, however, in the vast majority of positions" (1997, p. 113). This is true of most librarians, not only technical services librarians, and in recognition of this fact, most library schools offer courses in library management. However, these courses are often "general and theoretical in nature" and "do not provide a sound preparation for the decision-making process as required today" (Callahan and MacLeod 1996, p. 20). Because technological change has had, and continues to have, such a strong effect on the structure and workflow in technical services departments, it would be useful if this were addressed in library school coursework, either as part of a technical services course or as part of a management course.

One of the skills that Evans describes as being particularly shortchanged in library school curricula is authority work (1993, p. 53). Debra Hill also mentions it as highly desirable in a candidate for an entry-level cataloging position (1997, p. 82). Where are catalogers learning authority work and authority control? A survey of AUTOCAT list members done by Mugridge and Furniss revealed that only 18 of 49 respondents had learned authority control in library school, and many of those "included qualifying comments such as 'in general terms,' 'it was mentioned in my cataloging class, but we did not study it in any detail,' 'small part of cataloging core course' " (2002, pp. 236–237). The great majority learned authority control on the job, with additional help from professional reading or workshops. The majority thought that library schools should be teaching at least the fundamental theory and concepts of authority control, and some wanted to see more opportunity for hands-on practice. However, on-the-job training in authority control was seen as necessary, as even catalogers who have had training or experience in authority control will have to learn how to apply that to the particular cataloging system used by the library (Mugridge and Furniss 2002, p. 240).

The librarians surveyed by Mugridge and Furniss mentioned several forms of continuing education, including workshops, conferences, and professional literature, as a means for learning authority control, since it wasn't taught adequately in library school. Continuing education can be an important way for entry-level catalogers to make up for deficiencies in their education and for experienced catalogers to keep up with changes in the profession. Workshops and short courses are frequently offered by regional library networks, state library associations, library schools, and even individual libraries, on topics ranging from refresher courses in cataloging nonbook formats or authority work to the latest technical services organizational trends, such as outsourcing or local area networking (Jizba 1997, p. 126). Some of the best continuing education opportunities are offered by the Program for Cooperative Cataloging (PCC), which offers training for a designated coordinator for each member institution, who is then responsible for training the rest of the cataloging staff (Jizba 1997, p. 128). Reading professional journals and belonging to professional organizations can help practitioners keep up with current trends, and electronic discussion lists, such as AUTOCAT, can help catalogers find answers to specific questions, and can be especially useful for those who have little access to resources or colleagues at their own libraries (Hopkins 2002, p. 380). Because of the rapid changes in the field of technical services, continuing education opportunities are vital both to entry-level and experienced catalogers, and it is important for administrators to recognize this and support it by providing release time and funding, to the degree that budgets permit.

Technical services practitioners, including both entry-level catalogers and the supervisors who hire and train them, have repeatedly expressed dissatisfaction with cataloging education in most LIS programs. This dissatisfaction has sometimes been described as "theory versus practice," but that description oversimplifies the reality. Practitioners expect, and want, library schools to provide "a solid theoretical foundation, but they also would like to see job applicants with more direct, hands-on experience" (MacLeod and Callahan 1995, p. 164). This could be provided by means of a laboratory taught by a practitioner, more practice integrated with the course theory (where it would aid in understanding the theoretical concepts as well as providing real practice), or practica and internships. Some on-the-job training for entry-level catalogers, and even for experienced catalogers moving to a new library, will always be necessary, and the rapid pace of change makes continuing education important for all catalogers. What is most needed for the improvement of LIS education is better communication between practitioners and educators. Educators say they consult with practitioners, yet "there is still only casual contact between them while what is necessary is an organized, focused and in-depth discussion of issues" (Callahan and MacLeod 1996, p. 22). In addition to discussing issues, practitioners could participate in technical services education, providing practical experience to complement the theoretical background (Connaway 1992; Clack 1993, p. 33; Evans 1993, p. 57). With all the best intentions in the world, LIS programs cannot do it all; educators and practitioners need to work together in preparing entry-level catalogers for productive careers.

Educators' Perspectives

One of the most salient themes to emerge from the literature of the last decade was the need for technical services professionals to be prepared as managers (Fisher 2001; Connaway 1992; Bates 1999). Yet Callahan and MacLeod's survey (1996) revealed great disparity between how essential educators and practitioners thought management was in a good cataloging education. Learning to manage workflow and administering the department were rated significantly less important by the educators than by practitioners. Perhaps there is some implicit assumption here by educators that catalogers will remain catalogers and will not manage, will not address the broader issues, but this seems unlikely. Most catalogers do in fact need to be prepared for the bigger picture of technical services and attendant management responsibilities. In a study of tasks performed by catalogers in academic libraries, Connaway (1992) found that a significant portion of the professional cataloger's work is in fact administrative. If the profession is to counter Cronin's charge of a conflict of objectives, then management should in fact be given greater attention in the LIS curriculum to prepare professionals appropriately.

For future technical services professionals, management skills are perhaps even more critical. Diedrichs, a practitioner, states that library skills, management skills, and business skills will be of greater importance in the future: "This marriage of library skills, management skills, and business skills will have a plethora of uses in the library of the future. More and more areas within the library arena are controlled by contracts. . . . These individuals [acquisitions librarians] will need both business skills and library skills to navigate successfully the bureaucracies of all players: the institution, the library, and the contractor" (1998, p. 76).

Marcia Bates, a library educator, puts "Sophisticated Management and Policy" at the top of her list for an information school's curriculum. "Because we are in a time of revolutionary, not incremental, change we need people who can see the big picture, who can see the commonalities and the differences that really matter in a situation, rather than the surface conventions. In revolutionary times, you need the vision to translate the core values and service functions that are the heart of information service into the new circumstances" (Bates 1999).

While some educators and practitioners more generally emphasize management skills, educators of the last decade have been concerned with electronic resources and the challenges they pose to the professional. In a thorough analysis of metadata and electronic resources in cataloging education, Hsieh-Yee proposes a number of strategies for addressing this challenge (2003, pp. 210–214). Her findings are the foundation of a plan by ALA's ALCTS committee to help train metadata and cataloging educators (Hsieh-Yee 2003). The plan will operationalize Hsieh-Yee's findings by: announcing the task force's findings regarding the elements of bibliographic control expertise; assembling a "metadata basics" package for use by faculty and workshop leaders, creating a listserv for sharing news, setting up a Web clearinghouse for pedagogical resources, and holding a conference for educators and trainers to share expertise and ideas for integrating metadata topics into courses and workshops.

In addition to the need to prepare future professionals for handling of e-resources, Hsieh-Yee suggests that a broader scope is also needed, that educators need to talk beyond "library". "Cataloging education of the future will have a broader scope and examine information organization in various information environments, including libraries, museums, corporate information centers, and so on" (2003, p. 205).

The importance of expanding the scope of the profession's view is echoed by Bates. The profession, to survive, must teach beyond the concept of library, of place. By extension, technical services professionals may need to focus on content. Perhaps even focusing on e-resources is too narrow; perhaps the profession needs to not emphasize form but rather consider more deeply content and relationships, principles that will carry over to any medium. With a broader perspective and more inclusive scope, the profession might more actively "market" its skills and knowledge to other disciplines. Few outside the profession of LIS understand its contributions and its scope, and only those within it can educate, or more aggressively "market" these contributions, across domains and across media. Students need to be prepared to share the LIS world's knowledge. "In information schools we should be training our students to be able to translate all the core skills of information selection, organization, and access across all the media of the 21st century, not just the oldest" (Bates 1999).

Conclusion

The reports of the death of print (with apologies to Mark Twain) are greatly exaggerated. However, the proportion of information in digital form is steadily increasing, in libraries as well as in society as a whole. As Lynch says, "within a very few years virtually all new materials, and an ever-growing amount of previously published materials is going to be available in digital form as a routine matter" (2000). The increasingly digital library of the future will require more changes in LIS education, but perhaps these will not be as radical as many practitioners and educators fear. As Spink and Cool found in a survey of courses for digital libraries, they are "first and foremost libraries and, as such, any model curriculum should maintain a core set of courses that address the major functions and activities of libraries in general, in both digital and traditional forms" (1999).

What role might technical services librarians play in the brave new world of the digital (or more likely, the hybrid) library? If technical services professionals are not key to the design and maintenance of the digital library, its acquisitions, preservation, and organization, who will be? The Library of Congress has outlined a plan for creating digital libraries that include provisions for the usual technical services functions in altered forms, including preservation, descriptive data, and encoding schemes (Library of Congress 2002).

Clearly, those technical services functions that deal solely with the container of information (marking, shelving, binding) will not be needed. For the rest, much depends on the form that the digital library of the future might take. Acquisitions and collection management may become less important, but they are unlikely to disappear entirely. Not all digital information is, or is likely to become, available free to all over the Internet. Much high-quality information, especially that which has been subjected to peer review or other forms of "quality control," is available only by subscription, and this state of affairs is likely to continue. As long as it does, ordering, collection management, and budgeting will still be necessary. And given the volatility of digital information, preservation becomes more important than ever, even though its form changes dramatically.

It will also continue to be necessary to organize the information in some way to provide better access to users. Currently used cataloging and classification systems may not be ideal for the organization of a digital library, but technical services librarians have shown themselves able to adapt to new formats in the past, and will surely continue to do so. Descriptive cataloging would be less important and take different forms in the digital world, as the focus will necessarily be on the work rather than the container (a process that is already underway), but access points for persons, corporate bodies, and subjects will continue to be vital to allow users access to the materials. The form of these is likely to change, but the need for them will not.

Finally, will technical services remain wedded to the library as place? If technical services professionals fail to move beyond the physical and embrace the conceptual, they are perhaps sealing their fate as those charged with "Library housekeeping." But there is hope. Bing and Guangjun (1998) compare the activities of the traditional and the digital library. From their analysis, they find that the e-library requires more technical service responsibilities than the traditional library (1998, p. 6). In acquisitions, for example, added to the traditional tasks of understanding demands, ordering materials, monitoring deliveries, and approving payments, is conversion of existing materials into electronic form and copyright management. They suggest that there is indeed a lively future for technical services professionals in the digital library. We have much to learn from our Chinese colleagues, who conclude:

> During the evolutions from automation libraries into digital libraries, librarians should understand the impacts of digital library concepts and technologies on their libraries, analyze various changes concerning the working contents and procedures and even functions. They must accept their new roles and improve their information skills through education and training and life-long learning. Their today's efforts will guarantee their tomorrow's successes. (Bing and Guangjun 1998, p. 12)

References

Anglo-American Cataloguing Rules (AACR2R). 2nd ed. 1998. Chicago: American Library Association.

Anglo-American Cataloguing Rules (AACR2R). 2nd ed. 2002. Chicago: American Library Association, 2002.

Bates, Marcia J. 1999. *Congress on professional education: Focus on education of the first professional degree.* Available: http://www.ala.org/Content/ContentGroups/HRDR/1st_Congress_on_Professional_Education/1st_Congress__Panel_Presentation_by_Marcia_Bates.htm (Accessed May 29, 2003).

Bing, Wang, and Meng Guangjun. 1998. "The digital library: Its definitions and impacts on traditional libraries." *Journal of Information, Communication and Library Science* 5 (2, December): 3–13.

Callahan, Darren, and Judy MacLeod. 1994. "Recruiting and retention revisited: A study of entry-level catalogers." *Technical Services Quarterly* 11 (4): 27–43.

———. 1996. "Management issues and the challenge for cataloging education." *Technical Services Quarterly* 13 (2): 15–24.

Clack, Doris H. 1993. "Education for cataloging: A symposium paper." *Cataloging & Classification Quarterly* 16 (3): 28.

Conant, Ralph W. 1980. *The Conant report: A study of the education of librarians.* Cambridge, Mass.: MIT Press.

Connaway, Lynn Silipigni. 1992. "The levels of decisions and involvement in decision-making: Effectiveness and job satisfaction in academic library technical services." Ph.D. dissertation, University of Wisconsin.

Cronin, Blaise. 1982. *The education of library information professionals: A conflict of objectives?* Aslib Occasional Publication No. 28. London: Aslib.

Diedrichs, Carol Pitts. 1998. "Acquisitions: So what and where?" *The Journal of Academic Librarianship* (January): 74–76.

Evans, Anaclare F. 1993. "The education of catalogers: The view of the practitioner/educator." *Cataloging & Classification Quarterly* 16 (3): 49–57.

Fisher, William. 2001. "Core competencies for the acquisitions librarian." *Library Collection, Acquisitions, & Technical Services* 25: 179–190.

Freedman, Maurice J. 1984. "Automation and the future of technical services." *Library Journal* (June 15): 1197–1203.

Gorman, Michael, ed. 1998. *Technical services today and tomorrow.* 2nd ed. Englewood, Colo.: Libraries Unlimited.

Hill, Debra W. 1997. "Requisite skills of the entry-level cataloger: A supervisor's perspective." *Cataloging & Classification Quarterly* 23 (3/4): 75–83.

Hill, Janet Swan. 2000. "Why are there so few of us: Educating librarians for technical services." *Colorado Libraries* 26 1 (2000): 41–44.

———. 2002. "What else do you need to know? Practical skills for catalogers and managers." *Cataloging & Classification Quarterly* 34 (1/2) : 245–261.

Holley, Robert P. 2003. "The ivory tower as preparation for the trenches: The relationship between library education and library practice." *College & Research Libraries News* 64 (3): 172–175.

Hopkins, Judith. 2002. "The community of catalogers: Its role in the education of catalogers." *Cataloging & Classification Quarterly* 34 (3): 375–381.

Hsieh-Yee, Ingrid. 2002. "Cataloging and metadata education: Asserting a central role in information organization." *Cataloging & Classification Quarterly* 34 (1/2): 203–222.

———. 2003. *Cataloging and Metadata Education: A Proposal for Preparing Cataloging Professionals of the 21st Century. Final Report.* Available: http://www.loc.gov/catdir/bibcontrol/CatalogingandMetadataEducation.pdf (Accessed June 1, 2003).

Jizba, Laurel. 1997. "Everyone's job: Using and improving continuing education for technical services: a practitioner's perspective." *Technical Services Quarterly* 15 (1/2): 119–131.

Joudrey, Daniel N. 2002. "A new look at US graduate courses in bibliographic control." *Cataloging & Classification Quarterly* 34 (1/2): 57–99.

Lawton, Patricia A. 2002. "Retooling cataloguers and indexers for the information and knowledge management society: A needs assessment for continuing professional education in the UK and the US." In *Continuing Professional Education for the Information Society: The Fifth World Conference on Continuing Professional Education for the Library and Information Science Professions,* edited by Patricia Layzell Ward. Munchen: K.G. Saur.

Library of Congress. 2002. *National Digital Information Infrastructure and Preservation Program.* Available: http://www.digitalpreservation.gov/ndiipp/repor/repor_plan.html (Accessed May 23, 2003).

Lynch, Clifford. 2000. *The new context for bibliographic control in the new millennium.* Available: http://lcweb.loc.gov/catdir/bibcontrol/lynch_paper.html (Accessed June 1, 2003).

MacLeod, Judy, and Daren Callahan. 1995. "Educators and practitioners reply: An assessment of cataloging education." *Library Resources & Technical Services* 39 (2): 153–165.

McKechnie, Lynne (E. F.), and Karen E. Pettigrew. 2002. "Surveying the use of theory in library and information science research: A disciplinary perspective." *Library Trends* 50 (3, Winter): 406–417 (special issue: Current Theory in Library and Information Science).

Moran, Barbara B. 2001. "Practitioners vs. LIS educators: Time to reconnect." *Library Journal* 126 (18, November 1): 52–55.

Mugridge, Rebecca L., and Kevin A. Furniss. 2002. "Education for authority control: Whose responsibility is it?" *Cataloging & Classification Quarterly* 34 (1/2): 233–243.

Spink, Amanda, and Colleen Cool. 1999. "Education for digital libraries." *D-Lib Magazine* (May). Available: http://www.dlib.org/dlib/may99/05spink.html (Accessed June 1, 2003).

Tauber, Maurice F., and Associates. 1954. *Technical Services in Libraries*. New York: Columbia University Press.

Veblen, Thorstein. 1962. *The higher learning in America: A memorandum on the conduct of universities by business men*. New York: B. W. Huebsch.

Younger, Jennifer A. 1997. "An employer's perspective on LIS education." *Technical Services Quarterly* 15 (1/2): 109–118.

3

Staffing Trends in Academic Library Technical Services

Vicki Toy Smith*
Kathryn Etcheverria

Editor's note: The authors have compiled and conducted a survey directed at managers and directors of academic technical services departments. The sample was compiled from a select number of ARL and land grant libraries within the United States. Conclusions indicate that most technical services professionals feel that their work and professional development are unrecognized in their current environments. The authors present the findings from their survey, as well as their insights from further contact made with select individuals who participated in the survey.

Literature Review

The ranks of experienced librarians are thinning as large numbers of librarians trained in the 1960s contemplate and reach retirement. Statistics suggest that university librarians are older on average than librarians in general, and catalogers in ARL libraries are even older than the ARL population at large, a finding from ARL's 1994 and 1998 surveys (Wilder 2000, p. 3). Moreover, the pressures from ever-changing technology have compelled the technical services areas in libraries, once holding clear and straightforward roles, to move fluidly and change in the direction of those new technologies. Not surprisingly, when libraries seek new hires for newly configured positions, they find positions difficult, sometimes impossible, to fill.

In response to changes like these, library staffs are reconfiguring themselves to meet changing needs. Positions traditionally configured, such as cataloging and acquisitions librarians, are eliminated or reallocated to other job categories. Job advertisements for acquisitions librarians, for example, seek less special knowledge of traditional or particular formats, and more ability in emerging skills such as ability to negotiate licenses, work with automated systems, and monitor digital publishing trends (Withers 2001/2002, p. 73). New hires are frequently functional specialists; that is, skills are systems-related, fewer have library degrees and prior experience, and most command higher starting salaries than their librarian counterparts (Wilder 2000, p. 4).

Library staffs are on a steep learning curve to grasp and use the new technologies and specific applications, and one librarian who examined the human side of this trend likened the framework for change to "navigating white water"(McCarthy 1998, p. 368). In providing catalog access to electronic resources, many levels of staff now contribute to the effort, depending on local workloads. The roles and responsibilities of different levels of staff relating to these resources are not clearly delineated, as all levels of staff have grown and continue to grow in skills relating to access issues. The roles are blurred as they have been previously in processing print formats (Boydston and Leysen 2001, p. 137). This points to a movement away from traditional roles in technical services staffs at all levels; the bar is raised for everyone in relation to technology. Ouderkirk's article explores this notion further, so far as to identify types who will carry us forward: the creative visionary worker, as well as the rapid implementer/evaluator, both of whom will have viable roles in dramatic technological change in libraries (Ouderkirk 2000, pp. 343–356).

So where does that leave technical services staff members as they consider their worth to the library and their viability in the changing job market? How well do they function with the actuality of continuous and rapid change, and how do they feel about it?

The Survey

To collect a valid sample, we solicited responses from directors or managers in technical services departments of academic libraries, specifically from a sample of ARL and land grant libraries within the United States. Our hope was to gain information from technical services librarians with extensive knowledge of their own library's staff and technology changes during the past 10 years.

The survey was mailed to 106 people. About 100 are known to have received the survey at an institutional address. Respondents were asked to enter answers at a Web site developed by the University of Nevada, Reno's library Webmaster. Data and IP addresses were recorded for purposes of de-duping, but the anonymity of respondents was protected. Of the 100 staff members solicited, 25 entered valid responses. A copy of the survey used is in Appendix 3.1.

In gathering data, it was our goal to gain information about the perceptions of each respondent in the context of his or her library. The survey document (see Appendix 3.1) contained 16 questions. The first question looked at the types of duties that were included in various technical services departments. Question 2 through 4 addressed unit size, net increases, and net decreases over five- and ten-year periods respectively. Questions 5 and 6 looked at the position of the respondent and the number of years of library work experience. Questions 7 through14 inquired about job expansion and change, which were called workload and work roles, and asked for information regarding professionals and paraprofessionals in their respective units. Question 15 asked for an expression of satisfaction or dissatisfaction, as well as other emotions in relation to changes in the workplace. Finally, in question 16 the participant was asked if he or she would be willing to participate in a qualitative study exploring further his or her experiences and opinions regarding change in staffing and technology in the library.

After the survey data were compiled, questions were directed to selected participants for comment:

- What are the three biggest changes that have occurred in your unit in the last 5–10 years?

- What has been the greatest challenge to your unit regarding electronic resources? Please be as specific as possible.

Seven participants responded with comments that corroborated and added flesh to survey results. Their comments, full of insight, are interspersed throughout this chapter.

Results

Survey results indicated that most academic technical services units include a core of activities. All respondents' libraries included the core activities of order processing, serials processing, and cataloging. Most libraries (72 percent, 18 out of 25) reported electronic resources processes within their technical services units. Respondents had the opportunity to report other activities falling outside the realm of activities suggested. Categories reported indicated that most differences were related to terminology (activities such as marking and stacks management included different terms for similar activities). One large library reported a decentralized unit, that is, separate teams for different divisions of the library. But other information reported did not give evidence that this unit was radically different from other reporting libraries.

The survey was sent to responsible administrators. Their job titles included Dean of Libraries, Director of Technical Services, Associate Director of Technical Services, Assistant Director, Head of Cataloging, Collection Management Supervisor, and Coordinator of Technical Services. Not surprisingly, the majority of the respondents had a great deal of experience in libraries. Eighty percent of them held professional positions. Thirty-six percent had 21 or more years' experience in their current library, and a full 76 percent had 21 or more years of library experience total. Because we were interested in perceptions regarding academic libraries, we were seeking those with a good amount of both career and individual library experience. We felt it would increase the validity of the data.

Respondents reported growth in both the roles and workload in technical services units. Responses showed a perception of a growth in work roles for both professionals and paraprofessionals, 92 percent for both. More respondents perceived a growth in the workload for professionals than for paraprofessionals, 96 percent and 76 percent, respectively. These numbers may indicate that the growth in professional workloads has not translated to an equivalent growth in roles, for example, responsibility in the library for professionals.

In 80 percent of the responses, new responsibilities were new to the library, as differentiated from work moved or shifted from other departments. This suggests that new roles and new work come from new technologies applied in libraries, rather than from work shifted within the library. While the literature sometimes refers to the blurring of responsibilities between professional and paraprofessional, survey respondents perceived that all levels of staff had grown in their positions. According to comments by respondents, areas of growth for paraprofessionals included more high-level and original cataloging. Areas of growth for all staff included aspects of dealing with electronic resources, cataloging new formats, and growing in sophistication in use of integrated library systems (communications with respondents Ann Doyle, Robin Fradenburgh, and Susan Mueller, May 28–29, 2003).

Nearly all respondents reported increased levels of value in the job/viability in the job market for all levels of staff. It would appear to be no surprise that employees who are expanding in responsibility and work capacity view themselves as having increased value. It stands to reason that respondents perceive growth in capacity leading to increased viability in the job market and increased value in the library. It is hoped that library administrations are as readily acknowledging this value as technical services supervisors are.

Most respondents were from larger technical services units (nine were in units of 26 or more; 4 in units of 21 to 25 staff (see Figure 3.1). In most cases, technical services staffs had shrunk in size. Only 4 libraries reported any net increase at either 5 years or 10 years. The results indicate that the technical services units of many academic libraries are accomplishing more work with fewer people. Respondents in the follow-up referred to issues relating to decreased staff in technical services areas (Fradenburgh 2003; Mueller 2003).

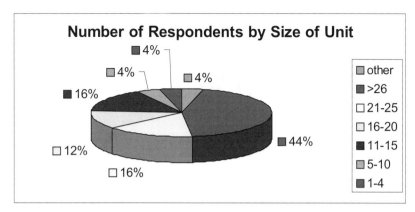

Figure 3.1. Number of Respondents by Size of Unit.

Respondents were fairly evenly divided in terms of satisfaction on the job. Twelve were satisfied, nine were dissatisfied, two were concerned, and two were indifferent. It is interesting that there was no particular correlation between perception of increased viability in the job market and value on the job and job satisfaction. Of 11 respondents who expressed dissatisfaction and concern regarding the job, 8 saw professionals as more viable and more valuable. That's not significantly different from 12 who were satisfied, 10 of whom saw professionals as more viable and more valuable. (See Figure 3.2.)

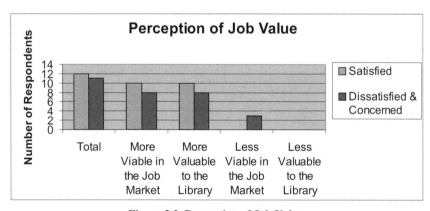

Figure 3.2. Perception of Job Value.

A correlation was found between unit size and satisfaction regarding the job. All respondents working in medium-sized technical services units (11–15 staff members) also reported satisfaction in light of staff changes (see Figure 3.3). The idea of an optimal size for technical services units is unavoidable in light of this finding, an idea discussed further in the Conclusion section.

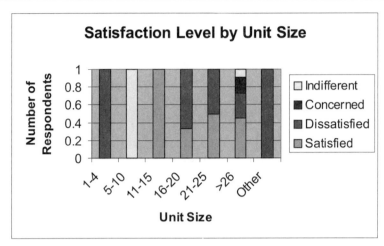

Figure 3.3. Satisfaction Level by Unit Size.

Of the 25 respondents, 14 responded affirmatively to the request to participate in a qualitative study in the form of an in-depth interview to follow this publication. We anticipate valuable insights to emerge from the accounts of a
number of these highly experienced librarians. A few respondents were chosen
to answer a brief list of follow-up questions to comment on their survey responses and situations in their libraries.

Insights from the Follow-up

Although all respondents in the brief follow-up had comments regarding
electronic resources, a specific challenge mentioned by all was changes wrought
by serials vendors. One mentioned the change of major serials vendor and the
challenge of handling more contracts and negotiations than ever before (Mueller
2003). Another pointed to the positive aspects of vendors in an electronic environment, able to perform more services and functions than before (Doyle 2003).

Another common theme regarded as a challenge was the inability of libraries
to provide unified access to electronic resources. Three respondents to the follow-up
mentioned problems associated with having at least two sources of serials information: Web site journal lists and library catalogs (Doyle 2003; Fradenburgh 2003;
Mueller 2003). They recognized it as a problem, but mentioned no silver bullet providing a definitive answer to the situation. One waxed eloquent, elaborating on the
problem of multiple sources: "The bifurcation of librarians about the role of the catalog: one tool, the equal of many others, or the primary mother-lode via which all
searching [is] channeled. Nobody wants to talk about it!" (Doyle 2003).

Responses showed innovation of many kinds—reorganization, creation of
new positions, writing new procedures to address the electronic environment—
and pointed out the need for further change. One respondent mentioned success
in reclassifying some positions in technical services from entry-level to

professional to utilize a more skilled pool of employees. Further, he described the creation of new procedures that worked more effectively in the electronic environment, but called for a change in the mindset of staff members so they would be able to grasp the worth of working in innovative ways (Nuzzo 2003). Another respondent described moving through the challenge of learning to deal with the new contracts in the electronic environment, to now tackling the new challenge: the complexity of coordinating all aspects of the new contracts and the huge amount of money involved. This effort calls for a giant step up in terms of collaboration and cooperation among library departments, university offices, publishers, consortia, and, upon occasion, even lawyers (Lewis 2003). One respondent described a real departure from the traditional acquisitions/cataloging departments of technical services, to an innovative reorganization that streamlined the entire processing of monographs from request to OPAC record. Called the MACC Unit (Monographic Acquisitions/Copy Cataloging), it is discussed in Chapter 14 of this book (Ramsay 2003).

Conclusions

Responses from academic librarians with years of experience provide a great deal of insight into the changing role technical services units are playing in academic libraries. Clearly, academic technical services has absorbed new technology and its related processes, specifically electronic resources, while also dealing with diminishing staffs as positions are eliminated or reassigned to other departments.

Responses point to a certain sense of self-worth among technical services staffs. Respondents pointed to growth and change in their units, both in terms of workloads and expanded roles in the library, as new technologies were introduced and new skills and processes were learned.

The situation of professionals in technical services units was difficult to ignore in the survey results. The perception of increased work with a lack of corresponding growth in library roles among professionals, coupled with a large segment reporting dissatisfaction, points to a real problem: professionals whose work and professional growth has possibly gone unrecognized in academic libraries. It is difficult to ignore the fact that an accomplished segment of the staff, those who trained paraprofessionals to take on increasing responsibility in cataloging and acquisitions processes, remains to be tapped for its wealth of experience and ability. Their future may be in positions of library administration, administering collaborative projects, or learning and teaching new processes related to electronic resources.

The highest level of satisfaction found in light of technical services staff changes was in mid-sized technical services units. This finding bears some thought, particularly for those in libraries with large staffs. There may be ways to reconfigure the work of technical services to maximize job satisfaction. Some ideas to consider are structuring work for less specialization and more cross training, and structuring departments in smaller work groups.

Note

*The authors are very grateful to Araby Greene for mounting the survey on the University of Nevada, Reno's Library Web site and for her valuable help in loading data into an SPSS file. Thanks is also due to Molly Mott for her work in generating graphs and tables.

References

Boydston, Jeanne M. K., and Joan M. Leysen. 2001. "Internet resources cataloging in ARL libraries: Staffing and access issues." In *E-Serials Cataloging: Access to Continuing and Integrating Resources via the Catalog and the Web.* New York: Haworth Information Press.

Doyle, Ann. 2003. Personal communication, May 29.

Fradenburgh, Robin. 2003. Personal communication, May 28.

Lewis, Linda. 2003. Personal communication, June 4.

McCarthy, Patrick. 1998. "Considering staff adaptation to change: A report from ALCTS Heads of Technical Services of Medium-Sized Academic Libraries Discussion Group." In *ALA Midwinter Conference Reports.* Chicago: American Library Association. PII S0364-6408(98)00064-7.

Mueller, Susan. 2003. Personal communication, May 28.

Nuzzo, David. 2003. Personal communication, June 4.

Ouderkirk, Jane Padham. 2000. "Staff assignments and workflow distribution at the end of the 20th century: Where we were, where we are and what we'll need to be," *Cataloging & Classification Quarterly* 30 (2/3): 343–356.

Ramsay, Karen. 2003. Personal communication, June 4.

Wilder, Stanley. 2000. "The changing profile of research library professional staff." *A Bimonthly Report on Research Library Issues and Actions from ARL, CNI and SPARC* 208/209 (February/April). Available: http://www.arl.org/newsltr/208_209/chgprofile.html (Accesssed May 6, 2003).

Withers, Rob. 2001/2002. "A decade of change—a study of acquisitions positions in libraries." *Against the Grain* (December/January): 73. Available: http://www.against-the-grain.com (Accessed May 6, 2003).

Appendix 3.1:
Technical Services Survey

1. In your library, technical services includes (check all that apply):

    ☐ Order processing   ☐ Serials processing ☐ Electronic resources ☐ Cataloging
    ☐ Marking   ☐ Interlibrary loan ☐ Other. Please specify ___

2. What is the size of your technical services unit (FTE; include students,
    part-time, full-time, all paid employees)?

    ☐ 1–4   ☐ 5–10   ☐ 11–15   ☐ 16–20   ☐ 21–25   ☐ 26 or more

3. Your technical services unit has had a net increase or decrease (FTE) of
    staff in the past:

    5 years: Increased: ☐ 1–2 ☐ 3–4 ☐ 5–6 ☐ 7–8 ☐ more—how many? ___
              Decreased: ☐ 1–2 ☐ 3–4 ☐ 5–6 ☐ 7–8 ☐ more—how many? ___

    10 years: Increased: ☐ 1–2 ☐ 3–4 ☐ 5–6 ☐ 7–8 ☐ more—how many? ___
              Decreased: ☐ 1–2 ☐ 3–4 ☐ 5–6 ☐ 7–8 ☐ more—how many? ___

4. In the past 10 years, these categories of staff have had a net increase or de-
    crease (FTE)

    Professional: Increased: ☐ 1–2 ☐ 3–4 ☐ 5–6 ☐ 7–8 ☐ more—how many? __
                   Decreased: ☐ 1–2 ☐ 3–4 ☐ 5–6 ☐ 7–8 ☐ more—how many? __

    Paraprofessional: Increased: ☐ 1–2 ☐ 3–4 ☐ 5–6 ☐ 7–8 ☐ more—how many? __
                      Decreased: ☐ 1–2 ☐ 3–4 ☐ 5–6 ☐ 7–8 ☐ more—how many? __

5. What is your position (check all that apply)

    ☐ Professional   ☐ Paraprofessional   ☐ Cataloging Supervisor
    ☐ Acquisitions Supervisor   ☐ Serials Supervisor
    ☐ Electronic Resources Supervisor   ☐ Other. Please specify: _____

6. The number of years of your work experience in libraries is as follows:

    In this library: ☐ 0–5 ☐ 6–10 ☐ 11–15 ☐ 16–20 ☐ 21 or more
    Total experience: ☐ 0–5 ☐ 6–10 ☐ 11–15 ☐ 16–20 ☐ 21 or more

7. Consider the roles/job descriptions of professionals in your technical services unit. In the last 10 years their roles have:

    □ Grown larger in scope/responsibility
    □ Grown smaller in scope/responsibility
    □ Shifted to other areas   □ Not changed

8. If the roles of professionals have grown larger, their new responsibilities are:

    □ Moved from other library departments
    □ New to the library

9. In the last 10 years, the work loads of professionals have:

    □ Grown larger
    □ Grown smaller
    □ Not changed

10. If roles of professionals have changed, professionals have become (check all that apply):

    □ More viable in the job market
    □ Less viable in the job market
    □ More valuable to the library
    □ Less valuable to the library

11. Consider the roles/job descriptions of paraprofessionals in your technical services unit. In the last 10 years their roles have:

    □ Grown larger in scope/responsibility
    □ Grown smaller in scope/responsibility
    □ Shifted to other areas   □ Not changed

12. If the roles of paraprofessionals have grown larger, their new responsibilities are:

    □ Moved from other library departments
    □ New to the library

13. In the last 10 years, the work loads of paraprofessionals have:

    □ Grown larger
    □ Grown smaller
    □ Not changed

14. If roles have changed, paraprofessionals have become (check all that apply):

☐ More viable in the job market
☐ Less viable in the job market
☐ More valuable to the library
☐ Less valuable to the library

15. When you think about staffing changes in your technical services unit, you feel (check all that apply):

☐ satisfied   ☐ dissatisfied   ☐ indifferent   ☐ angry   ☐ confused
☐ fearful   ☐ resentful   ☐ thankful   ☐ joyful   ☐ sad
☐ other, please specify _____

16. Would you be willing to participate in an in-depth interview exploring further aspects of staffing in your library and your experiences/observations regarding staffing?

4

Change and Adaptation in the Technical Services of a Group of Mid-sized Academic Libraries: A 14-Year Overview

Pamela Cline Howley

Editor's note: The author presents a multiple case study of evolution, adaptation, and change in the cataloguing and other technical services functions in a selected group of medium-sized academic libraries in the United States and Canada. The study was based on the analysis and comparison of the responses given by this group of libraries to what are essentially the same survey questions at a 14-year interval, first in 1989 and then in 2003. The author provides some interesting statistics between and among the results of the two surveys. The results are divided into three categories: technical services organization, changing responsibilities of librarians and staff, and responses to the new environment.

The Context of the Study

For the vast majority of academic libraries, the period since 1989 has seen the transition from local card catalogs and early online systems to fully implemented integrated library systems and sophisticated online catalogues, most of which are now Web-based and therefore accessible globally. Catalogers and cataloging departments have successfully managed, and indeed have guided and influenced, this fundamental environmental shift with flexibility, creativity, and imagination, while at the same time coping with ever-increasing demands for quality access to research and information resources of all types.

The past 14 years have been difficult ones for library technical services operations. It is a given that the whole of the library profession has been experiencing great change, and that this change is continuous. For librarians in the traditionally defined technical services areas of practice, in particular cataloging, the rate of this change has been especially great, and its trajectory has generally been discouraging. Cataloging, together with reference, was until recently accepted as fundamental to professional librarianship. In spite of that, we have witnessed a major decline in the number of cataloging positions in academic libraries. Indeed, as Wilder reports in his study of the changing profile of research library professional staff in ARL member libraries: "In 1998, there were 302 fewer cataloguers in ARL university libraries than in 1990 . . . a drop of 25 percent in just eight years" (2000, p. 3). Whether or not one agrees that it is a good thing, it is probably true, as Wilder asserts, that this decline is part of a larger shift in priorities among the ARL libraries. Nevertheless, the possibility of absorbing a decline of this magnitude has depended on the impact of what are well-recognized trends. These include the very positive effect that successful standardization and sophisticated technology have had on productivity (enabling and facilitating the shared cataloging that has led to a major falloff in the amount of original cataloging required by any given institution, and making the reference tools and information sources essential to the cataloging process easily accessible from the desktop); the pressure to increase the efficiency of operations brought on by shrinking library budgets; the resultant tendency to delegate previously professional level tasks to support staff; and the corresponding effort to redefine the cataloging professional as a manager rather than as a practitioner.

At the same time that the decline in the number of professional catalogers has been taking place, there has been no diminution in the amount of material to be cataloged. Even though many academic libraries have faced cuts in their materials budgets, there has been an increasing demand for more access and enhanced access to materials in all kinds of formats: maps, audiovisual materials, government documents, even gray literature and ephemera, and of course to electronic resources of all kinds. In addition there has been a burgeoning of roles and tasks that, although not defined in terms of the cataloger's traditional skill set, nevertheless demand expertise of the same kind—non-MARC database development, the devising and implementation of appropriate metadata schema, the provision of enhanced access to special collections, and so forth. The investigation and analysis of the ways in which organizational structures have changed and are changing provides some insight into how cataloging librarians and other technical services personnel have been enabled to meet the unprecedented demands placed on their operations over this time period. In an important survey of the changing role of professional catalogers, Eskoz (1990) included an examination of the common organizational patterns of cataloguing departments in ARL libraries in the mid- to late 1980s. The present study updates and complements the results of that earlier survey. Although more limited in terms of the number of libraries surveyed, the survey reported on here is more detailed in regard to organizational patterns and covers not only cataloging departments but also the larger context of technical services operations.

Methodology

As noted previously, the present study is based on the analysis and comparison of the responses given by the sample group of libraries to what are essentially the same survey questions initially asked in 1989 and again some 14 years later. The first survey was designed as an information-gathering tool with the purpose of discovering alternative approaches to organization for possible application at my own institution. Accordingly, the intent was not strictly to compare and quantify existing practices. The survey questions were therefore free text and open-ended.

A total of 72 survey questionnaires were mailed in May 1989, with follow-up letters sent to nonrespondents in July. A total of 37 full responses were received, a return rate of 51 percent. The surveyed libraries were selected from the 1989/1990 edition of the ALA *Directory* as "middle-sized" on the basis of enrollment, staff size, and reported holdings. In practice, "middle-sized" was defined quite broadly. Holdings of the selected libraries varied in size from a low of 462,000 to a high of 2,065,000. The average size was just over 1,200,000. Eleven libraries included are currently ARL members. An attempt was made to select libraries with a representative geographic spread.

The 1989 survey questionnaire comprised seven questions. The first three concentrated on the organizational structures themselves, and the other four explored the roles and responsibilities of the staff within those structures. In addition to these same seven questions, which were repeated in 2003, the follow-up survey included three supplementary questions designed specifically to address some major aspects of the changing environment: direct involvement in systems-related activities and the provision of access to digital resources, as well as a more general question regarding the emergence of new roles for cataloging and technical services personnel. Then, as a final question, survey contacts were asked what, in their opinion, had been the greatest change in cataloging since 1989 and what had been the catalyst of that change. Copies of the 1989 and 2003 survey questionnaires are included as Appendixes 4.1 and 4.2 respectively.

In January 2003, the follow-up survey was sent by e-mail to each of the libraries that had responded in 1989. A scanned copy of the questionnaire as completed in 1989 was included to provide context. Reminders were sent to nonrespondents in March. This time 29 full responses were received, for a response rate of 78.4 percent. Follow-up questions were directed to several respondents to clarify certain points in their responses. The results summarized here represent information provided in the responses from these 29 libraries. The 1989 responses from the eight libraries for which the second survey was not received have been eliminated from discussion, except that four of those libraries provided partial responses, mainly based on the fact that they were in the midst of a major reorganization and either did not have the time or felt that any responses would soon be out-of-date. Three of these libraries did, however, provide responses to the final survey question regarding the greatest change in their cataloging operations, and their responses are included in that section.

The survey questions were intended to elicit a picture not only of the organizational structure itself but also of the size, makeup, and responsibilities of staff within that structure. Although the detailed emphasis was on cataloging functions, the larger context of technical services organization and responsibility was also examined. Because the survey questions were free text and open-ended, a certain amount of interpretation is reflected in the analysis of the results. What follows is a series of comparative "snapshots" of the organizations in these 29 libraries, and comparisons of how they have evolved and adapted over the intervening years.

For the purposes of this discussion, the analysis of the results of the first three survey questions has been reordered to begin with the examination of the broader technical services organization, then move on to the organization and staffing of cataloging departments and their functional units, and finally discuss the roles and responsibilities of librarians and support staff in cataloging operations. Overall, the survey responses fall into three broad categories, and for convenience I review these under the following headings: technical services organization, changing responsibilities of librarians and staff, and responses to the new environment.

Technical Services Organization

Organization is a key element in establishing and maintaining a successful and flexible working environment, an environment that serves both to reflect and to influence the development of effective working relationships. The larger environment in which cataloging activities take place is, of course, the cluster of operations termed technical services. Gorman defines technical services as "all the tasks carried on in a library that are concerned with the processing of library materials in order to make them accessible to the users of the library" (1990, p. 2). In organizational terms, technical services is usually defined as some combination of the operations carried out in the acquisitions, cataloging, and serials departments or units. With the advent of integrated library systems the interaction and interrelationships among these functions have perforce become greater and more complex. Paradoxically, such interaction has also largely become easier, since the requirements imposed by systems processes make close cooperation both mandatory and natural. To develop a picture of the changes in this larger environment, the survey asked respondents how cataloging is related to other technical services functions. The 1990s saw a major trend toward the flattening of bureaucratic hierarchies in both public and private sector enterprises, a trend that led to the elimination of many middle-management level positions. To gauge the extent to which that trend was realized in academic library organizations, the survey also asked whether there was a head of technical services position in the library.

Head of Technical Services as Middle Management

In 1989, 23 libraries (79.3 percent) reported having a head of technical services or the equivalent, although one of these positions had been vacant for three years. All but one of these positions carried the designation "technical services" in its title. In the 2003 survey, this number had dropped to 16 (55.2 percent), once again with one position reported as vacant. Six libraries, including the one in which the position was unfilled in 1989, have eliminated this role as a recognizable component of their organizational hierarchies. In one other library reporting no "head of technical services," however, the administrative structure has been organized to split what are traditionally technical services functions between two different middle-management positions.

Of the 16 libraries retaining some version of the technical services position, 10 continued to apply the designation "technical services" in 2003, although one of these has expanded the title to include "information resources". The other positions now carry titles that for the most part reflect a broader mandate, with an emphasis on the management of activities surrounding the library's resources and collections. These titles include Associate University Librarian for Collections Services; Associate Director for Collection Management, Organization and Preservation; the above-mentioned Assistant Director for Information Resources and Technical Services; Associate Director for Resources and Collections Services and Associate Director for Information Systems and Access (technical services functions under both rubrics); Assistant Dean for Bibliographic and Access Services; and Head, Collection Management Services. Two libraries report having added the equivalent of a head of technical services since 1989. One of these positions, however, is currently vacant.

Functional Units Under Technical Services

The functions most often reported as separate administrative units under the mantle of technical services are still acquisitions and cataloging. In 2003, 24 of the responding libraries (82.7 percent) reported having administratively separate acquisitions and cataloging operations, compared to 27 of 29 (93.1 percent) in 1989. The persistence of the pattern of separate acquisitions and cataloging departments is rather surprising given that integrated library systems have made the interrelationship between these two basic functions especially close, with searching, verification, and the importation of bibliographic records constituting common activities within acquisitions. Indeed several libraries report that some basic cataloging, usually of titles with full LC copy, has been moved into acquisitions in rapid cataloging or cataloging-on-receipt operations.

Of the two other libraries in 1989, one reported combining acquisitions and cataloging in each of two separate departments, monographs and serials, while the second did not provide this information. In 2003, only three libraries reported having combined acquisitions and cataloging operations within a single department. One of these libraries has a single technical services division, with the functions divided internally into sections. Another has a combined acquisitions and cataloging department that also includes interlibrary loan. The library that had separate monographs and serials departments in 1989 now has a unified processing department divided into monographic and serials sections. All three of these departments include serials as well as monographs. A fourth library, however, now has separate monographs and serials departments, each of which combines cataloging and acquisitions functions by format and is headed by a librarian cataloger. One other library reports a team structure in which the discrete functions are unclear.

Serials is the third grouping of operations traditionally considered to fall under the jurisdiction of technical services. Already in 1989, the isolation of serials operations at the departmental level was reported in a minority, or 10, of the libraries (34.5 percent). This number had dropped to seven (24.1 percent) by 2003. One library has added a separate department for serials since 1989. In addition, one library reports having two separate serials departments: one for serials acquisitions and one for serials cataloging. In contrast are the two libraries noted above that have operations divided into monographic and serials units, in each of which cataloging and acquisitions are combined. Finally, one of the libraries that now has discrete cataloging and acquisitions departments is planning a reorganization into a materials- or format-based model configured as print and nonprint (including electronic) departments. This will be a unique configuration among this group of libraries.

Currently, the majority of the survey libraries integrate serials, and most often electronic resources as well, with monographs in both cataloging and acquisitions operations—this despite the fact that as serials are increasingly represented in electronic form, the ways in which they are handled have changed significantly. The integration of serials into cataloging and acquisitions departments has been incremental. In several libraries reporting separate departments in 1989, the cataloging component of serials management was carried out in the cataloging department, leaving the serials department to manage subscription and holdings matters. This is true of one of the separate departments in 2003 as well.

In the responses for 2003, both preservation (eight libraries) and collection development/management (seven libraries) were reported as departments under the rubric of technical services more often than was serials. Other departments included in technical services groupings were special collections (in three libraries), access services (circulation and interlibrary loan/document delivery), database management, and systems (in two libraries each).

In the survey group, the technical services divisions of 22 libraries (75.9 percent) have been reorganized since 1989, by adding, removing, dividing, and/or combining functions into new configurations. Interestingly, an examination of these changes reveals very few definite trends. As noted previously, in this group of libraries at least, the division of materials by format is becoming less common at the departmental level, although there are clear exceptions to this trend. More libraries are also combining activities that relate to resource management, such as collection development and preservation and special collections, with the traditional technical service areas. Access services, including circulation—which Gorman (1990, p. 3) includes in his defining list of technical service processes—and/or interlibrary loan/document delivery, have been combined with traditional technical services in only two libraries, and moved elsewhere in a third, even though these functions have a considerable commonality with technical services because of integrated systems and the utilization of large bibliographic databases.

One library has a particularly unconventional organizational structure: One associate director oversees acquisitions, cataloging, serials acquisitions, collection development, preservation, and special collections operations. A different associate director has responsibility for electronic resources, which includes serials cataloging, and also for documents management, all database management activities, and authorities maintenance. The wide administrative separation of functions that are essentially similar, and in the case of database management and authorities, interdependent with other technical services activities, is unparalleled and therefore particularly interesting. The survey response did not provide details of how the departments interact on a day-to-day basis, but it is reasonable to assume that cooperation is close and effective.

Organization of Cataloging Departments and Operations

In spite of the difficulties and challenges presented by the vast proliferation of information in all formats and the shrinking of academic library budgets, catalogers and cataloging departments do, as noted by Eskoz in 1990 (p. 390), continue to exist as recognizable and viable entities in today's academic libraries. It has doubtless been necessary for departments to reorganize in flexible and creative ways just to continue to fulfill their traditional functions while absorbing complex new responsibilities. Predictably, all of the cataloging functions in the survey have been the subject of organizational change since 1989. The greatest quantifiable change in cataloging departments has been the loss of staff, at both the professional and the support staff level. Clerical level positions, those that were dedicated to typing, card-filing, data inputting and labeling, have been eliminated by automation.

Staffing

The first survey question asked for a breakdown of staff in the cataloging department by level, as well as how many titles were cataloged annually. In the 29 libraries surveyed, the number of titles processed ranged from a high of 91,000 (actually reported as items) to a low of 6,000. The majority of libraries were, however, in the 20,000 to 50,000 title range, and the average annual production was 31,750. Some of the discrepancy in numbers is no doubt due in part to differences in the way institutions keep their statistics, for example, as titles or items and what kind of and how materials are counted. Staff sizes ranged surprisingly widely, from thirty to three and a half. To some degree these numbers also reflect differences in functional structures, in what activities and groupings are or are not included under the general rubric of the cataloging department. In cases where different functions were combined, the numbers are of those engaged in cataloging, in so far as it was possible to determine from the survey responses. One library has a considerable portion of its cataloging done by librarians outside the cataloging department, and these catalogers have been included in the numbers. Average staff size was just over fourteen; the average number of librarians per department was four. Librarians accounted for about 29 percent of the cataloging positions in this group of libraries. However, the proportion of librarians to support staff in cataloging departments ranged widely, from as low as 7 percent to as high as 56 percent.

The majority of these cataloging departments, 16 (55.2 percent), have had a decrease in overall staff size since 1989, several suffering dramatic losses of up to as much as 50 percent of positions. At the same time, however, eight of these same sixteen libraries reported substantial, even impressive, increases in productivity reflected in titles catalogued annually. Four more of the sixteen maintained the same level of productivity enjoyed in 1989. Six catalog departments reported staff of approximately the same size as in 1989, although the level and/or deployment of positions may have changed. On the other hand, seven libraries actually reported increases in staffing. This was, in at least two cases, in response to major increases to the library's materials budget. In others, the increase may be more the result of redeployment and restructuring than the addition of actual positions. Given the wide range of organizational change and restructuring that has taken place, staffing increases per se are perhaps not so surprising as at first glance.

Looked at another way, 14 cataloging departments (48.3 percent) report increases in productivity. Eight of these also report having suffered staff losses. Another seven libraries maintained the 1989 level of productivity, four with decreases in staff. Finally, two libraries did report a fall in productivity, one of these because serials were no longer included in the statistics. Comparative data from 1989 were not available for the other libraries.

Four libraries report outsourcing some portion of their cataloging work-load, mostly monographic copy. Interestingly, only two of these libraries report an actual decrease in cataloging staff, and one has even seen an increase. Several libraries also batch load vendor records, from aggregators for example, and these records may be reflected in their production statistics. Two libraries report-ing increased productivity volunteered the fact that they maintain large active backlogs—of two to three years in one case and of 20,000 titles in the other. Since both of these libraries make use of rapid cataloging procedures, the exis-tence of these backlogs demonstrates the enormous increase in materials to be cataloged.

As noted previously, these numbers are open to more than one interpreta-tion, and in many cases the situations in 1989 and 2003 are not comparable one to one. Nevertheless, the numbers do serve to demonstrate clearly that, for this sample group at least, cataloging departments are indeed managing to do more with less.

Organization of Cataloging Functions

As might be expected, in both 1989 and 2003, survey responses indicate a wide variety of organizational patterns, although all libraries reported carrying out cataloging activities within definable organizational structures. The histories and cultures of specific institutions no doubt have shaped the kinds of practical and creative organizational solutions developed in response to the challenges of both the internal and external academic library environment.

In her comparative study of the role of catalog librarians, Eskoz investi-gated the most common organizational patterns found in the catalog depart-ments of a group of American academic libraries. She identified three major patterns: 1) departments with a basically flat structure, having few internal sub-divisions; 2) departments divided into two basic sections: original and copy cat-aloging; and 3) departments with multiple formal internal sections (1990, pp. 383–384).

Although these three basic patterns were represented in the 1989 survey re-ported here, the departments described were often difficult to categorize distin-guishably in these terms. The majority of libraries, 17 (58.6 percent), had multiple internal divisions, although these divisions were formalized to varying degrees. Seven libraries (24.1 percent) had flat departmental organizations, and only two had the basic copy/original cataloging split. One additional library re-ported having two formal sections, but these were designated as "record cre-ation," including both copy and original records, and "record maintenance". But some libraries had less conventional organizations. One library combined serials cataloging and catalog maintenance in a department separate from monographic cataloging. Another library had separate departments for original cataloging and for database maintenance, while copy cataloging was a section under the pur-view of the head of the acquisitions department. Only one library in the 1989 survey had cataloging operations organized into teams, which in this case were structured according to broad academic disciplines.

Of the cataloging functions detailed in 1989, copy cataloging was most frequently defined more or less formally as a separate section within the department—in 15 libraries (or 51.7 percent). This was closely followed by database or catalogue maintenance in 14 libraries (48.3 percent) and original cataloguing in 11 (37.9 percent). Original catalogers were not formally organized in a distinct unit in five libraries, either because they worked independently or because they also had responsibility for other functional units. Six libraries (20.7 percent) reported separate sections for serials cataloging, while separate recon and physical processing sections were reported in several libraries. In general, with the exception of serials, the pattern for most of the 1989 survey libraries was an organization built around functions or types of activity within the cataloging operation, such as copy cataloging or database maintenance, rather than around format or type of material handled.

In 2003, the number of cataloging departments having basically flat organizations had grown from seven to eleven. Strikingly, only three of these eleven were among the seven libraries that had flat structures in 1989. The number of departments with multiple internal sections had declined from 17 to 11 (37.9 percent), and the nature of these sections had in many cases evolved. Although functional divisions based on type of activity are still relatively prevalent, there has been a definite trend toward what Eskoz (1990, p. 384) referred to as specialty "clusters," which for this group of libraries are based mostly on the type or format of material handled. Four of these libraries characterized their organized groups as "teams." The team structure shares many characteristics with the specialty cluster and may in practice be difficult to distinguish from it. In fact, in a 1994 survey of cataloging teams in academic libraries, Schuneman and Mohr defined the team "cataloging mode" as being essentially the same as Eskoz's cluster pattern. The "cluster" or "team" pattern combines original and some copy cataloging and is staffed by a mixture of librarians and nonprofessional staff (Schuneman and Mohr 1994, p. 257). Examples from the survey responses include groups dedicated to monographs, serials, electronic resources, documents, special formats, and/or combinations thereof. One of these libraries also has a group dedicated to East Asian materials and another a section dedicated to fine arts, while yet another organizes its teams predominantly around broad subject and language areas. This last library is not, incidentally, the same library that made use of discipline-centered teams in 1989. That library has since reorganized into a more conventional structure.

However, three other libraries that characterize their organization as team-based have operations that appear to be less clearly demarcated organizationally—organizations in which responsibilities and reporting lines as well as group boundaries seem to be more fluid and less clearly drawn, and where there appears to be an emphasis on group and cooperative action. For example, one of these libraries assigns librarians to primary and secondary responsibilities, so that one's place in the organization is more fluid.

In any case, although Eskoz (1990) found that in 1987 the cluster pattern seemed to be less common than it had been, the results of this survey would certainly indicate at least a temporary resurgence. Schuneman and Mohr (1997) also found that this pattern was not uncommon. Contrary to their finding, however, that subject-based teams were the most prevalent kind of cataloging team, the present study found that organization around format was the dominant approach.

In regard to the organization of specific cataloging functions, it is noteworthy that in contrast to the 1989 results, only four libraries (13.7 percent) reported having a separate section dedicated to copy cataloging in 2003. A fifth library, one of those employing a team organization, designates a discrete copy cataloging unit. Although, as noted previously, at least four of the survey libraries are outsourcing some portion of their monograph copy, copy cataloging is still being done in all the survey libraries. Responsibility for this work is attributed to specific groups of staff in the survey responses of the vast majority of libraries. In those libraries having internal divisions, copy cataloging is most often included with original cataloging in the specialty groupings discussed previously. It also should be mentioned that simple copy cataloging, usually defined as that using LC copy, is done as a "fastcat" or cataloging-on-receipt operation in the acquisitions department of at least two of the sample libraries and is being considered in two more. In two libraries LC copy cataloging is actually being done by student assistants. Finally, in two other libraries this level of copy is handled by database maintenance staff.

The second most common functional unit reported in 1989 was catalog or database management or maintenance. In 2003, 10 libraries (34.5 percent) still had separately designated sections or teams dedicated to this function. (One of these includes "enhancement" in the title of the section.) Five more libraries indicated specific responsibility for maintenance work among departmental staff. One library had a completely separate database management department. In contrast, 12 libraries did not indicate where database or catalog maintenance responsibilities reside. Because this area has changed dramatically with the advent of integrated systems and Web-based catalogs and portals, it may be that some libraries categorize this work more as a systems-related function. Several libraries, for example, reported making use of system-generated reports to check for errors and to monitor cataloging activity.

Other functional sections reported in 2003 include physical processing and preservation/conservation sections in three libraries, remote storage in one library, and interlibrary loan in one library. No libraries reported having separate recon sections, although recon is still ongoing in at least two of the responding libraries. Three libraries designate responsibility for metadata apart from broader electronic resources or serials cataloging. There is a fuller discussion of metadata-related activities in the digital/electronic resources section below.

In view of the deepened interest in and emphasis on the importance of authority control, particularly in the global environment of Web-based catalogs and Internet resources, it is surprising that authorities work is not more obviously represented in the organizations of the survey libraries. Only ten libraries indicate responsibility for authorities, in most cases (six) as part of the database maintenance operation. There are no sections dedicated to authority control itself, although individual responsibility is specifically assigned in four departments. In the case of the other libraries, it seems reasonable to assume that authority control activities are integrated with the processes of both cataloging itself and of database management, and consequently are not specifically highlighted.

Finally, serials cataloging is done in the cataloging departments of 22 of the survey libraries (75.9 percent), 10 of which have separate serials units or teams; two of these combine serials with electronic resources and one with catalog maintenance. Six of these departments have assumed responsibility for serials cataloguing since 1989. In only five libraries (17.4 percent) are serials still cataloged in a separate serials department. In one library, only original cataloging of serials is done in the cataloging department, while copy is in fact done in acquisitions. And one library having no cataloging department per se combines acquisitions and cataloging in a serials unit.

Summary—Organization

In searching for trends or patterns in the organizational changes that have taken place in this sample group of medium-sized academic libraries, one is struck by the fact that the only truly dominant pattern is change itself. This coincides with the findings of the earlier comparative study of cataloging departments, conducted in 1986–1987: "Regardless of the present structure of catalog departments, reorganization and experimentation with new procedures are ongoing. . . . One interviewee summarized it succinctly: 'Things continually shift.' The wide variations of such shifting can be epitomized by two examples. One administrator stated that several cataloguing sections have merged. Another reported that what was formerly one large department has been separated into four units" (Eskoz 1990, p. 385). The results of the present study demonstrate the continuing prevalence of this kind of organizational change in cataloging departments and in their parent technical services divisions. Loss of staff has of course had an impact on the flexibility that these units can exercise in establishing effective organizational structures. It seems reasonable to assume that the changing configurations that are documented here are the result of creative and thoughtful efforts to cope, within the constraints of their individual institutions, with the pressing, even relentless, demands placed on these operations by the changing world of information and research. In other words, they represent the results of successful and effective coping strategies rather than the results of the concerted attempt to structure ideal organizational frameworks.

Changing Responsibilities of Librarians and Staff

There is considerable literature on the changing nature of the role of the professional librarian, especially the professional cataloger. At least two recent surveys, one addressing professional catalogers (Buttlar and Garcha 1998) and the other paraprofessionals (Mohr and Schuneman 1997), have explored the ways in which the roles of these respective groups have been evolving.

Original Cataloging

At one time, original cataloging was generally considered, in academic libraries at least, primarily to be the role of professional librarians. The extent to which this responsibility in particular has been progressively delegated to paraprofessionals or support staff has been the subject of much discussion in the literature and is documented in the surveys noted previously. To gauge the degree to which this trend applies in the survey libraries, respondents were asked who was responsible for original cataloging in their institutions.

In 1989, just over half (16) of the responding libraries reported that original cataloging was the sole responsibility of librarians at their institutions. Of the remaining 13 libraries, 11 (37.9 percent) reported that support staff assumed some responsibility for this task. The share varied considerably: In six libraries, support staff did only specific and limited types of materials, for example, local theses, minimum level cataloging, literature (belles lettres), children's books, and editions for which copy for a variant was available. In one library, support staff prepared the description, then passed the title on to librarians for the assignment of access points. Four institutions gave experienced support staff responsibility for unspecified types of original cataloging. It could be argued that cataloging that is based on a variant edition, or performing simple description without establishing access points, does not really constitute original cataloging. This would leave 17 libraries (58.6 percent) in which professional librarians were solely responsible. In two libraries original cataloging was mainly the responsibility of support staff. One of these had its staff divided into very broad subject-oriented teams doing verification, copy cataloging, original cataloging, added copies and volumes, withdrawals, and shelflist maintenance. This was the only library where librarians did virtually no cataloging. At the other library, the bulk of the original cataloging was done by support staff, though librarians in the section also did some.

In 2003 there was nearly an even split: Thirteen libraries (44.8 percent) reported that, with the exception of adapting copy from variant editions—a practice characterized as "cloning" by one respondent—original cataloging is still the responsibility of librarians only. Fourteen libraries (48.2 percent) now have support staff doing some share of the original, two more than in 1989. The same two libraries that reported in 1989 that most original cataloging was done by support staff continue that practice. Eighteen libraries (62 percent) report no change in the assignment of this responsibility. The responsibility undertaken by support staff has increased in nine libraries, either because they are now doing some original cataloging where none was done in 1989, or because the amount and/or type of material undertaken has increased. In two libraries some original cataloging was done by nonlibrarians in 1989, but none is being done now. In both of these libraries, the delegation of responsibility had been quite limited.

Although these findings do support the trend toward increased delegation of original cataloging, the change has not been dramatic in this group of libraries. One might speculate on possible reasons for this. The amount of original cataloging overall has diminished substantially for all but the larger research institutions. What remains is often very specialized or esoteric in nature (Lee-Smeltzer 2000, p. 319). This, coupled with the fact that most of the libraries in the survey group have also seen losses of staff level positions but increases in materials to be cataloged, may mean that support staff have more than enough to handle already and that there is consequently a diminished need and a reduced scope to delegate further. Finally, the qualifications or indeed the pay scales of available staff may make the delegation of such highly demanding work impractical or unethical.

Revision

One of the concerns, justified or not, surrounding the use of support staff to perform original cataloging is maintaining a high level of quality control in cataloging. This concern is directly related to the issue of cataloging revision. The systematic review or revision of catalogers' work, usually prior to final entry into the catalog or database, has been a standard approach used by cataloging departments to ensure an acceptable level of quality control. With the shrinking of cataloging staffs and the pressures toward efficiency and streamlining, this final step would seem to be a likely candidate for elimination. This issue was addressed in the survey, with the following results.

In 1989, the level of routine, systematic revision after the training period was already relatively low, although revision during the training period was the norm. Twelve (41 percent) of the twenty-nine libraries reported some level of ongoing routine revision. The actual level of revision was in some cases difficult to determine from the responses. In four of these libraries, all or most work was revised, while only original cataloging was revised in six. Three libraries specified that original work done by support staff was revised. Notably, in two libraries original cataloging was revised by support staff. In one of these libraries nonlibrarian staff had sole responsibility for original cataloging, but in the other the work was done by librarians. In the libraries in which routine revision was not done, several reported using sampling, or spot-checking, or revising as the need was perceived by either the individual or the supervisor. Some libraries reported the practice of proofreading, often using shelflist cards. One library reported using its systems capability to flag new headings as a way to catch errors.

Seven (24.1 percent) libraries reported no regular efforts at revision or checking continued after the training period.

One might expect the amount of revision in 2003 to have declined sharply in light of improved standardization of copy and constant pressures to increase efficiency. Although there was a decrease overall, and 11 libraries (37.9 percent) reported that no continuing effort is placed on revision beyond the training period, an equal number of 11 libraries (37.9 percent) still engaged in some routine revision of work. This revision is limited to original cataloging in seven libraries, four of which specify that originals done by support staff are routinely revised. Notably, in two libraries revision takes the form of the review by librarians of system-generated reports of cataloging activity, through which problems are identified and addressed. This approach may be seen as a replacement for the older practice of proofreading shelflist cards. From this one might infer that this practice, or some variation of it, is in fact more prevalent than was explicitly reported on the survey. As in 1989, other libraries indicate the use of spot-checking or revision not as done routinely but in response to a perceived need.

The level and/or type of revision changed between 1989 and 2003 in 12 libraries. The level has been reduced in only five libraries, however. On the other hand, revision has actually been increased in four libraries. In two of these cases, original cataloging is now being revised where it was not previously. In both of these libraries, support staff have now been delegated a share of original work. In one library spot-checking has been introduced. Furthermore, one library that reported no systematic revision after training in 1989 now has all cataloging revised.

The results from this group of libraries tend to support the findings of Mohr and Schuneman (1997, p. 211) that the systematic revision of original cataloging was more likely to apply to the work of paraprofessionals than to that of librarians. Accordingly, in a significant number of the libraries surveyed, librarians continue to exercise control over the process of original cataloging through revision and oversight, even though the responsibility for that activity may now be shared with support staff.

The decline in the overall quality of cataloging records is often commented upon, although the validity of such concerns has not been convincingly demonstrated. In an environment where productivity depends so heavily on the cooperative sharing of catalog records through large databases such as OCLC, the potential for the replication of errors, sometimes serious errors, in individual catalogs is undoubtedly cause for concern. Whether or not some level of systematic revision can be an effective means to maintain the overall quality of cataloging records is a matter for further research.

Supervisory Roles of Librarians

Many in the profession believe that, as previously professional work is delegated to the paraprofessional group, the role of the professional librarian in cataloging should properly become that of a manager. Mohr and Schuneman referred to the "emerging thought about the proper role of the professional librarian in technical services—and in the profession in general—as managers, leaders, innovators, less involved than previously in day-to-day operations" (1997, p. 206). To discover the extent to which this trend is demonstrated in this survey group, contacts were asked how many and to what extent cataloging librarians are involved in supervisory or management roles vis-B-vis support staff.

In 1989, 19 institutions (65.5 percent) reported that one or more cataloging librarians below the level of the department head had formal supervisory/management roles, typically in section head positions. Nine libraries had either an assistant head or a principal cataloger. Among the other positions reported were Head of Copy Cataloguing or the equivalent (8 libraries); Head of Database Management or equivalent (5 libraries); Head, Serials (4 libraries); Head, Original Cataloguing (2 libraries); and Head, Recon Unit (2 libraries). Presumably, most of these positions also had a cataloging component.

Ten libraries (34.5 percent) reported that no formal supervisory responsibilities were delegated to librarians other than the department head. Five of these indicated that, although they had no formal responsibility, one or more of their line librarians were involved in providing direction, advice, and problem-solving for staff on an informal basis; that is, they filled the role of resource persons. Some of these did take part in staff training, monitoring workflow, or deputizing for regular supervisors. In 21 libraries (72.4 percent) at least one catalog librarian had no supervisory or management role. A total of 70 (48 percent) of the librarian positions in the survey group were nonsupervisory/managerial. The great majority of these were engaged in original cataloging.

In 2003, the same overall numbers still applied. Once again 19 libraries (65.5 percent) reported that in addition to the department head, one or more cataloging librarians have formal supervisory/management roles. In the other 10 libraries (34.5 percent), no formal supervisory responsibility was delegated, although informal, resource, and advisory roles were noted in five. The situation within some individual libraries has changed. Six libraries that reported delegating supervision in 1989 did not in 2003, whereas another six have delegated responsibility when they did not formerly do so. Much more indicative of the change is the fact that only 40 positions have no supervisory component, or just under 34 percent of the total positions reported. The number of professional librarians in these cataloging departments has fallen from 146 in 1989 to 118 today, a drop of 19 percent—not as large a drop as that reported in the ARL group as a whole (25 percent), but still very substantial. Clearly it has been the nonmanagerial positions that have sustained the greatest loss. That is, it is not necessarily so that more catalogers are becoming managers; rather, fewer nonmanagerial positions exist.

At a time when cataloging courses are no longer mandatory in many library schools, and there has been a marked decrease in the number of professional positions for cataloging practitioners, the question of where future librarians are to acquire the complex knowledge and skills needed to successfully manage large, multifaceted cataloging operations has no easy answer.

Participation of Support Staff in Policy and Decision Making

Survey respondents were asked whether there was any mechanism in place at their libraries to allow for the participation of support staff in policy and decision making. There was general consistency in both sets of responses to this question. Only one library in 1989 and none in 2003 indicated that there were no such channels or mechanisms in place. Responses generally expressed an openness to and a welcoming of staff input into cataloging issues, although at least two libraries qualified this to apply mainly to input in an advisory capacity and/or regarding procedural matters.

By far the commonest formal mechanism for staff participation was and still is the regular departmental, section, or unit meeting. Eighteen libraries reported using regular meetings in 1989, and fifteen did in 2003. Meetings of other formal library committees or groups such as library councils or staff organizations were specified by four libraries in 1989 and by seven in 2003. Other methods mentioned were direct input by staff supervisors and section heads, frequent consultation and active encouragement of participation by staff in at least the idea and opinion level, and the use of a collegial team approach. One library actually encourages initiative and innovation on the part of its staff by providing monetary rewards.

For the most part, the survey responses did not give a clear indication of the extent to which the input of staff into the policy and decision-making process has a real impact beyond the advisory on the policies and decisions made. Of course, the degree to which any management is truly responsive to direct influence from nonmanagement personnel is very much a matter of individual and institutional philosophy and style. Nevertheless, it is notable that, without exception, the 2003 responses do indicate that the ideas and opinions of support staff are valued, and in many cases are actively encouraged.

Summary—Changing Responsibilities

On the evidence of the 2003 survey responses, the changes in the responsibilities of librarians and staff in technical services have been considerable, but they have been evolutionary rather than revolutionary. In the survey group of libraries, there has certainly been an increase in the delegation of previously professional responsibility, most often of original cataloging, to the support staff

group. Nevertheless, original cataloging continues to be a primary role for catalog librarians even in those departments where this work is shared with staff. Although the practice of systematic, routine revision has declined, some revision is
still done in the majority of the survey libraries. More of the librarians left in cataloging departments are now engaged in some level of supervision, often leading and overseeing the activities of functional subunits. All the libraries in the
survey have formal and/or informal mechanisms in place to facilitate and
encourage the expression of ideas and opinions on the part of staff.

Responses to the New Environment

The responses to the final three questions, which were designed to address
the impacts of some of the major issues presented by the new information and research environment, as well as the fourth identifying the major changes and their
sources, shared an emphasis on the challenges of adapting to dramatic and rapid
advances in information technology both internally, with sophisticated library
systems, and externally, with the emerging dominance of the Internet and other
electronic resources.

Involvement in Systems Work

During the period covered by the two surveys, technical services librarians
have been confronted by a double conundrum: how best to employ the emerging
technology to ensure that it functions as an agent of efficiency and greater productivity, while at the same time absorbing the additional workload in terms of
both format and content presented by the proliferation of electronic research
materials.

Not surprisingly, the reported involvement of technical services personnel
in systems-related activities was relatively high, especially in relation to the implementation and maintenance of integrated systems. Nine libraries (31 percent)
did, however, report little or no involvement in systems work, although one of
these comments that people work closely with the library's systems staff, while
another has a cataloger maintaining the departmental Web site. It may be that the
question was interpreted more broadly in some cases than in others.

Eight libraries (27.6 percent) reported moderate involvement in which the
activities detailed include collaborating closely with systems units on ILS implementation and maintenance issues, and on such specific issues as coding and
indexing, record displays and information content, providing report specification and catalog profiles, as well as the testing of system upgrades. In addition,
two of these libraries are involved directly or indirectly in the development and
maintenance of departmental or staff Web pages and/or in efforts to establish
cataloging documentation online.

Two responding libraries did not elaborate on the extent or nature of activity but did indicate that professional staff were directly assigned to systems

work. In one, the current head of technical services also serves as systems librarian; in the other, the former head of cataloging has been reassigned to the systems unit with responsibility for technical services matters.

Finally, 10 libraries (34.5 percent) indicated that cataloging or other technical services staff are extensively or heavily involved in systems work, which includes responsibility for indexing and field structure and the maintenance of system tables for the ILS, direct responsibility for various ILS modules, the import and export of MARC records, data loading and extracting, writing systems loaders, updating the proxy for remote access, the creation and maintenance of databases using various metadata, developing Web-based interfaces, and addressing indexing and metadata solutions for digital resources. One of these libraries has a computing consultant position shared between cataloging and acquisitions, and in another the head of cataloging serves as backup for the systems librarian.

These findings clearly demonstrate the trend toward greater demand for computer and systems skills among catalogers and other technical services personnel. These skills are over and beyond those day-to-day skills virtually all staff in technical services must have to cope with and effectively adapt to the instability and near-constant change in the essential tools of a workplace that is overwhelmingly systems-dependent.

Provision of Access to Digital/Electronic Resources

The importance of providing access to digital resources in academic libraries is incontestable. Although there has been considerable discussion and debate over whether conventional cataloging practices are adequate to this task, the vast majority of libraries in the survey sample are in fact cataloging at least some category of electronic material. Many are also involved in creating and implementing alternative methods of access.

Only one of the 29 survey libraries reported no involvement in the provision of access to digital resources, commenting that although they should be involved, there has as yet been no time available. Of the other 28 libraries, at least 26 (89.7 percent) catalog digital resources, and the specific approach to access was unclear in the other two. Five libraries specified only cataloging e-serials. In addition, four libraries also maintain Web site access for e-journals, databases, and/or other Web materials. Three libraries indicated involvement in URL checking, although the method and extent of this checking was not detailed. Three libraries commented that they also make use of records from commercial sources (from aggregators or e-book suppliers, for example) to supplement their in-house cataloging.

In addition to standard cataloging, nine libraries (31 percent) also are involved in providing alternative access to digital resources and collections. These efforts include providing Dublin Core descriptive, administrative, and structural metadata for locally created digital resources; involvement in ETD developments; provision of access to databases of images, slides, or photographs; working with other areas to develop metadata standards and guidelines; playing a leading role in metadata implementation for digital library development—setting content standards, developing the search architecture and the search interface; and setting up a geospatial data repository.

In view of the loss of cataloging positions over the last decade, it is interesting to note that seven libraries in the sample group have professional positions dedicated to metadata and electronic resources. At least three of these are newly created positions rather than restructured existing positions. Despite different degrees of involvement by different respondents, it is evident that participation in the organization of access to electronic resources by cataloging departments is a trend that can be expected to grow substantially. There is much work to be done to devise and implement effective access to digital and electronic materials—work that is well-suited to the skills and expertise of a new generation of catalogers.

New Roles for Technical Services Personnel

Survey contacts were asked to describe any new roles that have developed for cataloging and other technical services staff. Predictably, there was considerable overlap between the answers to this question and those to the preceding two regarding systems involvement and especially access to digital resources. In fact, 25 libraries (86.2 percent) described new roles involving electronic resources, metadata, and/or systems-related work. The roles detailed included cataloging of electronic resources, of course, but there was also an emphasis on alternative access, especially metadata development, standards, implementation, and support. Some of the responses expand on those given previously, such as involvement in campuswide consultation on metadata standards and automation needs, creating a Web site for the distribution of staff information, the creation and development of SQL and other non-MARC databases, leading digital library projects and initiatives, contracting with vendors and registering databases and e-journals, managing descriptive metadata for a subject-enhanced table of contents for a full-text journal article database, and participation in the development of linking systems. Five libraries noted the purchasing and batch loading of vendor records for e-books and various collections.

Several libraries described other kinds of new roles. Among these were the management of documents and remote storage; the cataloging of maps, sound recordings, and other types of media; the practice of fiscally oriented management; and participation in information desk work. It was somewhat surprising that only one library mentioned information desk work as a new role for technical services personnel.

Major Changes in Cataloging Since 1989

Technology and systems were overwhelmingly considered the major cata-lysts of change in cataloging operations since 1989. The major changes them-selves named by respondents were divided nearly evenly between the implementation of integrated library systems (14 respondents) and issues sur-rounding the advent of Internet and other electronic resources (16 respondents). Nine respondents specified the development of sophisticated cataloging sources and tools such as bibliographic utilities and desktop access. Specific changes cited relating to systems and/or electronic resources included movement from a model dealing primarily with individual titles and items to one emphasizing the batch processing of data from various sources (three libraries); taking a more proactive role in the provision of access and the establishment of content stan-dards; the complexity that electronic resources have added to acquisitions proce-dures due to the contracting and licensing requirements; and the use of cataloging workstations that allow cataloging to be done outside the cataloging department, enabling adoption of a team organization and of cross-divisional appointments (one library each).

On a different note, eight responses cited reorganizations of departments and functions, two of these specifying the flattening of administrative structures. Related to this were three responses highlighting the development of a more col-legial organization, characterized by team action and the blurring of traditional roles. More basic changes cited included loss of staff (three libraries), greater delegation of responsibility to staff (three libraries), completion of recon or re-classification projects (three libraries), and outsourcing and the standardization that has made it possible (two libraries).

The loss of staff was the only major catalyst named that did not deal directly with systems and/or electronic resources, and even this may be seen as a related consequence of the impacts of information technology. Specific statements of the major catalysts for change included user demand for remote access, espe-cially to full-text; budgetary reallocation in support of digital projects; adminis-trative support for access versus ownership; and the determination not to be marginalized in the effort to meet changing user needs.

None of these statements regarding the major changes in cataloging opera-tions, their influence, and their causes, is surprising in the context of the survey results as a whole, or in that of the broader situation of today's academic libraries.

Conclusion

For cataloging and technical services operations, at least in this group of survey libraries, the past 14 years, though challenging and difficult, have never-theless been a period of continued success and productivity. Reorganization, re-structuring, and the realignment of roles and responsibilities have enabled librarians and staff in these operations to continue to function at a level sufficient to serve the changing needs of their users while mastering complex new technologies and a multiplicity of new resource formats. As demonstrated by the responses to this survey, many technical services librarians are already involved in exciting and challenging work that requires the application of their expertise beyond the MARC-based environment. With the globalization of our catalogs and databases, and with the growing movement toward a convergence among cultural institutions—universities, museums, and archives—particularly in such areas as authority control (*International Conference Authority Control* 2003), the demand for this expertise will certainly grow. But there is a finite limit to what can be accomplished through reorganization, automation, and ingenuity alone. Technical services librarians must be wary not to fall into the role of Boxer in George Orwell's *Animal Farm*, whose response to problems in productivity was always, "I must work harder" (or better, or smarter). Rather, a new generation of technical services librarians, above all catalogers, must be recruited—librarians able to continue to balance the complex in-depth expertise in MARC-based cataloging essential to understanding, interpreting, and transforming the future's online catalogs, with the ability to transfer that skill and expertise beyond the MARC environment to multiple alternative modes of resource description, discovery, and access.

References

Buttlar, Lois, and Rajinder Garcha. 1998. "Catalogers in academic libraries: Their evolving and expanding roles." *College & Research Libraries* 59 (4): 311–321.

Eskoz, Patricia A. 1990. "The catalog librarian—change or status quo? Results of a survey of academic libraries." *Library Resources and Technical Services* 34 (2): 380–392.

Gorman, Michael. 1990. "Technical services today." In *Technical Services Today and Tomorrow*, edited by Michael Gorman, 1–5. Englewood, Colo.: Libraries Unlimited.

International Conference Authority Control: Definition and International Experiences (2003: Florence, Italy). 2003. Available: http://www.unifi.it/biblioteche/ac/en/program.htm (Accessed June 2003).

Lee-Smeltzer, Kuang-Hwei (Janet). 2000. "Cataloging in three academic libraries: Operations, trends and perspectives." *Cataloging and Classification Quarterly* 30 (2/3): 315–330.

Mohr, Deborah A., and Anita Schuneman. 1997. "Changing roles: Original cataloguing by paraprofessionals in ARL libraries." *Library Resources and Technical Services* 41 (3): 205–218.

Schuneman, Anita, and Deborah A. Mohr. 1994. "Team cataloguing in academic libraries: An exploratory survey." *Library Resources and Technical Service* 38 (3): 257–266.

Wilder, Stanley. 2000. "The changing profile of research library professional staff." *ARL (Online)* 208/209 (February/April). Available: http://www.arl.org/newsltr/208_209/chgprofile.html (Accessed June 2003).

Appendix 4.1: 1989 Questionnaire

1. Please describe the general reporting structure of the cataloging department, including the overall size and the breakdown of staff by level (or attach an organization chart). Approximately how many titles are processed annually?

2. How is cataloging related to other technical services functions? Is there a head of technical services?

3. Briefly describe the functional units or sections in cataloging, including the number and level of staff in each.

4. Who is responsible for original cataloging—librarians? If not, what qualifications are required?

5. Are there mechanisms in place to allow for the participation of support staff in policy and decision making?

6. What type and extent of revision/supervision is routinely undertaken?

7. How many and to what extent are cataloging librarians involved in supervisory or management roles vis-B-vis support staff?

8. Other comments.

Appendix 4.2: 2003 Questionnaire

1. Please describe the general reporting structure of the cataloging department, including the overall size and the breakdown of staff by level (or attach an organization chart). Approximately how many titles are processed annually?

2. How is cataloging related to other technical services functions? Is there a head of technical services?

3. Briefly describe the functional units or sections in cataloging, including the number and level of staff in each.

4. Who is responsible for original cataloging—librarians? If not, what qualifications are required?

5. Are there mechanisms in place to allow for the participation of support staff in policy and decision making?

6. What type and extent of revision/supervision is routinely undertaken?

7. How many and to what extent are cataloging librarians involved in supervisory or management roles vis-B-vis support staff?

8. What is the nature and extent of direct involvement by cataloging and other technical services units in systems work?

9. Are technical services units involved in providing access to digital resources?

10. Describe any new roles that have developed for cataloging or other technical services personnel.

11. In your opinion, what is the greatest change in cataloging and technical services in your library since 1989? What has been the main catalyst of that change?

12. Other comments.

5

Quality Cataloging with Less:
Alternative and Innovative Methods

Mary L. Mastraccio

Editor's note: Providing quality cataloging to ensure better service has been a long-standing objective of library technical services departments. At the same time, pressure has been increasing to accomplish this objective with diminishing funds. The author of this chapter draws heavily upon her experiences in both academic and public libraries to illustrate ways libraries can cut costs without sacrificing quality in technical services. Areas for review include technical resources, staff options, procedures, and workflow. With the ideas presented here, directors and librarians in technical services departments should be stimulated to review their current practices and policies to find ways to reduce costs. Extensive appendixes provide access to the literature on topics discussed throughout the chapter.

More with less is not a new theme, nor is it unique to libraries. A quick search in a library catalog for *more with less* will locate materials on a wide variety of subjects. Books with this theme have been written on cooking, coal mining, engineering, dieting, and business. History indicates that the need to produce more with less is at least as old as the pharaohs. Managers and organizations in all businesses and industries want the biggest bang for their bucks, and library boards, directors, and users are certainly no exception. Libraries are required to provide more information resources, more access points, and more retrieval options. At the same time tightening budgets mean less money for both staff and cataloging.

Economic factors today make it imperative that librarians review current practices and procedures to see which areas can be changed to enable their libraries to produce more with less. When facing a serious crisis, it is critical to look for new ways to resolve old problems—to use a common figure of speech, it is necessary to "think outside the box." Thinking outside the box entails crawling out of the box and taking a step back to examine and compare both what is in the box as well as alternative options not previously adopted when only looking at what is in the box. One of my most enjoyable courses at library school was on creative management. The movie *Apollo 13* was showing at a local theater, so we went to see a graphic example of stepping back and re-looking at what is in the box. The NASA engineers' initial reaction was that it was impossible to bring the astronauts back alive, but—when forced to rethink their engineering presuppositions—the impossible was accomplished.

Difficult or impossible situations force us to consider all available options and can lead to innovative and alternative practices. Michael Heifetz—author, change consultant, and seminar leader—shows companies and organizations the value of difficult circumstances. It is when circumstances are painful that we are most likely to consider change. His list of potential growth areas through forced change contains the very goals libraries strive to achieve. Every library seeks to improve services and customer relations, be more efficient and cost effective, and ensure employee job satisfaction (Heifetz 1993).

Technical services tasks have many opportunities to improve overall library services, increase employee job satisfaction, and become more cost effective when faced with cutbacks in spending. The primary objective is to provide quality cataloging with decreased expenditures. Once this objective is established, it will be easier to determine steps to achieve it. Key areas to review are technical resources, local policies and practices, staffing options, and workflow.

Technical Resources

The resources used in technical services have a significant impact on staff allocation and workflow options and may lead to changes in local policies and practices, so it is advisable to review resources first. The term *technical resources* is used here to refer to any utility or source of catalog records or processing materials or related services. The options in this area are phenomenal and would require a book to adequately discuss them. Only a sampling of ideas will be discussed here, based primarily on resources that the author has used. An effort will be made to give attention to more innovative and alternative technical resources.

Outsourcing

When looking at resource options, a critical question to answer at the outset is whether outsourcing of some traditional technical service jobs is an option. The term *outsourcing* is used here in the broadest sense of contracting out work that would normally be done in the local library. The work may be as simple as providing packages of MARC records for new acquisitions or as extensive as full-fledged original cataloging for special collections. Some would argue that simply purchasing MARC records is really not outsourcing, because that is no different than purchasing catalog cards from the Library of Congress for new acquisitions. While I agree that purchasing MARC records is similar to purchasing catalog cards, this does not mean they are not outsourcing. I would argue that they are both forms of outsourcing, albeit a much simpler and cheaper form than outsourcing the cataloging of a special collection.

Ongoing cataloging is not the only form of outsourcing available to technical services. Libraries that convert existing collections from shelflists to the automated catalog (i.e., retrospective conversion) discover that the manual process is time-consuming, so they usually contract with a vendor to do this. Louisiana Tech University found the in-house process of converting and reclassifying the shelflist was not satisfactory because of the time delay for users of the online catalog. Fred Hamilton, the head of the Cataloging Department, said outsourcing of the retrospective conversion of Louisiana Tech University's shelflist to MARCIVE saved the library time and money (Meldrum 1995). Authorities processing is another labor-intensive task that is frequently outsourced, either as an initial clean-up or for ongoing maintenance. Reclassification of collections from one classification scheme to another is much more efficient in an outsourced project than in-house, one cart at a time (Meldrum 2002). Grove City College, Pennsylvania, reclassified the entire collection of over 118,000 titles in just 14 weeks because they outsourced the processing of the MARC data and the production of labels, according to Assistant Director Barbra Munnell (MARCIVE 2002). Indiana University of Pennsylvania had a similar experience converting 400,000 items to Library of Congress classification with little inconvenience to summer users (Steiner 2001). Production of labels and physical processing of materials can also be delegated to a vendor.

At this point, it is important to resist the knee-jerk reactions we tend to have when outsourcing is mentioned. As librarians, either a genetic disposition (to assume resultant certain disaster if control of the technical services process is taken from us) or experience prejudices us against the outsourcing option. Although there are reasons for this fear, it is important to look at the value of outsourcing, because the fear only indicates that there are problems, not that the problems are insurmountable or even inherent in the method.

A perusal of library literature and listservs identifies some problems libraries encounter when outsourcing. The most common complaints about outsourcing reflect more on the library's understanding of the purpose of outsourcing and the necessity for management of outsourcing projects than on the actual worth of outsourcing. Common responses to questions about libraries' experiences with outsourcing follow:

1. With outsourced cataloging there is still a need to edit the MARC records, add local call numbers, finish the bibliographic records (add local fields), and then type the same information in the holdings records.

2. Time is not budgeted for library and vendor interaction in profiling the outsourcing project as well as overseeing the actual project to ensure the end project is as expected.

3. With automated authority work some headings flip that should not flip and other headings expected to flip to an authorized form do not.

4. Call number options do not match some used in local libraries' collections.

5. It can be difficult to factor the cost of outsourcing a project accurately versus doing it in-house, so it is not always clear where the real savings are for the library.

These are all issues to address when considering outsourcing, to avoid poor choices, bad management, and unrealistic expectations.

Choices

Poor choices come from not taking the time to research properly what can and should be done, by whom, and what is needed in the local database. Vendors have different degrees of built-in flexibility of options and a willingness to do the unusual for a price. If a vendor gives an option to clean up something (i.e., obsolete MARC tags), investigate the pros and cons before declining or accepting the option. I recommend cleaning up as much as possible so that in the future, when a particular tag or code is critical, your data will reflect more current practices. All library systems are not created equal, however. The librarian must examine the local situation.

It is particularly important to have input from the technical services staff if outsourcing decisions are made by someone not directly involved with the cataloging module. In evaluating vendors it is also critical to realize that quality and value-added services are not always evident in the response to a request for information or request for proposal (RFP). Never assume, and never be in too much of a rush to inquire about anything, or to verify outcomes through test samples. For example, in outsourced cataloging, it is possible to have two vendors that offer MARC records with very different end products. The one vendor may provide the Library of Congress records and also offer similar quality in-house cataloging with value-added services such as customized call numbers, authority work, and enhanced records. The second vendor may provide a minimal cataloging record at best, with little of the fixed fields information supplied, little use of proper subfield coding in the variable fields, and no value-added services. Although these are two extremes and hopefully most of the vendors you consider will be better than the worst-case scenario, it is important to realize that things that sound the same are not always the same. A good RFP is critical to help with getting accurate information. A sample RFP for authority work is available at http://www.marcive.com/HOMEPAGE/Rfpauth.pdf. Detailed RFPs for book, journal, and cataloging services are available in *Outsourcing Library Technical Services: A How-to-Do-It Manual* (Hirshon and Winters 1996).

Failure to calculate properly the costs of cataloging and misunderstanding the costs of outsourcing cause many of the bad decisions in selecting outsourcing options. A number of print and online resources give details to calculate properly the costs of cataloging in-house and how that compares with various outsourcing options. The critical factor to remember is to compare all costs of each step that is being considered for outsourcing. Some resources to assist with calculating costs are found in Appendix 5.1.

Probably the most common mistake in selecting an outsourcing option is going with the lowest bidder without considering the end product. The lowest bid may or may not be the best option. Low bids do not necessarily mean poor-quality work; however, too often apples and oranges are being compared and the library ends up paying more as additional work is needed in the future. Do not be like the library director who went with the more expensive vendor because he assumed (without asking) that the lower-priced bid must be wrong and would require double the bid figure. The result was that he could have had the same quality work done for considerably less money if he had asked questions rather than assumed. As the profound Filipino proverb says, "The one who assumes, makes mistakes."

Management

Once an outsourcing choice has been made, someone at the library must take the responsibility to manage the project. Basically, this means working with the vendor to provide all the specifics of the desired end product as well as the required data in a timely manner. Outsourcing is a partnership between the library and vendor. Unless there is regular communication during the project, there will not be the necessary adjustments and desired improvements. Voices all along the spectrum of pros and cons for outsourcing recognize that oversight by a local librarian is critical to the success of any outsourcing project (Gorman 1995; Holt 1995; Dunkle 1996). The vendor is much like a satellite section of the technical services department. Competent workers do the bulk of the work that needs to be done, but a supervisor still needs to give attention to make sure local practices are understood and that the workflow is moving as desired. The workers (i.e., vendor) must be provided with the necessary materials (data) so they will be able to produce on the desired work schedule. Time taken to dialog with the vendor about the project will save time in the long run, and a greater level of satisfaction will be achieved.

Expectations

The anticipated contributions that outsourcing will provide to the library as well as expected impact on staffing have a lot to do with how successful the outsourcing project will be. When outsourcing is considered there are two common assumptions that predispose the library staff for bad, or less than ideal, experiences. Frequently, libraries only look at outsourcing in terms of reduced backlog and turnaround time from acquisition to circulation of materials. Time for management of the project is not budgeted in the anticipated new workflow. On the other hand, catalogers who do not focus on the reduced backlog often focus on the work that is being taken from them rather than the work they will now have time to accomplish. The loss of work keeps them frightened and defensive, so that rather than work as a team player in the outsourcing project, they look for "evidence" that the project is a failure. A successful outsourcing project will avoid both extremes by educating staff on what to expect.

Staff will spend less time on more routine cataloging tasks and so be freed up for database and service enhancements they could not do previously. Outsourcing is a tool that enables skilled staff to spend more of their time actually doing what only they can do with their specialized training. Tasks that can be outsourced rarely threaten the position of professional librarians (Meldrum 1995). Cataloging staff can now work on projects to enhance and modify bibliographic records and databases to meet local needs, design Web pages, and create resource guides (Waite 1995). It will not take long to come up with a full-time job's worth of enhancements that catalogers can provide if they do not have to spend the bulk of their time on the labor-intensive work of descriptive cataloging and authority work. Even when a library has a vendor enrich its basic records with tables of contents and summaries, many records remain that do not have that information available through an automated process. Special collections and growing digital resources require a skilled cataloger to make them easily accessible to the public. Links between citation databases and online catalogs are a critical area requiring in-house attention (Caswell et al. 1995). Additional or localized subject headings and authority records based on evidence gleaned from the transaction log can best be provided by the local cataloger and would greatly improve search results in the local catalog. Increasingly, there is discussion of the need for catalogers to become involved in interlibrary loan, document delivery, and electronic publishing as digital resources change the nature of library services (Potter 1998). The list is long and growing of neglected work that catalogers could move to the forefront of their daily duties if they used outside sources for some of the more routine tasks in technical services (see Appendix 5.2).

Outsourcing technical services is not having a fairy godmother wave a magic wand to turn your rags to riches—although it may seem like that if you have had a good experience with a database clean-up project. Any technical services outsourcing the library has done should be viewed as a power tool, not as a magic genie. A good analogy of the view of outsourcing is the way people look at a dishwasher. Those who remember the days of dirty dishes filling sinks and counters after a big party or family gathering are thankful for a dishwasher that can be filled in a few minutes, and the dishes be done by pushing some buttons and letting it wash. When it is done, the dishes can be put away. Frequently people forget this convenience and either complain about the occasional dirty spot on a dish or wonder why a dishwasher takes so much time to load and unload. The dishwasher is a tool, not a genie, so human involvement is still required. The same is true with any outsourcing project. Outsourcing saves time, but involvement is still needed at the local level.

Generally there is some type of trade-off in outsourcing. Vendors usually produce at a much higher rate than in-house staff to be profitable. To do this, streamlined processes are used. The degree of customization required and human intervention on the vendor's part will affect the cost of the project. When automated methods are used, more hands-on involvement is required at the local library, focusing on issues not easily addressed by an automated process. One skill or capability that catalogers have that is still needed is the hands-on, direct attention required in situations where a computer cannot discern what is wanted. For example, the local library's practice of assigning nonstandard call numbers may not be an available option when call numbers and holdings information are provided or labels are ordered. The library may need to enter holdings information and do some labels in-house or adjust its call number system to match the available options. In automated authority control some attention must be given to the process, although the issue of bad flips is overstated if a reliable vendor is used. The percentage of bad flips is very small or even nonexistent because good vendors have authority librarians and programmers working together to prevent this from happening. The high percentage of corrected and updated headings more than compensates for any errors. Reports of not-found headings as well as changed headings are usually available, so oversight is possible. The time expended reviewing reports and correcting headings or taking care of stray not-found headings is years away from what would be spent if all the authority work had to be done manually. Choosing whether to do authority work in-house or to use an automated system is like choosing whether to cut your lawn by hand or use a power mower and just trim the edges by hand. In all but the smallest of operations, the bulk of the work can and should be done with the available power tools technology has given us.

Richard Koch's *The 80/20 Principle* is must reading for librarians in management positions. His premise is that 80 percent of what is achieved comes from only 20 percent of the effort exerted (Koch 1998, p. 4). In the library setting this could translate to using automated processes available through reliable vendors to accomplish 80 percent (give or take, depending on the project) of the task that needs to be done. For example, the library that uses a vendor for initial authority clean-up and ongoing maintenance will only need to devote 20 percent of staff time to clean up 80 percent of the database. The remaining 80 percent of the catalogers' time will be available to focus on the remaining 20 percent of the clean-up tasks that cannot be addressed in an automated process. In other words, a good percentage of total staff time is spent tidying up and maintaining the really significant achievements that required only 20 percent of the time or resources. Of course, a library that does not outsource authority work is exerting 80 percent of its resources to achieve only 20 percent clean-up of the database because of the time required in a manual clean-up. Koch points out that the use of this principle can help us achieve more with less effort and less cost (1998, p. 3). The key to this achievement, according to Koch, is outsourcing and the maximum use of specialists (1998, pp. 38–39).

The most common argument against outsourcing is that the library has specialists among the catalogers hired in-house (Gorman 1995). The problem with this argument is that it does not address adequately the issue of needing to produce more with less. The increasing demand to produce more with less has severely crippled libraries that have not begun to "think outside the box." These libraries are no longer successfully fulfilling their missions because they can no longer "provide timely access to relevant information resources." Studies show "historic" backlogs (as opposed to backlogs that come and go in the normal flow of acquisitions) in large research libraries are frequently at least 20,000 volumes, and it is not uncommon to have a backlog of 70,000 volumes (Rogers 1991, p. 26). These materials are not accessible to the library patron, and of equal concern is that too many of these items will become dated and need to be discarded, hence never being available to users. A more recent survey on the use of outsourcing in academic libraries showed that the trend was still to try to do all cataloging in-house (Libby and Caudle 1997, p. 559). This is a very poor budgetary practice if the end result of in-house cataloging is a large "historic" backlog. A concerted effort must be made to find the best balance between in-house resources and outsourcing, to make all materials purchased available to users in a timely manner.

Technical services departments that take to heart Koch's principle will find positive outsourcing options to adopt. Each library must look at its individual situation to see which options are best. Each library is sure to find some method to save money on cataloging and processing of materials.

Without too much effort, a library can review the experiences of other libraries' outsourcing endeavors because this topic has become very popular in recent years. One source is a study for the American Library Association, *The Impact of Outsourcing and Privatization on Library Services and Management* (Martin 2000). Other works on outsourcing are listed in Appendix 5.3.

Cataloging (MARC Records and Card Sources)

Cataloging is a major technical services task and has the most options when addressing the issue of reducing cost and increasing benefits. The term "cataloging" in this discussion refers to the entire process of classifying, subject analysis, and producing a catalog record (or card) for an item. In smaller libraries all these steps are done by the same person, who is known as the cataloger, so this discussion does not limit the definition to creating a record. Although the primary focus of this discussion is automated libraries needing MARC records, the general guidelines also apply to libraries using cards. There are reasonable resources to help both the automated libraries and those that are not automated.

There are lists and reviews of the various means of obtaining MARC records; however, most lists are not all-inclusive, so the serious investigator needs to research more than one place. My experience has been that many worthy resources are not well publicized, and others echo that same concern (Tan 1996). The Library of Congress has made an effort to fill this void with their *MARC Record Services* and *MARC Specialized Tools* Web pages (see Appendix 5.4). Many of the resources listing vendor services focus on available acquisitions, cataloging, and collection development services, but they also include sources of MARC records. In most of these resources the list of vendors is more helpful than the details, since the details often become dated. A quality source of MARC records is critical to any library, as the time saved in searching for, creating, enhancing, and maintaining the MARC records can be like having an additional staff person (MARCIVE 2003).

CD-ROM

LC MARC records on CD-ROM are still available from some integrated library systems (ILS) and cataloging services vendors. There is usually a cost involved, which can make it less attractive than an online service with records updated more frequently. If you have never used anything else you may find this method satisfactory, especially if the CD-ROMs are provided at a minimal cost (or for free) by the library's ILS vendor. Catalogers experienced with online cataloging utilities find CD-ROMs cumbersome because of delays in updates as well as the need to switch CDs when formats or publication periods (current versus pre-1976) are changed. In addition, special hardware and networking issues need to be considered to allow for use of CD-ROMs. Also, surprisingly, the CD-ROM services may be just as expensive as some of the Internet cataloging options.

Z39.50 Harvesting

A very popular alternative to an expensive cataloging utility is Z39.50-based software that searches and downloads records from online catalogs of other libraries. The software may be a built-in feature of the ILS used, or stand-alones like *Bookwhere?*, a popular Z39.50 browser (http://www.webclarity.info/products/faq_bookwhere.html). For the small library with a tight budget, Z39.50 software greatly increases the pool of MARC records available. One nice feature of *Bookwhere?* is that the cataloger can choose the format in which to save the catalog record. For libraries that are dependent on cards, the records can be saved in text format and therefore save a lot of typing.

The downside to relying totally on Z39.50 software for cataloging is that the libraries you access may block you at the firewall because your frequent activity hinders their patrons from accessing the catalog. Free Z39.50 bibliographic records have become so popular that OCLC has decided to take action, encouraging member libraries to prevent non-OCLC member libraries from using their databases, so the pool of available libraries may soon rapidly shrink (Houk 2003). *Bookwhere?* specifically advises users to obtain permission from any library that they plan to use for exporting catalog records on a regular basis, but realistically this practice is rarely followed. Also, when servers are down for upgrades, or telecommunication problems occur in the libraries you frequent, you have to look elsewhere for records. Obviously this will slow down your cataloging, which increases labor costs. Some catalogers like to use a broader sweep when searching titles, and rather than limit by selected libraries they limit by state or type of library. Even with high-speed Internet access such broad searches can be too time-consuming and make searches of more than five libraries at a time impractical.

Web-Based Utilities

Online cataloging resources range from the very expensive to the amazingly reasonable. In this discussion we are primarily concerned with acquiring MARC records for ongoing cataloging. However, it is equally critical to look at all the alternatives for MARC bibliographic and authority records and conversion resources when changing or upgrading the library's automated system. ILS vendors may not always offer options of where to get the conversion and authority work done. The cost of the database clean-up is included in the pricing for the system or enhancement when the library adds the authority module. A close look at the pricing will show that often the service is outsourced to another vendor and there is an additional mark-up. Make sure to do some research on conversion and data clean-up options and go with what is best for the library in the long run. If the price is comparable, or less, it makes more sense to go with a MARC records vendor that is able to assist in ongoing maintenance of your database than with the integrated library systems vendor that will only do the initial work to put the data in its system.

When we investigated cataloging options at my last job in a public library, we found a Web-based cataloging service that was very affordable—in fact, MarciveWeb SELECT proved to be the most affordable utility. MARCIVE, Inc. has built up a good reputation for supplying MARC records since 1981 (http://www.marcive.com). There are no annual fees or search fees for the service with MarciveWeb SELECT; you just pay for the MARC records you order, and there is no minimum order. This online cataloging service includes records from the Library of Congress, the National Library of Medicine, National Library of Canada (NLC), U.S. Government Printing Office (GPO), A/V Access®, and the MARCIVE original cataloging databases. Copies of all records ordered are saved, functioning essentially as a backup database if you order all your records from the service. Value-added services make this particularly attractive. Libraries that need customized call numbers, labels, barcodes, cards, enhanced 505s, and authority work can have it all taken care of at one time. An added bonus for libraries that are training support staff in copy cataloging is that the initial display of the MARC records uses labels rather than tag numbers, and online help with coding is provided. Also, the file of cataloged records is retained for review until the order is finally submitted. This feature allows a trainee to catalog a number of items that can be reviewed and corrected by senior staff if necessary, before ordering the MARC records and adding them to the local database. Since there is no charge for connection time, multiple searches, or the temporary file, this is a good training tool.

Other companies are addressing the need for alternative cataloging sources. It certainly pays to do some investigating here. One innovative cataloging resource company is Librarycom.com (http://www.librarycom.com). This company does not do any authority work or record enrichment, but the service includes online cataloging, local OPAC, and circulation tracking, all conducted through the Web. The little library that cannot afford an automated library system and a systems librarian may find this Internet library catalog a solution. I have never used the service so cannot say how it works in a live environment, but the idea of only needing a computer and Web access to be able to catalog, have an online catalog, and circulate materials is an innovation needed in many libraries today.

Vendor Records

Book and audiovisual vendors as well as some cataloging utilities have begun addressing the problem of more money for acquisitions and less staff to catalog and process materials. Many jobbers supply at least some of the MARC records or minimal MARC records for books purchased from them. Majors, Rittenhouse, and Matthews are examples of book distributors that offer MARC records for books ordered from them. Each library should look at its needs and what services are available from its regular book jobbers, and at what price. Some vendors use available Library of Congress MARC records and others create their own records. Prices can vary considerably from one vendor to the next.

When we were working our way through a serious backlog at the Upper Dublin Public Library, we found it very helpful and reasonable to get the MARC records provided by three of our jobbers, Baker & Taylor, Grolier, and Recorded Books. We elected to accept CIP records if that was all that was available. This required more attention on our part to update partial records but was still much quicker than searching for records through a Z39.50 browser (we had not yet discovered MARCIVE's online cataloging service). When the bulk of the backlog was cleared up, we also went to a union catalog where the chances were high that another library in the consortium had already cataloged an item. Therefore, we stopped this form of outsourcing.

Another unique source of valuable MARC records is the *Documents Without Shelves* (http://www.marcive.com/HOMEPAGE/docswout.htm) service, which provides thousands of MARC records for online government documents. Monthly updates contribute hundreds of new records and maintain the URLs for these documents, providing quick and effortless access to valuable documents through the online catalog. In the early 1990s when the GPO made a radical change in its method of dissemination of government information, depository libraries expressed concern that the Federal Depository Library Program would be jeopardized (Cornwell 1994). Wayne P. Kelley, the Superintendent of Documents, recognized the need for a partnership of the GPO, the libraries, and others to enable the successful electronic dissemination of government documents (Kelley 1993). MARCIVE, Inc. saw a need and fulfilled it with a tool (*Documents Without Shelves*) to enable all libraries to have access to government documents with a great reduction in labor and capital expense.

Innovative and alternative resources for obtaining MARC records are available and should be considered. Budget shortfalls force us to review existing practices, and periodic reviews are necessary to keep from becoming stagnant. It is said that necessity is the mother of invention, so perhaps it is a good thing to have the status quo shaken to force us to rethink our presuppositions. There is room for alternative thinking not only in how we get our MARC records but also in the processing of materials and the workflow.

Processing (Materials and Vendors)

Processing is the physical preparation of an item for display and circulation (label printing, application of spine labels, pockets, barcodes, security strips or patches, protective coverings, etc.). Preparation of a library item for circulation is time-consuming but critical. Book vendors and MARC record utilities are available that provide labels and barcodes for items purchased from or cataloged through them. There are various levels of assistance available here. Some book vendors sell items shelf-ready with all labels, pockets, and security in place. Other levels of service only provide the spine, pocket, and barcode labels, and the library applies these locally. In selecting processing services it is critical to evaluate the nature and quality of the products (e.g., labels, barcodes) that will be attached to the cataloged item. Labels or barcodes that become unreadable over time or fall off are more expensive in staff time and replacement costs than beginning with a higher quality product. Along with durable printing and adhesive, it is important to select materials with low acidity. Products that are not acid-free will "burn" paper.

If you are fortunate enough to have some good, steady volunteers, or sufficient staff, you probably do not want to look at outsourcing any of these processes. However, if staffing is an issue, or there is not a good local system to create labels, then the cost of getting some or all of these processes done can make it worthwhile to outsource.

Policies and Practices

During the time that you are researching ways to reduce your cataloging costs through the use of various technical resources, you are likely to discover that some of your policies and practices are not the norm. If it has been a while since your library has reviewed its local policies and practices, now is a good time to review your methods. Often policies and practices have origins so old that no one currently working in the library knows when they started or why. Even if the reason something is being done is known, it wise to check periodically whether this is still the best solution for the library. In business and management literature, the point is made that America's best-run companies and organizations are flexible and are able to look beyond management systems and routines that over time can lose their connection to the core values that make the companies successful (Peters and Waterman 1982). Beneficial flexibility in organizations incorporates a systematic review of what is being done and proactive change, as necessary.

Review Process

Periodic reviews of an organization's processes (i.e., analysis of what is being done) ensures the most efficient use of resources and the fulfillment of the organization's mission. Business and library literatures both provide good resources for methods of reviewing organizational or departmental processes (see Appendix 5.5). The terms and details that describe organizational evaluation and analysis change as various management trends gain popularity or notoriety, but the core principles remain the same. A successful review of library processes depends on 1) the right person(s) being responsible for the review, 2) understanding the mission of the organization, 3) knowing the major processes of the organization, 4) clear guidelines and goals for the review, 5) a realistic completion date, and 6) clearly communicating specific findings and recommendations (Eustis and Kenney 1996; Hernon and McClure 1990).

Selecting the appropriate person(s) to oversee a process review may be as simple as requesting the immediate supervisor of a particular process to be responsible for the review. If an isolated process is all that is being reviewed and the supervisor has experience and skill in organizational analysis, this is sufficient. When the extent of the review encompasses multiple processes, or if it reaches across departments, however, it is critical to form a review team. The effort needed to gather data on current processes is reason enough to encourage team effort. In addition, teams bring multiple skills and perspectives to the review process, which helps ensure a balanced review. Teams should be composed of members from various areas under review, not only to bring their perspectives to the table but also to aid in communicating the results of the review throughout the organization. Consultants may be considered if the library is branching out into new territory where no one in-house has any experience, or when an outsider's opinion is required to ensure objectivity or to facilitate the review process. Consultants can be good facilitators and may bring new ideas to the discussion, but the burden of infusing the entire staff with the desire to embrace the change is on management and individuals within the organization (Perry and Woodworth 1995).

Management and key individuals within the library can set the direction of the review by beginning with a clear understanding of the library's mission statement. If that mission has not changed, then as each process is reviewed and changes are considered, the new process must be evaluated in light of how it will contribute to the fulfillment of the library's purpose. Ideally, the library will have a current set of organizational goals and objectives that can serve as a starting point for establishing areas to review.

In addition to the mission statement, the review committee should have a clear outline of all the processes under review. Unless the library already has extensive documentation on each area under review, producing the necessary outlines of these processes could require a year or more. Every library should start compiling data immediately, even if a review is not anticipated in the near future. The ideal time to begin gathering all of this information is not when a decision needs to be made about a particular process. Sufficient time is needed to review all the technical service's processes as well as the various solutions to ensure a successful change.

Get the staff involved in a brainstorming session to bring out possible processes that could change and why. Andrea Rabbia of Syracuse University suggests beginning the review process with the basic step of thinking through how the materials currently flow through the technical services department or library, and noting what you would like to change about the process (Rabbia 2002). During all the brainstorming sessions, keep in mind that the stated goal of the technical services department or section is what influences all decisions about maintenance or change of practices.

Local practice in supplying call numbers is a frequent reason given by libraries, especially public libraries, for not using vendor-supplied call numbers and labels. Many vendors have a reasonable degree of flexibility in the construction and convention of the call numbers that they supply, so if a local practice does not fit any of the available options, it may be well to review that practice. After all, what vendors provide in call numbers follows the practices of many other libraries, which is why they offer those options. What works in other libraries may well work in your local library and without too great a change from the current practice. From personal observation, library users as well as staff are able to adjust to change if they can see how it benefits them. When popular new titles are available in a shorter length of time than in the past, people will notice and be delighted.

Issues involved in processes include "what is done?", "when?", "where?", "how?", and "by whom?", and the crux of the decision will be the big question "why?" Everything must be reviewed, from acquisitions and cataloging to processing and database maintenance. No area should be left out of the review process. This does not mean that the technical services department is being torn apart. The review process can be reaffirming when an area is examined and found to be the perfect fit for the library at this time. Areas that are changed do not reflect negatively on the library or the staff; this is a reflection of the changing times. A process review is a tool to measure the performance of the library in the current environment and identify possible improvements.

Reengineering Stage

Once the review process is complete it is time to implement the changes. Do not be discouraged or surprised if this phase takes time. When the University of Illinois at Chicago considered changes for the acquisitions' notification slip ordering process, it took them 18 months of review and planning and then 9 months of implementation (Zuidema 1999, p. 50). Some changes will be quickly accepted by all and be smoothly accomplished; others will take some experimenting. Studies of reengineering efforts have shown that as many as 70 percent of the efforts do not achieve the desired results. Focusing primarily on the technical side of the redesign process results in a failure to communicate the vision for the change and a staff inadequately equipped to achieve the desired end. Successful reengineering projects realize that the key to effective change is the people involved. A reengineering stage that focuses on people includes time and steps to communicate to the staff the vision for, and the value of, the change; identifies new job competencies; and provides training (Wellins and Murphy 1995, p. 33). An organization that practices problem solving, experiments with processes, adopts lessons learned, and efficiently disseminates acquired knowledge throughout the organization has the greatest potential for smooth process changes (Garvin 1993).

Staff

Two issues need to be examined when considering staff resources and changing demands. They work hand-in-glove. The first question to be addressed is just what the staffing options are. In looking at the staffing options it is also necessary to consider the second issue of staff enrichment.

Staff Options

Remember to "dump everything out on the table" with no reservations because of existing or historical practices. Historically, there has been an assumption that the technical services and public services departments of the library were separate, and little or no crossover was possible (Jankowska and Young 2000). Generally, the only time these two departments interacted was when a librarian from technical services covered the reference desk or circulation desk in a pinch. One strong assumption has been that what happens behind the scenes in technical services does not affect the patrons. Since patrons are the priority in library services, public services issues have traditionally been given the focus of staffing allocation. Also, the complexity of AACR2 cataloging rules and MARC coding has fostered the assumption that only degreed librarians with cataloging experience should be allowed to do any cataloging. Later in this chapter it is stated that technical services is the number one patron service in the library. Since the services that the technical department renders to users are so vital, every avenue must be explored to find the staff to keep this area running smoothly. Large portions of the work in technical services can be done by individuals without professional degrees when they are trained and supervised by a cataloging librarian.

Professional and Support Staff

The question of the roles of professional and support staff in cataloging surfaces periodically in library literature. Whichever side of the issue you take, it is safe to assume that everyone is seeking the best mix to provide quality cataloging to patrons while reducing or preventing a backlog or overtaxing the library budget. The key is to have well-trained staff who understand the importance of their jobs, whether it be one portion of the cataloging process or the process in its entirety.

Understandably, catalogers object to the opinion that cataloging is merely clerical work that anyone can be trained to do. Another common concern is that the more times an item is handled, the more labor is involved, and the higher the labor costs. Libraries, however, have successfully increased their cataloging output (quality records with quantity) while depending on support staff (see Appendix 5.6). There are four areas in which people without a library degree can be trained to augment successfully the work of the cataloging librarian. These are discussed under "Staff Enrichment."

Technical Services and Public Services

In too many libraries there is a great divide between the technical services and the public services departments. A frequent comment in cataloging circles is that when the public services staff or librarians understand what goes on in a catalog they can better serve the patrons. The other side of the coin is also true. When catalogers know what the public service staff need to perform their jobs, the catalogers can better interpret cataloging rules to suit the local situation. It is encouraging to see the increase in recent articles showing how libraries are attempting to bring these two departments together so service to patrons is improved. Reference librarians have subject skills that could be used to enhance bibliographic records. Cataloging librarians have technical skills that can enable reference librarians to locate more quickly the type of materials sought by patrons (DeZelar-Tiedman 2000). Margaret Bing surmises that technical services is the critical portion of the library, as it is what makes public services possible (2000). Without cataloging, classification, and processing of materials, the public services portion of the library could not function. Miller stresses the importance of the relation of technical services to the core functions of the library by comparing public services to flowers. Public services without technical services is like cut flowers that do not last long (Miller 2000).

If you are in a library where the issue of greater cooperation between public and technical services needs to be addressed, recent publications provide critical input to the discussion (see Appendix 5.7). For a single resource, use *Integration in the Library Organization* (Thompson 2000). A theme repeated in many of the chapters is that teamwork must be fostered between technical services and public services.

When I began my last job as head of technical services in a public library, the only crossover between technical services and public services were the times I assisted public services with reference and circulation. By the time I left, most of the public services staff were involved in various tasks performed in technical services. There was a greater sense of teamwork and accomplishment as the resources for patrons dramatically increased. The use of the automated system in finding materials improved as well, as staff better understood MARC coding.

Full-Time and Part-Time

Full-time employees are critical to a well-run technical services department. Employees who invest more hours are more inclined to have a long-term commitment to the job and certainly have a better chance of seeing the big picture due to the increased exposure that they have. At least one full-time employee should oversee the technical services department for continuity. However, it is possible to run a good technical services department with the rest of the staff being part-time.

When a library cannot afford several full-time employees it is necessary to look at part-time help. Whether it be students or parents trying to work around a school schedule, or individuals wanting reduced hours for other reasons, there are some very competent people looking for part-time work. I have managed technical services departments in both academic and public library settings and found most of the part-time staff every bit as committed and competent as the full-time staff. Volunteers can also be a real asset as long as there is a qualified staff person to train and coach them in their work.

When I came into the cataloging position at Upper Dublin Public Library there were only three volunteers, who each came in about four hours a week to help, and a support staff person who entered and submitted orders to our main book jobber. The volunteers helped with the check-in of new acquisitions and the physical processing of books to make them shelf-ready. The cataloger, myself, did everything else, including systems management and assisting with public services. Not surprisingly, when I came into the job there was a serious backlog. Many items had been sitting on the cataloging shelf or in boxes for over two years. After giving myself time to become familiar with the local system and practices of the library, I began to make changes. The biggest change was to delegate as much as possible to others. My job was to train and coach the team and only handle the more difficult cataloging tasks. Through careful training and the restructuring of jobs to fit the skills of the already available individuals, we were able to increase our technical services staff to 15 volunteers and 12 public services staff, who assisted with various tasks related to acquiring, cataloging, and making materials shelf-ready. Although the new workflow required an item to be handled by several people (which is usually considered bad economy of labor), within the space of two years we cleared the two-year backlog, kept current with a healthy acquisitions budget, and managed multiple systems upgrades and changes.

Staff Enrichment

More with less does not have to be a negative experience for staff. The normal assumption when faced with the request to produce more with less is that it will demand more hours and responsibility for staff. Since personnel costs may make up 85 percent of many technical services budgets, perhaps the greatest fear is that staff reduction will be seen as the primary cost saver for libraries (Ruschoff 1995). In planning changes, however, staff members are a resource that should be viewed, not as a commodity to be traded or from which more can be squeezed, but rather as team players with potential for growth. The question is how each team member can experience the greatest professional and personal growth while meeting the needs of the library.

Variety

Although change, especially radical change in structure and practices, is often met with resistance, a common wish expressed by staff is for variety in their work setting. Expressions of a desire for change and to understand more of what is going on around them are the keys to expediting change in a manner that is both acceptable to and embraced by the staff. These catalysts for change are beneficial to staff and the library.

Processing. It may seem to be a given that support staff would be responsible for processing library materials. Unfortunately, there are catalogers who prefer to do the entire process of cataloging, labeling, etc., themselves. The argument is that it is better for one person to handle an item so that it is not picked up multiple times; therefore, labels and barcodes are applied as the librarian catalogs an item. However, these are steps that can easily be done by support staff to provide a better economy of staff management.

Processing materials can be a good starting place for staff interested in working in technical services. Observe the individuals' attention to detail, especially in following directions and catching mistakes. Many people who are good at processing materials are also good with other technical services tasks. However, it is critical to know your staff. Some people are excellent at finishing materials but cannot handle MARC records. Likewise, there are individuals who excel at online cataloging tasks who should not be given processing duties. Ask your staff if they would like to help with the finishing process of materials. Some will honestly tell you that when it comes to scissors and tape they are all thumbs, or, if they are able to do it, they do not like to do it. Others love to do things with their hands and have secretly longed for a break from their other tasks to do this enjoyable work. Making staff part of a team effort and rewarding them with time out from more taxing duties to label and cover new materials can benefit the library through a happier, more efficient staff.

Holdings information. Catalogers frequently add the holdings information at the time of cataloging. It is true that a skilled cataloger can enter the holdings details very quickly, especially when using an 852 field. However, the minutes spent entering holdings data represent a considerable amount of lost time for areas of cataloging that require experience and a higher degree of training. Many libraries have reduced backlogs by training support staff to enter the holdings information after librarians or trained copy catalogers have provided the MARC record. Training staff to enter holdings data is a good way to give the support staff a better understanding of library workings as well as to give them a sense of importance to the team. It is not unusual to see support staff who began entering holdings information eventually move on to increasingly difficult levels of copy cataloging and eventually go to library school.

Copy cataloging. Copy cataloging is the practice of borrowing other's work on MARC records to produce MARC records for the local library. The difficulty of copy cataloging has roughly three levels. The most simple is to recognize and select an exact match for the item in hand. One step more difficult is to find a MARC record that almost matches, but the publication information may differ in some way that requires editing the original MARC record to match the item in hand. Finally, a MARC record for a similar item, perhaps another book by the same author or a different format, may be used as the basis to construct a new record for the item that does not have a MARC record. Staff can be trained to recognize a good-quality record as well as a good match. Within each of these levels it is possible to differentiate further the learning process or skill levels. In matching MARC records the first level is to determine exact matches of good records. Over time, staff will be able to enhance a less-than-ideal matching bibliographic record. Once a staff member can quickly identify a good matching bibliographic record and make small additions such as local information, it is time to begin training that person to deal with more challenging editing of bibliographic records. More difficult editing can include correcting existing information, adding information, or altering similar records for different editions or publishers. Training staff to edit close matches should be done in degrees of difficulty. Records that only differ in edition statement are much easier than those that have a different publisher. Good records are obviously much easier than poorly constructed records. Finally, staff will become experienced enough to begin training on the highest level of copy cataloging. At this level, similar records are used as the basis for creating records for items for which there is no existing MARC record. With good documentation, experienced staff can increase their cataloging skills to further assist with cataloging. There is evidence that the core level record meets the needs of the average patron and should be acceptable in most cataloging (Banush 2001; Cromwell 1994; Stamm 2000).

The University of New Mexico General Library, when looking for ways to become more efficient, found that it needed to rethink the issue of using only highly trained and experienced catalogers for copy cataloging. Previously the library had assumed that copy cataloging was too difficult for anyone without years of training and experience. In 2000, after three years of using students to catalog all DLC copy, the library found it had been able to reduce its backlog of over 10,000 titles to less than 2,000. At the time of writing of the article on cataloging changes, the use of students to do copy cataloging was deemed successful (Benaud et al. 2000).

Brief records. Every library has a "step-child" collection that needs to be in the catalog for searching purposes as well as circulation tracking. These collections often contain materials that are expected to have a short-term use with high demand. In academic libraries this may be selected readings for coursework. Public libraries often have a paperback collection that is circulated on a generic record and card rather than on its own record and barcode. Brief records for use in the local catalog only can and should be created by support staff. Satellite collections such as those contained in academic reading rooms and departments may also need cataloging (Bell 1995). Most library systems allow templates to aid staff in constructing brief records. I have found that, with the aid of a template, a good guide sheet, and a little training, the support staff are able to enhance the catalog by creating brief records for materials that would not otherwise be accessible to patrons. Staff persons selected for this training should already be experienced with entering holdings information and possibly copy cataloging. Those that show real skill and an ability to look at the MARC record are the ones to give the opportunity to increase their cataloging skills by making brief records for local use.

Training

Well-trained staff members benefit both the library and the staff. It is easier to meet changing demands with a broader pool of skilled staff. The staff themselves find the work more rewarding when it is evident they have not hit a glass ceiling. Training staff will increase their sense of ownership of the services provided in the library. It is of interest to note that *Library Journal's*

"ParaProfessional of the Year 2003" award went to Susan Knoche, who was involved with the founding of the Paraprofessional Round Table of the Tennessee Library Association. She is a good example of support staff striving to become skilled in a variety of technical services tasks and being a catalyst for training opportunities for other non-MLS library staff to increase their value to the library team (Berry 2003).

In-house training is essential for learning how to do tasks in the local setting. Ruth Metz's 2002 book on coaching in the library is an excellent work on the why and how of training within the library setting. Library associations and consortiums are also good resources for local training opportunities. However, there are also training services provided on a national level that are good to consider. *The MARC of Quality* (TMQ) company is a popular training resource that conducts cataloging workshops, primarily in Florida but also across the country (http://www.marcofquality.com). TMQ also provides the subscription service to the software *MARC Report* that helps both the novice and the experienced cataloger pick up on details that are incorrect or lacking in the MARC record they are creating or editing.

A critical key to successful training is well-documented "cheat-sheets" for every task that is performed in technical services. Although everyone looks for quick guides for themselves when performing cataloging related tasks, my experience is that very few libraries take the time to prepare and maintain documentation or instruction sheets for staff. Libraries that do a good job in this area have a much higher success rate of training new people and cross-training existing staff (see Appendix 5.8).

When I left my job as head of technical services at the public library, the library had not yet found a replacement. This meant that there was no opportunity for me to give my replacement any orientation, and worse yet, the library needed to carry on with acquisitions and cataloging for an indefinite period of time without the normal oversight. All of the "technical services" staff were part-time and basically volunteers or public services staff enlisted to assist with specific tasks in technical services. It was three months before a new cataloger was found to oversee technical services. During those three months the library was able to continue purchasing and cataloging books because of the training, and especially because of the extensive documentation available for every task in technical services. When the new head of technical services librarian saw how things were running, she commented that she wondered at first why she was hired.

Workflow

Once it is determined what resources and staff options are available and what policies will change, it is time to consider how optimizing these resources, options, and policies will affect workflow. Usually there are good reasons for the way work progresses through the technical services department. However, as resources change, workflow changes may also be necessary. The need for change in workflow is not new, and in the last few years this topic has been addressed in a variety of library literature. As part of the process review discussed earlier, inquire what other libraries have done and learned in the process. Appendix 5.9 provides a starting point for learning about workflow changes.

It is important to note that each library found a solution that met its need at the time. There is no one solution that fits everyone or, as stated previously, no one solution that fits anyone all the time. When Cornell University Library looked at the organization of the technical services department in 1993, the library came to the same conclusion as the business and management literature: that flexibility was necessary to meet changes in personnel and conditions (Boissonnas 1997). The NLC reengineered its workflow using an assembly-line method in the early 1970s but in 1995 switched to integrated teams of catalogers that handled the entire process because their resources changed. As emerging technology continues to offer and require changes in cataloging, the NLC relies on organizational flexibility to maintain efficiency (McKeen and Parent 2000).

In the process of gathering ideas for change, remember that people are involved and a team spirit needs to be fostered. To get a workflow tailored to the local situation, the staff who will be implementing these ideas must be part of the planning process. Solicit ideas and reactions from the staff. Use the information gained in the process review to establish the new pattern of workflow. The overall workflow will be determined by the decisions on cataloging resources and staff issues, and the details of "where" and "when" should be worked out with a degree of flexibility as changes are implemented.

Conclusion

No library exists in a vacuum. Resources and needs change, and technical services must change to maintain a level of excellence in the services provided to the public and the public services librarians. Management principles that have served the business community well have application in the library environment. Libraries need to learn to outsource, restructure, and train staff so that they can better meet their objective of providing high-quality service to library users. When technical services departments are using and managing technical resources and staff options to the maximum, they will have quality cataloging for less.

References

Banush, David. 2001, June 11. *BIBCO core record study: Final report prepared for the PCC Policy Committee.* Library of Congress Program for Cooperative Cataloging. Available: http://www.loc.gov/catdir/pcc/bibco/coretudefinal. html#satcore (Accessed May 5, 2003).

Bell, Suzanne S. 1995. "Integrating access to formal and informal collections: What is important and what succeeds." *Journal of Academic Librarianship* 21 (3, May): 181–186.

Benaud, Claire-Lise, Elizabeth N. Steinhagen, and Sharon A. Moynahan. 2000. "Flexibility in the management of cataloging." In *Managing cataloging and the organization of information: philosophies, practices and challenges at the onset of the 21st century*, edited by Ruth C. Carter, 281–298. New York: Haworth Press.

Berry, John N., III. 2003. "ParaProfessional of the year 2003: Susan Knoche." *Library Journal* 128 (4, March 1): 40–41.

Bing, Margaret. 2000. "The false dualism: Technical services vs. public services." In *Integration in the library organization*, edited by Christine E. Thompson, 23–28. New York: Haworth Press.

Boissonnas, Christian M. 1997. "Managing technical services in a changing environment: The Cornell experience." *Library Resources & Technical Services* 41 (2, April): 147–154.

Caswell, Jerry V., Fred H. Gulden, Kathy A. Parsons, Dennis C. Wendell, and William H. Wiese. 1995. "Importance and use of holding links between citation databases and online catalogs." *Journal of Academic Librarianship* 21 (2, March): 92–96.

Cornwell, Gary. 1994. "On my mind: The Federal Depository Library Program: A call for action." *Journal of Academic Librarianship* 20 (2, May): 97.

Cromwell, Willy. "The core record: A new bibliographic standard." *Library Resources & Technical Services* 38 (4, October): 415–424.

DeZelar-Tiedman, Christine. 2000. "A perfect fit: Tailoring library positions to match individual skills." In *Integration in the library organization*, edited by Christine E. Thompson, 29–39. New York: Haworth Press.

Dunkle, Clare B. 1996. "Outsourcing the catalog department: A meditation inspired by the business and library literature." *Journal of Academic Librarianship* 22 (1): 33–43.

Eustis, Joanne D., and Donald J. Kenney. 1996. *Library reorganization and restructuring*. OMS SPEC Kit 215. Washington, D.C.: ARL.

Garvin, David A. 1993. "Building a learning organization." *Harvard Business Review* 71 (July–August): 78–91.

Gorman, Michael. 1995. "The corruption of cataloging." *Library Journal* 120 (15): 32–34.

Heifetz, Michael L. 1993. *Leading change, overcoming chaos: A seven stage process for making change succeed in your organization.* [Olympia, Wash.]: Threshold Institute; Berkeley, Calif.: Ten Speed Press.

Hernon, Peter, and Charles McClure. 1990. *Evaluation and library decision making.* Norwood, N.J.: Ablex.

Hirshon, Arnold, and Barbara Winters. 1996. *Outsourcing library technical services: A how-to-do-it manual.* New York: Neal-Schuman.

Holt, Glen. 1995. "Catalog outsourcing: No clear-cut choice." *Library Journal* 120 (15): 34.

Houk, Gary R. 2003, February 9. *The OCLC Cooperative: Non-member use of cataloging records presented to members council.* Available: http://www.oclc.org/oclc/uc/feb03/ppt/GaryHouk_NonMemberUseofRecords_file/frame.htm (Accessed April 24, 2003).

Jankowska, Maria Anna, and Nancy J. Young. 2000. "Blurred lines, clear future: Personal perspectives on the reference and cataloger partnership." In *Integration in the library organization,* edited by Christine E. Thompson, 7–20. New York: Haworth Press.

Kelley, Wayne P. 1993. "GPO: Moving to an electronic world." *Administrative Notes* 14 (10, May 15): 1–7.

Koch, Richard. 1998. *The 80/20 principle: The secret of achieving more with less.* New York: Currency.

Libby, Katherine A., and Dana M. Caudle. 1997. "A survey on the outsourcing of cataloging in academic libraries." *College & Research Libraries* 58 (6): 550–560.

MARCIVE, Inc. 2002. "College reclassifies 118,000 titles in 14 weeks." *MARCIVE Newsletter* 43 (October): 5. Available: http://www.marcive.com/HOMEPAGE/NL43.pdf (Accessed May 5, 2003).

———. 2003, March. "A practical guide to creating and maintaining a useful catalog in your church or synagogue library, p. 1." In *Cataloging for congregational libraries.* Available: http://www.marcive.com/HOMEPAGE/cong.pdf (Accessed May 8, 2003).

Martin, Robert S., ed. 2000, June. *The impact of outsourcing and privatization on library services and management: A study for the American Library Association.* [Denton, Tex.]: Texas Woman's University School of Library and Information Studies; [Washington, D.C.]: American Library Association. Available: http://www.ala.org/alaorg/ors/outsourcing/outsourcing_doc.pdf (Accessed January 9, 2003).

McKeen, Liz, and Ingrid Parent. 2000. "The National Library of Canada: Organizing information for the new millennium." In *Managing cataloging and the organization of information: philosophies, practices and challenges at the onset of the 21st century*, edited by Ruth C. Carter, 19–32. New York: Haworth Press.

Meldrum, Janifer. 1995. "Outsourcing issues stir conference attendees." *MARCIVE Newsletter* 23 (September): 1, 5. Available: http://www.marcive.com/HOMEPAGE/news0995.htm (Accessed May 5, 2003).

———. 2002. "Cost-effective approach to reclassifying a collection from Dewey to LC." *Marcive Newsletter* 43 (October): 1. Available: http://www.marcive.com/HOMEPAGE/NL43.pdf (Accesed May 5, 2003).

Metz, Ruth F. 2002. *Coaching in the library: A management strategy for achieving excellence*. Chicago and London: American Library Association.

Miller, David P. 2000. "Both sides now; or paradise now." In *Integration in the library organization*, edited by Christine E. Thompson, 41–46. New York: Haworth Press.

Perry, John, and Anne Woodworth. 1995. "Innovation and change: Can we learn from corporate models?" *Journal of Academic Librarianship* 21 (2, March): 117–120.

Peters, Thomas J., and Robert H. Waterman Jr. 1982. *In search of excellence: Lessons from America's best-run companies*. New York: Harper & Row.

Potter, William Gray. 1998. "Automation and technical services: The online catalogue in academic libraries." In *Technical services today and tomorrow*, edited by Michael Gorman, 141–155. Englewood, Colo.: Libraries Unlimited.

Rabbia, Andrea. 2002. "Syracuse University's adventures in re-engineering technical services." *Members' Briefing-AALL spectrum* 7 (2, October): 3–4.

Rogers, Sally A. 1991. "Backlog management: Estimating resources needed to eliminate arrearages." *Library Resources & Technical Services* 35 (1, January): 25–32.

Ruschoff, Carlen. 1995. "Cataloging's prospects: Responding to austerity with innovation." *The Journal of Academic Librarianship* 22 (1): 51–57.

Stamm, Andrea L. 2000. "The end of an era builds new team spirit: team playing at its best." In *Managing cataloging and the organization of information: philosophies, practices and challenges at the onset of the 21st century*, edited by Ruth C. Carter, 357–372. New York: Haworth Press.

Steiner, Ron. 2001. "LC conversion wrap-up." *Indiana University of Pennsylvania Libraries* [online] 1 (5, Fall):1. Available: http://www.lib.iup.edu/depts/admin/info/newsletters/fall percent202001 percent20newsletter.pdf (Accessed May 20, 2003).

Tan, Wendy. 1996, Spring. *Resources guide for outsourcing cataloging.* Syracuse, N.Y.: Syracuse University ISDP-IST561 Listserv posting (Accessed March 1, 1996).

Thompson, Christine E., ed. 2000. *Integration in the library organization.* New York: Haworth Press.

Waite, Ellen J. 1995. "Reinvent catalogers!" *Library Journal* 120 18, November 1): 36–37.

Wellins, Richard S., and Julie Schulz Murphy. 1995. "Reengineering: Plug into the human factor." *Training & Development* 49 (January): 33–37.

Zuidema, Karen Huwald. 1999. "Reengineering technical services processes." *Library Resources & Technical Services* 43 (1, January): 37–52.

Appendix 5.1: Cataloging Costs

Hopkins, Judith. "The ALCTS Commercial Technical Services Costs Committee." *Cataloging & Classification Quarterly* 15, no. 1 (1992): 106–109.

LaCava, Lydia, Jan Rothhaar, and Thom Saudargas. "Formula for calculating cataloging costs (Appendix A), p. 10." In *Outsourcing technical services : Broward Community College, Davie Campus Library: Considerations for LINCC libraries* [online]. Broward, Fla.: College Center for Library Automation, November 1999. Available: http://www.ccla.lib.fl.us/docs/reports/ outsourcing.pdf (Accessed February 20, 2003).

Martin, Robert S. *The impact of outsourcing and privatization on library services and management: A study for the American Library Association.* [Denton, Tex.]: Texas Woman's University School of Library and Information Studies, p. 108, Appendix D; [Washington, D.C.]: American Library Association, June 2000. Available: http://www.ala.org/ slsorg/ors/outsourcing/outsourcing_doc.pdf (accessed January 9, 2003).

Morris, Dilys E., et al. "Cataloging staff costs revisited." *Library Resources & Technical Services* 44, no. 2 (April 2000): 70–83.

Morris, E. "Staff time and costs for cataloging." *Library Resources & Technical Services* 36, no. 1 (January 1992): 79–95. With three years' samplings, this study shows the proportion of time spent at tasks, some trends in changes over time, and the per-title cataloging time and costs.

Tsui, Susan Lee, and Carol F. Hinders. "Cost-effectiveness and benefits of outsourcing authority control." *Cataloging & Classification Quarterly* 26, no. 4 (1999): 43–61.

Appendix 5.2: Promoting Catalogers

Ahronhein, Judith, and Lynn Marko. "Exploding out of the MARC box: Building new roles for cataloging departments." *Cataloging & Classification Quarterly* 30, nos. 2/3 (2000): 217–225.

Buttlar, Lois, and Rajinder Garcha. "Catalogers in academic libraries: Their evolving and expanding roles." *College & Research Libraries* 59, no. 4 (July 1998): 311–321.

Caswell, Jerry V., et al. "Importance and use of holding links between citation databases and online catalogs." *Journal of Academic Librarianship* 21, no. 2 (March 1995): 92–96.

Paiste, Marsha Starr, and Jane Mullins. "Job enrichment for catalogers." *College & Research Libraries News* 51, no. 1 (1990): 4–8.

Potter, William Gray. "Automation and technical services: the online catalogue in academic libraries." In *Technical services today and tomorrow*, edited by Michael Gorman, 141–155. Englewood, Colo.: Libraries Unlimited, 1998.

Waite, Ellen J. "Reinvent catalogers." *Library Journal* 120, no. 18 (November 1, 1995): 36–37.

Appendix 5.3: Outsourcing

American Library Association. "Guide to outsourcing in libraries." *Library Technology Reports* 34, no. 5 (September 1998): 72.

Banerjee, Kyle. "Taking advantage of outsourcing options: Using purchased record sets to maximize cataloging effectiveness." *Cataloging & Classification Quarterly* 32, no. 1 (2001): 55–64.

Bénaud, Claire-Lise, and Sever Bordeianu. *Outsourcing library operations in academic libraries: An overview of issues and outcomes.* Englewood, Colo.: Libraries Unlimited. 1998.

Berry, John N., III. "The measure of outsourcing." *Library Journal* 123, no. 2 (February 1, 1998): 1.

Block, Rick. J. "Cataloging outsourcing: Issues and options." *Serials Review* 20, no. 3 (Fall 1994): 73–77.

Brown, Lynne Branche. "Evaluating the outsourcing of technical services: How do you know if you're there if you don't know where you're going? A report of the ALCTS Commercial Technical Services Committee Program, American Library Association Annual Conference, Chicago, July 2000." *Technical Services Quarterly* 18, no. 4 (2001): 58–63.

Bush, Carmel C., Margo Sasse, and Patricia Smith. "Toward a new world order: A survey of outsourcing capabilities of vendors for acquisitions, cataloging and collection development services." *Library Acquisitions: Practice & Theory* 18, no. 4 (Winter 1994): 397–416. Discusses a survey of selected library materials jobbers, cataloging agents, and library consortia; concludes that communication standards, vendor and library automation, and new partnerships among vendors and libraries are leading to more opportunities for outsourcing acquisitions, cataloging, and collection development. Includes some issues to cover in an RFP.

Carter, Kathy. "Outsourced cataloguing and physical processing at the University of Alberta Library." In *Outsourcing library technical services operations: Practices in academic, public, and special libraries,* edited by Karen A. Wilson and Marylou Colver, 3–14. Chicago: American Library Association, 1997.

Dunkle, Clare B. "Outsourcing the catalog department: A meditation inspired by the business and library literature." *Journal of Academic Librarianship* 22, no. 1 (1996): 33–43.

Dworaczek, Marian. *Outsourcing of technical services in academic libraries: A bibliography.* November 30, 2001; updated September 10, 2002. Available: http://library.usask.ca/~dworacze/OUTSOURCING.HTM (Accessed January 9, 2003).

German, Lisa B. "In or out—in-house innovation and outsourcing technical services alternatives for the 90s: A report of an ALCTS program." *Library Acquisitions: Practice & Theory* 21 (1997): 77–79.

Hirshon, Arnold, and Barbara Winters. *Outsourcing library technical services: A how-to-do-it manual.* New York: Neal-Schuman, 1996.

Kascus, Marie A., and Dawn Hale, eds. *Outsourcing cataloging, authority work, and physical processing: A checklist of considerations.* Chicago: American Library Association, 1994.

LaCava, Lydia, Jan Rothhaar, and Thom Saudargas. *Outsourcing technical services: Broward Community College, Davie Campus Library: Considerations for LINCC libraries* [online]. Broward, Fla.: College Center for Library Automation, November 1999. Available: http://www.ccla.lib.fl.us/docs/reports/outsourcing.pdf (Accessed February 20, 2003).

Libby, Katherine A., and Dana M. Caudle. "A survey on the outsourcing of cataloging in academic libraries." *College & Research Libraries* 58, no. 6 (1997):550–560.

Library of Congress. "Contracting out: competitive sourcing." In *Handbook of federal librarianship*, ch. 5. Available: http://lcweb.loc.gov/flicc/hbfl/chap5.html (Accessed May 12, 2003).

Martin, Robert S, ed. *The impact of outsourcing and privatization on library services and management: A study for the American Library Association.* Denton, Tex.: Texas Woman's University, School of Library and Information Studies; [Washington, D.C.]: American Library Association, June 2000. Available: http://www.ala.org/slsorg/ors/outsourcing/outsourcing_doc.pdf (Accessed January 9, 2003).

Meldrum, Janifer. "Outsourcing issues stir conference attendees." *MARCIVE Newsletter* 23 (September 1995): 1, 5. Available: http://www.marcive.com/HOMEPAGE/news0995.pdf (Accessed May 5, 2003).

Ogburn, Joyce L. "An introduction to oursourcing." *Library Acquisitions: Practice & Theory* 18, no. 4 (Winter 1994): 363–366.

Stomberg, Lisa. "The underutilization of government document collections: Can outsourcing provide access solutions?" *Colorado Libraries* 22, no. Spring 1996): 42–43.

Wilson, Karen A. *Planning and implementing an outsourcing program.* Chicago: American Library Association, 1997. Available: http://www.ala.org/alcts/now/outsourcing4.html (Accessed January 9, 2003).

————. *Library technical services outsourcing: A select bibliography.* Chicago: American Library Association, 2002. Available: http://www.ala.org/alcts/now/outsourcing1.html (Accessed January 9, 2003).

Wilson, Karen A., and Marylou Colver, eds. *Outsourcing library technical services operations: Practices in public, academic, and special libraries.* Chicago: American Library Association, 1997.

See also Appendix 5.1: Cataloging Costs.
See also Appendix 5.4: MARC Record Resources.

Appendix 5.4: MARC Record Resources

Bush, Carmel C., Margo Sase, and Patricia Smith. "Toward a new world order: A survey of outsourcing capabilities of vendors for acquisitions, cataloging and collection development services." *Library Acquisitions: Practice & Theory* 18, no. 4 (1994): 397–416.

Documents without shelves. n.d. Available: http://www.marcive.com/ HOMEPAGE/dwsl.pdf; http://www.marcive.com/homepage/docswout.htm (Accessed May 5, 2003). An important resource of current, maintained MARC records, with hotlinks for thousands of government documents on the web.

Library of Congress MARC record services. n.d. Available: http://www. loc.gov/marc/marcrecsvrs.html (Accessed April 29, 2003). "This category includes any service that distributes MARC 21 records, such as records for copy cataloging, records supplied with materials, records used for recon purposes, updated records, conversion services, etc. Free services are indicated in the title of each listing." Hotlinks are provided to corresponding Web sites for further information.

Library of Congress MARC specialized tools. n.d. Available: http://www.loc. gov/marc/marctools.html (Accessed April 29, 2003). "Any software program that provides enhanced usability to MARC21 records and systems . . . conversion utilities and validation programs are included." Hotlinks are provided to corresponding Web sites for further information.

Martin, Robert S. *The impact of outsourcing and privatization on library services and management: A study for the American Library Association.* (Appendix E—Selected cataloging contractors). American Library Association, June 2000. Available: http://www.ala.org/slsorg/ors/outsourcing/ outsourcing_doc.pdf (Accessed January 9, 2003).

Meszaros, Rosemary L. "MarciveWeb DOCS." *Library Journal* 124, no. 7 (1999): 154–155.

Plaunt, James R. "Cataloging options for U.S. Government Printing Office documents." *Government Publications Review* 12 (1985): 449–456.

Appendix 5.5: Process Review

Barker, Joseph W. "Triggering constructive change by managing organizational culture in an academic library." *Library Acquisitions: Practice & Theory* 19, no. 1 (Spring 1995): 9–19.

Bregman, Alvan. *Second report on reengineering technical services: Reorganization of acquisitions and binding.* University of Illinois at Urbana-Champaign Library, June 3, 1998. Available: http://door.library/uiuc.edu/acq/report2.htm (Accessed May 2, 2003).

Carson, Kerry David, Paula Phillips Carson, and Joyce Schouest Phillips. *The ABCs of collaborative change: The manager's guide to library renewal.* Chicago: American Library Association, 1997.

Clement, Richard W. *Strategic planning in ARL libraries.* OMS SPEC Kit 210. Washington, D.C.: ARL, 1995. Sample strategic plans from research libraries.

Cook, Eleanor I., and Pat Farthing. "Technical services perspective of implementing an organizational review while simultaneously installing an integrated library system." *Library Acquisitions: Practice & Theory* 19, no. 4 (Winter 1995): 445–461.

Crist, Margo. "Structuring the academic library organization of the future: Some new paradigms." *Journal of Library Administration* 20, no. 2 (1994): 47–65.

Drake, Miriam A. "Technological innovation and organizational change." *Journal of Library Administration* 19, nos. 3–4 (1993): 39–53.

Eustis, Joanne D., and Donald J. Kenney. *Library reorganization & restructuring.* OMS SPEC Kit 215. Washington, D.C.: ARL, May 1996.This Systems and Procedures Exchange Center (SPEC) publication walks a library through steps for review and change and gives examples.

Faerman, Sue R. "Organizational change and leadership styles." *Journal of Library Administration* 19, nos. 3–4 (1993): 55–79.

Fitch, Donna K., Jean Thomason, and Elizabeth Crabtree Wells. "Turning the library upside down: Reorganizing using total quality management principles." *Journal of Academic Librarianship* 19, no. 5 (November 1993): 294–299. This article describes Stamford University's Davis Library's application of TQM principles to preparing for and implementing a restructuring of the Library and discusses the results of this reorganization.

Garvin, David A. "Building a learning organization." *Harvard Business Review* 71 (July–August 1993): 78–91.

Hammer, Michael, and James Champy. *Reengineering the corporation: A manifesto for business revolution*. New York: Harper Business, 1993.

Heifetz, Michael L. *Leading change, overcoming chaos: A seven stage process for making change succeed in your organization*. [Olympia, Wash.]: Threshold Institute; Berkeley, Calif.: Ten Speed Press, 1993.

Heller, James S. "Find a new balance: Technical services meets adidas." *AALL Spectrum Magazine* 7, no. 3 (November 2002): 16–17, 30.

Hernon, Peter, and Charles McClure. *Evaluation and library decision making*. Norwood, N.J.: Ablex, 1990.

Hoffman, Herbert H. *Small library cataloging*. 3rd ed. Lanham, Md: Scarecrow Press, 2002.

Jacob, M. E. L. *Strategic planning: A how-to-do-it manual for librarians*. New York: Neal-Schuman, 1990.

Lee, Susan. "Organizational change in the Harvard College Library: A continued struggle for redefinition and renewal." *Journal of Academic Librarianship* 19, no. 4 (September 1993): 225–230. Harvard College Library began a process of intense change in 1990. This article chronicles and analyzes the change process, focusing on eight key success factors for strategic planning in an environment of continual change.

Mayo, Diane, and Jeanne Goodrich. *Staffing for results: A guide to working smart*. Chicago: American Library Association, 2002.

Perry, John, and Anne Woodworth. "Innovation and change: Can we learn from corporate models?" *Journal of Academic Librarianship* 21, no. 2 (March 1995): 117–120.

Riggs, Donald E. *Strategic planning for library managers*. Phoenix, Ariz.: Oryx Press, 1984.

Senge, Peter. *The fifth discipline: The art and practice of the learning organization*. New York: Currency, 1994.

Shaughnessy, Thomas W. "Lessons from restructuring the library." *The Journal of Academic Librarianship* 22, no. 4 (July 1996): 251–254.

Silverman, Marc B., ed. *Teamwork and collaboration in libraries: Tools for theory and practice*. Binghamton, N.Y.: Haworth Press, 2001. Discusses issues and steps in planning, organizing, and administering library teamwork.

Thompson, Christine E., ed. *Integration in the library organization*. New York: Haworth Press, 2000.

Wallace, Danny P., and Connie van Fleet. *Library evaluation: A casebook and can-do guide*. Englewood, Colo.: Libraries Unlimited, 2001.

Wellins, Richard S., and Julie Schulz Murphy. "Reengineering: Plug into the human factor." *Training & Development* 49 (January 1995): 33–37.

Worrell, Diane. "The learning organization: Management theory for the information age or new age fad?" *Journal of Academic Librarianship* 21, no. 5 (September 1995): 351–357. The basic principles of a learning organization are examined in this article, which offers examples from and implications for library management practice.

See also Appendix 5.9: Workflow.

Appendix 5.6: Support Staff in Technical Services

Benaud, Clair-Lise. "The academic para-professional cataloger: Underappreciated?" *Cataloging & Classification Quarterly* 15 (1992): 81–92.

Berry, John N. III. " 'Professional' is only a label." *Library Journal* 120, no. 12 (July 1995): 6.

Davidson-Arnott, Frances, and Deborah Kay. "Library technician programs: Skills-oriented paraprofessional education." *Library Trends* 46, no. 3 (Winter 1998): 540–563.

Howarth, Lynne C. "The role of the paraprofessional in technical services in libraries." *Library Trends* 46, no. 3 (Winter 1998): 526–539.

Mohr, Deborah A., and Anita Schuneman. "Changing roles: Original cataloging by paraprofessionals in ARL libraries." *Library Resources & Technical Services* 41, no. 2 (July 1997): 205–218.

Nevin, Susanne. "Recruiting and training the paraprofessional cataloger: A program for college and undergraduate library supervisors." *College & Undergraduate Libraries* 4, no. 2 (1997): 65–92. An excellent article covering training methods and providing a model training program.

Rider, Mary M. "Developing new roles for paraprofessionals in cataloging." *Journal of Academic Librarianship* 22, no. 1 (1996): 26–32. The emphasis of this article is the importance of staff training and development to enable flexibility in staff assignment. Some methods for staff training are suggested.

Younger, Jennifer A. "Support staff and librarians in cataloging." *Cataloging & Classification Quarterly* 23, no. 1 (1996): 27–47.

Appendix 5.7: Technical Services and Public Services

Bazirjian, Rosann. "Automation and technical services organization." *Library Acquisitions: Practice & Theory* 17 (1993): 73–77.

Miller, David P. "Both sides now; or paradise now." In *Integration in the library organization*, edited by Christine E. Thompson, 41–46. New York: Haworth Press, 2000.

Stamm, Andrea L. "The end of an era builds new team spirit: Team playing at its best." In *Managing cataloging and the organization of information: Philosophies, practices and challenges at the onset of the 21st century*, edited by Ruth C. Carter, 357–372. New York: Haworth Press, 2000.

Thompson, Christine E. "The cataloging advisory group: A public/technical services forum." *Journal of Library Administration* 29, no. 2 (1999): 123–131.

Thompson, Christine E., ed. *Integration in the library organization*. New York: Haworth Press, 2000.

Appendix 5.8: Training

Avery, Elizabeth Fuseler, Terry Dahlin, and Deborah A. Carver. *Staff development: A practical guide*, 3rd ed. Chicago: American Library Association, 2001.

Beck, Sara Ramser, ed. *Library training for staff and customers*. New York: Haworth Press, 2000. An aid to librarians responsible for training issues from planning to presentation.

Blanchard, Ken, John P. Karlos, and Alan Randolph. *Empowerment takes more than a minute*. San Francisco: Berrett-Koehler Publishers, 1996.

Callahan, Daren, and Mark Watson. "Care of the organization: Training and development strategies." *The Journal of Academic Librarianship* 21, no. 5 (September 1995): 376–381.

Duda, Andrea L., and Rosemary L. Meszaros. "Staff empowerment: Effective training for greater responsibilities." *Technical Services Quarterly* 16, no. 4 (1999): 11–33.

Fritz, Deborah A. *Cataloging with AACR2 and USMARC: For books, computer files, serials, sound recordings and videorecords*. Chicago: American Library Association, 1998, revised May 1999.

Fritz, Deborah A., and Richard J. Fritz. *MARC21 for everyone: A practical guide*. Chicago: American Library Association, 2003.

Kao, Mary L. *Cataloging and classification for library technicians*, 2nd ed. New York: Haworth Press, 2001. Good training tool covering cataloging terminology, tools, and step-by-step instruction.

———. *Introduction to technical services for library technicians*, New York: Haworth Press, 2001.

Metz, Ruth F. *Coaching in the library: A management strategy for achieving excellence*. Chicago and London: American Library Association, 2002.

Nevin, Susanne. "Recruiting and training the paraprofessional cataloger: A program for college and undergraduate library supervisors." *College & Undergraduate Libraries* 4, no. 2 (1997): 65–92. An excellent article covering training methods and a model training program.

St. Clair, Guy, and Joan Williamson. "Training and continuing education for the one-person librarian." In *Managing the new one person library*, 2nd ed., 28–41. New York: Bowker, 1992.

Appendix 5.9: Workflow

Bregman, Alvan. *Second report on reengineering technical services: Reorganization of acquisitions and binding.* UIUC Library, June 3, 1998. Available: http://door.library.uiuc.edu/acq/report2.htm (Accessed May 2, 2003). A process review of acquisitions and binding at the UIUC Library, covering workflow implications and process recommendations.

Carter, Ruth C., ed. *Managing cataloging and the organization of information: Philsophies, practices and challenges at the onset of the 21s' century.* New York: Haworth Press, 2000 A collection of articles with practical solutions to staffing, organization, teamwork, and workflow issues that all libraries face.

Gomez, Joni, and Jeanne Harrell. "Technical services reorganization: Realities and reactions." *Technical Services Quarterly* 10, no. 2 (1992): 1–15.

Kaplan, Michael, ed. *Planning and implementing technical services workstations.* Chicago: American Library Association, 1997.

Meldrum, Janifer. "Labor-saving tips for barcoding your existing collection." *MARCIVE Newsletter* 38 (October 2000): 5. Available: http://www.marcive.com/HOMEPAGE/NEWS1000.htm#labor (Accessed April 24, 2003).

Wakiji, Eileen, and Kelly Janousek. "Five steps to redefining workload: An academic library case study in progress." In *Continuity & transformation: The promise of confluence: proceedings of the Seventh National Conference of the Association of College and Research Libraries, Pittsburg, Pennsylvania, March 29–April 1, 1995,* 187–195. Chicago: Association of College and Research Libraries, 1995.

Younger, Jennifer A., and D. Kaye Gapen. "Administration of technical services: Technical services organization." revised by Cecily Johns. In *Technical services today and tomorrow,* 2nd ed., edited by Michael Gorman, 165–181. Englewood, Colo.: Libraries Unlimited, 1998.

See also Appendix 5.5: Process Review.

Appendix 5.10: Additional Suggested Readings

Coing, Marga. *Effective communication: An essential tool to cope with the challenge of technological change.* Bangkok, Thailand: IFLA Annual Conference (65th), August 20–28, 1999.ERIC Clearinghouse No.:IR057694. Available: http://ericit.org/fulltext/IR545329.pdf or http://www.ifla.org/IV/ifla65/papers/024-101e.htm (Accessed August 7, 2002).

Duke, John K. "Acceptable copy: Quality in record selection and outsourcing: A report." *Library Acquisitions: Practice & Theory* 21, no. 4 (Winter 1997): 483–485.

Gorman, Michael. *Technical services: Today and tomorrow*, 2nd ed. Englewood, Colo.: Libraries Unlimited, 1998.

Kastner, Arno, and Judi Nadler. *Final report of the Task Force on Copy Cataloging Acceptance Policies.* Big Heads Discussion Group. December 14, 2001. Available: http://www.nyu.edu/library/bobst/research/tsd/catasurv.htm (Accessed May 20, 2003).

Novak, Jan. *Virtual libraries: Service realities.* Brisbane, Australia: Confer International Association of Technological University Libraries (IATUL) Conference, July 3–7, 2000. ERIC Clearinghouse No. IR057953. Full text available: http://educate.lib.chalmers.se/iatul/proceedcontents/qutpap/novak_full.html (May 5, 2003).

Smith, Stephen J. "Cataloging with copy: Methods for increasing productivity." *Technical Services Quarterly* 11, no. 4 (1994): 1–11.

6

The Name and Role of the Cataloger in the Twenty-First Century

Nadine P. Ellero

Editor's note: The author has reviewed the literature of the past 10 years and has compiled data from job descriptions for catalogers from late 1997 through May 2003. An extensive mapping of the results of these job descriptions is provided in tables. The information from these jobs helps to explain the present situation, as well as determine future trends. The author concludes that, while duties are changing, expanding, and becoming more integrated with library operations, the need for catalogers and their job duties is still essential for libraries in the future.

> *Change your opinions, keep to your principles; change your leaves, keep intact your roots.*—Victor Hugo

Introduction

Over the past 30 years we have seen our card catalogs and collections change from print to electronic, with some collection resources existing in both or several other nonprint formats. This change has been one of form/transformation, flexibility, and functionality. The once-stationary drawers containing cards have been transformed into electronic records/databases housed on computer hardware and network infrastructures. These electronic and often Web-accessible catalogs offer flexible service by not requiring a physical visit to the library. Functionality has been increased by providing library users with the ability to keyword search multiple fields and use Boolean operators to construct complex searches of a library's collection. Supporting, facilitating, and adapting to these changes are library technical services departments. Whether physically purchasing a printed book, licensing access for an electronic journal, creating MARC (Machine-Readable Cataloging) catalog records for the OPAC (online public access catalog), or marking-up digital objects with XML tags, library technical services have been weathering the challenges of technological change and embracing opportunities for service enhancements. This chapter explores the impact of change on a small subset of technical services: catalogers. The here and now of catalogers' endeavors is the twenty-first century, and the winds of change will continue to challenge how we catalog, the types of resources we catalog (print, nonprint, and digital), and where catalogers in library workflows are positioned.

The word "catalog" used to conjure up images of large majestic wooden cabinets with multitiered rows of drawers crammed with cards or a weighty printed tome such as the "Sears Catalog." When encountering this word, younger generations will more than likely not hold a physical image in their minds, only the vague concept of an inventory or directory. Dorner, writing on "Cataloging in the 21st Century," discussed the access versus ownership features of library resources and how this will affect the role and nature of the catalog even further (1999, p. 397). This leads to the question of what will happen to the word "catalog," and for this chapter's unfolding discussion, the word "cataloger." Will the term "cataloger" change? Will a cataloger's role transform dramatically, necessitating a totally different word or descriptive phrase? This author's position name in 1990 contained the phrase, "Bibliographic Control," the meaning of which implies much more than the word "cataloger" and was designed to encompass more than the act of cataloging, that is, authority control, union listing, as well as management responsibilities. Currently the author's position name contains the descriptive phrase, "Intellectual Access," an attempt to break away from a paper-centric tradition and forge into the digital future. The choice of the phrase "Intellectual Access" centered around the goal of resource access in a user-oriented milieu, an environment that was moving away from the bifurcation of technical and public services to a more harmonic whole viewing all library activities as services for the public. Another way to view the word "cataloger" could be Jane Padham Ouderkirk's proposal to define it "so that the full scope and range of activities for which we are responsible is more broadly understood" (2000, p. 353).

For this chapter, the literature of the past 10 years has been reviewed and data from job descriptions for catalogers have been collected from late 1997 through May 2003 to facilitate a mapping of the present terrain and determine future trends (see Table 6.1 for distribution by year). This author and others believe that significant information can be gleaned from analyzing job descriptions (Palmer, Xu, Copeland, Towsey, Hosoi, Chaudhry and Komathi, Lack, and Khurshid). Job descriptions are a data source or quarry from which one can mine information on current trends and unearth the treasures of organizational structures, duties expected, human/personality traits desired, and skills being sought by employers. All these elements are a window into the present time and a glimmer of what may lie ahead.

Table 6.1.
Breakdown by Numbers of Job Descriptions Analyzed in Each Year, 1997–2003, for Nonmanagement or Pure Cataloger Positions

Number Breakdown per Year (n=791)	Total
1997	21
1998	100
1999	169
2000	162
2001	137
2002	155
2003	47

Note: There are some overlaps in each year as positions are reposted or searches are extended; therefore the unique total is 754 positions and the composite total is 791.

In 1998 William E. Studwell wrote a short commentary, "New Millennium, New Names? On Changing the Names of Reference Librarians and Catalogers." Studwell suggested a more "meaningful" or functional name such as "library database data providers" or the abbreviated form of "data providers" (Studwell 1998, p. 80). In an earlier article he had stated that, "The terms "cataloging" and "catalogers," implying listing or putting things into their proper slots, are becoming ever more out of place and obsolescent with each passing year as well as each new change in technology and methodology" (1996, p. 17). Ellen J. Waite, writing in 1995, proposed a new role for the cataloger, one that emphasized cataloger services on the "front-line" and "assist[ance] in the development of our web pages and electronic finding tools and guides" (1995, p. 37). Sherry L. Vellucci suggested in 1996 that catalogers need to enter a "team ethos" and take on the role of "problem-solvers" (1996, p. 443). Indeed, the job descriptions analyzed for this chapter have shown trends validating these proposals. Some names have changed, and catalogers are being asked to serve in such roles as expert (or resource person), problem-solver, team participant, leader of initiatives, and monitor of trends in technology and new ways of organizing and accessing resources. In addition, catalogers are being asked to possess the temperament or ability to work independently and to have an aptitude for being detail-oriented. On the other hand, catalogers are also expected to possess flexibility, show initiative, cope with change, be innovative, exhibit creativity, and exude energy and enthusiasm. It seems that a balance of temperaments, introversion, and extroversion is highly sought as catalogers are working in more team-based, collegial, user-oriented environments.

The Data

Job descriptions were collected and analyzed for catalogers, heads of cataloging departments, heads of serial departments, and heads of technical services and obtained from AUTOCAT, INTERCAT, MEDCAT, SERIALST,[1] SILS-L (now called LIS-List, the ListServ of the author's alma mater, the Department of Library & Information Studies in the School of Informatics, University at Buffalo, State University of New York), VAVIRTUA (The ListServ for the Virtual Library of Virginia), and WEB4LIB. The decision to retrieve job advertisements from listservs, as opposed to printed journals was guided by the belief that a greater number of positions would be obtained from that venue, due to their popularity and timeliness (Nesbeitt 2003, p. 116). A future study comparing job advertisements in journals and listservs for comparable time periods would be required for verification of data compiled in this chapter.

A general set of parameters was used in selecting job descriptions for analysis: (1) positions in the United States and U.S. territories; (2) positions of full-time status only (grant positions, partial terms, special project positions, etc., were not included); (3) positions that required an MLS or either significant cataloging experience along with several courses or a related master's degree; and (4) positions that specifically stated knowledge of cataloging, cataloging tools, or experience in cataloging. The operational definition of cataloging used was the one proposed by Turvey and Letarte, "the spectrum of intellectual activities relating to the provision of bibliographic control, from traditional cataloging and classification to the use of metadata schemata and knowledge management" (2002, p. 167). Figure 6.1 contains other definitions used for this study's analysis. All types of libraries were included: academic (including research institutes, national libraries, and national archives), public (including state libraries), corporate/special (including museums, state legislative libraries, and special subject libraries such as the Folger-Shakespeare Library), and corporate/library service companies (such as Library Associates, OCLC, and SANAD Support Technologies). The author desired to "see" what actual changes in position names and responsibilities were evolving, along with respective rates of change in a consecutive, comprehensive and long-term (i.e. more than two years) collection of job advertisements. In other words, how great of an impact is technological change having on position names and responsibilities of "catalogers," as evidenced in advertised positions?

Corporate/Library Service Companies: Companies that provide various library services such as OCLC, SANAD Support Technologies, etc.

Digitization Projects/Digital or Virtual Library Involvement: Used to classify positions that indicated some role/involvement with uniquely organizing digital objects, application of non-MARC metadata schemes, or actual digitization performance or coordination, etc.

E-Resources: Any resource that is in electronic form. Examples include electronic journals, digital books, locally created digital objects, and Web sites.

Internet Skills: A suite of skills that have as their focus Web development/design. These skills include HTML, SGML, XML, databases designed for access of information/resources via the Web, etc., that have some kind of application and are more than Internet/Web searching skills.

Metadata Knowledge: Used to classify positions that mentioned metadata in a general sense or listed specific metadata types or structures such as Dublin Core, EAD, TEI, etc.

New Ways to Organize Resources/Information: A phrase used to classify positions that indicated a unique or innovative way to classify or organize resources within either an OPAC or a Web environment.

Pure Catalogers: Used to refer to positions classified as cataloging positions and are not heads of cataloging, serials, or technical services departments. They often do entail other responsibilities such as database maintenance/management, coordination of a unit operation or special format cataloging team (e.g. serials), supervision, training, etc.

Search Extended: A collective term used to classify positions that were extended in some manner, either intentionally or through a reposting spanning several months.

Figure 6.1. Definitions.

A Microsoft Access database was utilized for data containment and analysis. The elements collected and examined were date of job posting; position name or title; institution; state; whether cataloging electronic resources was required; whether the position required some Internet facility or Web development skills such as HMTL, SGML, etc.; salary or salary range if one was given; source of the job posting (e.g., AUTOCAT , SERIALST, etc.); general position notes (e.g., characteristics/elements and codes describing/illustrating job requirements and character/personality assets); environment notes (e.g., descriptions of the work environment); type of library (as described previously); and level of position (i.e., line cataloger, head of cataloging, head of serials, or head of technical services). Assistant heads of departments or technical services were categorized as heads of those respective areas, as were team coordinators whose responsibilities involved little or no performance of cataloging functions.

Several difficulties were encountered when conducting the analysis and processing of the job descriptions, and they have been recognized by other authors who have conducted similar studies (Copeland 1997, pp. 28–29; Towsey 1997, p. 63). One of the most challenging difficulties involved the removal of duplicates. Duplicate detection required (1) extra time and effort, (2) constant vigilance of position name changes that sometimes involved alterations in duties and/or slight increases in pay ranges, and (3) determinations of search extensions and repostings. Job positions were considered to be "search extensions" when they reappeared several months later with the dates for submission of applications changed or the appearance of phrases such as "open until position is filled." Many times, job descriptions posted on listservs contained URLs pointing to a fuller job description. Efforts were made to gather the fuller descriptions, but a few were missed and were coded as such. In this study there were 19 missing full job descriptions, representing 2 percent of the total analyzed.

Descriptive content analysis strategies were used for the process of analysis, and although many attempts were made to ensure accuracy, it is admitted that the potential exists for unintended omissions or errors during phases of the data collection, data coding, or data analysis. The author's strategy was to print out the job descriptions as they were received, analyze only 10 to 20 job positions at any one time, highlight the characteristics/elements with a highlighting marker on the printed job description, translate with codes when needed (see Table 6.2, page 126), and enter the data. Traditional content analysis strategies encourage the use of forms/worksheets, assignment of predetermined criteria rather than gleaning, and analysis and entry by several persons with one or more as reviewers (Allen and Reser 1990, pp. 257–260). The author's desire was to observe the trends personally as they emerged from the job descriptions, much as an archaeological expedition does in an excavation. This observational/ archaeological method required the author to maintain lists that tracked various types of data, such as character/personality assets/traits requested, skills sought, and roles acknowledged directly or indirectly. These lists facilitated the development of a concept, which then became encoded. Both classification analysis (assigning codes to classify concepts found in the data) and word frequency techniques were used, similar to the method utilized in the Lack study (2001, p. 14). One disadvantage of this archaeological method was frequent reediting and reanalysis of data as concepts emerged, and these needed to be incorporated into earlier analyses. The main advantage of this method, however, was the ability to view trends as they appeared and not as anticipated by the author, and in this way author bias was prevented. A single analyst examining each job description provided a unique opportunity to directly and personally observe all levels of changes, nuances, and variations found in the job descriptions. This personal experience facilitated the feel and depth of knowledge needed to witness trends and contemplate emerging future designs. The querying tools in Access aided the verification process as reports were created to enable error detection and correction. A proposed better and future process, along with the traditional methods of content analysis, would involve the collection of all job descriptions in their original electronic form and the application of XML tags for coding, retrieval, and analysis. This potential process is discussed in greater detail at the end of this chapter.

The "general notes" field of the database contained descriptive data for each job description, such as the type of cataloging skills required, expanded roles, and traits desired. A separate notes field, "environmental notes," captured descriptions of the work environment in which the position resided. Admittedly, the excavation and analysis of all these job elements was an enormous undertaking, and previous studies have focused on more limited samples with specific targeted goals. Palmer (1992) (1987–1989 sample) explored job advertisements for skills required of catalogers, while Xu (1996) (1971–1990 sample) examined the impact of automation and compared catalogers and reference librarians. Narrowing the focus by type of cataloger, Copeland (1997) (1980–1995 sample) viewed the changes in skills and knowledge needed for serials catalogers, and Towsey (1997) (1995–1996 sample) ventured out of the United States and contrasted trends in cataloging between the United States and the United Kingdom. Buttlar and Garcha (1998) (1997 sample) utilized surveys querying real world catalogers to study cataloging functions in academic libraries for areas of "significance" and change, while Hosoi (1999) (1999 sample), who also looked at academic libraries, focused on job qualifications to elicit trends and necessary skills and experience needed to obtain a cataloging position. Chaudhry and Komathi (2001) (1990–1999 sample) examined job positions and requirements needed for working in an electronic environment, while Lack (2001) (1999–2000 sample) looked at important "people skills" and technological competence. The most recent study as of this writing, Khurshid's (2003) (2000–2001 sample), examined required skills and the impact of new and emerging technological developments. A fuller discussion of these studies, contrasted with the author's study, is contained in the section "Comparison with Other Studies."

Table 6.2. Codes for Data Entry

Name of Element	Code to Use
General	
Job Description Changed	JDC2
Full Job Description Not Pulled from Web Page	NFD2
Job Position Not Filled Long (my guess)	NFL2
New Positions	NP2
Non-Traditional Cataloging Position	NTCP2
Search Extended (often guessed)	SE2
Personal Traits/Skills	
Analytical Skills	AS2
Communication Skills	CS2
Creative	CR2
Decision Making Skills	DMS2
Foreign Language Skills	FL2
Initiative	IN2
Interpersonal Skills	IS2
Organizational Skills	OS2
Problem Solving Skills	PS2
Project Management Skills	PJM2
Relational Database Skills	RD2
Second Masters	SM2
Special Subject Background	SS2
Tenure Track	TT2
Work Groups Skills/Team	WG2
Roles/Responsibilities	
Bibliographic Instruction	BI2
Collection Development	CD2
Content Management System	CMS2
Database Maintenance	DB2
Developing Thesauri	DT2
Emerging Technologies Knowledge	ET2
Intellectual Access	IA2
Intra-liaison	ILN2
Manage Operations	MO2
Professional Activities	PA2
New Integrated Library System	NILS2
New Ways to Organize	NWTO2
Quality Control/Quality Assurance	QC2
Quality Productivity Balance	QP2
System Administration (ILS)	SA2
Web Page Design	WPD2
Web Site Design/Development	WSD2
Environment	
Reorganized	RE2

The study conducted for this chapter focused on a much larger sampling of job descriptions that included all types of libraries, with in-depth analysis of job elements indicating present and future trends and departures from traditional cataloging roles and requirements. Some of the job elements, as written in the descriptions, required the author to make inferences so that comparisons and analysis could be applied across the sample. For example, when a job description stated the salary was in the "mid thirties," a $35,000 salary figure was entered, and when a phrase such as "cataloger prepares MARC records in all formats" was encountered, the inference was made that the cataloger was responsible for both original and complex copy cataloging.[2] Job elements that were clearly stated as wanted, desired, or needed were tracked and analyzed. The supposition was that clearly stated and defined elements were important, while job elements stated as "may be required or may involve xyz, etc." were considered less important, nonessential, and were not tracked or included in this study. For libraries with "team-based environments," "team leaders" were classified as analogous to department heads. Likewise, when terms such as "oversees" or "coordinates" were found in the job descriptions, the classification of "manager" or "manages operations" was applied.

Data Description and Analysis

The findings encountered in this study were closely aligned with previous studies and continue to show that change, while often felt acutely, is in reality manifested slowly. An examination of cataloger position names and roles proved this to be true. For purposes of discussion in this section and the next, "Comparison with Other Studies," intense analysis was conducted for pure cataloging positions only. The entire data set totaled 1,036 positions; pure cataloging positions, those not functioning primarily as managers or administrators, totaled 754, or 73 percent of the entire data set. Of the 754 job descriptions analyzed, 602 contained some form of "cataloger" in the title (80 percent), while 152 did not contain any form of "cataloger" in the title (20 percent). Seeing that 80 percent of all pure cataloging positions held titles with some version of the word "catalog," it logically follows that 90 percent of those positions entailed performance of cataloging operations. The remaining 10 percent functioned as experts (resource persons), overseers, planners, etc. Table 6.3 (pages 128–132) shows a selected distribution of unique position titles along with their frequency. All the higher numbers, except for "Technical Services Librarian," contain a version of "cataloger." Many more "catalogers" could be listed, as the multiple specialty ones were omitted, such as "Arabic Cataloger." Several newer and innovative titles appeared, like "Continuing Resources Cataloger Librarian," "Digital Resources Cataloger," "Information Architect," and "Knowledge Manager," but not frequently. The significance of catalogers, it seems, resides in what they accomplish and how they are perceived, not so much in what they are named. Lange, writing in 1991, stated, "Let us be known as inquisitive, as problem solvers, and innovators in using present and enhancing future information systems" (p. 15). Looking at the responsibilities of original and complex copy cataloging, 678 (90 percent of the pure cataloger subset) positions required this as a major responsibility/role. Catalogers with management and/or supervisory responsibility totaled 298 (40 percent of the subset), those with supervisory roles totaled 240 (32 percent of the subset), and those functioning as an "expert" or "resource person" totaled 113 (15 percent of the subset). Positions classified as "Non-traditional", that is, involving major roles in either digital library infrastructures, digitization, heavy-duty metadata applications or Perl programming, for example, numbered 12 (2 percent), revealing that traditional cataloging is needed, central to knowledge management (i.e., based on timeless principles of intellectual access), and here to stay whether the persons ("catalogers") are renamed or the term is revitalized.

Table 6.3. Selected Breakdown of Position Titles: Uniqueness and Frequency

Position Title	Totals
Assistant Catalog Librarian	4
Assistant Catalog/Reference Librarian	1
Assistant Cataloger	2
Assistant Database Management Authorities Librarian	1
Assistant Federal Documents Cataloger	1
Assistant Librarian	4
Assistant Librarian for Public and Technical Services	1
Assistant Librarian for Technical Services	1
Assistant Librarian [and other specially named sections]	2
Assistant Technical Services Librarian	1
Audiovisual Cataloger	3
Audiovisual/Special Materials Cataloger	1
Authority Control Librarian	1
Authority Control/Database Maintenance Librarian	1
Authority Section Head	1
Automated Library Services-Authority Control Librarian	1
Automation and Cataloging Librarian	1
AV Cataloger	1
AV Catalogers & Medical Catalogers	1
Bibliographic & Metadata Services Coordinator	1
Bibliographic Access Librarian	1
Bibliographic Control Librarian	1
Bibliographic Records Librarian (Cataloger)	1

Position Title	Totals
Bibliographic Services Librarian	1
Bibliographic Specialist	1
Biomedical Information Specialist/Serials Cataloger	1
Cartographic Materials Catalog Librarian	1
Catalog Librarian	76
Catalog Librarian [and other specially named sections]	26
Catalog Librarian/Head of Catalog Maintenance	1
Catalog Maintenance Librarian	1
Catalog Management Librarian	2
Catalog Manager	1
Catalog/Archives Librarian	1
Catalog/Electronic Access Librarian	2
Catalog/Government Documents Librarian	1
Catalog/Reference Librarian	2
Cataloger (Cataloguer=1)	76
Cataloger [and other specially named sections]	11
Cataloger Librarian	6
Cataloger/Annotator	1
Cataloger/Metadata Librarian	2
Cataloger/Metadata Specialist	1
Cataloger/Project Manager	2
Cataloger/Reference	5
Cataloging	2
Cataloging and Authority Control	1
Cataloging and Collection Development Librarian	1
Cataloging and Database Management Librarian	2
Cataloging and Metadata Quality Control	1
Cataloging and Metadata Services Librarian	1
Cataloging and Reference	1
Cataloging Associate Librarian, Original Cataloging	1
Cataloging Department Head	1
Cataloging Librarian	32
Cataloging Librarian, Serials and Electronic	1
Cataloging Librarian [and other special sections like serials]	1
Cataloging Manager, Bibliographic Access Management	1
Cataloging Position (Senior Library Information Specialist)	1
Cataloging Services Librarian	4
Cataloging Services Librarian (Monographs)	1
Cataloging Supervisor	1
Cataloging Team Librarian	1

(*Continued*)

Position Title	Totals
Cataloging/Automation Librarian	1
Cataloging/Database Management Librarian	1
Cataloging/Indexing Librarian	2
Cataloging/Reference Librarian	1
Cataloging/Systems Support Librarian	1
Cataloging/Technical Services	1
Cataloging/Technical Services Librarian	3
Cataloging/Technology Librarian	1
Cataloging/Web Librarian	1
faautoCataloguing & Acquisitions Librarian	1
Continuing Resources Cataloger Librarian	1
Coordinator for the Development of Bibliographic Control	1
Coordinator of Bibliographic Control (Cataloging Coordinator)	1
Coordinator of Cataloging and Serials Management	1
Database and Authority Control Librarian	1
Database Maintenance Librarian	1
Database Maintenance/Specialized Monographs Cataloging Librarian	1
Database Management Cataloger	1
Database Management Librarian	2
Database Management Librarian/Cataloger	1
Database Quality Coordinator	1
Digital Libraries/Cataloging Team Librarian	1
Digital Resources Cataloger	1
Electronic Access/Cataloging Librarian	1
Electronic Access/Serials Librarian	1
Electronic Cataloging and Metadata Coordinator	1
Electronic Resources & Serials Cataloger	1
Electronic Resources Access Librarian	2
Electronic Resources Access Specialist (Electronic Resources Cataloger)	1
Electronic Resources and Serials Cataloging Librarian	1
Electronic Resources and Special Formats Cataloger	1
Electronic Resources Catalog Librarian	5
Electronic Resources Cataloger	11
Electronic Resources Cataloging Librarian	1
Electronic Resources Librarian	5
Electronic Resources Librarian for Technical Services	1
Electronic Resources Serials Librarian	1
Electronic Resources Technical Services Librarian	2
Electronic Resources/[special format designated]	4

(Continued)

Position Title	Totals
Electronic Serials Librarian	1
Electronic/Digital Resources Cataloging Librarian	1
Head Cataloger	4
Head Cataloger for Automated Library Services	1
Head Cataloger/System Librarian	1
Head of Database Development	1
Head of Technical Services/Webmaster	1
Head, Data Control Unit	1
Head, Database Maintenance Section (of Collection Services/Cataloging)	1
Head, Metadata Unit	1
Information Analyst	1
Information Architect	1
Information Architect/Classification and Indexing Specialist	1
Information Organization Librarian	1
Integrated Systems Coordinator/Catalog Librarian	1
Knowledge Manager	1
Librarian (Cataloger)	20
Librarian: Cataloging and Reference	1
Librarian: Lexical Specialist	1
Library Cataloger	2
MARC Database Manager	1
Metadata Analyst	1
Metadata Librarian	9
Metadata Librarian, Cataloging Department	1
Metadata Librarian/Archivist & Digital Library Project Manager Rare and Manuscript Collections (RMC)	1
Metadata Specialist 2	1
Monographic Cataloger	5
Monographic Cataloger [other basic versions of this]	10
Monographs Original Cataloger	2
Multiple Formats Cataloger	1
Music Cataloger	3
Music Cataloger and Music Archives Librarian	1
Nonbook Cataloger/Metadata Librarian	1
Non-Book Cataloging Coordinator	1

(Continued)

Position Title	Totals
Non-Print Cataloger	1
Original Cataloger	2
Original Cataloger [special sections]	6
Original Cataloger/Authorities Coordinator	1
Original Cataloger/Information Architect/Cataloger	1
Periodicals/Cataloging Librarian	1
Principal Catalog Librarian	1
Principal Cataloger	2
Principal Electronic Resources/Special Formats Processing Librarian	1
Print and Digital Monographic Cataloger	1
Professional Cataloger	1
Professional Librarian Catalog Department	1
QC Librarian	1
Rare/Nonbook Cataloger-Special Projects & Collections	1
Reference & Cataloging	1
Reference Librarian/Social Sciences Subject Specialist and Cataloger	1
Reference/Cataloger Librarian	1
Resource Management Librarian	1
Romance Languages Cataloger	1
Senior Assistant Librarian, Central Technical Service (Cataloging Department)	1
Senior Catalog Librarian	2
Senior Cataloger or Senior Cataloging Librarian	5
Serial Cataloger Librarian	1
Serials & Metadata Cataloger	1
Serials and Electronic Resources Cataloger	3
Serials Cataloger	31
Serials Cataloging/Metadata Librarian	1
Serials/Electronic Resources Cataloging Coordinator	1
Special Formats Cataloger	4
Technical Services Librarian	23
Technical Services Librarian/Cataloger	1
Technical Services Manager/Cataloger	1
Technical Services/Cataloging	1

As with the findings of other studies, the large majority of job positions in this study were in academic libraries, 796 (77 percent) (see Table 6.4 for comparison of all library types). Likewise, the types of positions showed an overwhelming majority to be pure cataloger positions, 754 (73 percent) (see Table 6.5 for comparison of types of library positions and Table 6.1, page 121, for total numbers of job descriptions analyzed in each year from late 1997 through May 2003).

Table 6.4. Breakdown by Types of Libraries

Library Type	Totals, Entire Data Set (n=1,036) (Includes "Senior" Levels)	Totals, Pure Catalogers Only (n=754)
Academic	796 (77%)	586 (78%)
Public	125 (12%)	92 (12%)
Special	48 (5%)	33 (4%)
Corporate/Library Service Companies	46 (4%)	43 (6%)

Table 6.5. Breakdown by Types of Cataloging Positions

Position Type (n=1036)	Total
Pure Catalogers/Non-Department Heads	754 (73%)
Heads of Technical Services	144 (14%)
Heads of Cataloging	116 (11 %)
Heads of Serials*	24 (2 %)

Note: These were classified by function and not by position title.
*All included cataloging responsibilities and/or management of cataloging efforts.

This study also looked at the descriptions of the library "environment" (see Table 6.6, page 134) as they were given in the context of job responsibilities, required qualifications, and preferred qualifications. It was interesting to find that only 268 (36 percent) of the job descriptions highlighted the type of environment, beyond a general description of the library as a whole, in which the cataloger would be engaged. In recent years, many articles and speakers have emphasized the degree and frequency of "change" in work environments, and yet the job descriptions did not reflect a high concern with describing any "new" environment. Likewise, only 50 (7 percent) of the positions described a need for the cataloger to be able to cope with change, and 142 (19 percent) expressed a strong desire for the cataloger to be "flexible" (Steinhagen and Moynahan 1998, pp. 5, 16; Ayres 1996, p. 4). Ironically, back in 1950 Mary D. Herrick, writing on the "Status of Worker Morale Among College Catalogers," described a need for " 'flexible procedures' and 'cordial intrastaff relationships' " (1950, pp. 35–36). This ability to be flexible within the context of rapid change and shifting work priorities is a key skill and asset. Mering wrote in 1998 that, " catalogers must learn to be flexible in this transitional period and participate in the development and use of new technologies" (1998a, p. 85). Freeborn and Mugridge, describing a new reorganization of monographic cataloging at the Pennsylvania State University libraries, also discussed the necessity of flexibility and tolerance for change (2002, p. 36). Interestingly, of the entire 1,036 job positions collected, 15 (1 percent) mentioned an organizational restructuring change, reinforcing the argument that the "change" being observed and felt is primarily due to technological changes in library OPACs, cataloging tools, and library materials.

Table 6.6. Characteristics of Library Environments for Nonmanagement, "Pure" Cataloging Positions

Library Environments (n=754; Total mentioning specifics about environment = 268, 36%)	Total
Changing Environment	94 (12%)
Team Environment	86 (11%)
Dynamic Environment	41 (5%)
Collegial/Collaborative Environment	40 (5%)
Production-Centered Environment	28 (4%)
Complex Environment	10 (1%)
Evolving Environment	4 (.5%)

Many of the prior studies traced the type and numbers of traditional skills and knowledge (e.g., MARC, AACR2), tools (OCLC/RLIN, LCSH, MESH, etc.) and automation skills (PCs, spreadsheets, etc.). This study focused on new, variant, or upcoming responsibilities, roles, and personality traits desired for current positions.(Table 6.7, on page 136, lists in descending order the various emerging roles and responsibilities discovered, and Table 6.8, on page 137, lists in descending order the desired personal skills and traits of catalogers.) Not surprising was the high number of occurrences for the responsibility of cataloging electronic resources, 339 (45 percent). Electronic resources included both resources found/discovered on the Web as well as those "born digitally," which often emanate from the digitization of rare and archival objects and documents. To further demonstrate impact in the cataloging of electronic resources, the author desired to obtain from OCLC (Online Computer Library Center, Inc.) the numbers and types of electronic resources added to the database, for each year in the 1997–2003 span, but was informed via an e-mail response that these data were not available.[3] OCLC's *Annual Reports* contain statistics by format, such as books, serials, computer files, etc.; however, in June 1997 the format or type of record designation ("m") was limited to encompass computer software, numeric data, computer-oriented multimedia, and online systems or services only, rendering conclusions for electronic resources unobtainable via the "computer files" breakdown (Weitz 2002, p. 2). According to the findings, OCLC was the preferred bibliographic utility and therefore would have been the best source to obtain information regarding the quantities of MARC-based electronic resources that have been cataloged.

The relatively low numbers of catalogers with roles in the "digital or virtual library" or with digitization projects, 63 (8 percent), or with gateways or portals, 4 (.5 percent), as found in this study, was surprising and did not follow the sweeping changes noted in work environment characteristics, 94 (12 percent, see Table 6.6, page 134), the number of jobs requesting Internet skills, 130 (17 percent), or the desire for metadata knowledge or experience, 132 (18 percent). One reason for this discrepancy may be attributed to the level or type of cataloging job being advertised, and a survey conducted on existing job positions and responsibilities might show that many catalogers are actively working on or engaged in some aspect of digitization projects, gateways or portals, etc. It may also be that the "change" often discussed refers to accelerated changes associated with technological advancements. Hill noted the phenomenon of accelerated change by commenting that "the skills that catalogers have today won't carry them through their careers. They'll only carry them through today" (2002, p. 258). The need and desire for continual learning will become, if they are not already, a basic staple for the present and future cataloger, and the data studied found 16 (2 percent) job positions specifically expressing this necessity. Although this percentage is low, it is one of several traits to be watched and to be encouraged. Roy Tennant (1998) listed several traits in "The Most Important Management Decision: Hiring Staff for the New Millennium," learning being one of them, that will be crucial for present and future catalogers:

- the capacity to learn constantly and quickly
- flexibility
- an innate skepticism
- a propensity to take risks
- an abiding public service perspective [service/user oriented]
- an appreciation of what others bring to the effort and an ability to work with them effectively [team oriented]
- skill at enabling and fostering change, and the capacity and desire to work independently (1998, p. 102)

Many of these traits can also be viewed as "roles," such as "team initiator" for a new project or "change implementer" for revamping an old workflow or embracing a new technology.

Table 6.7. Emerging Roles and Responsibilities
in Descending Order

Emerging Roles and Responsibilities (n=754)	Total
Electronic Resources Cataloging	339 (45%)
Reference Responsibilities	141 (19%)
Managerial Roles	137 (18%) *including supervision, 298 (40%)
Metadata Knowledge/Application	132 (18%) [Dublin Core=64; EAD=34; TEI=32]
Internet Skills of Various Types	130 (17%) [HTML=60; XML=43; SGML=30; "Mark-up Languages"=11]
Monitoring Trends	129 (17%)
Liaison with other Departments within the Institution and Outside the Institution	103 (14%) [Vendor Liaison=24, 3%]
Leadership Role	95 (13%) [Vision=3, .4%]
Collection Development Responsibilities	93 (12%)
Digitization Projects/Digital or Virtual Library Involvement	63 (8%)
Web Page/Site Responsibilities	58 (8%)
Liaison Role with Internal Library Departments/Groups	52 (7%)
Bibliographic Instruction	43 (6%)
General Database Skills	33 (4%)
New Ways to Organize Resources	20 (3%)
Thesauri/Taxonomies	18 (2%)
Licensing Responsibility	18 (2%)
URL Maintenance	18 (2%)
System Administration	16 (2%)
Outsourcing Responsibilities	15 (2%)
Intellectual/Enhance Access	14 (2%)
General Public Services Role	9 (1%)
Grant Writing	4 (0.5%)
Involvement with Library Gateways or Portals	4 (0.5%)

Table 6.8. Person-Based Skills and Traits
of Nonmanagement, Pure Catalogers (n=754)

Skill/Trait	Total
Communication Skills	485 (64%)
Foreign Language Skills	382 (51%)
Interpersonal Skills	281 (37%)
Problem Solving Skills	189 (25%)
Analytical Skills	172 (23%)
Able to Work Independently	171 (23%)
Organizational Skills	163 (22%)
Flexibility	142 (19%)
Team Oriented	135 (18%)
User/Service Oriented	109 (14%)
Energetic/Enthusiastic/Dynamic	72 (10%)
Second Masters Now and/or Eventually for Tenure	70 (9%)
Creative	67 (9%)
Innovative/Forward Thinking	64 (8%)
Detail Oriented	62 (8%)
Able to Cope with Change	50 (7%)
Initiative	48 (6%)
Accuracy in Cataloging	21 (3%)
Ability/Desire for Constant Learning	16 (2%)
Decision Making Skills	11 (1%)
Ability to Work under Pressure	4 (0.5%)
Has Humor	4 (0.5%)

A continuing expanded role for catalogers is participation in some component of reference or public services work. (Table 6.9, on page 139, displays this role and several others for each year of the study.) The data show little significant change for reference activity, and reveal similar incremental increases for Internet skills, digitization, and metadata efforts. Several authors, chiefly Eskoz (1991) and Folsom (2000), have written extensively on catalogers engaging in reference activities, and the present study confirmed that 141 (19 percent) of the job descriptions require reference participation. Other activities such as collection development came in at 93 (12 percent), and bibliographic instruction at 43 (6 percent), both falling below management, metadata, trends, liaison, and leadership roles.

Although there are several emerging roles in addition to public service roles, such as leader, visionary, metadata expert, monitor of trends, Web page developer/designer, and vendor liaison, the core role of cataloging in providing and enhancing access to resources continued to be a forerunner, with 678 positions (90 percent) requiring this role and associated skills. In addition, the trait of being able to work "independently," 164 (21 percent); the ability to "problem-solve," 189 (25 percent); the possession of foreign language skills, 382 (51 percent); and the need for analytical skills, 172 (23 percent) continued to be expressed. Possessing acute analytical skills and detail-oriented perceptions remain hallmarks of excellent catalogers. Analytical skills were especially highlighted in Mering's (1998a) article on the future of professional catalogers as an important quality for the new cataloger to possess (p. 85). Likewise, Wendler strongly emphasized the cataloger's role in leading intellectual control with developments of metadata standards (1999, pp. 44, 50–51), and Hoerman pleaded for the importance of "improving access" as the guiding principal for all cataloging discussions and catalog designs, which may also energize and attract more persons to the cataloging profession (Hoerman 2002, pp. 39–40).

Many personal assets, such as communication skills, interpersonal skills, team orientation, flexibility, and user/service focus, are either holding steady or increasingly being requested, along with the traditional knowledge, principles, and tools of cataloging. (Table 6.10 shows a view through the years of selected personal traits.) These personal assets are indicative of the changing work climate, where constant evolution of resources and technology is occurring. To keep pace with this evolution, catalogers are being sought who possess collegiality (collaboration), self-motivation (initiative), energy, enthusiasm, dynamic spirits, innovative minds, creative ideas, and the ability and desire for continual learning. Eden and Bierman, in addressing knowledge access management at the Lied Library and OCLC's Knowledge Access Management Seminars, pointed out "the importance of proactivity and initiative in the incorporation of knowledge access management concepts in the library's organizational culture" (2002, p. 91; see also McCombs 1997, p. 134; Mering 1998b, p. 58).

Table 6.9. Selected Emerging Roles: View Through the Years 1997–2003

Year	Electronic Resources Cataloging		Metadata		Web Page or Site Responsibility		Internet Skills		Digitization Projects		New Ways to Organize Information		Reference (*does not include bibliographic instruction)		Managerial Roles (*does not include supervision)	
1997* n=21	11	53%	2	10%	4	19%	9	43%	1	5%	2	10%	4	19%	6	29%
1998 n=100	33	33%	8	8%	10	10%	20	20%	5	5%	2	2%	22	22%	12	12%
1999 n=169	63	37%	18	11%	17	10%	27	16%	5	3%	5	3%	38	22%	29	17%
2000 n=162	65	40%	30	19%	15	9%	21	13%	8	5%	3	2%	29	18%	35	22%
2001 n=137	78	57%	40	29%	13	9%	26	19%	18	13%	5	4%	28	20%	21	15%
2002 n=155	83	54%	35	23%	17	11%	32	21%	23	15%	4	3%	22	14%	33	21%
2003* n=47	24	51%	9	19%	4	9%	8	17%	7	15%	0	0	5	11%	6	13%

Note: 1997 and 2003 data are not from complete years.

Table 6.10. Selected Personal Traits and Skills: View Through the Years 1997–2003

Year	Communication Skills		Interpersonal Skills		Flexibility		Team Oriented		Independent		Detail Oriented		Problem-Solving Skills	
1997* n=21	16	76%	8	38%	9	43%	3	14%	4	19%	0	0	5	24%
1998 n=100	63	63%	33	33%	25	25%	21	21%	31	31%	2	2%	26	26%
1999 n=169	105	62%	67	40%	38	22%	33	20%	33	20%	9	5%	42	25%
2000 n=162	98	60%	70	43%	28	17%	27	17%	31	19%	15	9%	49	30%
2001 n=137	91	66%	50	36%	24	18%	27	20%	37	27%	15	11%	33	24%
2002 n=155	107	69%	52	34%	27	17%	21	14%	30	19%	17	11%	33	21%
2003* n=47	28	60%	16	34%	6	13%	7	15%	13	28%	6	13%	7	15%

Note: 1997 and 2003 data are not from complete years.

Among the top ranking person-based skills were communication (64 percent), interpersonal (37 percent), problem solving (25 percent), and team-based skills (18 percent). Along with these top ranking people skills were the traditional skills of foreign language facility (51 percent), ability to work independently (23 percent), and organizational and analytical skills at a proximal 22 and 23 percent.

Finding and attracting these highly flexible, skilled communicators, and effective team players, who are also equipped with foreign language skills, the ability to work independently, appeared to be somewhat challenging, as 80 (11 percent) of the job positions were extended or reposted and often re-advertised with slightly higher salaries. In general, salaries reported from this study's job postings were relatively low but still within predictable ranges. The lowest median appeared in 1998 at $35,946 and the highest median in 2001 at $57,447. According to the *2001 National Occupational Employment and Wage Estimates* from the Bureau of Labor Statistics, the median librarian salary was $42,670, within a range of $24,730–$65,240 (U.S. Bureau of Labor Statistics 2002, Section 25–4021 Librarians). The *ARL Annual Salary Survey, 2001–02,* showed the median salaries for U.S. librarians from 1998 to 2001/2002 ranging from $44,544 to $51,806 and the average salary for catalogers in FY 2001/2002 ranging from $38,072 to $50,961, depending on years of experience (Kyrillidou and Young 2002, p. 18, 40). Real world data are much more reliable, but the salary data for postings reveals what employers want to pay and in some cases are able to pay. (Table 6.11 shows the low, median, and high salaries obtained for each year, noting that there are incomplete coverage for years 1997 and 2003.) It is encouraging to observe, however, that the salary data for the first five months of 2003 revealed the lowest beginning salary at $30,000. The salary data obtained by this method must be carefully considered, as 29 percent of the job postings did not list a salary or range, and most say "commensurate with experience." A future study could investigate the salaries paid for each job that was posted and successfully filled.

Comparison with Other Studies

Tables 6.12 through 6.19 compare general roles and skills, expanded roles and skills, person-based skills and traits, and salaries for the present and other recently conducted studies. Most of the studies concentrated on U.S. academic libraries, with the Hosoi and Lack studies clearly stating that parameter. The others were less specific, but the assumption can be made from their sources, *American Libraries* and *C& RL News,* that the job positions were largely academic and located in the United States. (Table 6.12, on page 142, presents a comparative demographic breakdown.) It can be seen that the Palmer, Towsey, and Chaudhry studies also included public and special libraries. Percentages of academic libraries, 78 percent for the present study, and special libraries, 4 percent, are in keeping with the other studies and showed little variability, suggesting either a constant or slowly changing environment.

Table 6.11. Comparative Analysis—Salaries

Study	Positions Listing Salary	Positions Not Listing Salary	Low	Median	High	Salary Ranges
Palmer 1987-1989 n=340	-	-	-	-	-	-
Xu 1971–1990 n=262	-	-	-	-	-	-
Copeland 1980–1995 n=?*	-	-	-	-	-	-
Towsey* March 1995– February 1996 n=180	75%	25%	29,000 low point mean	31,000 mid point mean	33,000 high point mean	20,000– 72,000
Buttlar & Garcha 1997 n=271	-	-	-	-	-	-
Hosoi 1999 n=124	-	-	-	-	-	-
Chaudhry 1990–1999 n=131	-	-	-	-	-	-
Lack October 1999– October 2000 n= 77	-	-	-	-	-	-
Khurshid 2000–2001 n=151	-	-	-	-	-	-
Ellero 1997–2003 n=754	535 (71%)	219 (29%)	1997 26,510 1998 20,747 1999 23,316 2000 21,528 2001 24,089 2002 23,795 2003 30,000	1997 42,254 1998 35,946 1999 45,658 2000 49,264 2001 57,447 2002 48,583 2003 46,496	1997 57,998 1998 51,144 1999 68,000 2000 77,000 2001 90,804 2002 73,370 2003 62,991	20,747– 90,804

*United States data only taken from the Towsey study.

Table 6.12. Comparative Analysis—Demographics

Study	Academic	Public	Special	Library Corporate	Line/"Pure" Cataloger	Technical Services	Search Extended	Entry Level	New Positions
Palmer 1987–1989 n=340	71%	14%	15%	-	52%	16%	-	-	-
Xu 1971–1990 n=262	-	-	-	-	-	-	-	-	-
Copeland 1980–1995 n=?*	-	-	-	-	-	-	-	-	-
Towsey March 1995–February 1996 n=180	147 (82%)	19 (19%)	14 (8%)	-	-	-	-	-	-
Buttlar & Garcha 1997 n=271	271 (100%)	-	-	-	-	-	-	-	-
Hosoi 1999 n=124	124 (100%)	-	-	-	-	-	Not considered	-	-
Chaudhry 1990–1999 n=131	69 % 9% (colleges, schools)	9%	5%	8% called "other"	-	-	-	68%	-
Lack October 1999–October 2000 n=77	77 (100%)	-	-	-	-	-	5 (6%)	-	-
Khurshid 2000–2001 n=151	-	-	-	-	-	-	-	-	-
Ellero 1997–2003 n=754	586 (78%)	92 (12%)	33 (4 %)	43 (6%)	754 (100%)	Head of Technical Services=144 (14% of larger dataset, 1036)	80 (11%)	70 (9%)	18 (2%)

Xu: Original data set included catalogers and reference librarians. Cataloger data only was pulled for this table. Xu included temporary positions of at least nine months duration as well as senior level positions.

Copeland: Total in study not stated; focused only on serial catalogers' job descriptions from *American Libraries* and *C&RL News*.

Towsey: Included temporary and part time positions and senior level positions; data for United States used in this table.

Buttlar & Garcha: Surveyed catalogers in positions as opposed to analyzing job descriptions.

Hosoi: United States academic only, includes senior level, temporary and part-time positions from *American Libraries* and *C&RL News.*

Chaudhry: Analyzed job descriptions from *American Libraries* only.

Lack: Analyzed job descriptions from *American Libraries* only, focused on United States academic positions including senior level and excluding Law and Medicine as they were not classified in the "Academic Library Section".

Khurshid: Analyzed job descriptions in *American Libraries, College & Research Library News*, along with some from AUTOCAT and included positions not requiring an MLS.

Ellero: Analyzed job descriptions from Listservs such as AUTOCAT, SERIALST, etc. and focused on nonmanagement level cataloging positions.

True comparisons are difficult to obtain, and several caveats need to be stated. First, the categorization assigned by investigators will often differ. Second, the concepts used to describe data/phenomena will often vary. Third, the unique focus taken by any investigation will often illuminate different aspects. The focus of this investigation was twofold: (1) a selection of job advertisements representing "pure catalogers" primarily and (2) an emphasis on new/different and/or continuing roles and traits of catalogers. While heads of departments and divisions were or presently are catalogers, the assumption was made that the majority of their work entailed managerial/administrative tasks and was not representative or descriptive of the trends and roles emerging or continuing for the performers of actual cataloging work (referred to as pure catalogers). Cataloging work requested of senior level positions totaled 37 (13 percent) out of a total of 284. The author does note however, that many "real" positions are intentionally hybrids, combining reference work and cataloging, systems administration and cataloging, and in a few instances, Webmaster and cataloging. Many of the positions encompassed the leading or coordinating of a specific format such as "serials" or function such as "authority control" or "database maintenance," which challenged the "pure cataloger" classification. None of the other studies made this distinction for "pure catalogers," following the theory that much of the routine work of cataloging was performed by paraprofessionals and/or outsourced and that much of the cataloger's work is now inherently "managerial" (Hosoi 1999, p. 14). Although this author does not dispute this fact (see Tables 6.13 and 6.14, pages 144–145), the present study showed 18 percent (137; if including supervision, 298, or 40 percent) of the catalogers functioning in management roles. The belief is maintained that the special expertise and skills of a professional cataloger are needed and will be in demand as library Web pages increase in complexity, more resources become digitized, and technology becomes more sophisticated. Hill and Intner, writing on cataloging education, observed, "Most librarians employed in a cataloging or other technical services operation in a library are involved to some extent in management . . . which involve[s] creative thinking, writing, and communicating, and interpreting a wide variety of events, statements, documents, and data in order to make decisions" (1999, p. 12).

Table 6.13. Comparative Analysis—General Roles, Part A

Study	Original Cataloging	Supervise	Manage	Train Staff	OCLC/RLIN	Expert Advisor	Leadership Vision
Palmer 1987–1989 n=340	-	50%	-	17%	-	-	-
Xu 1971–1990 n=262	-	105 (40%) Includes administration	18 (7%) Called coordination	-	188 (72%)	-	-
Copeland 1980–1995 n=?*	-	-	-	-	Discussed on page 30.	-	Discussed on page 29.
Towsey March 1995–February 1996 n=180	74 (41%)	87 (40%)	4 (2%) Called coordination	-	115 (64%)	1 (.5%)	-
Buttlar & Garcha 1997 n=271	-	Professional=85 (32%) Support=207 (78%) Students=132 (50%) Subordinates=183 (69%)	95 (56%) Called coordination	78 (46%) Of copy catalogers	OCLC=249 (92%) RLIn=52 (19%) WLn=7 (3%) Other=19 (7%)	-	-
Hosoi 1999 n=124	-	71 (57%)	62 (50%)	47 (38%)	-	-	-
Chaudhry 1990–1999 n=131	-	56 (43%)	77%	-	-	-	-
Lack October 1999–October 2000 n=77	-	-	59 (77%)	-	-	-	-
Khurshid 2000–2001 n=151	-	-	-	-	-	-	-
Ellero 1997–2003 n=754	678 (90%) Includes complex copy 127 (17%) only original	240 (32%)	137 (18%)	192 (25%)	OCLC=329 (44%) RLIN=14 (2%) OCLC or RLIN, Other=74 (10%)	113 (15%)	95 (13%) Vision=3 (.4%)

Table 6.14. Comparative Analysis—General Roles, Part B

Study	Problem Solver	Policy and Procedures	CONSER NACO, PCC, SACO	System Administration New ILS	Workflow Design or Management	Database Maintenance	Quality Assurance or Controls	Outsourcing
Palmer 1987–1989 n=340	-	-	-	-	-	-	-	-
Xu 1971–1990 n=262	-	-	-	-	-	-	-	-
Copeland 1980–1995 n=?*	-	—	-	-	-	-	-	-
Towsey March 1995–February 1996 n=180	8 (4%)		-	-	-		Discussed on page 78	-
Buttlar & Garcha 1997 n=271	55 (33%) "Edits problem records"	Cataloging=206 (78%) Technical Services=122 (46%)	-	8 (5%)	189 (71%)	199 (75%)	Discussed on page 319	73 (27%)
Hosoi 1999 n=124		48 (39%) Includes workflow	26 (21%)	-	48 (39%) Includes Policy & Procedures	69 (53%) Includes Authority Control		
Chaudhry 1990–1999 n=131	-	-	-	-	-	-	-	-
Lack October 1999–October 2000 n=77	-	-	-	-	-	-	-	-
Khurshid 2000–2001 n=151	-	-	-	-	-	-	-	-
Ellero 1997–2003 n=754	189 (25%)	234 (31%)	172 (23%)	System Administration =16 (2%) New ILS=17 (2%)	95 (13%)	129 (17%) *only specifically stated as such, does not include authority control	109 (14%)	15 (2%)

The number of entry-level positions showed a drastic difference, with Chaudhry and Komathi's (2001) rate at 68 percent and the present study at 9 percent. This may be an example of differing definitions, with Chaudhry classifying all positions as either entry-level, middle management, or managerial, and this study classifying entry-level as those that did not require much or any prior experience, were specifically stated as entry level, or expressed that an MLS degree must be completed by the employment/appointment date. New positions, exhibited by 2 percent of the "pure catalogers" subtotal, were tracked by this study and not by any of the others.

Another difference, and one central to this chapter, was the label "cataloger" (see Table 6.15). The findings for this study showed that 80 percent of the names contained some form of "cataloger" in the position title, contrasted with Hosoi's (1999) 27 percent, Lack's (2001) 29 percent, and Khurshid's (2003) 38 percent. All other names, however, such as those for electronic resources or metadata, were well within similar ranges. One possible reason for this discrepancy may be the difference in sample sizes or the focus of the present study on "pure catalogers." However, a query on any form of the word "catalog" in the position title for the larger data set of 1,036, which included senior levels, showed 69 percent (714 positions). The same set of reasons may be applied to the differences in percentages of original cataloging, management roles, and the development of policies and procedures. The Buttlar and Garcha study (1998), which exhibited vast differences for roles in managing/handling workflow, database maintenance, policies and procedures, and outsourcing, may be attributed to the fact that their study was a survey of persons in real positions and not job advertisements. A study comparing actual positions versus job postings would be beneficial in determining how close job postings are to real world positions. An older study conducted by Furuta (1990) recognized the challenges of analyzing imprecise and varying data that are often found in job descriptions (1990, pp. 224, 250), and Xu expounded on this: "First, a brief job description cannot fully embody the complete requirements and responsibilities of a particular librarian. Second, there are differences in requirements between postings and the real applicants. . . . Third, once certain sorts of requirements or responsibilities have become relatively commonplace, they might not always be mentioned in job descriptions. . . . Moreover, the wording of advertisements often reflect compromises among members of the search committee" 1996, pp. 29–30). In addition, Copeland commented that, "terminology throughout the advertisements is inconsistent" (1997, p. 28).

Table 6.15. Comparative Analysis—Position Names/Titles

Study	"Catalog" in Title	Electronic Special Formats	Serials Cataloger	Head of Cataloging	Head of Technical Services	Rare Book Special Collections, Etc.	Database Manager	"Metadata" in Title
Palmer 1987–1989 n=340	-	-	-	-	-	-	-	-
Xu 1971–1990 n=262	-	-	-	-	-	-	-	-
Copeland 1980–1995 n=?*	-	-	-	-	-	-	-	-
Towsey March 1995–February 1996 n=180	-	-	-	-	-	-	-	-
Buttlar & Garcha 1997 n=271	-	-	-	-	-	-	-	-
Hosoi 1999 n=124	33 (27%)	9 (7%)	17 (14%)	12 (10%)	9 (7%)	16 (13%)	-	-
Chaudhry 1990–1999 n=131	-	-	-	-	-	-	-	-
Lack October 1999–October 2000 n= 77	23 (29%)	7 (9%)	7 (9%)	9 (12%)	-	-	3 (4%)	2 (3%)
Khurshid 2000–2001 n=151	58 (38%)	10 (6%)	16 (11%)	11 (7%)	-	-	1 (.6%)	6 (4%)
Ellero 1997–2003 n=754	602 (80%) 152 (20%) w/o	50 (7%) e-resources only 68 (9%) not including the e-resources only titles	91 (12%)	116 (11%)* From 1036 total	144 (14%)* From 1036 total	35 (5%)	19 (3%) with "data" in title but not "metadata". 15 (2%) for Database Management or Maintenance	24 (3%)

Results were fairly similar across the studies for several expanded roles, especially considering that the other studies included senior management level positions and this study did not. The similar roles were cataloging electronic resources and HTML/SGML expertise (see Tables 6.16 and 6.17, page 150). Larger differences were seen for bibliographic instruction, reference, and collection development in comparison with the Buttlar and Garcha data. Metadata knowledge or skills was lower in this study than the others and could be attributed to the demographic coverage of this study, which included all libraries and not just academic libraries. It can be safely assumed that work with metadata has been more prominent in academic libraries; however, this may change in the future and will be interesting to track for a future investigation. The present study resulted in 92 percent (58 positions) of the digitization projects residing in academic libraries. Table 6.9 (page 139) shows a steady increase in digitization projects, and it is no doubt in these endeavors that "metadata" is being heavily employed.

Communication and interpersonal skills (see Tables 6.18 and 6.19, pages 151–152) continue to be of great importance. Chaudhry wrote that, "To work effectively, one must convey his or her thoughts and ideas clearly and precisely. This also includes having healthy relationships with fellow coworkers, as a cataloger cannot work in isolation. He or she must work with others in good comradeship to get the job done" (Chaudhry and Komathi 2001, p. 17). No one person can master every tool, the intricacies of all types of databases, or the facility of all metadata applications from Dublin Core to XML descriptive tagging. A team of professionals, like in an operating room, is needed to give birth to initiatives or revive physical and/or intellectual access to lost, damaged, or brittle resources. Each team member has a specialty to share and a unique insight to offer that will bring a vitality and variety that no individual person working alone can provide.

Table 6.16. Comparative Analysis—Expanded Roles and Skills, Part A

Study	E-Resources Digital Documents	Internet or Web Skills	Metadata	Bibliographic Instruction	Reference	Collection Development	Monitor Trends	Grants
Palmer 1987–1989 n=340	-	-	-	6%	27%	18%	-	2%
Xu 1971–1990 n=262	-	-	-	-	-	-	-	-
Copeland 1980–1995 n=?*	-	-	-	-	-	-	-	-
Towsey March 1995–February 1996 n=180	17 (9%)	31 (17%) Combined Internet and Hypertext skills	2 (1%)	-	17 (9%)	18 (10%)	-	-
Butlar & Garcha 1997 n=271	Digital Documents=117 (44%) E-resources=83 (31%)	6 (2%) 4=web page design 2=Internet training HTML=88 (33%)	-	84 (32%)	124 (47%)	126 (48%)	-	4 (2%) Called fund raising
Hosoi 1999 n=124	48 (39%)	31 (25%) Includes HTML	-	26 (21%)	40 (32%)	34 (28%)	-	-
Chaudhry 1990–1999 n=131	-	16 (12%)	7 (5%)	-	-	-	14 (11%)	-
Lack October 1999–October 2000 n=77	24 (31%)	7 (9%)	23 (30%) Required=5 Preferred=15 Responsibility=3	-	-	-	-	-
Khurshid 2000–2001 n=151	-	6 (4%)	58 (38%)	-	-	-	-	-
Ellero 1997–2003 n=754	339 (45%) Combined Digital Documents & E-resources	130 (17%)	132 (17%)	43 (6%)	141 (19%)	93 (12%)	129 (17%)	4 (.5%)

Table 6.17. Comparative Analysis—Expanded Roles and Skills, Part B

Study	HTML	SGML	XML	TEI	EAD	General Markup Language Specified as Such	Mentor	URL Maintenance
Palmer 1987–1989 n=340	-	-	-	-	-	-	-	-
Xu 1971–1990 n=262	-	-	-	-	-	-	-	-
Copeland 1980–1995 n=?*	-	-	-	-	-	-	-	-
Towsey March 1995–February 1996 n=180	1 (5%)	-	-	-	-	-	-	-
Buttlar & Garcha 1997 n=271	88 (33%)	12 (4%)	-	-	-	-	-	-
Hosoi 1999 n=124	20 (21%)	-	-	-	-	-	-	-
Chaudhry 1990–1999 n=131	-	-	-	-	-	-	-	-
Lack October 1999–October 2000 n=77	-	-	-	-	-	-	-	-
Khurshid 2000–2001 n=151	-	-	-	-	-	-	-	-
Ellero 1997–2003 n=754	60 (8%)	30 (4%)	43 (6%)	32 (4%)	34 (5%)	11 (1%)	17 (2%)	18 (2%)

Table 6.18. Comparative Analysis—Person-Based Skills and Traits, Part A

Study	Communication Skills	Interpersonal Skills	Team or Group Skills	Flexibility	Ability to Cope with Change	Organizational Skills	Analytical Skills	Detail Oriented	Innovative, Forward Thinking
Palmer 1987–1989 n=340	-	-	-	-	-	-	-	-	-
Xu 1971–1990 n=262	49 (19%)	-	-	Discussed on p. 13	-	-	-	-	-
Copeland 1980–1995 n=?*	-	-	Discussed on p. 33–34.	Discussed on p. 32–33	Discussed on p. 29	-	-	-	-
Towsey March 1995–February 1996 n=180	91 (51%) Includes Interpersonal Skills	-	79 (44%)	-	-	-	-	-	3 (2%)
n0 Buttlar & Garcha 1997 n=271	-	-	-	Discussed on p. 320	-	-	-	-	-
Hosoi 1999 n=124	-	-	-	"Versatility" is discussed on p. 16 and 20	-	-	-	-	-
Chaudhry 1990–1999 n=131	102 (78%)	37 (28%)	30 (23 %)	-	-	-	-	-	-
Lack October 1999–October 2000 n=77	54 (70%)	42 (55%)	-	-	-	20 (26%)	16 (21%)	-	-
Khurshid 2000–2001 n=151	99 (66%)	50 (33%)	-	-	-	-	-	-	-
Ellero 1997–2003 n=754	485 (64%)	281 (37%)	135 (18%)	142 (19%)	50 (7%)	163 (22%)	172 (23%)	62 (8%)	Innovative=50 (7%) Forward Thinking=14 (2%) Total=64 (8%)

Table 6.19. Comparative Analysis—Person-Based Skills and Traits, Part B

Study	Able to Work Independently	Foreign Language Skills	Second Master's Degree	User or Service Oriented	Initiative Self-Motivation	Creative	Energetic, Enthusiastic, Dynamic	Ability/Desire for Continual Learning
Palmer 1987–1989 n=340	-	-	-	-	-	-	-	-
Xu 1971–1990 n=262	-	-	28 (11%) 1980–1990=7.5%	Discussed on p. 13	-	-	-	-
Copeland 1980–1995 n=?*	Discussed on p. 29	-		-		-	-	-
Towsey March 1995–February 1996 n=180	-	-			-	-	-	-
Buttlar & Garcha 1997 n=271	-	60 (48%) Required=41 (33%) Included Foreign Language Cataloging	31 (25%) Required=5 (4%) Preferred-26 (21%)		-	-	-	Education and training mentioned on p. 319
Hosoi 1999 n=124	-			-	-	-	-	-
Chaudhry 1990–1999 n=131	-	61 (47%)		-	-	-	-	-
Lack October 1999–October 2000 n= 77	-	-	19 (25%)	-	-	-	-	-
Khurshid 2000–2001 n=151	-	75 (50%)	17 (11%)	-	-	-	-	-
Ellero 1997–2003 n=754	171 (23%)	382 (51%)	70 (9%)	109 (14%)	Initiative=48 (6%) Self-Motivated=43 (6%) Total=91 (12%)	67 (9%)	Energetic=47 (6%) Enthusiastic=14 (2%) Dynamic=11 (1%) Total=72 (10%)	16 (2%) Professional Activities=153 (20%) Monitoring Trends=129 (17%)

Conclusion

Although there is no doubt that position responsibilities are changing, expanding, and becoming more integrated with library operations as a whole, change is still slower than is often thought. The label "cataloger" is alive and well, with 602 (80 percent) job positions containing some form of the word "catalog" in the title. The main duties and temperaments/personality traits of catalogers continue to be valued as evidenced by the desire for "detail"-oriented persons, 62 (8 percent), and the ability to work independently, 171 (23 percent). On the other hand, there is transformation regarding the "how or manner in which" catalogers are being asked to work, and that is with flexibility 142 (19 percent), in teams, 135 (18 percent), and with other library personnel (Chaudhry and Komathi, 2001 p. 17). Michael Gorman wrote in 1984 that the potential growth toward or transformation of the "Ecumenical Library," where each librarian would perform largely professional duties encompassing all aspects of librarianship from acquisitions to reference service, may be forthcoming. The data in this study showed such an ecumenical transformation to be slow in evolving, if indeed it will ever reach the total state of holistic integration Gorman envisioned or Thomas proposed, where it "should lead to better, wider appreciation by all library staff of the contribution of cataloging" (Thomas 1997, p. 11). Eskoz's data showed a small percentage of technical and public services merging responsibilities, and she concluded that "a complete merger of technical and public services duties is probably impractical." Eskoz also noted a need for flexibility: "What can be advocated without qualification is an atmosphere of flexibility of increasing use of individual talents, interests, and abilities" (1991, p. 85). Likewise, Xu, stated that, "the differences in major responsibilities and knowledge or skills needed reveal that the completely holistic librarian as Gorman [Gorman, 1983, p. 56] has described, might be some time in arriving" (1996, p. 29). Ogburn's theory of "cultural lag," highlighted and discussed by Xu, was well supported by this author's analysis.[4] Technology is advancing and changing how and what we do, but not so dramatically as the perception of change may suggest.

Predicting the future is always a difficult task, and now more than ever as the rate in technological change increases each year (McCombs 1997, p. 131). The signs of the times will require vigilance, and future studies will be needed to follow the changes and mark enduring skills and traits. This present study used a hybrid of automation and paper printouts for job advertisements. Future studies could capture job descriptions in electronic form from listservs and/or digitally scan them from printed sources. The electronic documents could be encoded with content descriptive XML tags, and reports and tabulations made with a speed and ease to make follow-up and additional efforts attractive for future investigators. More investigation is needed to answer such questions as (1) Are listservs advertising all the potential cataloging jobs, or are traditional journal sources needed in addition? (2) Will "pure catalogers" fade out in time and be replaced by more or only hybrid or holistic positions? (3) How many current cataloging positions are involved in digitization projects? (4) Will salaries be improved as more technological roles and skills become required and central to the work of cataloging? (5) Are cataloging duties and responsibilities moving down to the support staff level, and if so, what about appropriate compensation?

The traditional tasks of cataloging, resource description, classification, name authority control, subject access, and indexing of library resources, enabling simple and/or complex searches, are the heart of the art and trade of catalogers, whether in a print-centric or digital-centric world. This core mission and these values cannot be ignored, budgeted away, or lost in the increasing prevalence and popularity of Internet search engines producing improved keyword searches. There is and will remain a vital role for "catalogers," and the importance their work enhances resource discovery and retrieval. According to Bob Ainsbury, cataloging is making a comeback (2002, pp. 27–31); however, the ways in which "catalogers" accomplish these goals will change and hopefully become better, faster, and integrated with other information delivery systems. Chaudhry and Komathi concluded that "cataloging skills remain relevant in the electronic environment, and in fact there is an increasing need for them" (2001, p. 14). Libraries, through either formal or informal structures, are becoming more team-based in the hope of utilizing and integrating talents and ensuring greater productivity. Bazirjian, who wrote on the reorganization of cataloging services at the Pennsylvania State University libraries and the division of cataloging services into five teams, concluded that, "Although no firm baseline data against which to measure the outcome and productivity of the team organization are available, there is a strong belief that our students, academic faculty, and other library users benefit from the efficiencies of this organization, such as good communication, collaboration, and a strong sense of responsibility and quality awareness" (2003, p. 36). Likewise, Dorner wrote that "Drabenstott and Burman predict flatter structures with staff having flexible positions working in service clusters or project teams to provide customized service or to perform particular tasks" (2000, p. 83).

The principles of and the need for "cataloging" (intellectual access/knowledge management, resource description, etc.) will continue to prevail along with rapid changes and improvements in surface structures and tools such as MARC, XML, and RDF. The ways in which these tasks are accomplished will continue to involve and require more technology, flexibility, and teams of professionals working together. However, the ability to work independently, to give attention to detail, and to solve complicated problems of access, are some of the most vital traditional roles and skills that will always be required of "catalogers," whatever they may be labeled. Position names may change, come and go, return, or be redefined, but the creation, verification, standardization, and assurance of multiple access avenues for all types of library resources will be eternal, and these avenues will hopefully become ever more user-friendly and user-oriented.

Eden and Bierman capture the twenty-first-century essence of cataloging well:

> The role of cataloging in the emerging new world of librarianship and libraries is up for grabs–it is ours for the making and the taking. Proactive and participatory discussion and planning by cataloging librarians and staff both locally and nationally is essential to forging an exciting new role for catalogers to play in the emerging digital information world . . . The possibilities for the future in the emerging digital information world are limited only by our imagination and initiative (2002, pp. 93, 100).

The heart of the cataloger's work is everlasting, stable, and alive, providing the life-blood for resource discovery and access. Just as muscles provide flexibility for the human body to bend and move in multiple ways, catalogers must be flexible and ready to respond and thrive in a rapidly changing environment of continuous technological evolution.

Notes

1. Allison Sleeman, Head Serials Cataloger, Alderman Library, University of Virginia, aided in the gathering of job descriptions from SERIALST.

2. From Job Number 750 in the author's database.

3. Jennifer Bielewski, "RE: VAM Electronic Resources Inquiry 5/21/2003," e-mail regarding the number and types of electronic resources in OCLC question, May 22, 2003.

4. Hong Xu, "The Impact of Automation on Job Requirements and Qualifications for Catalogers and Reference Librarians in Academic Libraries," *Library Resources a& Technical Services* 40 (1996): 10, 29. Regarding cultural lag, Xu wrote, "there is a time gap from the implementation of new technology in libraries to the corresponding changes in library professional duties and responsibilities. 'Cultural lag,' as proposed by American sociologist William Ogburn in his influential book *Social Change with Respect to Culture and Original Nature* (1922), might be the reason. Ogburn stated that normative and social relationship changes cannot occur instantaneously to keep pace with technological innovations; in fact they might change very slowly" (1996, p. 10).

References

Ainsbury, Bob. 2002. "Cataloging's comeback: Classifying and organizing corporate documents." *Online* 26: 27–31.

Allen, Bryce, and David Reser. 1990. "Content analysis in library and information science research." *Library & Information Science Research* 12: 251–262.

Ayres, Fred. 1996. "What is the future for catalogues and cataloguers?" *Catalogue & Index* 122: 1–5.

Bazirjian, Rosann. 2003. "Role of library faculty in a team environment." *Library Administration & Management* 17: 33–38.

Buttlar, Lois, and Rajinder Garcha. 1998. "Catalogers in academic libraries: their evolving and expanding roles." *College and Research Libraries* 59: 311–321.

Chaudhry, Abdus Sattar, and N. C. Komathi. 2001. "Requirements for cataloguing positions in the electronic environment." *Technical Services Quarterly* 19: 1–23.

Copeland, Ann W. 1997. "The demand for serials catalogers: An analysis of job advertisements, 1980–1995." *The Serials Librarian* 32: 27–37.

Dorner, Dan. 1999. "Cataloging in the 21st century-part 1: Contextual issues." *Library Collections, Acquisitions & Technical Services* 23: 393–399.

———. 2000. "Cataloging in the 21st century-part 2: Digitization and information standards." *Library Collections, Acquisitions, & Technical Services* 24: 73–87.

Eden, Brad, and Kenneth J. Bierman. 2002. "Knowledge access management at Lied Library: Cataloging and web site reengineering." *Library Hi Tech* 20: 90–103.

Eskoz, Patricia A. 1991. "Catalog librarians and public services-a changing role?" *Library Resources & Technical Services* 35: 76–86.

Folsom, Sandy L. 2000. "Out of the nest: the cataloger in a public services role." *Library Collections, Acquisitions, & Technical Services* 24: 65–71.

Freeborn, Robert B., and Rebecca L. Mugridge. 2002. "The reorganization of monographic cataloging processes at Penn State University Libraries." *Library Collections, Acquisitions, & Technical Services* 26: 35–45.

Furuta, Kenneth. 1990. "The impact of automation on professional catalogers." *Information Technology and Libraries* 9: 242–252.

Gorman, Michael. 1983. "The ecumenical library." *The Reference Librarian* 9: 55–64.

Herrick, Mary D. 1950. "Status of worker morale among college catalogers." *College and Research Libraries* 11: 33–39.

Hill, Janet Swan. 2002. "What else do you need to know? Practical skills for catalogers and managers." *Cataloging & Classification Quarterly* 34: 245–261.

Hill, Janet Swan, and Sheila S. Intner. 1999. *Preparing for a cataloging career: From cataloging to knowledge management.* Available: http://www. ala.org/Content/ContentGroups/HRDR/1st_Congress_on_Professional_ Education/1st_Congress__Preparing_for_a_Cataloging_Career.htm (Accessed May 21, 2003).

Hoerman, Heidi Lee. 2002. "Why does everybody hate cataloging?" *Cataloging & Classification Quarterly* 34: 31–41.

Hosoi, Mihoko. 1999. "Cataloging positions in U.S. academic libraries: An analysis of job advertisements." Master's thesis, University of North Carolina at Chapel Hill.

Khurshid, Zahiruddin. 2003. "The impact of information technology on job requirements and qualifications for catalogers." *Information Technology and Libraries* 22: 18–21.

Kyrillidou, Martha, and Mark Young, eds. 2002. *ARL annual salary survey 2001–02.* Available: http://www.arl.org/stats/pubpdf/ss01.pdf (Accessed May 21, 2003).

Lack, Adina R. 2001. " 'People skills' and technological mastery: What U.S. academic libraries require of catalogers in these areas." Master's thesis, University of North Carolina at Chapel Hill.

Lange, Holley R. 1991. "Catalogers, is it time for a (title) change?" *Technicalities* 11: 14–15.

McCombs, Gillian M. 1997. "WEBolution: Rethinking the technical services knowledge base and culture in a web-based information environment." *Cataloging & Classification Quarterly* 24: 129–140.

Mering, Margaret. 1998a. "Future of professional catalogers: A report of the ALCTS creative ideas in technical services discussion group meeting, American Library Association midwinter meeting, Washington, DC, February 1997." *Technical Services Quarterly* 15: 84–86.

———. 1998b. "The role of professional catalogers in organizing the Internet: A report of the ALCTS creative ideas in technical services discussion group meeting, American Library Association's annual meeting, San Francisco, June 1997." *Technical Services Quarterly* 16: 57–59.

Nesbeitt, Sarah. 2003. "Librarian recruitment process at home in the wired nation: online job advertising is now the norm, survey reveals." *American Libraries* 34: 116–118.

Ouderkirk, Jane Padham. 2000. "Staff assignments and workflow distribution at the end of the 20th century: where we were, where we are, and what we'll need to be." *Cataloging & Classification Quarterly* 30: 343–355.

Palmer, Joseph W. 1992. "Job advertisements and cataloging skills." *Journal of Education for Library and Information Science* 33: 61–63.

Steinhagen, Elizabeth N., and Sharon A. Moynahan. 1998. "Catalogers must change! Surviving between the rock and the hard place." *Cataloging & Classification Quarterly* 26: 3–20.

Studwell, William E. 1996. "Perfection and permanency in an imperfect and non-permanent environment: toward a new description of cataloging." *Technicalities* 16: 16–17.

———. 1998. "New millennium, new names? On changing the names of reference librarians and catalogers." *Behavioral & Social Sciences Librarian* 16: 79–80.

Tennant, Roy. 1998. "The most important management decision: hiring staff for the new millennium." *Library Journal* 123: 102.

Thomas, Alan R.1997. "The work-wide web: A cataloging career for every librarian?" *Cataloging & Classification Quarterly* 24: 5–22.

Towsey, Michael. 1997. "Nice work if you can get it? A study of patterns and trends in cataloguing employment in the USA and the UK in the mid-1990s." *Cataloging & Classification Quarterly* 24: 61–79.

Turvey, Michelle R., and Karen M. Letarte. 2002. "Cataloging or knowledge management: perspectives of library educators on cataloging education for entry-level academic librarians." *Cataloging & Classification Quarterly* 34: 165–187.

U.S. Bureau of Labor Statistics. 2002. *2001 National occupational employment and wage estimates.* Available: http://stats.bls.gov/oes/2001/oes254021.htm (Accessed May 21, 2003).

Vellucci, Sherry L. 1996. "Future catalogers: Essential colleagues or anachronisms?" *College & Research Libraries News* 7: 442–443.

Waite, Ellen J. 1995. "Reinvent catalogers!" *Library Journal* 120: 36–37.

Weitz, Jay. 2002. *Cataloging electronic resources: OCLC-MARC coding guidelines.* Available: http://www.oclc.org/connexion/documentation/type.htm (Accessed May 28, 2003).

Wendler, Robin.1999. "Branching out: Cataloging skills and functions in the digital age." *Journal of Internet Cataloging* 2: 43–54.

Xu, Hong.1996. "The impact of automation on job requirements and qualifications for catalogers and reference librarians in academic libraries." *Library Resources & Technical Services* 40: 9–31.

Part 2

Case Studies

7

Redesign of Database Management at Rutgers University Libraries

Ruth A. Bogan

Editor's note: The author discusses the redesign of database management at a large academic research library. The core competency model is discussed, as well as how it was used and applied to help initiate change in workflow, perception, and self-worth in both individuals and a department looking for meaning and value in their organization. By envisioning the future, the Database Management Section at Rutgers University Libraries was able to identify their core competencies, and actively took risks to explore, experiment, and find their place within their library and their organization, and position themselves securely for the future.

All library technical services managers face an essential question: How does one direct a workforce toward a future that cannot be seen? Technical services managers in large research and university libraries have a particular challenge in trying to reconcile their institution's research in the fields of library and information science with the ongoing work of the library. Subject specialist librarians create digital library projects, and researchers investigate new models for digital and data systems. Such projects and models may contrast disconcertingly with the daily activities of the library units that managers oversee. This is the case at Rutgers, the State University of New Jersey. A handful of Rutgers librarians and information scientists are developing and testing new conceptual models for archiving, accessing, and preserving information in digital form, while much of the staff continues to provide traditional library services, such as acquisitions, cataloging, and interlibrary loan.

In early 2003 the Rutgers University Libraries (RUL) arranged a half-day Digital Futures information session for all library personnel. A dozen speakers summarized their progress in various digital library projects, digital content management systems, and associated metadata schemes. Staff members from the RUL Database Management Section (DBM)—one unit of the Cataloging Department—who attended the session returned to their desks wondering what, if anything, it all had to do with them. It was difficult for staff to see how their own work might fit into the new models. Most decided that it had nothing at all to do with them. They concluded that one of two things would happen. On the one hand, their work might change significantly one day in the future; when that happened, they would be expected to do new work, presumably unrelated to what they were presently doing. On the other hand, they might simply find themselves with no work at all. This was a demoralizing and stress-inducing state of mind for library staff. It was also an unfortunate environment for the library as an organization.

Library managers have a responsibility to deal with the gulf that separates the comfortable status quo from the uncertain future. Evidence of this mandate comes from a spate of competency documents developed over the last decade. Acknowledging the proactive role of library managers as change agents, the University of Nebraska-Lincoln includes, in its description of leadership competency for senior level staff, the following indicators of proficiency:

- Envisions future trends and establishes appropriate goals to support changes in priorities or direction

- Facilitates optimal department or unit performance that is in alignment with library vision and strategies. (McNeil 2002, p. 77)

Like many competency statements, this list focuses on the behavior of the individual. It prescribes how a good manager should behave. Personal development, however, is not the only issue, nor is it the most critical one. The library is more than an aggregation of the skills and knowledge of talented individuals. Great ideas do not make a great library. The institution as a whole needs to evolve. For this to happen, all library managers must be agents of proactive, evolutionary change within their areas of responsibility. Even the most innovative ideas in the library ultimately are implemented and maintained by skilled and knowledgeable staff.

Library technical services managers must ensure the viability of the skills and knowledge of their staff members over time. This expertise is integral to the institution's knowledge base. The technical services manager's challenge is to *envision* how library roles might evolve; *identify* the skills, knowledge, and attitudes that will contribute to that evolution; and *build* the organizational competencies. To realize the idealized information models emerging within their institutions, technical services managers must employ an organizational model that promotes incremental change at every level of the institution.

One such model is the core competency of the corporation, articulated by C. K. Prahalad and Gary Hamel and elaborated by Dorothy Leonard-Barton (Prahalad and Hamel 1990; Leonard-Barton 1995). Their core competency model focuses on building and sustaining the complex amalgam of skills, knowledge, technology, management structures, and values that create and maintain the value of an organization as a whole. The model emphasizes that the activities of the workforce build an organization's knowledge base. The value of the core competency model for libraries is its focus on systemwide, rather than personal, competencies.

The Core Competency Model

In "The Core Competence of the Corporation," C. K. Prahalad and Gary Hamel predict that the leaders of American business will need to identify and develop their companies' core competencies to be competitive in a global market. According to the authors, a corporation's core competency should

- provide potential access to a wide variety of markets,

- make a significant contribution to the perceived customer benefits of the end product, and

- be difficult for competitors to imitate. (Prahalad and Hamel, 1990, pp. 83–84)

The authors illustrate the core competency concept with the case study of NEC, a company that in 1988 was a strong player in the fields of semiconductors and telecommunications. NEC grew their business to world-class status by *envisioning* the future convergence of computers and communications, *identifying* the company's core competencies in telecommunications, and, finally, *building* on the firm's existing skills and knowledge to develop and acquire new skills in semiconductors (Prahalad and Hamel 1990, pp. 80–81). In *Wellsprings of Knowledge*, Dorothy Leonard-Barton characterizes core competencies as interdependent systems of technologies, skills/knowledge, managerial systems, and values. She explains that organizational core competencies

- constitute a competitive advantage,

- are built up over time, and

- cannot be easily imitated. (1995, p. 4)

According to Leonard-Barton, a core competency is developed through knowledge-building activities. Conceptualizing, modeling, and even training are potentially valuable; however, only when they are translated into activities do they increase the organization's knowledge base. The author is specific about the kinds of activities that contribute to strengthening core competencies. They are

- shared creative problem solving,

- implementing and integrating new methodologies and tools,

- formal and informal experimentation, and

- pulling in expertise from outside. (Leonard-Barton 1995, p. 8)

The author balances her discussion of core competencies with a discussion of core rigidities. Capabilities, she warns, have a way of becoming rigidities—too much of a good thing. When the environment of an organization changes, or when staff move past skill into habit, managers may find themselves struggling against the very things that made the organization successful. Core rigidities result from the notion that if something is good, more of the same is better (Leonard-Barton 1995, p. 32).

The components of an organization's core competencies: technology, managerial systems, skills/knowledge, and values are naturally resistant to change in varying degrees. By now most libraries have experienced the move from one integrated library system to another, and the consequent realization that the former system had dictated a way of working that the new system could not support. In a case like this, efficient practices become barriers to change almost overnight. As another example, managerial systems, such as the library's job classification structure, which are devised to reward staff and encourage excellence, become deterrents to change if they are not regularly updated. Library technical services activities, in particular cataloging, are susceptible to becoming rigid because of the high degree of knowledge—cataloging codes, classification schemes, controlled vocabularies—required for the work, and the emphasis on values in the form of local, national, and international standards.

Despite its corporate world origins, the concept of organizational core competencies has relevance for libraries. Before exploring that, however, it is necessary to point out that the managerial concept of core competencies differs from the more familiar curricular model of competencies, which is widely recognized within the library community.

The Core Competency Model and Libraries

Librarians have been talking about competencies since the 1970s. Major studies have defined and validated competencies to guide the education of professional librarians (Friedrich 1985; Griffiths and King 1986; Rehman 2000). Professional organizations as well as state agencies and associations have written competency documents or designed competency-based educational programs for their constituents (SLA 1996; CLA 1998; NJLA 1999). Individual institutions incorporate competency guidelines into training programs and formal evaluation exercises (McNeil 2002). In general, these activities adhere to the definition of a competency as a measurement of personal development. In contrast, the management model sees competencies at the level of the corporation or organization. It is the latter—the organizational management model—that the Rutgers' Database Management Section adopted.

Libraries and library units do not look for markets; they offer services. To be effective, the core competency model needs to be recast in language that makes sense in libraries. Paraphrasing Prahalad and Hamel, a library's core competency should affect or make possible a range of services. A competency developed for a single service, which cannot be extended to other services, is probably not a core competency. Being able to capture MARC-encoded catalog records from a bibliographic utility using a proprietary Z39.50 cataloging interface is no longer a core competency for the library. The ability of staff to find, identify, select, and obtain metadata records from a variety of sources using a variety of interfaces gives the library the flexibility to move across a broader landscape; it is a true core competency.

The second indicator of a core competency—that it should make a significant contribution to the perceived customer benefits of the end product—is a reminder that commerce keeps its eye on the customers. Leonard-Barton, in her explanation of how core rigidities develop, tells a story that makes the point more relevant to libraries. Cross, the manufacturer of fine pens, refined its quality control to such an extent over the years that workers were rejecting pens with almost invisible surface blemishes. The employees' assertion that customers demanded flawless pens at any price was countered when management researched and found that customers really wanted functionality before good looks (Leonard-Barton 1995, pp. 52–53). While a core competency delivers value to the user, the perception of what constitutes value must be validated. A true core competency delivers what users expect as well as what they value. Maintenance of bibliographic records is a traditional library function, but it can be a core competency only to the degree that it delivers value to the user. If users expect reasonably prompt delivery of resources, while internal processes impose unreasonable delays, the processes are negating the core competency. In recent years, a number of large university libraries have adopted streamlined processes, such as classifying books and sending them to the shelves without waiting for full cataloging. Certainly none of these libraries would question that cataloging is a competency. Their processes suggest, however, that they recognize that cataloging by itself is not a core competency for their libraries. Their sophisticated cataloging workflows, customized to move the majority of resources to the shelves within a targeted time frame, deliver benefits their users expect.

Finally, organizational core competencies are difficult to imitate because they are complex interactions of knowledge, skills, and behaviors built up over time. Google tutorials enable individuals to use an Internet search engine. Imparting information literacy to first-year students at Rutgers, however, is a complex process—a core competency.

Libraries, like businesses, must *envision* the future, *identify* their core competencies, and *build* knowledge for the future. The context is different, but the questions are not. What are the evolving trends that libraries need to watch? What needs do libraries fill better than other organizations? What core competencies should libraries develop to remain viable? Several writers have noted the applicability of the business core competency model to libraries. Susan Jurow references both the Prahalad and Hamel article and Leonard-Barton's book in an article about the work of the academic library. She suggests that core competencies need to be defined within the institution as well as for the profession (Jurow 1996). Richard Naylor (2000) discusses how an institution's core competencies, once identified, can structure the library's program of staff development. Both authors consider core competencies important for strategic planning.

The public library community makes use of the organizational core competency model—though not by name—in *The New Planning for Results*, which leads library administrators and staff through an exercise of community scanning to identify the library's service responses (Nelson 2001). The program documentation suggests a number of possible service responses, for example Basic Literacy, Commons, Cultural Awareness, Information Literacy, and Lifelong Learning. The library must *envision* its community's future needs, assess how well suited it is to meet a given need, and determine whether other organizations are addressing the need. In effect, library planners *identify* their institution's core competency—literacy, community building, education (Nelson 2001). A sister publication, *Managing for Results*, is a roadmap for *building* the complex web of skills, knowledge, technology, collections, and facilities to strengthen the library's service responses, and consequently its core competencies (Nelson, Altman, and Mayo 2000).

The Core Competency Model and DBM

What follows is a description of how the Database Management Section of Rutgers University Libraries has made use of the core competency model—*envision* the future, *identify* the core competency, and *build* knowledge—to ensure that the unit can play a significant role in the future of RUL. In contrast to accounts of departmental reorganization, this is not a tale with a beginning and a conclusion; it is an account of an ongoing process.

When DBM chose to implement the model, it struck out on a lightly traveled path. Case studies describing core competency exercises occur in the literature of business management; few, if any, appear in the literature of librarianship. Jurow proposes the core competency model as a tool to help academic libraries decide what services and activities to retain and build and which to let go (Jurow 1996). She suggests that the model is a strategic planning tool. Certainly it is that. DBM, however, saw in the model a way to engage each of its valued members in actively building the unit's future. The core competency model connects DBM to the future of the Rutgers Libraries. It is hoped that the DBM experience will, over time, validate the usefulness of the organizational core competency model in a library setting.

The Database Management Section

DBM is a paraprofessional unit of six full-time staff classified as library assistants and library associates, with a full-time library supervisor. In November 2001 RUL appointed a professional librarian to head the unit, boosting the membership of the section to eight. DBM is a large unit within the Cataloging Department; one-third of all permanent Cataloging Department staff members work in DBM.

A description of the unit's duties, written in 1999, documented DBM's involvement in a range of typical bibliographic record maintenance activities and clean-up projects, from correction of MARC filing indicators to recataloging. The unit was and is responsible for retrospective conversion of print format metadata to MARC. In 1999 DBM maintained a card series authority file for the Cataloging Department and subsequently assumed responsibility for the online name and subject authority files of the RUL integrated library system. In addition, since contracting with an authorities vendor, DBM has been responsible for post-cataloging authority control. Other large university and research libraries maintain database management units under various names, with duties generally similar to those of Rutgers' DBM Section.

In 2002 the Database Management Section began to look more critically at its work and its worth within the Rutgers Libraries system. Before the unit could identify its core competency, the DBM members needed to have a sense of their unit's unique identity. As part of the Cataloging Department, DBM staff members thought of themselves as copy catalogers. Although they performed some functions similar to those of various cataloging units, DBM had different responsibilities. These responsibilities included authority control, retrospective conversion, and MARC record maintenance, and necessitated different skills, training, and ways of measuring success. While the RUL catalogers' skills and knowledge tended to be vertical—concentrated and detailed understanding of a consistently applied cataloging code—DBM's knowledge and skills were more horizontal. The hallmark of DBM's work was its variety. DBM staff members understood this in concept, but observation of their workflow and attention to their comments hinted at some confusion.

The second challenge was that DBM perceived its job to be the resolution of day-to-day, uncoordinated requests for unrelated clean-up jobs from individuals throughout the RUL system. "We are," as one DBM staff member noted, "the unit that cleans up mistakes." A series of unit self-evaluation exercises, in which the staff members were asked to reflect on DBM and its activities, confirmed that the unit recognized some of the undesirable effects of these situations.

To move them toward identifying their competency, DBM staff members were encouraged to consider what they did well. In general the staff viewed themselves as skilled problem solvers, responsive to the requests of library staff members and online catalog users, who called upon them to revise or correct bibliographic and holdings information in the integrated library system. They generally agreed that the work they did was useful. In particular, DBM members valued the variety of their tasks. On the other hand, some of them saw their work as being uncoordinated, since they were expected to attend to whatever project happened to be the priority at the time. They generally complained that this situation made it impossible to completely finish a project before being instructed to start another. When asked what they most wanted for DBM, they suggested higher visibility in the RUL community, recognition and compensation for their work, better training, and new challenges. They agreed that the Libraries needed to finish retrospective conversion, particularly for Alexander Library, the largest unit library, and that this responsibility fell squarely on the shoulders of the Database Management Section.

The need for a clear identity for DBM and for some control over its activities presented familiar management challenges. The fact that the Libraries decided to hire a professional librarian with faculty status to head the Database Management Section reinforced both the value of the unit and RUL's commitment to strengthening DBM's unique role. The DBM self-assessment resulted in some consciousness raising both within and outside of the unit. DBM staff began to develop priorities for its myriad of tasks and shared these with the library community at Rutgers. They stopped looking for mistakes to clean up and began to plan their work in terms of months rather than days. They started to pay attention to the work of other units, watching for points of convergence with their own work. There were few protests from outside the unit; in fact, librarians and staff expressed appreciation for the clarification.

Envisioning the Future

To make use of the core competency model, Database Management would have to do the impossible—forecast the future. By listening to visionaries and scanning the horizon, they decided they could make some educated predictions. DBM acknowledged that the unit would have to repeat the exercise of future scanning regularly to keep up with the changes happening within and beyond the Rutgers Libraries. To get a sense of the direction in which DBM might evolve, it was necessary to weave together predictions about libraries in general, the academic library, library technical services, the specific library functions that typically take place in a unit like DBM, and finally, given the unit's makeup, the role of support staff in the library.

Many predictions about libraries offer broad and general counsel about responding to change. The California Library Association's Task Force on the Future of Librarianship (1996), for example, urges libraries to be flexible and adaptive to change. Peter Brophy admits that the future role of the academic library is unclear; however, he notes six trends that academic libraries should expect to see, among them more intensive use of digital resources, continuing demand for books and other traditional resources, and reduced levels of staffing (2001, p. 25).

With regard to library technical services, Jennifer Younger and D. Kaye Gapen note that the kind of future that Brophy predicts will compel technical services units to make their activities more cost effective, adopt a user-centered focus, accomplish their work with smaller staffs, and learn to deal with accelerating change. They see technical services units responding with increased use of technology, streamlined workflows, and revised cataloging standards (Younger and Gapen 1998). Michael Gorman predicts that the future of library technical services "lies in adapting our tools and methods" but holding to the mission of the library (1998, p. 201).

Considering the future role of support staff, Lynne Howarth speculates that library paraprofessionals will survive by defining a niche. She says "it may be dangerous to be less than distinct, ill-advised to be vaguely definable or possibly overlapping" (Howarth 1998). Hers is an especially sobering warning for units like DBM, which, spawned in days of generously staffed technical services departments, have drifted into a subordinate role as general clean-up units. Other futurists simply envision increasing responsibility for library support staff in more diverse roles. The authors of *The Academic Library in the Information Age,* although they propose to address the changing roles of all library personnel, simply confirm that the work of library staff will change and grow (C.E.T.U.S. 1997). William Gray Potter makes two brief but interesting predictions that are pertinent to Rutgers' DBM Section. He proposes that the clerical functions performed by library support staff will disappear, to be replaced by more truly paraprofessional activities. He also acknowledges that the evolution of more complex library online catalogs will require a more skilled workforce, and he hints that this greater complexity merits professional oversight (Potter 1998). Potter is one of the few futurists to acknowledge that technical services managers need to be concerned about developing a competent workforce to maintain the library's complex repositories.

Finding specific guidance in the predictions of library futurists, particularly for technical services, is difficult. Certain themes, however, are common:

- Libraries will be increasingly user-centered.

- There will be more and more varied resources to keep track of, using more diverse metadata schemes.

- Support staff will take on more responsibilities that were once reserved for professional librarians.

Identifying a Core Competency

The most important step in addressing the core competency model with DBM was articulating the unit's unique expertise. Discovering exactly what made DBM valuable to the Libraries and what distinguished it from other units proved to be an interesting and valuable exercise. The unit began by asking, "What does DBM do best?" The answers were disappointingly uninspired: fix problems, clean up mistakes. They tried another tack. The Database Management Section has been, over the years, the designated or de facto retrospective conversion unit at RUL. Shelflist conversion activity has surged and retrenched, much of it involving DBM or one of its former iterations. The conversion process at Rutgers required a certain litany of steps. Regardless of new workflows, streamlined processes, outsourcing, use of new technologies, and dressing up old activities with new names, the basic steps remained. Every DBM staff member knew them. So DBM considered retrospective conversion and asked the question, "Which of these steps could we trust to others, and which would we need to keep as our own?" Once they got past the anticipated response, "We have to do it all," they agreed that any work that involved searching Rutgers Libraries' complex database to locate and precisely identify bibliographic and holdings information was their job. They also acknowledged that the basic level skills needed to locate MARC records to match existing shelflist data could be taught to others, but that the skills and knowledge required for complex matching tasks belonged to the DBM unit. It was clear that the staff saw their competency as their intimate knowledge of the existing bibliographic and holdings data for the libraries' collections, along with knowledge of how to convert data from print to MARC format. That was a good start. It followed that DBM's role as keeper of both the manual series authority file, and later of the online name and subject authority files, extended the scope of their competency. Transferring critical series treatment decisions from cards to the local MARC name authority file was simply another form of record management and conversion.

Still the identified competency lacked something. It was missing the piece that, in the corporate world, might be called the competitive edge or the customer satisfaction component. Core competencies are what the organization does better than its competitors in the interest of meeting customer, or user, demands. For this, DBM looked to the strategic plans of RUL and the Cataloging Department. One of the Libraries' goals for the fiscal year cited retrospective conversion. Librarians were reporting questions and complaints from faculty about unconverted catalog data. The first goal of Cataloging was responsiveness to user needs. DBM took note of these two goals and reconsidered its work. Being knowledgeable about the RUL database and its records was a competency of the Database Management Section but not a core competency for RUL. Being intensely focused on making corrections to individual catalog records was not winning DBM much credit when users simply expected them to get the shelflist conversion finished. So, if DBM could be smart, reasonably accurate, and highly productive, especially with the spotlight turned on conversion, they would be demonstrating a true core competency for the organization. That competency could be expressed as *fast and accurate maintenance and conversion of bibliographic and related metadata to support the Rutgers University Libraries' resources.*

The DBM competency definition meets Prahalad and Hamel's three requirements. Fully developed, it allows DBM to participate in a wide array of RUL activities. It acknowledges user demand for accuracy balanced with timeliness. Finally, the particular mix of skills and knowledge on which the competency is grounded is complex and not easily imitated either inside or outside Rutgers. The next step in adopting the core competency model was to enhance DBM's expertise through knowledge-building activities.

Building Knowledge

What makes Dorothy Leonard-Barton's view of organizational core competencies so compelling is her emphasis on the unique ability of activities (rather than goals, incentives, or even skills that are not integrated into the workflow) to build knowledge. Plans, models, mission statements, and objectives all have value; only activities, however, ultimately create and strengthen the library's competencies. The challenge is to infuse incremental change into today's activities. DBM needed to incorporate potentially critical new skills and knowledge into the unit's work. Leonard-Barton specifically identifies four key activities for building organizational core competencies: shared, creative problem solving, integrating new tools and processes, experimentation, and incorporating expertise from outside the organization (1995, p. 8).

The following descriptions of DBM activities are a representative sample. The categories of activities are not mutually exclusive. Knowledge acquired from outside the unit becomes incorporated into unit processes. Experimentation generates the need for shared problem solving, and so on. Because tomorrow's strength builds squarely on today's activities, the knowledge-building activities described here fall somewhat short of the cutting edge. Many of the activities center on print to MARC metadata conversion, an activity that has generally lost its futuristic patina. Conversion was and continues to be, for the near future, one of the major responsibilities of the DBM Section. Rather than decry the situation, DBM used conversion as its base and worked to stretch the concept of metadata management and conversion through carefully considered activities.

Shared, Creative Problem Solving

In 2001, when DBM began its internal assessment, the unit's culture did not encourage shared, creative problem solving. Questions and problems were directed up the chain of command; answers were sent back down. Before the unit could incorporate collaborative problem solving into its activities, the staff needed to feel comfortable working laterally to generate solutions. One particularly effective method of encouraging this blossomed from an innocent seed.

Early in the process of redesigning the workflow for shelflist conversion, the DBM Supervisor designated two-person teams for daily trips to the stacks. Once the teams became comfortable with the routine, they began to identify ways to improve the workflow. They brought their ideas back to the unit for discussion. At first, ideas and recommendations went to management, but over time problem solving became a more horizontal process. The pairs persisted into subsequent projects. After training on a new software package, problems were directed first to team partners or other staff members. Breakthroughs were shared and celebrated. Informal coaching became commonplace. The importance of shared problem solving to the management of knowledge within DBM was reinforced when one of the staff members suggested that, after a week of working with new software, it was time for the whole section to get together to share their tips and tricks.

Implementing and Integrating New Methodologies

Implementing new processes runs counter to the popular injunction against fixing what isn't broken. It is difficult to encourage process change when there is not an immediate, visible need. Processes, once they are in place, tend to resist change. This was true of DBM as it is with many organizations. The conversion workflow in place in 2001 was designed to maintain a minimum level of activity with careful attention to details. DBM's maintenance level conversion process mirrored the procedures designed for catalogers reviewing cataloging copy for new books. This entailed record-by-record searches of a bibliographic utility using a Z39.50 interface, followed by comparison of the record with a title page/verso surrogate submitted by staff from various units. In effect, DBM was cataloging the already cataloged, according to detailed copy cataloging standards. The unit considered that this high level of attention to individual titles was the standard of quality and was expected and appreciated by library users. In fact, the users—librarians, staff, and faculty, to name the most vocal—wanted to pick up the pace. New methods were needed that would simultaneously increase the conversion rate and broaden the unit's expertise.

DBM, in response, developed three new conversion workflows, each one taking advantage of a hitherto untried procedure, technology, or vendor service. They abandoned the practice of having boxes of books and photocopies of title pages sent from the Alexander Library in New Brunswick for conversion (DBM works in Piscataway, a neighboring town across the Raritan River from New Brunswick). In collaboration with the Collection Services unit at Alexander Library, DBM developed a retrospective conversion process in which minimal MARC records, created by staff at Alexander Library, were harvested out of the library's database, matched by a vendor to full MARC records, and returned to the database. DBM could devote its time and expertise to the more complex work of dealing with unmatched records rather than to routine record-by-record matching.

A second process was developed and tested to use vendor services almost exclusively. A third methodology incorporated use of cataloging software and collaboration with the Systems Department in batch file management. Specific conversion standards for matching and revising cataloging copy, tailored to the work of DBM and the expectations of the RUL community, were adopted. The immediate objective of these changes was to move conversion along at a faster pace. At the same time DBM was strengthening its ability to develop and implement multiple, simultaneous processes. The staff was beginning to understand the value of their new processes as models for similar projects. They were developing the ability to transfer their expertise quickly to new situations.

Process change has a dark side. Change can make people feel incompetent. One reason people resist process change is the inevitable slowdown in work and the sense of awkwardness that they feel when trying to learn new ways of doing things. DBM staff began to exhibit signs of change anxiety; they worried about not getting their work done and asked for clarification of priorities. Once the staff understood that the unit's managers would support them through their temporary awkwardness, they developed a more positive attitude toward change.

Experimenting

Experimentation, the third activity, is difficult to distinguish from the previously described activity, new process implementation, because successful experimentation eventually turns into process. Most DBM process revisions incorporated some degree of experimentation. The following activities are easily identified as experiments because they failed. Successful experimentation becomes process; unsuccessful experimentation becomes history, or the foundation of the next experiment.

DBM speculated that having a laptop computer in the stacks for the inventory phase of conversion might expedite the task. After one trial the experiment was universally, but articulately, voted down as being the wrong place for a technology solution. In the process of testing, however, the unit increased their knowledge of the library's computer network and the physical layout of the Alexander Library where they were working.

Another example of building unit competency through experimentation involved the Cataloging Department queue of uncataloged books. The Associate University Librarian (AUL) for Digital Library Services, who also heads the Cataloging Department of which DBM is a part, speculated that many of the uncataloged new books might have Library of Congress copy available and could be moved quickly to the stacks. DBM volunteered to test her premise. (The lure of new books is irresistible to a unit consigned to years of retrospective conversion.) At the same time DBM would be able to experiment with OCLC batch searching, editing, and label-making software. The DBM staff supervisor quickly developed guidelines and a schedule, allowing time to evaluate the results. The experiment lasted a week—certainly insufficient time to allow DBM staff to master the software programs—and did not result in any near-term changes in new book cataloging. However, that short experiment gave DBM a chance to try something new that might have implications for their own work. Although they had not mastered the process, they could envision its use in other situations. Within the year they were able to put that knowledge to use in other contexts.

Importing Knowledge

In early 2002, the AUL mandated a workflow analysis for the three units under her direction: Acquisitions, Cataloging, and Systems. This presented the DBM staff with an opportunity to examine the unit's workflows in detail to spot redundancies and bottlenecks. That was, in itself, an instructive and valuable exercise. As a follow-up, the AUL proposed to hire a consultant from outside the library field to analyze the results of the workflow study and suggest improvements. Budget reductions across the university forced the hiring of a consultant to the back burner. Unfortunately DBM, along with the rest of the staff, lost a rare opportunity to import knowledge that could have been beneficial.

Consultants represent one external source of knowledge for a library. Expertise is more commonly gained through recruiting to fill positions. While libraries do import outside expertise, it is more likely to happen at a higher level in the institutional hierarchy than DBM. For example, late in 2002 Rutgers' Technical and Automated Services hired a database programmer to enhance the Libraries' knowledge base to quickly build a grant-funded digital library project—a good example of importing knowledge to enhance an organizational core competency.

In essence, every recruitment and hiring of a new staff member affords the library the potential for importing knowledge it needs or wants. As mentioned previously, the Cataloging Department recruited a librarian to be head of DBM. In doing so they proved the validity of William Potter's suggestion that oversight of the maintenance of the library's online catalog, and by extension other library repositories, would likely become a professional responsibility, as maintenance becomes a more complex and critical job. The Cataloging Department, in effect, imported skills and knowledge in the interest of strengthening an important organizational core competency—metadata maintenance.

Future Directions

DBM has enormous potential. To fully realize that potential, the unit will need to be alert to roadblocks. The first is the danger of overstating its identity. One of the beneficial outcomes of the unit's core competency exercise was a better understanding of itself as a unique entity within the Cataloging Department and RUL as a whole. This could work against the unit if the members choose to aggressively defend their traditional boundaries and, in so doing, fail to recognize opportunities to apply their unique expertise outside their circumscribed limits of RUL's organizational hierarchy. The next logical extension of DBM's competency might be outside the Cataloging Department, or even outside the Libraries

DBM will need to remember that it takes activity to build competency. Faced with the unfamiliar look and feel of the digital future, the unit will be tempted to take on work that completely bypasses the rich knowledge and skills resident in DBM. This is not to say that DBM should not learn new skills, but that those skills should build, rather than replace, their expertise. In addition, training for new skills does not build organizational competency until the skills have practical application. It is activity that builds competency. For example, DBM expects to build its core competency by developing skills in metadata schemes other than MARC. To that end, some of the DBM staff attended a Dublin Core workshop, where they were given an overview of the DC metadata scheme and created several Dublin Core metadata records. They left the workshop with new knowledge. Activities—experimentation and incorporation of the new skills into the unit's work—will build the unit's core competency.

Finally, DBM will need to be alert to how easily a core competency can become a core rigidity. To combat this, DBM must constantly scan the horizon to see what is evolving inside and outside of the Libraries. The unit must constantly look for the intersection of new models and projects with its own expertise. To avoid building walls around its core competency, DBM must be continually and dispassionately evaluating its work. Innovation and flexibility prevent competency from becoming rigid.

DBM is large, expert, and energetic. Their once reactive role as general clean-up crew has become a proactive role in line with RUL's strategic plan. DBM cannot wait until all the digital and data architectures are in place to determine what work will need to be done in the library, how it will be done, and what precise role the unit will play. DBM must recognize and seize the opportunities as they emerge. The library's future builds on innovations achieved today, by units like DBM. When technical services staff members see glimpses of the future, as the DBM staff did at the RUL Digital Futures session, but cannot see themselves in that future, the library organization is imperiled. Technical services managers must find a way to link the expertise of today's library to the future, even if the precise shape of that future is uncertain. The core competency model, defined by Prahalad and Hamel and explored in depth by Dorothy Leonard-Barton, is suited to help libraries and their staffs innovate for the future. Its central theme is the nurturing of an organization's knowledge assets. Those assets, embodied in an interwoven fabric of skills, processes, administrative systems, and values, give an organization and its work units inimitable core competencies.

To ensure its flexibility and continued value to RUL, DBM assessed its role in the library and defined its core competency to be *fast and accurate maintenance and conversion of bibliographic and related metadata to support Rutgers University Libraries' resources.* The expertise embodied in the unit and articulated in its statement of competency is critical to the Libraries' mission. It is being stewarded and developed to evolve as the RUL landscape becomes more digital. The expertise of DBM will be increasingly valuable as metadata proliferates across an increasing number of repositories. DBM's knowledge-building activities—shared problem solving, implementation of new processes, experimentation, and importing knowledge—strengthen the unit's ability to respond quickly to emerging opportunities. Such opportunities are not likely to be radical shifts requiring the rebuilding of skills from the ground up; rather, they will be logical extensions of the expertise embodied in the unit.

References

Brophy, Peter. 2001. *The library in the twenty-first century.* London: Library Association Publishing.

California Library Association (CLA), Library Education and Recruitment Committee. 1998. *Competencies for California librarians in the 21st century.* Available: http://www.cla-net.org/resources/r_competencies.php (Accessed May 25, 2003).

California Library Association (CLA), Task Force on the Future of Librarianship. 1996. *The future of librarianship.* Sacramento: CLA.

Consortium for Educational Technology for University Systems (C.E.T.U.S.). 1997. *The academic library in the Information Age.* Seal Beach: California State University. Available: http://www.calstatela.edu/academic/infocomp/learning/teachcetus.htm (Accessed May 25, 2003).

Friedrich, Adele E. 1985. *Competencies for the information professional in the coming decade.* Pittsburgh: University of Pittsburgh.

Gorman, Michael. 1998. "Technical services tomorrow." In *Technical services today and tomorrow,* 2nd ed. Englewood, Colo.: Libraries Unlimited.

Griffiths, José-Marie, and Donald W. King. 1986. *New directions in library and information science education.* White Plains, N.Y.: Knowledge Industry Publications for the American Society for Information Science.

Howarth, Lynne C. 1998. "The role of the paraprofessional in technical services in libraries." *Library Trends* 46: 526–539.

Jurow, Susan. 1996. "Core competencies." *Journal of Academic Librarianship* 22: 300–302.

Leonard-Barton, Dorothy. 1995. *Wellsprings of knowledge*. Boston: Harvard Business School Press.

McNeil, Beth, comp. 2002. *Core competencies*. SPEC Kit, no. 270. Washington, D.C.: Association of Research Libraries.

Naylor, Richard J. 2000. "Core competencies." *Public Libraries* 39 (2): 108–114.

Nelson, Sandra. 2001. *The new planning for results*. Chicago: American Library Association.

Nelson, Sandra, Ellen Altman, and Diane Mayo. 2000. *Managing for results*. Chicago: American Library Association.

New Jersey Library Association (NJLA). 1999. *NJLA core competencies for librarians*. Available: http://www.njla.org/statements/competencies.html (Accessed May 25, 2003).

Potter, William Gray. 1998. "The online catalogue in academic libraries." In *Technical services today and tomorrow,* 2nd ed. Englewood, Colo.: Libraries Unlimited.

Prahalad, C. K., and Gary Hamel. 1990. "The core competence of the corporation." *Harvard Business Review* 68 (3): 79–91.

Rehman, Sajjad ur. 2000. *Preparing the information professional*. Contributions in Librarianship and Information Science, no. 93. Westport, Conn.: Greenwood Press.

Special Libraries Association (SLA), Special Committee on Competencies for Special Librarians. 1996. *Competencies for special librarians of the 21st century*. Available: http://www.sla.org/content/SLA/professional/meaning/comp.cfm (Accessed May 25, 2003).

Younger, Jennifer A., and D. Kaye Gapen. 1998. "Technical services organization." Revised by Cecily Johns. In *Technical services today and tomorrow,* 2nd ed. Englewood, Colo.: Libraries Unlimited.

8

Successfully Merging Workflow and Personnel in Technical Services: A Management Perspective

Ann Branton

Editor's note: The author documents reorganization of the Bibliographic Services Department at the University of Southern Mississippi. Due to economic hardships, organizational change, and a new integrated library system, much of the workflow of the department was examined, resulting in a more efficient use of personnel, procedures, and collaborative and cooperative management practices. The author provides information on how acquisitions, cataloging, authority control and database maintenance, and serials workflows and personnel assignments were affected by reorganization of the department, as well as comments from a managerial perspective on individual and departmental change.

Something old, something new—like a marriage, the beginning of a new partnership that blends all the traditional departments in technical services (TS) into one department requires some time for everyone to understand the big picture and learn to operate as a greater whole. Time is needed to get to know one another and to demonstrate enough good will to make the new relationship perform with integrity, efficiency, and harmony. Accustomed to working separately and relatively independently of one another, personnel in TS departments that are reorganized to function as one must perform tasks with greater cooperation in a team environment. Personnel must learn to blend their traditional functions and responsibilities with innovative organizational ideas designed to improve processes and workflow, some old, some new.

Institutional Profile

The University of Southern Mississippi (USM) is a medium-sized institution and the only major university in the southern part of the state of Mississippi. The university was recently reorganized into five degree-awarding colleges and is a Carnegie classification Doctoral/Research-Extensive institution. Current enrollment is approximately 15,000 students divided among its two campuses and several auxiliary research facilities. USM Libraries consist of three libraries: Cook Library, the central library on the main campus; McCain Library and Archives, which houses special collections; and the Gulf Coast Library on a growing branch campus. Together they employ 34 librarians, 47 support staff, and 75 to 90 student assistants during the academic year, and they also offer three graduate assistantships per year. The Libraries support the university's distance education programs and online courses via electronic resources and databases, which include electronic journals and books.

Library Organization

Administrative leadership in the Libraries has been relatively stable, with little turnover in senior positions for more than 10 years. Until 1999, the Libraries were organized in the traditional way, with a library dean and several directors over public services, technical services, systems, the multimedia center, and special collections, in addition to the director of the Gulf Coast branch campus. Under each directorship, there were one or several departments, each with a department head. Reference, circulation, and interlibrary loan were under the directorship of public services (PS); collection management, including acquisitions and serials, and cataloging were under a centralized technical services (TS) serving all three libraries. The head of technical services personally managed collection development activities for the main campus with support from the head of collection management. Systems included all responsibilities related to the Libraries' online catalog and provided technical support for all computer and electronic equipment as well. The multimedia center offered training and expertise in computer software and graphic arts and managed the circulating materials of a growing audiovisual collection. Special collections included primary sources, manuscripts, rare books, historical maps, and materials about Mississippi. The directors and department heads met regularly as a team to confer about policies and general library issues and participated in two off-site retreats per year to reevaluate services and activities that supported the Libraries' mission and plan for the future. A strong collegial relationship had been built over 10 years of relative administrative stability, meeting fiscal challenges with success and confidence.

Economic Hardships

By mid-1999, however, a number of factors were challenging this status quo. In a major effort to upgrade computer technology on campus, the systems department was transferred out of the main library to a separate office of technology resources (OTR), with the loss of three positions including the systems director and two support staff. In addition, the multimedia center was divided, the circulating media collection was moved into the main library facility, and the graphic and training component was moved to OTR with the loss of its director and four support positions. In 2001, the head of technical services was expected to retire at the end of the fiscal year. In addition, due to a significant statewide economic downturn, the university administration had frozen all open positions on campus and cut library materials allocations as well, in a cost-cutting effort to save money for the state. By the end of fiscal year 2003, due to continued economic stress, additional retirements, resignations, and hiring freezes, over one-third of the remaining librarian positions were unfilled.

Organizational Change

During an annual management retreat in early 2000, the Libraries' administration recognized the need to make changes to the overall structure of the organization and reallocate responsibilities to better serve the academic community. Several positions were reevaluated and reassigned to absorb the loss of personnel in leadership and subordinate roles. Some auxiliary collections were moved into the main library to offer greater hours of access and merge support personnel into areas of greater need. After a year of discussion and planning among the remaining senior administrators, library management was finally reorganized in the spring of 2001. In response to the retirement of the director of technical services, the two senior director positions were merged and an associate dean appointed. Department heads of reference, circulation, and cataloging were appointed heads of departments that had been realigned and renamed Information Services, Access Services, and Bibliographic Services, respectively. A newly formed position of collection development coordinator was also assigned supervisory responsibilities for a reading room on the second floor of the main library that included serials, microforms, and multimedia resources. Special collections was expanded to include a digitization lab, and a catalog librarian position was transferred to support this initiative. Later, the systems department was reinstated in the main library after the campus technology upgrade was completed and stable in 2002. These changes to the Libraries' organizational structure in 2001 also followed a year after the implementation of a new integrated library system, Sirsi Unicorn™.

Technical Services

New computer technology had facilitated the need for changes in technical services as early as the 1980s. Automation replaced many of the traditionally manual tasks, such as typing catalog cards, and automated processes proved to be more accurate and more efficient than previous procedures. By 1994, all personnel in technical services had their own desktop computer with much of the software needed to perform their jobs. After major renovation of the main library in 1996, every staff workstation had access to word processing software, the local OPAC and its technical services modules, and the OCLC bibliographic utility. After a new system was implemented in 1999, all work was performed in a Windows environment. This in itself streamlined every function in technical services.

But total integration of TS modules in a Windows operating system only occurred when Sirsi Unicorn™, with its WorkFlows™ technical services interface, was installed. The new system enabled all functions in technical services to be customized and routine processes to cross over traditional boundaries between acquisitions, cataloging, and serials. Implementation of a library system can be a very stressful course of action, as many details and procedures in the workflow must be analyzed. Some immediate changes were unavoidable. At USM Libraries, it took at least a year for everyone to become comfortable enough and knowledgeable enough to implement the more sophisticated elements of the system.

Pre-Merger Performance

During early briefings with the new department head in Bibliographic Services, the Libraries' administration expressed serious concerns about areas of unsatisfactory performance within the old organization of technical services that historically seemed to be insurmountable problems. The primary concern was the number of manual processes that were still in place in spite of several years of automation. Considerable lag time between the date an order card was submitted for order to the date the item was actually received and cataloged seriously undermined the confidence of the teaching faculty in the Libraries' ability to serve their academic and research needs. A sizable backlog of materials in special formats still remained 10 years after the Libraries were first automated. Cataloging electronic journals had become an additional burden to the serials librarian, who increasingly spent more time maintaining them and registering the authorizations to provide online access. Clearly, the departments were not taking full advantage of the Libraries' state-of-the-art integrated automated system, Sirsi Unicorn™. There was very little evidence to demonstrate that the separate technical services departments shared information or worked as a team on any activity or project. Except for preorder cataloging, which required cooperation between the acquisitions and cataloging staff during the annual ordering cycle, personnel from different departments rarely worked together to meet a common goal or deadline. Communication between the department heads regarding workflow among their respective departments was minimal or on a "need to know" basis.

Implementing Shared Governance

Goals were set for the two merged departments, formerly Collection Management and Cataloging, now organized as one department named Bibliographic Services, with three units: Acquisitions, Cataloging, and Serials. Under the new organization, the librarians in the separate units had a share in the overall management of the department and did not have administrative titles, emphasizing that Bibliographic Services was the only department and that the several units within the department were equal and interdependent in the decision-making and problem-solving processes. Librarians now collaborated in determining policies and procedures, with a focus on the overall goals of the department. Each unit contributed to the success of the department as a whole. This eliminated territorial attitudes that often impeded cooperation and collaboration among personnel. A new management vision was put in place and communicated to the newly organized department, with the following goals:

- Provide leadership in creating an atmosphere of mutual trust and respect, and a positive, service-oriented work ethic in a cooperative, collaborative work environment.

- Communicate the vision and goals for the department to all personnel as a whole, to work groups and to individuals.

- Evaluate fiscal workflows for all units, determining peak and low points in each cycle.

- Cross-train personnel in all technical services modules: acquisitions, cataloging, and serials.

- Revise all job descriptions to reflect changes in the workflow and work assignments; perform desk audits for positions as needed.

- Provide continuing education opportunities in training workshops and team-building activities for the department personnel.

- Significantly improve the efficiency and timeliness of ordering and receiving library materials during the fiscal cycle.

- Evaluate quality and quantity standards in cataloging to reach greater balance between detail and productivity.

- Evaluate all manual and electronic procedures, eliminating duplication of effort and bottlenecks in the workflow.

- Provide reports that analyze statistics of monthly and annual productivity and relate the progress of projects and achievement successes.

- Provide an ergonomic and healthy work environment, with adequate and appropriate computer hardware and software to accomplish assigned tasks.

Bibliographic Services

The Bibliographic Services Department of USM Libraries currently employs 4 librarians (a reduction from nine librarians during the past two years), 18 support staff, 1 graduate assistant, and 12 student assistants. The department is managed by a single department head, while the remaining three librarians serve in supervisory roles that facilitate day to day management of the three units: Acquisitions, Cataloging, and Serials. These librarians do not hold titles of authority, yet they supervise in a more organic sense. They each have separate work assignments and also serve in a supervisory role, providing training and support in their respective areas of expertise as needed during the normal routine cycle of ordering, receiving, cataloging, and processing materials. The units are defined by these principal responsibilities, and personnel derive their primary work identity from assignment to a specific unit. However, personnel are cross-trained in all of the technical services modules for acquisitions, cataloging, and serials. This training plan enables all staff to perform ancillary assignments across unit lines.

Integrated Workflow

All units participate in all aspects of bibliographic services, and almost all individuals are assigned tasks that require them to be knowledgeable in the three technical services modules of the library automated system, Sirsi Unicorn™. Sirsi Unicorn WorkFlows™ software is fully integrated and provides unique capabilities in the way that it allows access to the functionality of all modules simultaneously. The WorkFlows™ toolbar can be customized to individual tasks and individual levels of responsibility that make it feasible to blend the traditional components in technical services into a more streamlined workflow. In addition, personnel work in a fully integrated Windows environment with access to the OCLC bibliographic utility and CatMicroEnhancer™, OCLC Spell-Checker™, Validator™, MacroExpress™, WordPad™, and the MSOffice™ software suite. Each workstation has access to the Internet and a number of library databases useful in providing verification of data, in addition to the department's well-developed home page of local policies and practices. The Internet also provides access to inventories on vendors' Web sites and to online ordering services such as Amazon.com, Barnes & Noble.com, and a large number of small out-of-print services. These technological improvements enhance the Libraries' ability to provide a complete workstation for employees.

The units remain unique and discrete; primary affiliation with their particular unit is maintained. The tasks and their skill sets are integrated, and there is daily communication with the other TS units. As their projects and assignments require, personnel from these three units collaborate in their work as much as possible.

While some tasks such as those that include financial responsibilities may be too complex and sensitive to allow complete cross-training, most tasks do require knowledge of all the TS modules. This big picture approach fosters appreciation of all of the functionality in the TS modules and helps employees to see how their assignments fit within the Libraries' mission of providing access to library materials. Assignments are made according to the skill sets of individual employees and the unit with which they are affiliated. Everyone has been trained to understand how an item is ordered, received, and cataloged, to know the construction of the MARC record, and to be familiar with *Bibliographic Formats and Standards*, and they must read at least the first two chapters of AACR2R. With this foundation, all personnel can be trained in additional special skill sets and customized to more challenging work assignments.

The unique aspect of an integrated department manifests itself when additional personnel are needed for peak periods of any of these primary objectives. Personnel from all units can incorporate into their daily routine additional assignments without training and restructure of the sister unit. Each unit shares in the decision-making and problem-solving processes, adapting to the ebb and flow of the annual work cycles. Each unit has unique cycles within the annual cycles that often require sharing of personnel to meet deadlines or accomplish special projects in shorter time periods within the fiscal year. While the units perform traditional tasks and activities, they have all assumed a broader scope of duties that cross over the more commonly understood lines of responsibility.

Role of the Librarian

A librarian serves as a liaison for each unit or integrated work group to the department head, whose primary role is to elicit the skills and expertise needed to facilitate success in the overarching goals of the department. Librarians in the department may select staff from any unit who have the skills to accomplish the objectives of a project. Many of these objectives are traditional: spend the allocation before the end of the fiscal year, catalog all new materials in a timely manner, and evaluate journal titles during the annual add/drop cycle before payment is due.

All librarians have assumed greater roles in management of the department, contributing to the planning and supervision of projects that include working more directly with subordinate staff, delegating routine assignments, and performing annual evaluations. Technical staff have accepted more responsibilities as well, in supervising and directing student employees who support their assignments. Many routine processes, which traditionally were performed or supervised by professional librarians, are now being managed by support staff.

Physical Support

The three units share a large work area that is housed on the second floor of the main library. The area has large windows, providing an abundance of natural light. Equipment is state-of-the-art, well maintained, and ergonomically appropriate to each individual. The department has a commodities budget of $20,000 per year in addition to an annual binding budget of over $60,000. Librarians work in individual private offices; support staff and student assistants work in modular workstations that have been customized to their assignments as much as possible.

The departments' wages budget for student assistants is about $30,000 per year. Student assistants are paid minimum wage their first year of employment and are given small raises each subsequent year they are employed. Some individuals are promoted to student supervisor, with wages to compensate for the additional responsibilities. When possible, some are employed full-time to benefit from the university's six-hour tuition waiver for full-time employees; some are hired upon graduation. This has proved to be an excellent recruitment practice, as several of the student assistants have later become librarians in their own right. In addition to the student assistants, one graduate assistantship is awarded to a student from the USM School of Library and Information Science program each year.

Documentation

Written procedures are critical to maintain standards, document local practice, provide training resources, and communicate policies and procedures for all department assignments. Documentation is provided to all personnel online in a well-developed Web page. First created in 1995 for the cataloging unit, it now reflects the policies and procedures of all units. Many external links to technical services tools and resources are provided. Currently, the department's Web pages are being redesigned to serve as a Web portal, offering more sophisticated searching capabilities. Revision and maintenance are ongoing. In addition to many standard resources to support daily activities in Bibliographic Services, several tools have been created that contribute to national TS resources as well. A MARC21 tutorial was developed and national access provided online to train new employees in basic MARC theory. Another tool that was created and is widely used by catalogers nationally is a list of free floating headings valid in the subfield lv of the 6XX fields. In an effort to establish and control the many Cutters assigned to a vast number of composers, a music Cutter list was created locally and made available online. More than 700 pages have been created for the department to maintain standards and provide access to elements necessary to perform our work well.

Acquisitions Unit: Integrated Management

The acquisitions unit performs all the ordering activities for the two campuses, monitoring their separate budget allocations for library materials. Until 2001, the acquisitions and serials units were known as the Collection Management department, which consisted of two librarians, a department head and the serials librarian, and two senior staff who were responsible for traditional supervision and evaluation of eight subordinate staff. Since the merger of all technical services departments, the acquisitions unit has undergone reorganization requiring revisions in workflow, job descriptions, and especially the work environment. Although the new department head was well known to the acquisitions staff, the hands-on management style was very new to them. As there were no written procedures for routine tasks or a documented fiscal plan, group meetings to determine everyone's responsibilities were held frequently during the first few weeks of the new organization. The primary focus during the first year of new management was understanding the ordering cycle; evaluating vendor profiles and material fill rates of the Libraries' three primary book vendors; revising and reorganizing workflow and job assignments; streamlining and eliminating duplicate efforts in placing, tracking, and canceling orders; and collecting data in general.

Current Practice

The acquisitions unit has retained their traditionally separate identity but has shared responsibilities with the cataloging and serials units. Due to cross-training in the TS modules, there is greater understanding of the duties and responsibilities of the other two units, and consequently greater respect for the expertise each unit contributes to the overall departmental workflow. Direct supervision and evaluation of personnel is the responsibility of a librarian who serves in a daily role of unit facilitator, trainer, and coach, meeting weekly with the unit to assess problems and share in their resolution and address productivity concerns during peak times of the ordering cycle. All members of the work group share in discussions and together determine work assignments to successfully achieve the goal of spending the materials allocation wisely, efficiently, and in a timely manner before the end of the fiscal year. All participate in evaluating current practices and procedures. New ideas are submitted and tested to discover ways to improve productivity and the quality of services provided to faculty regarding new orders and the annual allocation of funds, encumbered and paid, received or canceled. Currently there are five support staff who form the core work group of the unit. The current acquisitions budget of $2.5 million is monitored by a senior staff member in acquisitions, who processes the invoices to be paid, while other members of the unit create orders and select the appropriate MARC records, generate purchase orders, and monitor and note the status of orders over the following four to six weeks before 90 percent of the materials are delivered. One staff member is also responsible for receiving and processing gifts and exchanges for the library collections.

Integrated Work Group

The best example of the success of the department's integration of functions is the cataloging at point-of-order (CAPO) team. There are two components to the team. Members of the core group are those assigned to the unit and are responsible for tasks. They are also expected to contribute to weekly meetings typically associated with acquisitions: supervising the monitoring and expending of the materials allocation, handling special ordering requests, and receiving and processing invoices to be paid.

During the nine months that the unit is engaged in ordering and receiving the bulk of the orders for the fiscal year, as many as five additional employees from cataloging and serials are assigned to the work group. They participate equally in performing the tasks and contribute to weekly meetings to evaluate team progress, resolving problems such as bottlenecks in the workflow, clarification of policies and procedures, and communicating needs and concerns. Written minutes of the meetings are taken and distributed to all units so everyone is aware of progress made, and the assignments of staff temporarily assigned to the work group are understood by all, particularly supervising librarians in cataloging or serials. The whole department shares in this activity during the fiscal year directly or indirectly, shifting priorities and personnel as needed to complete this major initiative.

Several steps were taken to streamline the ordering process. Search and verification steps were eliminated for titles published within the last two years, and the system was set to catch duplicate orders or incorrect MARC records at the point the records were loaded into the system twice a day. Tighter control of allocations was exercised, monitoring expenditures, encumbrances, and amounts paid on a weekly timetable. In the last three fiscal ordering cycles, 2001–2003, the cycle has been completed progressively earlier each year; FY 2002/2003 was finished three months before the end of the fiscal year.

In streamlining the ordering process, both acquisitions and cataloging staff learned to function in both modules to perform all of the same tasks. During the time that it takes to expend the materials allocation, about 10 employees participate in the ordering and precataloging of materials. When materials arrive, all team members receive materials, perform edit cataloging as needed, barcode and link the items, and forward materials to be labeled and processed. Exceptions are nonprint/media and scores; these are sent directly to librarians and staff with special training to order, receive, and catalog them.

Orders with publication dates older than the most current two years are searched on vendors' inventory Web sites. This both verifies the bibliographic data and determines from whom the item should be ordered. This saves time and ensures delivery in the shortest possible time, with a reduced likelihood of a cancellation or out-of-print status report.

Current Initiatives

An in-house electronic ordering form has been created, and beta testing of the new e-order process was completed in spring of 2003. The design of the order form was a collaborative effort between the Libraries' Webmaster and the acquisitions staff as several prototypes of the form were reviewed, critiqued, and revised. Where orders were created card by card in the past, orders in batches of 10, 50, and 100 will be created with simultaneous searching for the MARC records for download into the OPAC via batched ISBN number searches in OCLC CatME™, expediting the order cycle process dramatically. The teaching faculty and/or their library faculty collection development liaison can submit orders. The new e-order form provides access to a number of searching tools to ensure that valid bibliographic data are supplied in the order form. Data are collected to chart the effectiveness of the new procedures in the coming year. Every effort has been made to replace manual and paper dominant activities with electronic procedures. There is considerable support in software to track and maintain data related to the ordering and receiving of library materials. USM has installed PeopleSoft™ software across campus, and the Sirsi™ system acquisitions module is compatible with this financial management software. System-generated reports provide data that are converted to MSOffice Excel™ to be manipulated and produce reports to reflect current status of allocations: free balance, funds encumbered, funds paid. This is particularly important during the last quarter of the ordering cycle.

Development of the acquisitions Web page is ongoing, to make all policies and procedures related to tasks in the ordering cycle and acquisitions workflow available online. An online manual is being developed to track progress of the ordering cycle and to serve as a monthly planner for the many deadlines that must be met during the cycle. Additional research is being done to evaluate the best practice of internal processes and to compare vendor performance and selection in an effort to make every dollar count.

Cataloging: Collaborative Management

The cataloging unit centrally manages cataloging activities for the two campuses and all their collections. The unit consists of seven support staff and three librarians who perform traditional functions in cataloging: original and edit cataloging, database maintenance and repair, and authority cataloging and control. Each of these specific areas in the unit has evolved during the past two years of change. Until 2001, the department had been stable in its leadership, with one department head for over 10 years, two senior catalog librarians, and four catalog librarians, typically entry-level; however, there has been considerable turnover at this junior level of cataloging personnel over the past dozen years. Typically, entry-level librarians are trained for one year, performing original cataloging for dissertations and theses. After a year, their work is evaluated and additional assignments are made according to priority, matching skill with interest when possible.

All catalog librarians perform original and complex editing for all formats. They also serve as a liaison to those who manage the collection(s) for which they catalog. They meet regularly with personnel from the various public service areas to discuss priorities, improvement of access to materials, or any concern they may have about their area as it relates to the materials that are cataloged for their collection. This has proven to be invaluable in communicating concerns, revising processing procedures, and the like. A 24-hour rush cataloging service is also available, and requests are often completed in far shorter time.

Since USM has an ALA-accredited library and information science program, several of the staff in cataloging are also LIS graduate students. Due to their academic and/or practical training, some are performing original cataloging, primarily dissertations and state documents, in addition to others who perform a significant amount of editing and new cataloging for materials in both print and nonprint formats.

As a charter member of the CORC Project, USM's catalog librarians have been trained in cataloging electronic resources, primarily of state government and nonprofit Web sites in Mississippi. The librarians participate in all of these cataloging activities.

Current Practices

Each of the three catalog librarians supervises two or three staff members in cataloging, operating as a team on similar assignments, either by collection or by format. Each librarian provides the team with assignments and the necessary training to achieve them and is generally available to provide direction as needed or requested. For the most part, support staff manage their assignments during the month with clear guidelines about what needs to be achieved by the end of the month. As most of the new monograph materials are cataloged by those assigned to the acquisitions unit and the CAPO work group, the cataloging staff and librarians catalog nonprint and special formats, including rare books, and perform original cataloging as needed. The unit is not subdivided into print and nonprint; staff are trained in print and at least one nonprint or special format such as VHS or DVD videorecordings and books with an accompanying CD-ROM, or scores and LP or CD sound recordings. Consequently, the support staff are more flexible and more skilled when new projects or assignments are made.

DLC and member copy are accepted as one and the same. Duplication of the classification number will be caught when the record is loaded and an error message reports that the number already exists. This occurs a very small percentage of the time and therefore does not warrant checking every classification number to screen out the few conflicts. No attempt is made after the item is received in hand to find a better or enhanced record to replace the one used for ordering. This record is edited in the local system. Some MARC records are not acceptable in the CAPO process, and those materials must be cataloged in a conventional manner upon receipt of the item in hand. Enhancements are later made to the substandard MARC records that are selected, adding classification numbers, subject headings, and other added values such as the table of contents. Original cataloging and enhanced editing are also performed for pre-AACR2 MARC records for older works from a backlog of retrospective materials. For the past several years, by adding a new call number, content notes or subject headings, and by upgrading older pre-AACR2 MARC records, the unit has saved on average over $10,000 in earned credits from OCLC. For every two dollars spent on OCLC utility charges, one dollar is earned back in credit through the permanent enhancements made in MARC records.

Authority Control and Database Maintenance

Authority work is completed for original cataloging; for edit cataloging the system reports exceptions for names or subjects without an authority record. Work on new headings added to the catalog is performed on a regular monthly maintenance schedule. The database was authorized by a vendor in spring of 2002; clean-up of exceptions identified by the vendor is an ongoing project. The number of staff trained to perform authority work has been increased to allow concentration on authority control during slack periods of the ordering cycle. In the fall of 2001, librarians were trained to participate in NACO and have made a commitment to perform original authority cataloging with an emphasis on personal and corporate names, particularly those from Mississippi publications.

All bibliographic records are given a spell-check before loading into the OPAC; periodically, a standard list of misspelled words is checked in the database. Repair of problems encountered as a result of system migration is ongoing as well.

Now that the integrated modules are fully utilized and personnel are cross-trained in them, there is more time to devote to this critical database maintenance and repair activity.

Current Initiatives

Working with electronic and digital formats is the newest skill added to the units' cataloging repertoire. While the librarians received basic training in cataloging electronic resources several years ago, managing them has become more challenging. In addition to cataloging hundreds of e-journals in separate records,

MARC cataloging is provided for reference databases, Web pages, e-books, and digital resources, such as oral histories generated by the digitization lab in the special collections department.

Initially, the catalog librarians set standards for the way access is provided to these new formats. It was determined that separate MARC records would best provide full access to every unique "edition" of an electronic item. Compromises have been made regarding the retrieval of multiple records with the same serial title in different formats by adding uniform titles where warranted and some other creative "out of the box" thinking to accommodate the needs of public services while adhering to cataloging best practices. A uniform title with a format qualifier has been added to each bibliographic record for serials owned in nonprint formats. The URL for the electronic work displays above the title when retrieved in the public catalog.

An in-house thesaurus was adapted to perform subject analysis for a collection of digitized civil rights-related oral histories to provide access to these primary sources online. Utilizing Dublin Core elements in the XML document, visible to the viewer and fully searchable, LC subject headings were substituted where possible, or local authority records were created where necessary to ensure the integrity of access in the OPAC and the special collections Web site. This collaborative relationship is very encouraging, and catalog librarians are eager to participate in electronic cataloging utilizing XML and other related encoding software.

In an initiative to cut costs in authority cataloging, a software product called *Validator*™ was purchased. *Validator*™, a quarterly publication in CD-ROM format, contains Library of Congress (LC) authority records that may be downloaded to the local system just as bibliographic records are downloaded from OCLC. Introducing other software products, such as MacroExpress™, has also streamlined some routine steps in cataloging. Improving the workflow is an ongoing process of tweaking routines and balancing effectiveness with efficiency.

Serials: Cooperative Management

The serials unit is managed by the serials librarian. Three technicians are employed to perform the many technical activities necessary to manage serials: periodicals, newspapers, loose-leaf, standing orders, and continuations. One technician is responsible for binding operations for both serials and book formats. USM Libraries subscribes to approximately 5,000 serial titles, electronic journals and databases, JSTOR, and several online aggregators. Ebsco is the primary jobber for serials subscriptions in addition to the Libraries' direct subscriptions. The serials librarian has supervisory responsibilities for the unit, revises job descriptions, performs annual evaluations, and provides training, assigning tasks as appropriate. In addition to use of the serials module, staff all have access to and use of the cataloging and acquisitions modules. It was decided that it was best to supervise serials processing centrally in the Bibliographic Services department. Overall, the serials unit experienced the least amount of change; cross-training in all TS modules was already in place. Cataloging assignments in microform collections, both cataloging and database maintenance of the MARC records for the collection, were the most significant addition to the workflow.

Current Practices

Due to the nature of serials management and the unique differences in database maintenance of the collection, few nonserials unit technicians participate in serials work. The few exceptions are those technicians, from both acquisitions and cataloging staff, with excellent skills in attention to detail and an appreciation for the many possible variables in serials control. They have been trained to check in journals, post invoices, and recognize title changes. A cataloging technician who performs serials check-in for the state journals and state documents housed in special collections, in addition to her monograph cataloging assignments for the same collections, is just one example of this cooperative arrangement. By working closely with the serials unit, the cataloging technician is also able to provide special collections staff with an additional contact point to inquire about all of their materials.

Serials and a few cataloging technicians are now cross-trained to provide mutual support during the year to assist with projects that require both cataloging and serials module expertise. All serials staff are familiar with the cataloging module, and during less intense work periods they routinely perform database MARC and item repair for the microform collections. Continuations are cataloged by the serials unit senior technician. Many monographic series are cataloged as individual books when they are received and given appropriate series statements and classification numbers to retrieve them together. In addition, the senior serials technician also performs copy and edit cataloging for microforms during spare moments, as many of the Libraries' microsets do not have bibliographic records available for purchase.

Serials and acquisitions personnel cooperate in assisting with the annual add/drop cycle and with posting invoices and processing them to be paid. Serials personnel post serial invoices, and the serials allocation is monitored by the serials librarian in cooperation with the acquisitions accountant. This annual task requires knowledge of the acquisitions and serials module.

The serials unit staff do not have public service desk duties but do work cooperatively with personnel in Journals and Media Services (JMS). JMS houses journals, microforms, and the multimedia collections. JMS is supervised by a librarian who also serves as the collection development coordinator. Support staff from both public and technical services work cooperatively on routine activities and on several annual projects during the year; serials unit staff assist greatly in shelf maintenance in JMS.

In 1991, the Libraries' administration decided to classify all journals and integrate them into the circulating stacks, although journals do not circulate. This merging of collections has been very successful, in part because the most current four to five years of bound journals are held in JMS alongside the loose issues, providing easier access to current materials most frequently requested. Each fall semester there is a major shift of the older bound volumes to the stacks. The serials unit is fully responsible for the shift and all of the database maintenance the shift requires to correctly reflect the move. Serials unit personnel are also responsible for routine maintenance of the shelves in JMS. The bindery technician gives close attention to the loose issues to be sure that missing issues are claimed and replaced if possible, to send complete runs to the bindery.

Current Initiatives

Open positions in the cataloging unit provided the opportunity to reevaluate job assignments. In addition to electronic books and subject Web pages, cataloging electronic journals has been reassigned from the serials librarian to a cataloger responsible for all electronic resources. The serials unit librarian will supervise this cataloging activity and will be able to devote more time to electronic journal maintenance and related auxiliary tasks, to provide stable access to the electronic journals and databases.

A project under discussion is a first-time inventory of the government documents collection. The project will require cooperation between librarians and staff from several departments, primarily Bibliographic Services and Information Services. A great deal of planning will go into assignment of responsibilities for every step of the process. A significant percentage of the documents have no MARC records in the OPAC, or there is a MARC record and the item is lost or shelved in error. Personnel in serials and cataloging have been trained to address any problem that may arise.

More and more sophisticated databases are being added to the Libraries' collection of electronic resources. The electronic services librarian is responsible for maintaining the Web interface for electronic resources. Due to the nature of their assignments and responsibilities, the serials librarian and acquisitions staff must work cooperatively with the electronic services librarian to provide stable access to new electronic databases. Ordering new subscriptions and monitoring renewals are managed by acquisitions staff, while the cataloging and setting up control records in the serials module are performed in the serials unit. When reference librarians have problems with access to databases, the electronic services librarian brings their concerns to the serials librarian. In this way, each serves the other as liaison for their respective areas in a new relationship established to answer questions and address issues about anything related to serials.

Final Thoughts on Management

For change to be successful there must be a foundation to support the implementation of new ideas and new methods of work. Change does not come about in a vacuum but results from procedures or organizational structures that no longer serve the mission of the institution. Change in any library is meant to be a good thing that benefits the majority of the community the library serves. In the best-case scenarios, change is ongoing to continually improve the services provided.

Constant evaluation of policies and procedures creates an atmosphere conducive to change, great or small. Group participation in the problem-solving and decision-making processes develops a sense of shared ownership of the outcomes. Success is the result of mutual trust and shared governance; failure is the result of a lack of leadership in the process.

In the fall of 2002, the Bibliographic Services Department participated in a benchmarking exercise to identify all who performed tasks in two or more TS modules. Die-cuts were distributed to represent the different units/modules that each person worked in. A green frog represented acquisitions, a yellow cat represented cataloging, and a blue bird represented serials. If a technician performed any task in any one or more of the modules, he or she was given a token for that task. By the end of the exercise, everyone had at least two different representations of the TS modules in which they work. The exercise inspired discussion about lines of communication, and it was clear that everyone had input in the decision-making process on a daily basis. Librarians were not always the first persons with authority to give advice or share information related to the task at hand. A clear picture of interdependency and integration of tasks was illustrated by the exercise.

Cycles Within the Fiscal Cycle

Each unit has a unique cycle of its own, but all are closely related to the fiscal year buying cycle. The first unit to begin the fiscal year in earnest, once the materials allocation has been determined, is the serials unit during the annual journal add/drop/renewal phase. This process must be completed by mid-September. There are several critical deadlines that must be met to benefit from discounts and to ensure timely cancellation and renewal of subscriptions. USM faculty participate in the add/drop selection at the very beginning of each semester. As soon as the serials allocation can be estimated, allocations for library materials can be distributed by deans to their respective departments. Firm orders for books and other library materials begin to be processed and placed by November, when the serials invoices are being posted. By the end of December, 50 percent of the firm orders for both print and nonprint are complete. During the holidays, library materials are delivered and will be received and cataloged when staff return in January.

By the time the new materials have been processed and shelved, the second deadline for the remaining materials budget has arrived, in mid-February. Firm orders are complete by the end of April, and almost all of the new materials will have arrived and been processed at the same time. Particularly during the spring months, the serials unit has completed the most critical part of its cycle, and the staff are generally free to take on additional assignments as needed. During the latter months of spring, the acquisitions unit must do general housekeeping of records and files, canceling orders over 120 days old and noting the status of others in preparation for the annual rollover of accounts to begin the next fiscal year. No orders of any kind are placed between mid-June and the end of July to allow for a smooth transition of accounts. Generally, the summer is a good time to give auxiliary assignments, such as authority control and maintenance of the database, to the acquisitions staff. The cataloging unit is less affected by these cyclic ups and downs; it steadily performs cataloging for collections from the backlog when not participating in the preorder cataloging/receiving cycle. No new materials have been added to the backlog in over 10 years.

Ideally, with resources and energy focused on completing even routine tasks more wisely, work can be done more efficiently and economically. A new model of blended units from old, more traditional departmental divisions in technical services supersedes the cumbersome workflow between departments that once required the maintenance of a paper trail for every transaction. By cross-training and merging tasks and by utilizing new technologies, there are no bottlenecks to clog the ordering process, no need to hand off order cards between departments, and no need to send 90 percent of the new monographs to cataloging staff. There is better utilization of personnel, who are cross-trained and able to tackle any project with skill and confidence. With greater understanding of all the units in bibliographic services, greater respect exists for the expertise each unit can contribute in performing all assignments, from placing the order to making an item accessible to the library user.

Conclusion

The success enjoyed by the newly organized Bibliographic Services Department could not have been achieved without the good will of every individual affected by the merger. Change can be stressful in the best of situations; good will was an indispensable factor in achieving the goals set forward by the Libraries' administration in 2001. If productivity increases and meeting deadlines far sooner than ever before are measures of success, then the merger has indeed been a success. Due to economic and organizational factors during the past several years, USM Libraries has experienced significant change. Reorganization of departments in both public and technical services areas has been accomplished, and lines of responsibility have been adjusted to maintain standard services. While traditional library roles have been preserved for the most part, personnel titles are more generic and therefore more flexible in accommodating future change and new lines of accountability, responsibility, and communication.

References

Chambers, Juilleen, Jennifer Martin, and Beverly Reynolds. 2000. "Defying conventional wisdom: Innovation and culture change from down under." *Cataloging and Classification Quarterly* 30 (1): 35–50.

Freeborn, Robert, and R. Mugridge. 2002. "The reorganization of monographic cataloging processes at Penn State University Libraries." *Library Collections, Acquisitions & Technical Services* 26 (1): 35–45.

Gorman, Michael. 1998. *Technical services today and tomorrow.* Englewood, Colo.: Libraries Unlimited.

Kaplan, Michael, ed. 1997. *Planning and implementing technical services workstations.* Chicago: American Library Association.

Maxwell, John C. 2001. *The 17 indisputable laws of teamwork: Embrace them and empower your team.* Nashville, Tenn.: Thomas Nelson.

Wakimoto, Jina Choi, and Gina R. Hsiung. 2000. "Blurring the boundaries between professional and para-professional catalogers at California State University, Northridge." *Library Collections, Acquisitions, & Technical Services* 24 (3): 171–188.

Zuidema, Karen, 1999. "Reengineering technical services processes." *Library Resources and Technical Services* 43 (1): 37–52.

9

Workflow Analysis as a Basis for Organizational Redesign at McMaster University Library

Cheryl Martin

Editor's note: The author discusses how workflow analysis was used as a basis for change and redesign in the Bibliographic Services Division of a large Canadian academic library. The process of flowcharting is examined, as well as the general feelings and anxieties expressed by personnel during the process of change. Issues regarding communication and the increasing volume of electronic resources, as well as knowledge requirements and work assignments, led to the Division being organized into two teams divided by format, with librarians as team leaders. The author provides extensive documentation in the appendixes of memos and decisions directly related to the reorganization.

McMaster University Library (Hamilton, Ontario) has a centralized Bibliographic Services Division with 21 staff members, organized into copy cataloging, original cataloging, and maintenance/authorities sections. The original cataloging and maintenance sections are team-based, while the copy catalogers have a supervisor. In addition to cataloging, maintenance, and authority work, staff in the Division are also responsible for preorder searching and for entering order information in the catalog. This organization evolved over time and had been driven mostly by budget issues and retirements. The original cataloging team was formed in 1992 and had originally been made up of both librarians and library assistants. Over the years, all of the librarian cataloger positions were eliminated as a result of retirements and budget issues, which necessitated their transfer to public service areas. The remaining library assistants performed all of the original and difficult copy cataloging, with the assistance of one librarian from the science and technology library who cataloged one day a week. The maintenance/authority section had a supervisor until the end of 1998, but she retired at the same time as the director of Bibliographic Services. The supervisor and director positions were combined, and the maintenance/authority group was made a team. The copy cataloging section has traditionally had a supervisor, and this section continued as in the past (see Appendix 9.1).

There were several problems inherent in this organizational structure. One was the organization of the teams, which had no formal team leader. Each member of the team took a turn being the "team leader," who organized the workflow and meetings and communicated team issues to the Division. The person in this team leader position was a unionized staff member with no supervisory responsibility, and the team leader changed every few months. There was resistance from the staff to changing the term of the team leader to provide more continuity. The director supervised all of the members of the teams, and it was difficult for her to encourage the teams to organize and do their work but also have enough involvement to ensure that the work was being done and provide direction when necessary. This arrangement became even more problematic once the staff became unionized, because of the difficulties of having union members supervise their unionized colleagues, even in an informal way.

Communication within the Division was also an issue. The team members consulted freely with each other and with staff members in other areas of the library, but the staff members in the supervised section did not have as much opportunity to consult or to be consulted. Also, because the "team leaders" had no supervisory responsibilities, the hierarchy of the library system was not set up to allow them to participate in workshops and meetings or to receive communications meant for supervisors. The director functioned as their supervisor, but it was difficult to include the team leaders in some meetings and at other times to meet with the other supervisor about supervisory matters. It was an awkward situation that didn't seem to have any easy solution in the existing structure. Team members wanted constant communication and to be involved in all decisions, and they looked on the "private" meetings at which supervisory decisions were made with some suspicion. There was a lot of one-way communication from the director to the teams but not a great deal of information being shared by them. The teams understood that they needed to communicate with each other, but not that they also needed to communicate with their supervisor on a regular basis, and this created an ongoing conflict. It was difficult for the director to balance ongoing relationships with members of the team and with management activities that had become more complex and extensive and were expected to increase.

The main problem with the organizational structure was that it impeded workflow. Staff members working on the same format were divided by the level of the work being done, and the copy and original catalogers were not working to the same standards. Some staff members were checking exhaustively for authorities, but others were not checking them at all, even in authority-intensive formats such as music. Some complex copy for government publications, music, and maps had been assigned to the copy catalogers, who had only basic training in these formats. On the other hand, more complex copy for other formats and subject areas was given to the original catalogers. This imbalance of responsibilities created morale problems that could not be easily resolved in the existing structure. These situations had evolved over time and had not been examined to see if the work was being done effectively and to resolve the issue of what work should be done by each level of staff. Work was being replicated because staff members were not always working together effectively to solve problems. For example, the copy catalogers would search for copy at the point of order, then search again when the item arrived if LC copy had not been found. The original catalogers, who also did most of the non-LC copy, might search for better or different copy at the point of cataloging.

Staff members believed that they were providing excellent service to our users because they were creating the best, most complete records in the catalog and ensuring that the highest standards were followed. Unfortunately, this standard of cataloging takes time, and time was becoming a problem, especially with the large increase in the volume of electronic resources. The Library had entered a national consortium called the Canadian National Site Licensing Project (CNSLP) and a provincial consortium of academic libraries, in order to purchase access to electronic resources. These resources began arriving quickly, and sometimes the Libraries suddenly had access to hundreds or even thousands of new electronic journals. We received an increasing number of complaints from public service staff and from users that it was taking too long for material to reach the shelves and for electronic resources to be made accessible through the catalog. Monographs and other material with full LC copy moved quickly through the Division, but all other materials went to the original catalogers. The existing policy was that most materials without complete LC copy went to the original catalogers, who examined every item in great detail, even if it had good copy that could be done quickly. The original catalogers were not achieving an acceptable work output. This was partly due to their work practices and partly because of the time taken to perform their team responsibilities and provide assistance to other staff members.

With the existing organizational structure, most of the work of providing access to electronic resources fell to the five members of the maintenance and authorities team, who were responsible for maintenance of records for the equivalent print titles. Adding the URL to an existing record was defined as maintenance. As this became more of a priority for the Library, there was great pressure to provide immediate access to electronic materials as quickly as possible, and we were not able to do this. We purchased copy for most of our electronic products, loaded it, and edited it as necessary, but it was still taking too long for the records to be usable and still meet our users' needs for timely access. There was a general belief in the Division that users' demands for immediate access to electronic resources were unrealistic, and that they could not expect to have access until we had edited the records to standard. Library management was not willing to accept this delay. A fundamental change in philosophy was required.

There were cataloging policies and procedures that were not adding value for the user but that were long-standing and had not been examined for efficiencies. As an example, staff members were changing the Cutters on already-cataloged materials to preserve an LC Cutter on newly arrived monograph copy, on the assumption that it was too difficult for copy catalogers to adjust Cutters to fit into the call number index. It was doubtful if this added any value for the user, and relabeling materials so that an LC Cutter could be preserved seemed wasteful and inefficient, when training the copy catalogers to adjust the Cutter seemed relatively simple. All of these policies and procedures needed to be examined and changed as necessary, to ensure that materials could move as quickly as possible to the shelves and that work was not redone unless absolutely necessary.

In the summer of 2000, a decision was made to critically examine the organizational structure, environment, and work practices in a comprehensive way with the goal of making whatever changes were necessary to improve service, workflow, and communication. Because of the numerous problems and their interrelation, it seemed reasonable to examine the entire structure at once, rather than trying to resolve each issue individually. These problems were not anyone's fault, merely the end product of many years of work carried out without any critical examination of the underlying processes and standards. With budget constraints and increasing pressure to work faster, finding efficiencies became a priority.

Planning of the Reorganization

In September 2000, the process by which these issues would be examined was presented to staff in the Bibliographic Services Division, with a timetable for change (Martin 2000). There was general consensus that this was a good idea, although some staff members were nervous about what the ultimate outcome might mean for them and for their jobs. The workforce in the Division was very stable; most staff members had been with the Library for anywhere from 15 to 25 years. While this was an advantage for training and for knowledge of past practice, it was sometimes a liability. Staff members had been comfortable in transferring manual processes to an automated environment but still used the same processes, procedures, and standards that they had been taught many years before. Many processes had merely been automated, without considering whether they could be done a different way to take best advantage of the technology. For example, call numbers were still written in the backs of books and labels were produced using a word processing program instead of using the information already stored in the bibliographic record, along with appropriate software, to produce the labels directly from the record. Past attitudes toward users' needs were also not reflective of the current faster-paced environment. Users were demanding more of us, and we were not capable of responding with appropriate speed.

There was some confusion about how some processes were being performed, why staff members were performing the same process to different standards and in different ways, and why some processes had not been examined for many years. Flowcharting and analyzing existing processes provided a good idea of where change was indicated. It would be onerous work that would take many months, but it seemed to be the best way for everyone to thoroughly understand what work was being done and to elicit ideas from the staff about how things might be changed for the better. Most staff members were not going to be convinced that change was necessary unless they were proactively involved and were given the opportunity to participate in the change.

There are many advocates of the "bottom-up" approach to change management. According to Geraldine O'Brien, "change needs to occur at the level of the employee's job rather than as a consequence of senior management's edicts. . . . Senior management's role in 'bottom-up' change is to specify the general direction and provide a climate for change"(2002, p. 443). The document presented to the staff at the outset of the review gave a general outline of the process and provided an opportunity for them to be actively involved in the change process.

There was some initial mistrust of the entire review process and of a possible "hidden agenda" of some kind. The only way to overcome this was to engage the staff in the process at the outset and let them see that the only agenda on the table was to identify ways of working more efficiently. We had to ensure that the process went slowly enough so staff members could become accustomed to talking about what was being done, how it might best work if it could be changed, and how it could be changed. This was not a process that most staff members were used to. They had traditionally been given direction and had not had much input into decisions about workflow. Even the staff in the teams had limited experience with this type of activity. Part of the agenda was to get them to look at "the big picture" and see how their activities contributed to the work of the Library and the university community as a whole, so that they could help to make better decisions in the future.

The reality was that this project would lead to a climate of continuing change, in which we would have to respond quickly and appropriately to changes in the demands placed on us. According to Sauser and Sauser, "the most successful organizations in the long run are those that continuously adapt to changes in the competitive environment. . . . It has become essential to manage change as a continuing process, not as a discrete event or even a series of discrete events"(2002, p. 34).

Three staff members, the librarian supervisor, and the director formed a steering committee to oversee the process through the initial stages of flowcharting and workflow analysis. They organized and participated in the flowchart meetings and provided advice about other aspects of the process. The distribution of steering committee minutes to all staff members, plus the presence of three staff members on the planning team, helped to reassure staff members of their full involvement in the process. When people are in-volved in change, they are more committed. But, as Patricia McLagan states,

> involvement won't save a change that doesn't add value or is imple-mented unfairly. Involvement must have a purpose. If it's just a way to manipulate people and has no potential impact on decisions, don't go through the motions. That only breeds cynicism. . . . [Participants] do need to trust the people setting the goals, believe that the goals will lead to greater performance, have access to feedback, and have control and ownership of the steps and actions for achieving the goals. In other words, there needs to be participation at the level of getting things done. Successful changes always involve the people affected because they have important contributions to defining or implementing the change. (2002, p. 44)

The basic parameters of this project had been decided before it was pre-sented to the staff. There needed to be a clear plan in place to ensure that the out-comes would gather pertinent information that could be used to make decisions regarding a new organizational structure. Staff members had neither the experi-ence nor the background to decide how the project should work, but they could actively participate in helping to define what changes would be made. The steps involved in the project were to

- flowchart the current processes;

- review the current workflows and the organization structure;

- examine policies, procedures, and standards;

- make decisions about what and how changes would be made;

- implement the changes; and

- review the results of the changes.

These steps were each assigned a timeline, and we expected to be at the point of making decisions about reorganization at the end of 2001. A five-week labor disruption during the spring of 2001 made this original timetable unwork-able and caused many tensions that made it inadvisable to make reorganization decisions until the stress of the strike had diminished. It was not until the fall of 2002 that the decision was made regarding how to reorganize staff resources, and the new organization came into being in January 2003.

Workflow Analysis

Most staff members were unfamiliar with flowcharting, so a trainer con-ducted a session on how to flowchart processes. It was beneficial for staff mem-bers to see that this was a normal way to analyze and make decisions about processes, and that it was based on the knowledge that they already had about their job duties. We then began to make a list of everything that needed to be flowcharted.

In most cases, we divided long processes into shorter flowcharts so that they were more manageable. For example, we did not flowchart the entire process of cataloging a book with LC copy from start to finish. Instead, we made separate flowcharts for searching for copy, cataloging a monograph with LC copy, physical processing, authorities checking, etc. This resulted in a lot of flowcharts but made the actual flowcharting process easier because we could concentrate on one detail of a process at a time.

Between August and November 2001, we created a total of 87 flowcharts. This may seem like an enormous number, but it reflects the complexity of the activities involved in cataloging, maintenance, and physical processing in an average-sized cataloging department. The staff members directly involved in a given process met to flowchart it, guided by one of the members of the steering committee. Sometimes all staff members in the Division were involved, sometimes only two or three. One person (usually the steering committee member) would then record the process using a flowcharting program and document any relevant notes. Everyone who had been at the meeting would check the final product for accuracy, at which point the flowchart could be marked as "done" (see Appendix 9.2 for an example).

Flowcharting was only the first step of this process. Analyzing the workflow and identifying areas for change was by far the most challenging aspect. Staff members were always told at the beginning of a meeting that we were not interested in changing things that worked well, only those that were cumbersome and inefficient, or that didn't add value for the user, or that were preventing material from reaching the shelves as efficiently as possible. To guide the analysis, the same questions were considered at each analysis meeting:

- What works well with this process? Are there any obvious problems or issues? If so, brainstorm ideas to change or resolve the problem.

- Does everyone involved follow the same process? If not, document personal variations, with reasons for the differences.

- What changes could make it more efficient? This should not be confined to what anyone thinks is possible; brainstorm ideas for how this could be done more efficiently.

- Are there any local practices in this process (i.e., those not required by official standards). This should include those that are "required" because of our system (either the integrated library system or the organization).

- Why are we doing it, and what would happen if we stopped or changed it?

We decided not to have 87 separate discussions. Instead, the flowcharts were grouped in related areas and discussed during one meeting. For example, all of the flowcharts related to map cataloging were discussed together. This enabled us to see the entire process for a particular category of material. Everyone who had been at the flowcharting meeting attended the analysis meeting, and any other staff members who were interested in the process were welcome to attend any of the meetings. The director chaired each flowchart analysis meeting and guided the discussion. Since she was to make the ultimate decision about what changes would be implemented, it was essential that she be present for each discussion.

Quite a few interesting discussions took place during the analysis process. Some staff members had never been asked how they thought things should be done, and many contributed very good ideas for how things might be done differently. Staff members benefited from the opportunity to learn how to present their ideas for change to others—a new experience for some of them. A great deal of the dialogue centered around issues that affected people outside the Division, and how they might have to change their service expectations should a decision be made to change divisional policies and procedures.

All of the information compiled in the flowchart and analysis discussions was compiled into a progress report that could be used as a basis for future activities (Martin 2002). Many of the issues that needed further discussion involved people outside the Division. This provided tangible proof of the interrelationship of the Division with the rest of the Library and was a surprise for many people both within and outside the Division. The perception of a great divide between technical and public services was obviously no longer valid in our organization.

Tact and diplomacy were required to compile a document that presented ideas for change that might take place throughout the Library and that could enable many staff members to work more effectively. Because of the sensitive nature of the document, it was presented to management staff first, and they had the opportunity to ask for some things to be taken out and for some wording to be changed. Their suggestions were most welcome and were incorporated into the document before it was presented to all staff in the Library. We wanted to provide an opportunity to discuss positive change, not to criticize or embarrass staff members in other areas (see Appendix 9.3 for a copy of the Bibliographic Services Progress Report).

Results of Workflow Analysis

Following the publication of the progress report, further work was required to align staff resources with the work to be accomplished. Bibliographic Services Division staff members needed to discuss

- what changes would be made in our work policies, procedures, and standards;

- whether the type and volume of work was matched with staff resources; and

- the appropriateness of the current organizational structure of the Division.

The director would decide which changes would be implemented and how the Division would be structured following from these discussions, taking all opinions into consideration.

It was understood that long-standing policies, procedures, and standards could not be changed quickly; more information was often required, and further analysis or discussion of some issues needed to take place. There was further work to be done on the evaluation of policies and standards. Some information was gathered during the flowchart analysis, but further discussion of issues such as levels of cataloging and local policies was planned before definite decisions were made. Although it was important to have these discussions, they did not affect some of the other initiatives, suggestions, and conclusions that were presented in the progress report.

We needed to closely match our staff resources with the volume and type of work to be done and organize our work structure to facilitate the achievement of our goals. A full discussion and understanding of the issues raised in the flowchart analysis, with the active participation of all affected, would help with these discussions.

During the flowchart analysis, five main topics recurred as issues for further analysis:

- serials maintenance,

- electronic resources cataloging and maintenance,

- government publications cataloging,

- ordering, and

- physical processing.

Only one person had been assigned to serials maintenance work, and with the proliferation of electronic resources there was too much work for one person to manage effectively. Electronic resources cataloging and maintenance work was expected to increase and was of high priority for the Library, although the volume was unpredictable. Government publications cataloging was being done by several people who would benefit from a closer working relationship, both with each other and with those assigned to serials cataloging and maintenance, since many government publications are serials. The ordering process had worked well in the past, but change was needed: Orders were being passed back and forth between technical services areas and the workflow was fragmented. Physical processing, especially label production, was not as cost-efficient as it could be, and a more efficient labeling program was needed.

From our discussions, it was also clear that a comprehensive review of standards should begin as soon as possible. The process would include decisions about copy searching standards and procedures; responsibility for the cataloging of various formats and levels of material; and standards for copy and original cataloging, authority establishment and verification, and physical processing.

A "Bibliographic Services Liaison Group" was formed with representation from all public and technical services areas, and chaired by the director of Bibliographic Services. This group was to provide a forum for discussion of issues, including any decisions or project plans that would affect the catalog, prioritizing of material, and scheduling of projects. The group was also to form a plan and timeline to address the cross-divisional issues documented in the report. All staff members in the Library were welcome to attend any meeting, and the minutes were posted on our Web site.

The most important decision to be made within the Division was how the staff resources would be organized. After looking at incoming material in all formats, cataloging and processing statistics for copy and original cataloging, maintenance, and projects, several options were considered. Three different options seemed possible:

1. Maintain the existing structure.

2. Divide up the maintenance and authorities team, by moving serials maintenance and authorities to original cataloging and general maintenance and project work to copy cataloging; this option would keep staff of approximately equal job classification together.

3. Organize the teams by format: one team for monographs and special materials (maps, music, and rare materials) and project work, and one team for serials, government publications, electronic resources, and authorities; this option would provide for staff members at a variety of job classification levels in each team.

Because of the previously discussed issues surrounding the team leader positions in the teams, it was decided that librarians would become the permanent team leaders, taking this responsibility away from the library assistants. A successful case was made to hire another librarian to lead one of the teams, and the librarian who had supervised the copy catalogers would be the other team leader. This would give the director more time for management and planning responsibilities. A further advantage to this was that the support staff members could be relieved of the duties of organizing workflow and discussion of problems; the team leader would take on this work and leave them more time for primary duties. Many staff members in the teams enjoyed working in what they considered a self-directed team and were not pleased with this change. However, this reassignment of responsibilities would enable them to focus on their primary role—providing access to material. The needs of the Library had to be balanced with the perceived job satisfaction of some staff members.

In the third option listed above, it was difficult to decide which team should have the responsibility for authority work; the staff could have been assigned to either team. In the end, it made the most sense to assign the staff so that the numbers in each team were approximately equal. These three options were presented to the staff for their input. The document outlining the options and their advantages and disadvantages can be found in Appendix 9.4.

When we met to discuss these options, staff members were sure that the decision had already been made and their opinions were irrelevant. It was clear in the document that was presented to them that option 3 resolved most of the identified problems and seemed to be the best solution. They were assured that no final decision had been made, although there was a strong case to be made for the third option. They were told that their input was valuable; if they had compelling reasons why one of the other options (or one not presented) would be more effective, then they were strongly encouraged to present them. Interestingly enough, there was little support for leaving things the way they were. On the other hand, the main objection to the most radical change was that it was so radical; there were no specific reasons put forward as to why it should not be implemented. Staff members in the original cataloging team mostly preferred the option that would keep them together as a team, but their reasons were based on their belief that they worked well together and should not be separated. They had little feedback about how the other identified issues would be resolved if option 2 was chosen.

In the end, there were no convincing arguments presented to consider a different solution, and option 3 was selected. Over the following weeks, individual meetings were held between each staff member and the director to discuss the work that was most appropriate to the person's skills. Everyone was allowed to express a preference for a section, but placement in that section could not be guaranteed because the number of people in each team at each classification level had to be taken into consideration. At the end of this process, each staff member was notified about the decision, and the result was that all staff members who expressed a preference were placed in their preferred teams. A chart of the new organizational structure is included as Appendix 9.5.

The transition period between the old and new organizations necessitated team training for the new teams, planning for workflow and other details needed for the new structure, planning and implementation of physical space changes, and interviewing and choosing the person for the new librarian position. It was quite difficult to find a suitable candidate to fill this new librarian team leader position. We began to interview in July 2002 but were not able to conclude this process until November. It seemed sensible to wait until the new team leader was chosen before implementing the changes to the organization, so the reorganization came into effect on January 1, 2003. The physical space changes required some construction, which was completed in February 2003.

In the meantime, we had been discussing the ordering workflow with the Collection Management and Development Division ("Collections") staff, to decide if the ordering process could be performed more effectively. While the division of work between Collections and Bibliographic Services had worked in the past, it was clear that it was no longer viable. A decision was made to move the entire ordering function to Collections. A time study helped determine that the ordering process done in Bibliographic Services was the equivalent of approximately one FTE staff member. One position, therefore, was moved from copy cataloging to Acquisitions, and one person volunteered to take on this new role.

Conclusion

Staff members began to work in their new teams in January 2003, and they continue to adjust to the changes to workflow and to their own work assignments. Some are skeptical that the changes were necessary. Some hope that everything will go back to the way it was. Some see the advantages and have received positive feedback from staff members outside the Division. An evaluation of the reorganization is planned for the fall of 2003. An increase in our ability to provide timely access to electronic resources is already evident. A larger group of people have been assigned to this work on a regular basis, and they are able to concentrate on effectively providing access to electronic resources. The physical reorganization took place near the end of the fiscal year, when large amounts of the monograph budget were being expended. When these monographs arrived, it seemed as if the staff members assigned to that team would not be able to handle the work, since the number of people assigned to derived monograph cataloging is smaller than it was in the previous structure. Everyone in the Division agreed to catalog monographs for a couple of days, and the situation was rapidly brought under control. This team approach to resolving problems that affect a group in the Division is a positive outcome of the reorganization process.

Communication within the Library about cataloging issues has been greatly improved as a result of the reorganization. Staff members from outside the Division can see that it is possible to openly discuss cataloging issues as well as solutions that enable everyone to work more effectively. The resulting positive changes have added to the overall credibility of the process. The discussions that have taken place in the Bibliographic Services Liaison Group have been very useful, in that they have facilitated a broader understanding of each others' priorities and points of view, and benefit from the advice of staff members throughout the Library. As this process continues it is less likely that decisions will be made within the Division that adversely affect collective achievement of the Library's mission.

It was difficult to keep the momentum of this process. It took place in addition to all other activities in the Division, and at times it was a challenge to ensure that the process moved forward while we continued to provide all of our services in a timely manner. The labor disruption also greatly affected the momentum, likely to a greater degree than it might have if it had not been the first occurrence of its kind for the Library. The timeline slipped much more than it should have as a result, and a process that was to take 14 months took almost two years. The amount of time that it takes to plan and coordinate this type of project should not be underestimated, especially if most of the planning work is being done by a small group of people in addition to their regular duties.

This change process relied mainly on the leadership and vision of the director, who found it a difficult task to convince everyone else that it was the right thing to do. Sometimes it seemed that it might have been easier to give up and let everything stay as it was. The support of other management and supervisory staff for this process, however, helped a great deal. It is much easier to provide leadership for change when it is supported by colleagues and by library management. Some staff members had a more positive attitude toward the change as they saw that their ideas were considered and encouraged, and would be implemented. Staff members saw how they could be involved in improving their work environment by active participation in problem solving, by discussing ideas to work more efficiently, and by learning more about what users really want from us and making their needs our priorities.

References

Buckland, Michael. 1992. *Redesigning library services: A manifesto.* Chicago: American Library Association.

Evans, Margaret Kinnell, Bob Usherwood, and Kathryn Jones. 1999. *Improving library and information services through self-assessment: A guide for senior managers and staff developers.* London: Library Association.

International network of public libraries. 1999. Edited by Bettina Windau. Lanham, Md.: Scarecrow Press.

Kezar, Adrianna, and Peter D. Eckel. 2002. "The effect of institutional culture on change strategies in higher education: Universal principles or culturally responsive concepts?" *Journal of Higher Education* 73 (July–August): 435–461.

Martin, Cheryl. 2000. *Planning for a changing future.* Available: http://library. lib.mcmaster.ca/cat-coll/futplan.htm (Accessed June 7, 2003).

———. 2002. *Bibliographic services progress report.* Available: http://library. lib.mcmaster.ca/cat-coll/planweb.htm (Accessed June 7, 2003).

McLagan, Patricia A. 2002. "Success with change." *T+D* 56 (2): 44–54.

O'Brien, Geraldine. 2002. "Participation as the key to successful change: A public sector case study." *Leadership & Organization Development Journal* 23: 442–455.

Sauser, William I., and Lane D. Sauser. 2002. "Changing the way we manage change." *SAM Advanced Management Journal* 67 (4, Autumn): 34–40.

Appendix 9.1:
University Library Bibliographic Services Division

Planning for a Changing Future

1. Introduction

Both the work and the environment in which Bibliographic Services Division staff members work change constantly, and these changes have accelerated in recent years. Until a few years ago, the catalogue was maintained by typing and filing cards, and manual corrections to paper shelf lists. Now, automated processes have changed many of these duties. We have adapted to changes in cataloguing codes and standards, and have integrated new formats, such as the increasing variety of electronic resources, into our work. As to the environment, the retirements of the former Director of the Division and the Principal Cataloguer resulted in a redistribution of responsibilities, and increased emphasis has been placed on individual and group or team responsibilities. We continue to experience budget pressures, such that we have a limited number of staff and a finite amount of money, neither of which is likely to increase in the near future.

From time to time, it is necessary for us as a division to take stock of where we have come from, where we are, and in which direction we need to go. We need to examine and discuss both our work and our environment in the context of the "big picture". We need to ask ourselves some basic questions, and devise systematic ways to discuss them constructively, so that all of us have opportunities to express ideas and opinions, and we ultimately reach the best decisions possible.

Looking at our work practices, we need to ask questions such as:

- Are our policies and procedures appropriate to computer-assisted—as opposed to manual—cataloguing?

- How can policies and procedures be changed to make results more effective?

- Is our workflow sufficiently flexible to be responsive to service needs?

- Are "exceptions" that we make in following rules and standards worth the cost and effort?

In considering our environment, some of the issues are:

- Are there barriers to communication and working together to solve problems?

- How successful have we been in achieving broader involvement in planning and decision making through organization in teams?

- How can we better foster a climate wherein a climate of mutual respect and trust is actively promoted?

- Given the change to team structures, do all staff have sufficient skills and practice in decision making, consultation and constructive criticism?

As we do not work directly with the public, it is sometimes difficult for us to see the effects of what we do (or don't do) in creating and maintaining the catalogue. It is possible for us to lose sight of our primary mission of providing efficient and effective access to Library materials.

The three fundamental purposes of the catalogue are:

- to uniquely identify what we have;

- to provide access points so that materials can be found in the catalogue; *and,*

- to provide a call number so that the item can be found on the shelf, or a URL so that access can be provided through an external link

These activities create information for our users to access materials in the library, using the catalogue. Everything that we do should relate in some way to one of these purposes.

In this document, we will examine what steps we can take to ensure that we continue to contribute to the achievement of the Library's vision and mission in a dynamic way. We need to develop a vision of our individual and collective work that will allow us to examine, evaluate and implement beneficial changes. This will also enable us to influence our environment to achieve continual improvement for the common good.

2.   Opportunities and Desired Outcomes

The primary goal of the Bibliographic Services Division is:

> to provide efficient, effective and integrated access to all of the information made available by or through the library, making the best use of allocated resources.

This goal flows directly from the second strategic goal of the University Library:

> To maintain and develop services so that Library users have integrated access to information resources, both local and remote, in a manner appropriate to their needs.

All staff members in the division need to have a common understanding of this primary goal of the division, and to appreciate how the work of all individuals and groups contributes to its achievement. If we are to take full advantage of the many opportunities inherent in contemporary bibliographic divisions and access systems, we need to:

- systematically *review procedures* to identify and resolve barriers which prevent materials being integrated into the collection as quickly as possible;

- *identify and balance work priorities* in such a way that core materials move through efficiently, and projects and changing needs can be accommodated;

- *examine the level of cataloguing* that we use for certain classes of materials to determine if changes can be made, so that the workload is reduced, and materials are available for use more quickly with records that still meet an acceptable level of quality and consistency;

- *enhance the team-work environment* such that initiative and the effective expression of opinions by all staff are encouraged, issues are discussed rationally and fully, and logical decisions that are reached collaboratively and by consensus are supported by all;

- *understand the range of decision making*, the responsibilities that attach to decisions, and the scope of decision making at each organizational level;

- *communicate our goals* to other divisions in the Library and to our other users, and be adaptable to changing our priorities as theirs change.

3.   The chart on page 217 identifies several objectives towards which we need to work so that the division can reach its primary goal. For each objective, a set of steps that will be necessary to achieve it and the outcomes (or results) that will flow from achieving it are noted. The achievement of these objectives will directly contribute to the improvements in our future work and environment. My vision of the future, which is reflected in the objectives, is as follows:

- materials move quickly through the division as a result of decisions being made by the appropriate person, in a timely manner

- materials are organized so that they can be located quickly when necessary

- work is performed only once, and in accordance with applicable standards and policies

- policies and standards which we use, and the decisions we make, will result from careful and balanced consideration of all factors (cost, efficiency, staff time, and users' needs)

- all of us will understand our individual roles in providing access to materials

- all of us are involved in the formation of the processes we use, and the decisions we make

- comments, opinions and constructive criticism are welcomed by all because we all have the ability to express our concerns in an appropriate manner

- we all help each other to achieve our individual and common goals.

4.   Processes to Achieve our Objectives

A steering committee will oversee this project to monitor our progress toward the expected outcomes. The committee will be chaired by the Division Director, and will consist of the Database Development Librarian, and one member of each of the two teams. This committee will begin its work in September 2000.

The chart on page 218 identifies the activities, steps, and time frames that are initially proposed. These will be fully discussed and modified as necessary prior to finalization, so that all staff understand the work that lies ahead. To ensure that our work contributes positively to the achievement of the Library's mission, we must continually be aware of opportunities to make that work more effective. This implies continuous change. It does not mean that the change has to be radical, or that there will be constant upheaval. Rather, it means that we need to thoughtfully assess what we presently do, to look for ways to do things better, and to understand how what is done will benefit the users of our catalogue and library.

These are not easy tasks. They require us to look critically at everything we do and how we do it, and begin from the premise that all issues can be openly and constructively discussed. When we are not used to this type of critical examination, it can be difficult and stressful. We need to remember, however, how much things have changed already, and the success we have had in adapting to those changes. We provided access to materials through card catalogue until just a few years ago, and we have already adapted to the changes that were imposed on us by the advent of automated cataloguing systems, the change from AACR1 to AACR2, and the advent of new formats and types of electronic materials. We have every reason to be confident in our ability to deal successfully with future change.

Divisional Objectives and Anticipated Outcomes

OBJECTIVE	STEPS TO ACHIEVE THE OBJECTIVE	OUTCOMES (RESULTS)
Workflow is improved and better integrated	• examine current processes and develop better alternatives • examine whether we need to do some of the things we currently do	• materials will move more quickly through the division to the user • problems will be resolved at the earliest appropriate level
The work environment is enhanced	• ensure that all staff have the skills to address problems • identify training that may be needed	• all staff members work together effectively • problems are addressed in a constructive and positive way
Users' needs are better met	• examine how our policies and procedures affect the user through a commonsense appraisal and consultation with public services staff • ensure that materials are processed as rapidly as possible	• greater appreciation of the work we perform by both users and other library staff • work clearly contributes to the achievement of library goals
Work is performed only once, and in the unit best positioned to do it	• enhance personal responsibility for individual work effectiveness • identify knowledge gaps, and initiate training as necessary • review work procedures, revise as necessary, and broaden understanding of their relationships • examine alternative organizational models	• greater sense of independence and accomplishment in individual work • improved organizational structure • staff in other divisions have confidence in the quality of our work
Technology is used to its fullest potential	• critically examine new ways of doing things by researching the literature and consulting with colleagues • use the full capabilities of the new workstations • create and maintain a web page for cataloguing resources • maintain policies and procedures in one place, up-to-date, and universally accessible	• automated, simplified processes work better than complex manual ones • staff freed from routine tasks to use unique knowledge and skills • equipment and software is used to its fullest potential
New forms of materials are readily integrated into the processing stream	• discuss ideas for handling new formats • discuss priorities for electronic products with public services staff • learn how other libraries deal with new formats	• ensures all formats of materials are dealt with in a timely manner • users' need for "the latest" or "the newest" is met

Processes to Achieve the Objectives

PROCESS	ACTIVITIES	TIME FRAME
Document the processes we are currently using, using flowcharts	• organize training on the purpose and use of flowcharts, and how to create them • decide what will be documented • prepare the flowcharts	• September, 2000 to January, 2001
Review the current work flows and the organization structure	• are they (work flows) straightforward and efficient? • do they make the best use of staff skills and time? • what tasks could be organized differently? • what "exceptions" cause delays? • is the size/volume of work matched with staff resources? • is our current organization optimal?	• February, 2001 to July, 2001
Examine our policies, procedures and standards	• evaluate service and access requirements • develop criteria for the review of policies, procedures, standards (*e.g.* Is an action required by local, national, or international standards? Does an action have a potential for use in a future system? etc.) • systematically evaluate policies, procedures and standards	• February, 2001 to July, 2001
Make decisions about what and how changes will be made	• consult with other staff and users • use the information gathered to make decisions • implement decisions, or recommend implementation to Library Administrative Committee, as appropriate	• September, 2001 to October, 2001
Review the results of the changes	• devise an evaluation plan to ensure that changes have achieved the expected results • fine-tune some things, or return to an issue for in-depth examination, as necessary	• December, 2001 to February, 2002

Appendix 9.2: Monograph with Partial Copy

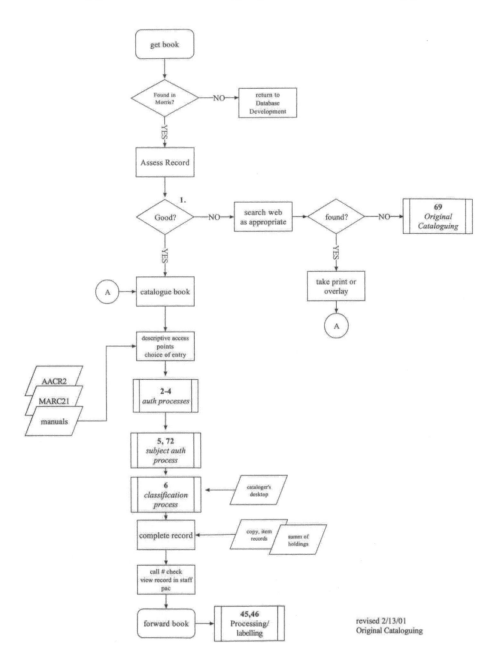

revised 2/13/01
Original Cataloguing

Appendix 9.3:
Bibliographic Services Plan: Progress Report

Prepared by Cheryl Martin, Director of Bibliographic Services
Date: April 4, 2002 (with regular updates to project status)–last update July 15/02

I. Introduction

II. Issues discussed in the flowchart analysis meetings

III. Next phase of the project

IV. Conclusion

Appendix: Specific issues discussed in the flowchart analysis meetings

I. Introduction

In 2000, Bibliographic Services staff members embarked on an ambitious plan to analyze work practices and the organization, to ensure that both supported our goal of providing effective service. It seemed an appropriate time for us as a division to take stock of where we have come from, where we are, and in which direction we need to go. The work that Bibliographic Services staff members do in providing and maintaining access to resources is of vital importance to the Library, which in turn forms an important core of the University's teaching and research functions. For the University to succeed in its mission, Library services and resources must be of the highest possible quality. Our work directly supports the service and resources offered to our users.

To ensure that our work practices and environment support effective service goals, several things needed to be done. To examine work practices, the steps included:

- review procedures to identify and resolve barriers to an efficient workflow (i.e., having materials available for use as quickly as possible)

- identify and balance work priorities so that regular work flows efficiently, and projects and changing needs can be accommodated

- examine the level of cataloguing, and make changes if necessary.

To begin to examine our environment and organization, there were "focus group" sessions in which all staff members in the Division were invited to discuss what is working well, what could be changed, and suggestions for improving or changing the situation. A consultant was hired to facilitate these sessions. They provided useful information about the positive aspects, problems and issues perceived by all staff who participated. Further training will be arranged, in order to support the goals and outcomes of this project.

This progress report documents issues raised in the discussions, and suggestions and conclusions which have been made based on the information gathered. Plans for further action are also documented.

Work Objectives

Bibliographic Services staff prepared flowcharts for many of the processes which take place in the Division, and analyzed the workflows to determine what is working well, if any changes needed to be made, or if there were any external factors affecting the efficiency of the workflow. The work of flowcharting and analyzing the resulting flowcharts was spread out over many months, and involved all staff in the Division. In all, 87 flowcharts were prepared from October 2000 to June 2001. The analysis meetings took place from August to December 2001.

Effective Service

To provide the most effective service to all our stakeholders, we must have a vision of how the Division should operate. As presented in the original document, the vision for Bibliographic Services includes:

- materials move quickly through the division as a result of decisions being made by the appropriate person, in a timely manner

- materials are organized so that they can be located quickly when necessary

- work is performed only once, and in accordance with applicable standards and policies

- policies and standards which are established, and the decisions we make, result from careful and balanced consideration of all factors (cost, efficiency, staff time, and users' needs)

- we understand our individual roles in providing access to materials

- we are involved in the formation of processes and decisions

- comments, opinions and constructive criticism are welcomed by all because we all have the ability to express our concerns in an appropriate manner

- we all help each other to achieve our individual and common goals.

When we talk to our stakeholders (other Library staff, students, faculty members, other McMaster staff, other universities and libraries, and the general public who use the library), they also have goals for us:

- make all materials available for use as quickly as possible

- materials should be easily located on the shelf or in the catalogue

- there are no errors in the cataloguing or physical processing that affect access and retrieval.

Our goals and those of our stakeholders are compatible, so it is reasonable to conclude that we have correctly established our goals.

II. Issues Discussed in the Flowchart Analysis Meetings

The flowchart analysis meetings took place over a period of several months. To reduce the number of meetings, related flowcharts were discussed at the same time, whenever possible. Usually, all staff members involved in the work of a particular flowchart participated in the analysis meeting. All staff members in the Division had the opportunity to be involved in the discussion of any flowchart, either by attending the meeting or by submitting comments.

The flowchart meetings were guided by a list of questions, meant to initiate discussion and ensure that similar information was gathered in each meeting. We wanted to document whether a particular process worked, both by itself and with its related processes. We also wanted to know if there were aspects of the process that should be changed, how it might be changed, and what effect this might have on other processes, both inside and outside the Division. It was difficult to discuss the process without discussing the work, and a great deal of information was gathered about work practices, policies, procedures, and standards.

The information gathered in the flowchart analysis has been summarized in the appendix to this report.

III. Next Phase of the Project

Based on the information gathered, it is clear that there are many things which can be done to create a more effective work environment in Bibliographic Services. Some of these are fairly easy to implement; others will take more time.

a) Within Bibliographic Services

The next steps in this process are:

- discuss and decide what changes will be made in the work

- evaluate whether the type and volume of work is matched with staff resources, and

- assess the appropriateness of the current organizational structure of the Division

Our next step is to discuss the information compiled, and make decisions about what changes will be made. Further information will likely be required, and more analysis or discussion of some issues will take place. There is still work to be done on the evaluation of policies and standards; some information was gathered during the flowchart analysis, but further discussion of issues such as levels of cataloguing and local policies must take place. While these discussions are important, they will not impact on some of the other initiatives, suggestions, and conclusions that are presented in this document.

We need to closely match our staff resources with the volume and type of work to be done, and organize our work structure to facilitate the achievement of our goals. A full discussion and understanding of the issues raised in the flowchart analysis will help with these discussions.

During the flowchart analysis, five main topics recurred as issues for further analysis:

- serials maintenance

- electronic resources cataloguing and maintenance

- government publications cataloguing

- ordering

- physical processing.

Our data suggests that there are some imbalances in the number of staff assigned to these areas, or in the workflow, which create barriers to the achievement of our goal of effective service. The volume of serials maintenance work cannot be dealt with when only one person is assigned to it. Electronic resources cataloguing and maintenance work will continue to increase and is of high priority for the Library, although the volume is impossible to predict at this time. We know that, at the very least, we must add URLs to records for government publications and maintain the URLs in the catalogue in a timely manner. Government publications cataloguing is done by several people who would benefit from a closer working relationship, both with each other and with those assigned to serials cataloguing and maintenance, since many government publications are serials. The order workflow would be more effective if the orders were not passed back and forth between Acquisitions and Bibliographic Services. There is a variety of physical processing being done throughout the Library, and this could be done more effectively if all physical processing was done to the same standard, and probably by the same group of people.

From our discussions, it is also clear that a comprehensive review of standards should begin as soon as possible. The process will include decisions about:

- should we change our copy searching standards and procedures?

- who should catalogue various formats and levels of material?

- what level and standards should be used for both copy and original cataloguing?

- what standards should be applied to authority establishment and verification?

- what standards should be established for physical processing?

Staff members will be involved in discussions in these areas. A time line and plan to address these issues will be developed in the near future.

b) Outside Bibliographic Services

Many of the problems which were identified in the flowchart analysis relate to the work of staff members in other Divisions. We all make decisions on the best solution to a problem or issue from our own perspective. Sometimes we don't take all aspects of the problem into consideration, or understand the impact on the work of other staff members. Sometimes the goals of the Bibliographic Services Division are incompatible with the goals of other Divisions: for example, a project done in another Division may create maintenance work in Bibliographic Services that we haven't included in our priorities. There are things that we do which might have been perfectly appropriate in the past but are no longer necessary given current technology, or not cost-effective based on our limited resources, or staff may not be available to perform some tasks.

A committee will be formed with representation from Reader Services, Collections, and Bibliographic Services, and chaired by the Director of Bibliographic Services. This will provide a forum for discussion of issues such as: decisions that affect the catalogue, prioritizing of material, and scheduling of projects. The committee will also form a plan and time line to address the issues documented in the appendix that involve divisions other than Bibliographic Services.

IV. Conclusions

A comprehensive review of the issues defined above, and discussions with staff members in other areas, will allow us to determine which procedures and special arrangements should be continued, and which ones should be ended. It will also help to determine cataloguing levels for all categories of material. Ideally, we would have unlimited resources to make any kinds of changes or special arrangements requested, and to catalogue everything at the highest level of completeness. In reality, our resources are limited and if we are to move ahead with projects and activities such as providing access to electronic resources, decisions need to be made concerning the most effective use of our time. This may mean that we stop doing some things because we cannot afford to do them, or denying some requests that we would have automatically granted in the past, or finding another way to complete the work. The cost of staff time is an important consideration in determining standards and levels for cataloguing and processing tasks. The volume of incoming materials in many areas of cataloguing and maintenance varies widely, and these changes in volume must be dealt with on an ongoing basis.

In 2001, the Library Users Committees identified several factors which affect their use of the Library. They are specifically concerned about the amount of time it takes for materials to be available for use. Brainstorming sessions were held with Acquisitions and Bibliographic Services staff to generate ideas on how materials could move more quickly through the order and cataloguing process. These ideas are being discussed by the management and supervisory staff in Acquisitions and Bibliographic Services. Some of the ideas and issues discussed in this document overlap with those discussed in the brainstorming sessions, so we are working on a consolidated approach to issues which affect the ordering and cataloguing processes.

The information gathered has shown that some changes are needed to ensure effective use of staff resources in Bibliographic Services. Some are small procedural changes, and others are more wide-ranging. The next step is to discuss these changes with staff members in Bibliographic Services, to ensure that they understand the need for change, the impact that it will have on them, and the benefits of more effective use of resources. This may require some training in new tasks or processes, especially since some of the changes potentially involve the reorganization of staff and evaluation of the team structure.

This report and subsequent plans will also be discussed with the Library Management Group, to ensure that they understand and support the kinds of changes being contemplated, and the impact of these changes on the Library.

Effective use of staff resources and an enhanced work environment in the Bibliographic Services Division will lead to greater satisfaction in the work accomplished, and satisfaction that our stakeholders are well served. Changes will also be felt in other areas of the Library, which may contribute to effective use of staff and physical resources throughout the Library.

Cheryl Martin
April 4, 2002

Appendix: Issues Discussed in the Flowchart Analysis Meetings

The goals to be achieved are as follows:

- the workflow is improved and better integrated

- work environment is enhanced

- work is performed only once, by the people best positioned to do it

- technology is used to its fullest potential

- new materials are readily integrated into the processing stream.

The issues have been organized by stakeholders:

• Bibliographic Services only (no other areas directly involved)

• Acquisitions

• All Library Divisions

• Outside the Library

The issues are listed in order of time to implement: short (less than six months) medium (6-12 months), or long term (more than 12 months). This is the time to implement from beginning the task. The details of each issue are explained, the stakeholders are listed, and a solution is suggested. Please note that these are suggested solutions, and will require discussion before any decisions are made.

Note that the term "stakeholders" assumes that Bibliographic Services staff members are included, so they have not been listed.

a) Bibliographic Services

Issue:	Searching for copy
Details:	Records used for ordering may not always be the best record to use for cataloguing the material. There are various interpretations of what is a "good" record, depending on the material and the cataloguer. Materials may be held for several months to see if copy appears. We should make full use of technology available to find copy.
Solution:	The process of searching for cataloguing copy must be reevaluated. We will establish guidelines that allow materials to move as quickly as possible with a minimum number of searches. Using copy is less expensive than original cataloguing, but waiting for copy past a certain time is counterproductive. Establish a cut-off time for copy searching, then catalogue the material with the record provided. Ensure that we are taking advantage of ways to search for copy, to find high-quality copy as quickly as possible.
Time:	Short
Status:	

Issue: Documentation of local policies for classification practice

Details: Develop an automated way of recording local practices for classifica-
                tion so that the cataloguer doesn't have to research the correct number.

Solution: Classification Web, when it is available, should resolve this issue. All
                staff members in Bibliographic Services have access to this product,
                but some training may be required.

Time: Short

Status: Class Web is available but we don't have our subscription as of July
                15/02. When it arrives we will begin on this project.

Issue: Sharing information

Details: Cataloguing tools should be reviewed at cataloguing meetings so that
                everyone is aware of changes and understands their application.

Solution: Subject headings lists, CSB and other information should be circu-
                lated to everyone. Staff members should take collective responsibility
                to bring changes or peculiarities to the attention of other staff mem-
                bers at cataloguing meetings.

Time: Short

Status: Have begun doing this as of July 15/02.

Issue: Changing materials in the collection to accept an LC cutter

Details: The practice has been to accept an LC cutter for all materials, and redo
                materials already in the collection to fit into the LC call no. index. This
                is a good practice in the literature collection because of the potentially
                large amount of material by the same author, but doesn't seem an ef-
                fective use of staff time when working in other areas of the collection.

Solution: Except in the literature collection, adjust all cutters to fit into the call
                no. index. Do not change cutters on material already in the collection
                unless there is a problem with the filing order.

Time: Short

Status:

Issue:	Some authorities are not up to date in Horizon
Details:	Authorities, especially for series and subjects, are not always up to date. Cataloguers may not be able to use the most current headings, or may ask more than once for corrections to the same heading. We can make more use of Validator and other products to add authorities to Horizon.
Solution:	Evaluate the processes used for series and subject authorities, and make changes necessary to ensure that the work is completed as quickly as possible. All staff members could download simple names from Validator, freeing the time of authorities staff to deal with more complex problems.
Time:	Medium
Status:	

Issue:	Knowledge of LC classification schedules
Details:	Some staff members have not been taught how to use the LC classification schedules, or have not been required to use them. Staff members sometimes don't notice errors because they are not familiar with the schedules.
Solution:	Provide training in the structure and formation of LC classification, to all staff members who need this knowledge.
Time:	Medium
Status:	

Issue:	Cutter conflicts
Details:	Database Development staff accept the cutter on LC copy, but if it doesn't fit in the call no. index they give it to a supervisor for resolution. Everyone should be able to adjust simple cutters to fit into the call no. index.
Solution:	There is general agreement that this is a reasonable solution. Only complex issues, such as double-cuttered material, should be referred to the supervisor.
Time:	Medium
Status:	

Issue:	Cataloguing of copy for different editions, copyright dates, publishers
Details:	These materials are presently done in Original Cataloguing, although they were catalogued in Database Development in the past. This function could be moved to back to Database Development.
Solution:	Assess training needs and move this function to Database Development. Often the copy is correct except for the publication information.
Time:	Medium
Status:	

Issue:	Treatment of non-LC copy
Details:	Non-LC copy is catalogued in Original Cataloguing or in Database Development, depending on the format; recon and replacements are the responsibility of Catalogue Services staff. Standards are inconsistent, especially for authority-controlled fields.
Solution:	Examine standards and ensure consistency. Decide who should catalogue non-LC copy, and provide training as required.
Time:	Medium
Status:	

Issue:	Authority checking and verification
Details:	The checking and verification of authorities should be consistent across the Division.
Solution:	Establish standards for authority work that apply to all materials. Develop training as necessary.
Time:	Long
Status:	

b) Collections (Acquisitions, Library Development, Collection Development, Shipping & Receiving)

Issue:	Changes of procedures in Acquisitions
Details:	Sometimes procedures are changed and we are not notified, or staff are asked to try something new without consultation with a Bibliographic Services supervisor.
Stakeholders:	Acquisitions
Solution:	Ongoing communication about policies and procedures, and consultation between supervisors when changes are contemplated, would help to ensure the best use of staff time.
Time:	Short
Status:	

Issue:	Duplicate serials
Details:	Serials are not always identified as duplicates, especially if they are received as gifts.
Stakeholders:	Development, Acquisitions
Solution:	Duplicate issues should be identified as such, no matter how they are acquired, so that they are processed correctly.
Time:	Short
Status:	

Issue:	Summary of holdings
Details:	A summary of holdings is created for all serials, and then deleted if the title has automated check-in.
Stakeholders:	Acquisitions
Solution:	Decide at point of receipt if the title will be automated, and do not create a summary of holdings unless necessary.
Time:	Short
Status:	

Issue: Use of pop-up notes in serials check-in

Details: Pop-up notes are used inconsistently in serials check-in. Materials with problems are sometimes given to Bibliographic Services staff instead of being resolved at the check-in stage.

Stakeholders: Acquisitions

Solution: Establish uniform standards for pop-up notes. Ensure that this information is provided when necessary so that the check-in process is as fast as possible, and only unresolved problems are sent to Bibliographic Services.

Time: Short

Status:

Issue: Printing of purchase orders

Details: The form presently used may not be necessary. Printing purchase orders using the laser printer would save an average of 5-6 hours of staff time per week.

Stakeholders: Acquisitions, Library Administrator

Solution: The Library Administrator should consult with the auditor to determine what records need to be kept, and in what format. Procedures can be changed depending on the decision.

Time: Short

Status:

Issue: Sorting of incoming material

Details: Sorting of material is time-consuming. Material is not always streamed to the correct location within the Division.

Stakeholders: Acquisitions

Solution: Discuss if there are any ways to stream material more accurately. Possibly, have all staff in Database Development sort the material as they change the status.

Time: Short

Status:

Issue:	Fund no. vs. location
Details:	The fund number is sometimes the only location information supplied on orders. This does not give us adequate location information for cataloguing. The fund number also does not tell us the library in which the material is to be located; some fund numbers are for material that could be in more than one library.
Stakeholders:	Collections, Acquisitions, Library reps
Solution:	The correct collection code and library location should be provided at the time of order or receipt, so work is done once and we don't have to stop to consult with Acquisitions or other staff members.
Time:	Medium
Status:	

Issue:	Processing of supplementary materials
Details:	Supplementary materials accompanying serials and monographs are treated differently.
Stakeholders:	Acquisitions
Solution:	All supplementary materials should be processed using the same standards, whenever possible.
Time:	Medium
Status:	

Issue:	Binding of music scores
Details:	Parts are bound separately. The score and parts must be sent back to Bibliographic Services for labelling after binding.
Stakeholders:	Shipping & Receiving
Solution:	Examine whether this process is cost-effective and takes full advantage of current binding technology. Consult with the vendor to determine if another method of binding/labelling is possible.
Time:	Medium
Status:	

Issue: Serials problems identified in Acquisitions

Details: Serials problems are sometimes given directly to staff in Biblio-
                    graphic Services, instead of being resolved by Acquisitions staff.
                    This includes problems identified at check-in, and decisions about
                    the retention of accompanying material.

Stakeholders: Acquisitions

Solution: Whenever possible, give problems to a supervisor or designated
                    staff member in Acquisitions; only pass on problems that need to
                    be resolved in Bibliographic Services. Consider whether access to
                    the cataloguing module would help.

Time: Medium to long

Status:

c) All Divisions in the Library (UL)

Issue: Use of range nos. for Thode periodicals

Details: Users complain that titles are not kept together when the title
                    changes. Bibliographic Services staff spend many hours updating
                    range numbers in the catalogue. Thode library staff spend many
                    hours moving materials around to create room for new titles.

Stakeholders: Thode staff, Thode library users

Solution: This is an issue with a long history of debate among Thode library
                    users. If titles must be kept in alphabetic order, discontinue range
                    numbers in the catalogue.

Time: Short

Status: Kathy and Cheryl to discuss.

Issue: Physical movement of materials

Details: Materials should be given to the appropriate person, whether it is
                    new material or something being returned for corrections.

Stakeholders: Acquisitions, Reader Services, Research Collections

Solution: Sorting of new material should be done at the point of receipt to
                    ensure that it is given to the appropriate person. All material being
                    returned from other Divisions for corrections should be sent to
                    Catalogue Services, not to a particular person.

Time:	Short
Status:	Liaison group to discuss.

Issue:	Reclassification policy
Details:	The present policy is that all editions of a work should be in the same class no. because users look for all editions to be in the same place. We must identify these and consult to see if other editions are to be withdrawn. Current material waits for a decision on material already in the collection.
Stakeholders:	Reader Services staff (mostly Heads of Circulation), Library users
Solution:	Ignore earlier editions with different class numbers when cataloguing. This will ensure that new material moves as quickly as possible. Other editions can be located using the catalogue.
Time:	Short
Status:	Elise, Vivian, Kathy and Cheryl will discuss.

Issue:	Barcode placement
Details:	At present, the barcode for non-circulating monographs is placed in the back of the book. All barcodes should be placed on the front cover of monographs.
Stakeholders:	Reader Services staff
Solution:	It is expensive and time-consuming to replace barcodes when material is moved to and from Reference. Horizon has a block on reference collection codes, so they cannot be signed out accidentally. Having all barcodes in the same place ensures consistency and eliminates the possibility of error in placing the barcode. Changes in labelling procedures for non-circulating material may also be necessary.
Time:	Short
Status:	Elise, Joan, Vivian and Cheryl will discuss.

Issue:	Use of flags

Details:	Flags are placed in material for various reasons. They are useful for locating material and ensuring that correct location is on the call no. label.
Stakeholders:	Acquisitions, Stacks Control
Solution:	We will continue to use flags for rush, Research Collections, Reference Thode, and Innis material. We will discontinue the use of other flags, such as the "do not check in" flag. Having all material checked in will solve the problem of "in process" or material checked out to Bibliographic Services being reshelved.
Time:	Short
Status:	Steven, Elise, Anne, Joan, and Vivian will discuss.

Issue:	Insurance forms and annotation of bibliographies for Research Collections materials
Details:	The cataloguer fills out insurance forms. She is also to annotate bibliographies in Research Collections. It's unclear why these duties should be performed by Bibliographic Services staff.
Stakeholders:	Research Collections
Solution:	Research Collections staff should fill out insurance forms. The cataloguer no longer annotates bibliographies.
Time:	Short
Status:	Carl and Cheryl discussed this on July 13/02. It was agreed that the cataloguer will continue to fill out the forms but the binders will be kept in Research Collections.

Issue:	Sorting of government publications
Details:	Serials are not always separated from monographs.
Stakeholders:	Gov pubs librarians, Acquisitions
Solution:	When sorting, gov pubs librarians should ensure that serials are sorted out, so they can be checked in and processed correctly.
Time:	Short
Status:	Donna Millard, gov pubs librarians, Donna Thomson and Cheryl will discuss.

Issue:	Project work in other Divisions
Details:	We need to know what projects are being planned in other Divisions, especially when they might affect the catalogue (for example, large stacks moves, amalgamation or separation of collections, recon projects, large donations).
Stakeholders:	Reader Services, Collections, Research Collections
Solution:	We need to assess the impact on the catalogue and on staff resources during the planning phase, to ensure that our part of the project can be completed in a timely manner. Sometimes substantial work must be done that we have not incorporated into our cataloguing, project, or maintenance schedules. A committee will be formed to discuss Bibliographic Services priorities and provide a forum for discussion of these issues (see p. 4 of this document).
Time:	Short
Status:	Liaison group will discuss.

Issue:	Public service databases or web pages
Details:	There are some conflicts between information contained in public service databases/web pages and the catalogue. We sometimes are expected to adapt our procedures or do extra work to ensure that information in the other product is correct. This has occurred with several local products, including the Research Collections web page and the submission of fonds records to ARCHEION, the Map Library database, and the gateway database.
Stakeholders:	Reader Services, Research Collections
Solution:	Horizon is the catalogue of record for the Library. We cannot support locally-developed products unless the decision to do so is made at the management level. When a decision has been made to support a product, we will work together to ensure that a minimum of extra work is required.
Time:	Short
Status:	Liaison group will discuss.

Issue: Requests for changes to the catalogue

Details: We receive requests with incomplete information. We also receive requests that should not be sent, or for which the staff member has not done the necessary research beforehand. Examples: requests to move or catalogue earlier issues of periodicals when we only keep the current issue, or to reclassify monographs without sending the material to us for relabelling.

Stakeholders: Reader Services, Research Collections

Solution: We will develop a form for bibliographic change requests. Requests that are incomplete will be returned. Some staff members need training in using the catalogue, especially in understanding serial records. If training or retraining needs are identified, the staff member and his/her supervisor will be notified.

Time: Short to Medium

Status: Liaison group will discuss.

Issue: Collection development structure

Details: Materials are ordered for the collection without vital information being supplied, such as determining if it's an added copy or volume, if it belongs in a reference collection, or what should be done with older editions of the work. We are also not explicitly told which library the material is for, and sometimes this is not clear.

Stakeholders: Collections, Acquisitions, Reader services, Library reps

Solution: The correct collection code and location information should be provided at the time of order or receipt. Work will be done once and we won't have to stop to consult with other staff members, or redo work because it's later decided that the material should be in a different location.

Time: Medium

Status: Deferred

Issue: Movement of rare Research Collections materials

Details: Materials do not follow the same procedure as all others, which affects workflow and causes extra work in retrieving materials. All materials are sent to Research Collections, and then the cataloguer must retrieve them.

Stakeholders: Research Collections

Solution: Provide the cataloguer with a locked cabinet to store rare or ex-
                  pensive materials in process, so they don't have to be transported
                  to and from Research Collections during the cataloguing process.

Time: Medium

Status: During our reorganization, we will provide the cataloguer with a
                  locked cabinet to store materials being worked on. (Cheryl and
                  Carl, July 13/02)

Issue: Maps as periodical supplements

Details: Maps are separated from their periodicals and sent to the Map Li-
                  brary. Other supplementary materials stay with their titles.

Stakeholders: Map Librarian, other Reader Services staff members, Library us-
                  ers

Solution: Examine whether the extra work involved in separating maps
                  from other supplementary material and treating them differently is
                  an efficient use of staff resources.

Time: Medium

Status: Cathy Moulder and Cheryl will discuss.

Issue: Examine score binding

Details: The present score binding method is expensive and cumbersome,
                  and creates extra work for staff members and users. Staff mem-
                  bers must create multiple item records and labels, and shelve mul-
                  tiple thin items with the call no. label on the front. Users looking
                  for music with many parts must spend time locating the score and
                  all of the parts, which may not be shelved together.

Stakeholders: Stacks Control, Bindery assistant, Music collection users

Solution: Examine a cost-effective and user-friendly method, such as putt-
                  ing the parts in a pocket in the back of the score. Have the binder
                  put the call no. on the spine of the score, to aid in shelving and re-
                  trieval. Consult with the binder about alternative options for bind-
                  ing music scores.

Time: Medium to long

Status: Elise, Nora, Lorna and Steven will discuss.

Issue: Local practices

Details: Local practices cause extra work. Material moves most quickly when local practices are kept to a minimum. It is less efficient to have local practices which are not decided upon until the material is catalogued and processed (for example, the use of "Z" in class numbers).

Stakeholders: Reader Services, Acquisitions, Research Collections, Library users

Solution: Reduce or eliminate local practices, with the goal of cataloguing and processing material as quickly as possible. Any local practices which must be applied must be decided upon at point of order or receipt.

Time: Medium to long

Status: Liaison group will discuss.

Issue: Responsibility for physical processing

Details: Various types of physical processing are done throughout the Libraries, using various standards of processing and materials (tape, other labels, etc.) When something is moved to another location, we must remove the local processing, and new local processing may be added when the item arrives.

Stakeholders: Reader Services, Acquisitions

Solution: All processing done outside Bibliographic Services should be discontinued. We will identify the types of local processing being done, and work with staff members in other Divisions to eliminate it altogether, or have the work done when the material is processed to avoid rework.

Time: Medium

Status: Liaison group will discuss.

Issue: Consultation between staff members

Details: Various issues about who to consult about what

Stakeholders: Reader Services, Collections, Research Collections, Systems

Solution:	Staff members outside the Division should talk to a Bibliographic Services supervisor before asking a staff member in the Division to change a policy or procedure, or informing a staff member that one of their policies or procedures has changed, or doing major work on hardware or software. This will ensure that the implications of a solution are adequately addressed, and that all affected are informed or consulted.
Time:	Medium
Status:	

Issue:	Collection policy for retention of supplements and special issues, and reporting missing issues
Details:	The collection policy about what is kept and what is thrown out is unclear, especially for material such as annual buyers' guides and other supplements. There are no clear guidelines for reporting missing issues so that they are indicated in MORRIS.
Stakeholders:	Periodicals, Collections
Solution:	The collection policies should be explicit about what is kept, so that a decision does not have to be made for each title. We will develop a problem reporting form to be used to report missing issues.
Time:	Medium
Status:	

Issue:	Barcode number problems
Details:	Barcodes do not have a check digit, so problems in entry can easily occur. Scanners are inaccurate and sometimes scan the number incorrectly, either because of the quality of the scanner or the quality of the barcodes.
Stakeholders:	Systems, Mills Circulation Manager
Solution:	Investigate whether the barcodes or the scanners are causing the problem. If possible, use barcodes with a check digit. Purchase high-quality scanners which read the number with a lower error rate than those currently used.
Time:	Medium
Status:	Check digit has been activated.

Issue: Access to other modules

Details: Staff members should have access to all other modules, to see in-
                  formation that they might not see in their "usual" module. Most
                  staff members could make use of a MARC display and the serials
                  modules if they were available to them, and could resolve prob-
                  lems themselves.

Stakeholders: Acquisitions, Reader Services, Research Collections, Systems

Solution: Investigate whether a MARC display can be provided in iPac. If
                  not, give read-only access to the cataloguing and serials modules
                  to all staff. Provide training as necessary.

Time: Medium

Status:

Issue: Use of label program

Details: The label program does not transfer complete information; the la-
                  bel must be edited so that we must continue to write the call no. in
                  the back of the book. It cannot be used for CODOC numbers be-
                  cause they don't transfer properly. It is also not used for serials.

Stakeholders: Acquisitions, Systems

Solution: Explore the development of a more effective label program. Ex-
                  pand the use of the program to other materials, if possible.

Time: Medium to long

Status:

Issue: Labels and security

Details: We use a large number of labels, stamps, and security strips, espe-
                  cially for non-book materials. The cost involved may not be justi-
                  fied, and a reduced level might achieve the same result.

Stakeholders: Reader Services

Solution: Consult with other libraries about their security and labelling practices.
                  Ensure that the minimum of labels, stamps, and security are used.

Time: Medium to long

Status:

Issue:	Electronic resources
Details:	Information about electronic resources is not always available, or shared. Sometimes other aspects of the acquisition of products are not considered, such as the retention and location of manuals and other paper accompanying materials.
Stakeholders:	Systems, Acquisitions
Solution:	Create a form (either paper or web-based) to ensure that all information about a product is recorded and available for everyone to see. This information will be more easily available when the gateway database is fully developed.
Time:	Medium to long
Status:	

Issue:	Wider sharing of policies
Details:	All Divisions need to share policies that affect others. Reader Services policies concerning the use of "Z" in the classification number, and what music materials belong in each of the reference collections, are not fully understood. Material which is sent back to Bibliographic Services for reclassification and/or relabelling could be done correctly the first time if these decisions were made at the point of order or receipt.
Stakeholders:	Reader Services, Collections, Research Collections
Solution:	Greater use should be made of Division web sites and the staff web site. Policies should be shared, and affected staff members should be consulted and/or informed when policies change. Policies should also be made by departments or Divisions as much as possible, not by individuals, to ensure consistency.
Time:	Medium to long
Status:	

d) Outside the Library (Other Parts of the University, HSL)

Issue:	Theses
Details:	Bibliographic Services staff check the accuracy of the paperwork that accompanies theses, and ensure that the student has graduated before cataloguing his/her thesis.
Stakeholders:	Graduate Studies
Solution:	Graduate Studies is responsible for ensuring that the paperwork is complete, and that only theses for graduating students are submitted to the Library. They will be consulted about whether we also need to check this work.
Time:	Short
Status:	

Issue:	Coordinate standards, policies and procedures with HSL
Details:	Different standards, policies and procedures make the catalogue confusing, especially for faculty and students who use both UL and HSL resources. When we want to extract data to use in other places such as the gateway database, the differences cause problems in extracting data and making full use of it. We use separate records for all materials except electronic resources.
Stakeholders:	HSL
Solution:	We should work towards the goal of having uniform policies, procedures and standards, and using one record for identical items. Regular discussion and decision meetings would ensure the coordination of standards and policies.
Time:	Medium
Status:	Mary Anne and Cheryl will have regular meetings (at least every 2 months) and ensure that rule interpretations, policies, etc. are similar.

Appendix 9.4: Bibliographic Services Division, Options for Organizational Structure, April 2002

ORGANIZATIONAL OBJECTIVE OR ISSUE/PROBLEM TO BE RESOLVED	OPTION A 3 SECTIONS (Current Structure)	OPTION B 2 SECTIONS: ① Original/Serials/Authorities ② Copy/Maintenance/Projects	OPTION C 2 SECTIONS: ① Monographs/Spec. Mat'ls./Projects/Maintenance ② Serials/Gov. Pub'ns./Electronic/Authorities
① Consistent standards can be applied across all formats	✓ (maybe)	✓ (maybe)	✔
② Staff cataloguing the same formats have a close working relationship and can benefit from the knowledge and experience of others	✓ (maybe)	✓ (maybe)	✔
③ Staff develop greater expertise in a smaller number of formats	✗	✗	✔
④ Principal cataloguer role is supported	✗	✗	✔
⑤ Ability to adapt easily to changing priorities for cataloguing and maintenance	✓ (maybe)	✓ (maybe)	✔
⑥ Serials maintenance function has appropriate number of staff assigned	✗	✗	✔
⑦ Electronic maintenance: ability to respond to changing volume and complete work quickly	✓ (maybe)	✗	✔
⑧ Staff working on gov. publ'ns. have a close working relationship with each other and with serials cataloguing and maintenance	✗	✗	✔
⑨ Easier to create cross-training opportunities and ability to help with priority tasks	✗	✓ (maybe)	✓ (maybe)

> ✓ = Maybe, or partly ▪ ✗ = No ▪ ✔ = Yes

April 23, 2002

Appendix 9.5: Bibliographic Services Division, Organization Chart (1999–2002)

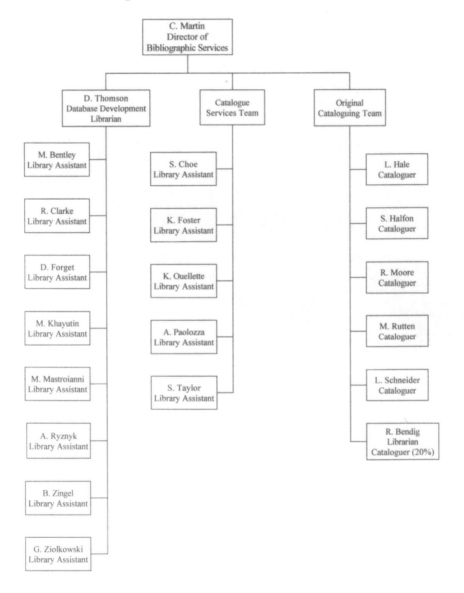

Appendix 9.6: Bibliographic Services Division, Organization Chart (2003–)

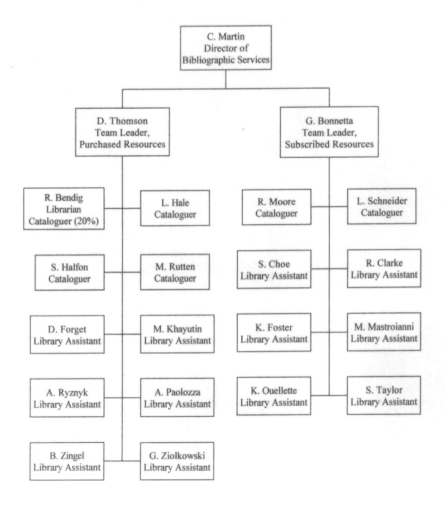

10

Centering Technical Services: Developing a Vision for Change at Union College

Annette M. LeClair

Editor's note: The author describes how proactive change and examination of challenges can be used to position a library department for an active and important role in its organization. Initiating the power of a vision for the future, or a vision statement, in which leadership, collaboration, and flexibility are the rule instead of the exception, the author documents actual examples of successfully getting a new position in the department, beginning the process of training/retraining support staff, and influence on the space planning and floor plans of new workspaces for the department. This chapter is an excellent case study of the power of proactive planning and leadership, rather than reactive response and action, as a model for dealing with change and reorganization.

Change has been a constant in the long history of the Technical Services department at Union College's Schaffer Library. As part of an innovative liberal arts institution that has a 200-year history of its own, the library's information processing team has frequently had to transform itself in response to changes in the College's priorities, publishing practices, and standards for bibliographic control. Long before the electronic information explosion, long even before the advent of the interactive bibliographic networks that revolutionized day-to-day cataloging operations, the library was constantly expanding the types of resources it collected and searching for better ways to organize them. Handwritten lists of the books acquired while Union was pioneering the integration of science, engineering, modern languages, and political studies into the classical curriculum in the nineteenth century gradually became handwritten catalog cards, then typed or preprinted ones, before the online catalog became the primary means of finding the ever more diverse material in the library's collections. Every set of national cataloging rules, starting with the 1889 edition of Charles Cutter's *Rules for a Dictionary Catalogue*, was carefully acquired, analyzed, and adapted to meet local needs. Use of the Dewey Decimal Classification system for the general collections gave way to that of the Library of Congress in the 1970s. Throughout these decades of change, and under a variety of names and management styles, a well-staffed Technical Services department emerged to provide a wide variety of acquisitions, cataloging, and serials management services to the library and the campus community. By the mid-1990s its four professional librarians and seven full-time support staff members (out of a total library staff of 13 librarians and 15 full-time support staff) were expert both in their work and in the process of adapting themselves to institutional and professional change.

Despite this record of success, the department faced unprecedented challenges in the last decade of the twentieth century that demanded a new approach to the ways in which it managed change. Some of these challenges were particular to Union College, others were common among libraries of many types and sizes, but all presented themselves simultaneously in the middle years of the decade. Within the Schaffer Library Technical Services department, a hierarchical organizational structure once established to highlight the professional expertise of its Catalog librarian had begun to prove isolating and an awkward fit for new information management needs. The sudden and tragic loss of several long-term staff members revealed gaps in documentation as well as in the department's ability to handle all varieties of incoming material in a knowledgeable, efficient manner. In the same time period, the library began work on a major building renovation and construction project. This project required the relocation of the Technical Services department throughout construction as well as hard thinking about the ways in which staff space would be allocated in the new building.

Meanwhile, the College was placing new emphasis on its long-standing tradition of promoting research by its approximately 2,000 FTE undergraduates. To support this emphasis, all librarians were invited to participate in expanded instructional programs, much as they were already participating in weekend service at the reference desk. The College was also beginning to emphasize greater efficiency in its administrative operations. Although fundraising for the library building and other College projects was proceeding well, the practice of outsourcing selected library functions was gaining national attention, and the library was asked to consider whether aspects of its technical processing services might be candidates for this approach to reduce ongoing operational expenses. In addition, any staff vacancies were to be carefully reexamined before permission to fill would be considered. All of these issues were being raised at the same time that the Internet was becoming a central source of information for academic research. Schaffer Library sought first to integrate access to electronic information with access to its more traditional research material, and then to become a presence on the Internet itself. Yet, with the College's lean approach to staffing at the end of the century, it was clear that no additional personnel could be hired to assume these growing responsibilities.

What was new in the approach that the Technical Services department took in response to these many challenges was threefold. First, the department decided to take the initiative in developing proposals for change, rather than simply reacting to the challenges directed its way. This is not to say that the department had never been proactive in the past. But it began extending its reach in the mid-1990s consciously, energetically, and consistently. For example, the problems of how to incorporate electronic resources into the library's collections and develop an effective library Web site were—and remain—library-wide issues. But rather than waiting to be asked what they might contribute, the Technical Services librarians proposed and committed resources to a working solution that consciously transformed the department's mission while still affirming the value of the services that it had been providing all along. This decision to become proactive energized the department at many times when the problems it faced might otherwise have seemed overwhelming. Second, the department developed a vision of its future that assumed that *change* would remain the primary constant in its work. When tackling any administrative task, the librarians decided that they would meet the immediate need but also assume that even more radical change might be needed ahead. This vision had the effect of ensuring that each challenge would be met with the broadest kind of thinking, not only about the problem at hand but about what Technical Services at Union College might and should become in the future. Third, the librarians decided to face these challenges collegially in all senses of the word. They would operate and make department-wide decisions as a team of colleagues, and they would do so with a focus centered on their role within the College community.

Flexibility in serving the mission of the College as a whole quickly became the standard by which any response to a challenge would be measured. The Technical Services department's investigation of options for outsourcing provides an example of how this thinking worked. Following a detailed study of its operations, the department was able to demonstrate to itself as well as to the library and College administrations that it was already outsourcing all of the work that it effectively could by utilizing OCLC, book and serial vendors, and the functionality of its ILS. But it also determined that one of the chief factors preventing it from outsourcing much of anything else was the nature and history of the College itself. The library's extensive Special Collections department contains many rare materials (particularly those in the College archives or produced by student researchers) that require a knowledgeable College employee to catalog and process. Reaffirming its role in providing access to these unique materials, the Technical Services department also recognized that its future might well involve the development of additional services to this busy area. Perhaps it could begin processing manuscript collections as part of its acquisitions services or help create finding aids in the Cataloging unit. Rather than threatening department operations, additional outsourcing of routine tasks could free up the time of skilled staff members to begin working on these new enterprises. Thus the department has remained flexible on the topic of outsourcing, on the alert for appropriate opportunities, knowing that in future it could become the means by which improved access may be offered to important research materials that are currently known only to a few at the College.

At no time from the mid-1990s through the present has the Technical Services department created a single master plan or blueprint for the future that covered all aspects of its operations. But its determination to be proactive, prepare for change, and keep its attention focused on the particular kinds of contributions that it can make to the library and the College has helped it to implement a number of major projects that have affirmed the centrality of its place in both. In the process, the department has transformed itself from a hierarchical organization best equipped to handle traditional research materials into a cooperative unit that provides leadership to the campus and beyond in organizing and accessing all kinds of information resources. This transformation has had three closely related aspects: professional staff reorganization and development, support staff development, and space planning and design. Coordinated by constant discussion of how the department might extend its reach beyond its traditional roles and into the future, these projects were all instigated and largely accomplished by the staff of the Technical Services department itself.

Professional Staff Reorganization and Development

The organization in place in the Technical Services department at the beginning of the 1990s divided its work into two main branches, Cataloging and Acquisition/Periodicals (see Figure 10.1). Two professional librarians were in the Cataloging unit, one in Acquisitions/Periodicals. All three librarians nominally reported to the head of Technical Services. Within the Cataloging unit, however, the professional catalog librarian also reported to, and received all work direction from, the head of Cataloging. All support staff in the Cataloging unit also reported to the head of Cataloging; the Catalog librarian directed the work of no other staff members. This arrangement had been developed to free the attention of the catalog librarian to create original catalog records, oversee authority control processes, and solve complex cataloging problems. But it often created conflicting lines of authority when support staff assistance or questions were involved. In addition, the Catalog librarian was the only librarian at the College who reported to a librarian other than the library director or a department head. No matter how cordial relations might be within the department, the Catalog librarian often felt overlooked within the library as a whole and worried that the position, rather than seeming privileged, looked like one of secondary importance within the hierarchy.

The reasons behind the librarians' differing levels of autonomy were particularly difficult to articulate given the fact that the head of Cataloging and the

Catalog librarian shared responsibility for processing Special Collections material and thus for creating some kinds of original catalog records, as well as for aspects of authority control. By the time that the library was beginning to acquire electronic resources and a wider range of multimedia titles in the mid-1990s, it was becoming increasingly difficult to assign professional responsibilities equitably and to train and organize support staff accordingly.

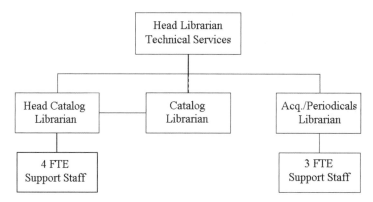

Figure 10.1. Schaffer Library Technical Services Organization, Early 1990s.

An unexpected vacancy in the head of Cataloging position precipitated another kind of crisis. Not only had much of the long-term memory of department projects and procedures vanished; the library could no longer be assured that the vacancy would be filled. Instead of trying to defend or restore the status quo, however, the remaining librarians in Technical Services met to discuss what their long-term focus should be and to consider whether a different organizational structure might serve it better. They quickly reached a number of conclusions about the kinds of challenges they would be facing in the years ahead. Regular cataloging work (as the recent exploration of outsourcing options had confirmed) was becoming an ever more efficient process, requiring less and less intervention by a librarian on staff. However, electronic and multimedia information products were presenting the library with complex organization-and-access issues. Such information formats were also likely to predominate in future. Technical expertise was already badly needed for the library to develop a Web site that would fully represent all that it had to offer. Special Collections would continue to require onsite cataloging expertise, in an expanded form if possible, well into the future. Collaborative work with the Public Services librarians on Web site development and on promoting special collections would become increasingly important. To face all of these challenges, it was clear that the librarians in Technical Services would need to organize themselves as a team of equals, all equally engaged in developing the kinds of services that the library would need.

The most immediate outcome of this discussion was a proposal from the Technical Services department in 1995 that the head of Cataloging position be replaced with a new position, which was eventually given the title "Electronic Media Librarian". The new librarian's primary responsibilities would be developing access to electronic and multimedia sources, including coordinating the establishment and maintenance of the library's Web site. The Catalog librarian would become the new administrator of the Cataloging unit and receive assistance from the head of Technical Services in developing services to Special Collections. Both the Electronic Media and Catalog librarians would have their own support staff assistants, who would report to them directly. The Acquisitions/Periodicals librarian's responsibilities would remain largely unchanged, but all four librarians would begin meeting on a regular basis to discuss new enterprises and to begin making better use of the current and potential connections among staff and procedures at all levels in the department.

The Schaffer Library administration had no difficulty in first approving this reorganization of its Technical Services department and then obtaining permission from the College to fill the new Electronic Media librarian position. The benefits of being able to hire a professional librarian to work on electronic products and on the library's Web site without having to add to total staff levels were obvious. Imbedded in the new job description, however, were two additional experimental responsibilities whose origin was in the department's vision that further changes in its role within the library and on the campus might well prove fruitful to all. One was that the Electronic Media librarian was to "serve as a primary link between the Technical and Public Service departments for the processing and distribution of electronic and multimedia information sources" and the other was that the new librarian would place a high emphasis on "train[ing] other Technical Services and library staff as well as the College community" in electronic products and applications. These efforts at bridge-building and outreach were consciously made to try to move the expertise of the Technical Services staff beyond its previous boundaries and to make its personnel more visible partners within the library and on campus. But it was also hoped that the department's services would become better informed and could hence be improved through closer contacts between its staff and the other librarians, faculty, and students for whom those services are designed.

A number of small adjustments to the reorganization have been made since it was first proposed. These have generally been in the area of support staff assignments and oversight for the processing of standing orders, which continue to require coordination among all areas of Technical Services. But the new three-unit organization—Cataloging, Electronic Media, and Acquisitions/Periodicals—still thrives, as do the principles that all librarians have equal standing, work as a team, and have independent responsibility for supervising members of the support staff (see Figure 10.2).

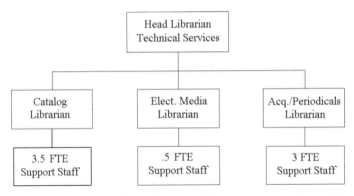

Figure 10.2. Schaffer Library Technical Services Organization, 2003.

The rewards of the department's new collaborative approach and of its leadership in providing access to electronic resources have been wide-ranging. First among them is increased participation by all librarians in department decision making and project planning. Biweekly meetings of the four librarians are now organized and facilitated by each of the librarians on a rotating basis, a system that encourages everyone to participate in agenda-setting and discussion of department concerns. Pursuing together the department's vision that closer contacts with the public are mutually productive, the Technical Services librarians as a group have also increased the level of their participation in reference, bibliographic instruction, and campuswide training programs. Even before the reorganization, all of the librarians at Schaffer Library had shared responsibility for weekend reference desk service, but afterwards a number in Technical Services began to volunteer for up to four additional weekday hours to improve their skills or help out at busy times. During one academic year, the Catalog librarian also contributed 10 hours a week to front-line services in the Special Collections department. This experiment had as its goal better understanding of the information access needs in that area of the library, so that Technical Services as a whole could begin thinking more knowledgeably about developing new kinds of support. All four librarians also voluntarily participate in bibliographic instruction and/or library orientation programs. Depending on their other commitments, their participation may be minimal or extensive during any given term. But the Public Services staff has come to know that they can count on their colleagues in Technical Services to help meet the demand for instruction services to the College's increasingly active body of student researchers, who not only regularly present their work in campus symposia but typically constitute one of the largest groups at the annual National Conference on Undergraduate Research.

The Electronic Media librarian in particular has also become a leader in campuswide instruction services. From offering one-on-one sessions in faculty offices on new electronic products to co-teaching (with staff from the College's Information Technology Services department) week-long classes for faculty on developing course-related Web sites, this librarian has taken the training aspect of the position well beyond its "back room" beginnings. Following the department's new collaborative planning model, the Electronic Media librarian has also worked with staff from several library departments to test new information processing and delivery systems. Among these experiments has been the participation by librarians from a number of different departments in the founding phase of the OCLC CORC project and the successful application for a grant to test methodologies for digitizing images in the Special Collections department.

Most successful of these collaborations has been the Electronic Media librarian's work with the Public Services and Systems librarians on the development of the Schaffer Library Web site (http://www.union.edu/library). The development of this site has been a team effort from the beginning, coordinated by a committee under the direction of the Electronic Media librarian and informed by input from all areas of the library. Continual enhancement of Web site content has made the working relationship between the Electronic Media and Bibliographic Instruction librarians particularly close. Combining technical expertise with a vision centered on the educational mission of the College, this team has produced a far-reaching site that both reflects and serves the diverse interests of the academic program and the campus community. Its high quality and breadth of coverage have already won the site and members of its design team four national awards for different aspects of its development, including a Reference and Adult Services Division of the American Library Association/Facts on File award for its presentation of primary source documents on current affairs (1995), a *Library Hi Tech* award in the "General Reference" category (1998), a Gale Research/Ethnic and Multicultural Information and Exchange Round Table award of the American Library Association for its links to multicultural resources (1999), and a *netConnect* Library Web Site Award for the contribution that the site has made to the organization of the Web as a whole (2002).

Support Staff Development

The librarians in Technical Services could not have re-imagined and reorganized themselves as a team, much less found the time to work on these new enterprises, without finding more efficient ways to manage the day-to-day work of the department. This necessity has been particularly acute in the Cataloging unit, where the most significant reorganization occurred. The department first realized significant time savings when it stopped producing and maintaining redundant card files. The librarians also revised selected procedures, such as those for withdrawing books from the collection, to delegate more of the routine work to student assistants. But the most important factor in the transformation of the department, other than the reorganization at the professional librarian level, has been retraining the support staff and providing them with the means to handle a wider array of contemporary information formats themselves.

As a first step, the time of one of the assistants in Cataloging was redefined to assist with the maintenance of electronic resources and of the Web site in particular. The individual selected for this split position had already worked in the unit for many years but was comfortable with change and willing to learn. A training program focused on Web authoring tools and other pertinent protocols, and software was developed by the Electronic Media librarian, utilizing off-site as well as on-campus instruction programs whenever possible. The new skills associated with this position have proved invaluable tools in meeting the department's new commitment to maintaining electronic information resources. Ongoing duties of the position include adding selected electronic titles and full text journals to the online catalog, reviewing URL checker reports, and updating links in the catalog and on the library's Web site. Future possibilities include scanning documents in aid of Special Collections digitization projects and taking on some of the more routine tasks associated with the administration of electronic subscription services.

Initially, the idea of creating other specialized positions of this kind seemed attractive because it was easy to train one person at a time and fund off-site training opportunities when necessary. Consequently, when the Technical Services reorganization was first implemented, the department assigned the processing of all audiovisual and multiformat materials to an individual support staff member as well. The notion of proliferating specialized assignments quickly became unworkable, however, when tested against the standard that *change* is inevitable in all aspects of technical service work. It was clear that the skills of any staff member accustomed only to print would become outmoded very rapidly in a world of rapidly changing information formats. In addition, the Technical Services department had been working throughout the reorganization period to upgrade its support staff positions, emphasizing the sophistication of the staff members' information processing skills and their overall contributions to the organization of knowledge both at the College and around the world via OCLC. These efforts had met with considerable success: Four of the seven support staff positions were upgraded mid-decade, one in Cataloging, one in the split Cataloging/Electronic Media position, and two in Acquisitions/Periodicals. But this very success made it seem likely that, in future, the careers of individuals in traditional positions would once again start falling behind those of colleagues working with newer formats and challenges.

Looking even further ahead, it also seemed likely that the department would need to increase the number of support staff hours or even positions assigned to electronic and multimedia formats as the universe of digital information continues to expand. Since the possibility of being able to add positions to the library remains remote, any skills needed in future would probably have to be developed among current staff. Ultimately, the Technical Services librarians felt that all support staff should participate in the changes occurring around them. It simply made sense to train everyone so that materials in all formats could be processed efficiently no matter who might be in the office or on vacation at any time during the year. Undertaking the retraining program would also help the department to prepare proactively for its own imagined future. And on an individual level, it seemed the only equitable way to encourage collegiality among staff members, continue to increase their standing within the institution, and keep each one of them competitive on the wider job market.

Thus the decision was made in the late 1990s to retrain all support staff members in Cataloging so that no one would be left behind and all would become knowledgeable, adept handlers of all information formats. This effort took over two years as each format (videotapes, DVDs, compact discs, books with accompanying software, and so on) was addressed in turn. A series of in-house staff meetings, training sessions, and practice "weeks" was devoted to the project. By far the most effective aspect of the retraining program, however, was the development of Web-based, interactive documentation for processing materials in each of the nonprint formats currently collected by the College. The documentation for each format covers general cataloging policies and procedures; specific editing instructions for MARC bibliographic records; and step-by-step, illustrated directions for physical processing. All of the librarians contributed at various times to the drafting and coding of these procedures, which are now under the oversight of the Catalog librarian. Mounted on the Technical Services section of the library's Web site, with hotlinks to related documentation at Union as well as at remote sites, they are frequently updated but provide a stable point of reference whenever procedures change or new formats need to be added. The initial investment by the librarians in designing the retraining program and preparing the Web-based documentation has paid off in the increased efficiency and independence with which both support staff and students process materials that used to wait for a professional librarian's attention. But it has also had unexpected dividends in extending the influence of the Technical Services department beyond Union College. Colleagues at regional meetings have commented that they often turn to Schaffer Library's documentation on nonprint materials when faced with an unfamiliar format, using the hospitality of the Web to access instructions designed with that very situation in mind.

Space Planning and Design

The third and perhaps most permanent form of transformation in the Technical Services department over the past decade has been in the physical space that it occupies. The $18 million building renovation project undertaken by Union College in the mid-1990s affected all areas of library service. The oldest part of the building was gutted and reconfigured, the section formerly housing Technical Services was demolished, and a new three-story extension was added. Technical Services staff and operations were relocated to another building on campus during the entire construction phase from 1996 through 1998. This massive fundraising and planning project was managed by College and Schaffer Library administrative staff. The overall building design was by the firm of Perry Dean Rogers. But input from faculty, students, and the library staff on space needs and layout was solicited from the project's inception, and the Technical Services staff had a direct impact on the final design in two key areas: the location of the Technical Services office and the interior arrangement of the office itself. The Technical Services team was ultimately persuasive on these points by once again being proactive, focusing on their vision for change, and promoting a view of the department that was centered on the essential services that it provides to the College community.

The initial proposal from the architects was that the Technical Services office be located on the second floor of the library, along an outside wall that had pleasant views but was shut off from the rest of the library by a large block of book stacks. The Technical Services staff, accustomed to a "rear guard" location in the old building that was, however, on the first floor along with the Reference and Circulation desks and other public service points, immediately felt that this location was isolating as well as inconvenient for the flow of materials throughout the building. The remote location was certainly workable in a technical sense, especially given the fact that during the construction project the department would prove that basic processing services could be run from an entirely different building if needed. But what the Technical Services librarians in particular found troubling was the way in which the second floor location "hid" them as partners in the academic enterprise and perpetuated the notion that technical services are only about processing materials behind the scenes. Absent from the design was any ease in sending faculty or students to speak to someone in Technical Services about a book order, missing periodical, or upcoming bibliographic instruction session. Absent was any ready ability on the part of the Technical Services department to offer on-the-spot support to colleagues at the Reference Desk who might be pursuing a question about the catalog, or seeking help in accessing a newly acquired electronic product. Absent most of all was any physical representation of the department's own vision of itself as a changing enterprise, one that could help the academic program to thrive by interweaving technical and instructional expertise in an ever-growing number of direct services to the campus community.

The Technical Services librarians' protest at the lack of visibility and flexibility in the second floor location, combined with their practical concern about the inconvenience of managing materials in nonadjacent areas of the library, eventually persuaded the designers to find space for the Technical Services office on the first floor of the new addition. The office is now centrally located among a suite of service points that includes the Government Document librarian's office as well as the Reference Desk, the Circulation Desk, and a large Periodicals Reading Room whose current materials are maintained by the Acquisitions/Periodicals unit (see Figure 10.3, page 258). To fit into this area, which is slightly smaller than the area it had requested in the new building program, the Technical Services department sacrificed space within its walls for a preservation lab that it had planned to host for both general and special collections. This lab was built on the third floor of the renovated library instead, in a location near the Special Collections department that is arguably just as convenient for the range of activities that now take place there. Technical Services personnel remained very much involved in planning and outfitting the lab, and in consequence it now houses sophisticated scanning and other computer equipment needed for the digital reproduction of documents as well as the more traditional tools needed for book repair.

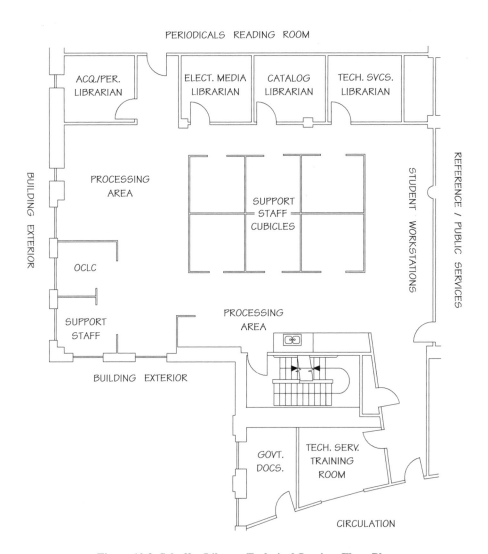

Figure 10.3. Schaffer Library Technical Services Floor Plan.

Once the question of basic location was settled, work began on the interior arrangement of the Technical Services area. In keeping with plans for other professional librarian offices in the building, the program called for the installation of separate offices (120 square feet each) for each of the four librarians in the department. An early suggestion from the building design team was that these four offices be arranged along the exterior walls of the Technical Services room, where large windows—the ceilings in this area of the building being 16 feet high—would create a bright working environment. A fixed counter in the middle of the room would create an open space for student assistants to work at various processing and computer tasks, and staff cubicles could be located for ease in supervising the students nearby. Again, however, the librarians and support staff within Technical Services felt that a more flexible arrangement would better meet the needs of the department and enhance its ability to function as a true service point both now and in future. With generosity and patience the architects and building planners listened to Technical Services staff concerns, eventually taking the rough sketches drawn by the staff of the department and making them the basis for the final design.

The primary goal of the redesigned space was to keep the central office area as open as possible. The librarians and staff asked that no fixed walls or counters be built except around the librarians' offices and next to a small sink area. This arrangement ensured that the majority of the space within the department might be reconfigured easily, even dramatically, should the changing roles or responsibilities of the Technical Services department ever warrant it. To reinforce a feeling of openness throughout the space, the librarian offices were moved into a new position along an interior wall shared with the Periodicals Reading Room. This move allowed the maximum amount of natural light from the high exterior windows to reach all areas of the office. Each of the four professional offices was also equipped with a large window overlooking the central office space and one or two high windows along the shared wall that also let in natural light via the central office windows and the reading room respectively.

All furniture and equipment was also scheduled for replacement at the time of the renovation project, so the entire Technical Services staff met to consider the question of the best height to use for the panels that surrounded the support staff cubicles and define student work areas. The consensus among the staff was that all movable panels should be the same height, so that they might be reused easily in any new office arrangements. The height that the department chose was a relatively low 52 inches, again to enhance the openness of the office and promote a feeling of collegiality rather than isolation throughout the room. For similar reasons, a central OCLC cataloging station was retained for some kinds of work, even though the department's switch from dedicated lines to TCP/IP connections distributed its access to OCLC to workstations everywhere in the office. Situating this shared processing station next to the high exterior windows made it possible for everyone to step away from their own desks and workstations for an hour or two a day and to enjoy a view of the campus, while the campus would get a glimpse of what goes on in the department. On the other hand, workstations for student assistants in the Cataloging unit were deliberately located on the opposite side of the office away from the windows, along an interior wall that adjoins the atrium where the Reference Desk is located. At the suggestion of the Technical Services staff, this wall was heavily "wired" on the Technical Services office side. This was done so that the space that is now used by student workers might be converted into an easily accessible research and instruction area should the growth of electronic resources further expand the department's role in student training programs.

The evolution of its current training programs and its collegial management style also created demand in the Technical Services department for a small but separate instruction and conference space within the office itself. Indeed, a "training room" topped the department's wish list for the new Technical Services area. Constant revisions in cataloging procedures and standards over the decades, as well as frequent planning meetings, made the staff acutely aware of the limitations of trying to hold complex discussions in the middle of an active work area or of trying to demonstrate a software enhancement to multiple staff members hunched around a single computer screen. The alternative—vacating the office while meetings and training sessions were held on another floor—was equally problematic, since student workers still had to be supervised and it was difficult to predict when a staff member might be needed. If it were not for the high visibility of the training sessions already being offered by the Electronic Media librarian, however, the technical services training room might never have been constructed. The case was successfully made that the department would function more efficiently and have more to offer as well as gain from such a facility were it to be built as suggested. Thus a fully wired and equipped instruction and conference room, capable of housing eleven persons at a meeting but best suited to groups of five or six, was created within the Technical Services department directly adjacent to the Reference Desk/Circulation corridor.

The size and location of the technical services training room makes it one of the most popular and heavily used spaces in the building. It can be reserved for a meeting or small group training session by any member of the library staff, although Technical Services staff still tend to be the first to fill in the calendar. Currently, its facilities include wireless as well as wired network connections, a laptop computer, projector, conference phone, video monitor connected to the campus distributed video and satellite downlink system, VCR, retractable screen, white board, bulletin board, bookshelf, table, and chairs. This room provides convenient space for project planning; vendor visits; staff development and training; and small group instruction sessions for librarians, students, and faculty using electronic resources for their research. Like the OCLC workstation by the window in the central office area, it also allows visitors a glimpse of Technical Services operations and reinforces the notion that the department is an important part of the life of the library.

Conclusion

In sum, the department's accomplishments in the area of professional staff reorganization and development, support staff development, and space planning and design are many and multifaceted. But it is the common approach to change that underlies them—the intertwining of proactive thinking, conviction that change is inevitable, and commitment to collegiality—that is the department's true strength. Having developed their vision of what should inform the department's decisions no matter what the immediate challenge may be, the librarians and staff in Technical Services have been able to make confident progress toward a future that is still only partially visible to them. They have been quick to take advantage of opportunities for change and have been successful in implementing them, largely because their vision is more about how the department should act than about what tradition says its actions should be. In the process, they have extended the department's reach not only to serve the campus and the profession but also to educate others about the importance of the role that technical services can play in an academic community.

Work on these issues continues at many levels nearly 10 years after the Technical Services department first began thinking about them. Educating the campus about the history, extent, and significance of the department's contributions is an ongoing project. The department recently hosted the dean of the College, who spent a lively afternoon in the office talking to librarians and staff and learning firsthand about the services they provide. All staff members have also participated in gathering materials for a library exhibit on the kinds of work that the Technical Services department has done in the past and what it is doing now. A thorough revision of the Technical Services section of the library's Web site is also underway to make it easier to use and to bring all aspects of it up-to-date. Finally, Schaffer Library's migration to a new ILS in 2003 is engaging the entire department in a review of new possibilities for using the online catalog to create better connections among print, electronic, multimedia, and locally digitized information resources.

But the results of the work accomplished thus far have been happy for those within the department as well as for the wider campus community. The Technical Services librarians in particular are an engaged and optimistic group—not the least because, after a nearly 20-year period during which no Technical Services professional passed a sixth year, tenure-like review, both librarians who came up for such reviews within the past decade passed them readily. The Technical Services librarians believe, in short, that they have made a persuasive case at Union College that their services are not only still relevant but fundamental to the institution as a whole. By centering their attention on their place in the academic community and developing a flexible, proactive vision for change, they have kept the Technical Services department at the center of the action as well.

11

Merging Departments in a Small Academic Library

Rhonda R. Glazier
Dr. Jack D. Glazier

Editor's note: The authors examine the process of strategic planning and merging of departments in a small academic library. Staff reactions to the process and subsequent reorganization are detailed, along with areas of concern that still need to be addressed. The challenges of managing change with workflow and personnel are also discussed, as well as how important communication is throughout any type of redesign or reorganization. The authors conclude by stating the importance of emphasizing the need for continual change and reorganization to staff, so that they are prepared for fluidity and flexibility in the future.

William Allen White Library, on the campus of Emporia (Kansas) State University, is an academic library serving a campus that has approximately 6,000 students, the majority undergraduates. Emporia State offers several degree programs through distance education, and a campus that has been emphasizing distance education over the past four years. As do the other small campuses, Emporia State hopes that its distance education program will serve as a means to stabilize its student numbers and help it stay competitive in a state with three similarly situated smaller universities and three larger state universities.

In 2001, with the new emphasis on distance education and the entry of a new director, William Allen White Library decided to undergo a strategic planning process to help establish a plan for the next five years. One of the goals set at the beginning of the strategic planning process was a reorganization of the library. For technical services, this resulted in a significant increase in its responsibilities.

Prior to 2001, the technical services department consisted of cataloging, acquisitions, and bindery/preservation. Cataloging encompassed the functions of original and copy cataloging, collection maintenance, authority work, and database clean-up. Acquisitions included book purchasing, serials acquisition, and payment of all bills for binding books and periodicals because these invoices were paid from the materials budget. It was also the clearinghouse for gift materials. Bindery/preservation encompassed serials check-in, bindery preparation, and book repair.

Along with technical services, there were access services, reference, government documents, media resources, special collections, and archives. Access services included circulation, interlibrary loan, and periodicals check-in and reference. Reference included reference services and library instruction; one of the professional librarians in this department was responsible for the library's Web page. Government documents included cataloging and reference. Media resources included media booking and selection. Special collections included the May Massee Collection (a collection of original artwork from children's books), the William Allen White Special Collection (a collection of papers belonging to a Pulitzer prize-winning newspaper editor, William Allen White), and rare books. Finally, the university archives was part of the library organization but housed in another building.

Following the 2001 strategic planning meetings, circulation, interlibrary loan, government document cataloging, and periodicals check-in were put under the direction of the head of technical services. Responsibility for periodical reference and government documents reference was assigned to the reference department. Special collections administration was placed under the direction of the head of the university archives. One of the reference librarians was moved out of reference and became responsible for collection development, media resources, and the library's Web pages, and became the distance coordinator for the library. This position reported to the dean of the library.

The Transition

The restructuring of technical services brought about a number of unique problems. First, the move put together staff who did not usually interact with each another. Second, the workflows for each area were different. Finally, they were physically located on different floors.

Prior to the reorganization, staff interaction was based on long-term relationships developed by staff members who had gone years without a change in work assignment and therefore had developed specific ways of interacting. In addition, their work assignments frequently had a physical location element associated with them. That is, not only were they in different parts of the building, but because of workflow issues, these staff members tended to rely on a narrow set of colleagues for problem resolution. This meant that because of their varying job responsibilities, workers tended to interact with the same person. One consequence of these patterns was that staffers made assumptions, frequently erroneous, about others' abilities, knowledge, and responsibilities.

Cataloging, bindery/preservation, and acquisitions had workflow patterns that were fairly constant and did not fluctuate with the academic school year, unlike circulation and interlibrary loan. In addition, they were located together in the same general work space and had worked together for years. On the other hand, circulation and interlibrary loan had similar work space and interaction issues but tended to have a different workflow. Their workflow differences emanated from the fact that they tended to be busiest during the academic year when classes were in session.

Government documents cataloging was a different situation as well. Originally, it was a part-time work situation in which the staff member also did government documents reference. The cataloging part and serials check-in responsibilities were made into a full-time position, and a staff member who had done both tasks was assigned to that area. This position was moved to technical services and began reporting directly to the head of that department.

Finally, cataloging and acquisitions were moved to a different part of the building to free up more public space in reference. Any time a department is moved it can be a complex undertaking, but a move at the same time as reorganization added layers of complexity to the process. First, planning had to be done to determine where everyone was to be located for workflow purposes in the new space. Since at least two of the staff members were completely new to the area, a workflow had to be determined before the move, and assumptions had to be made about job responsibilities before staff members were actually in the jobs doing their daily tasks. Second, the new area had to be rewired for computers and phones. Third, the new area to which cataloging and acquisitions was moving was only about one-third the size they had previously occupied.

The Process

Once the new organizational structure had been announced by the dean, she met with individual staff members, along with their new supervisor, to go over the logic behind their new assignments and how they fit into the organizational structure. For most staff members, their duties did not change, but in some cases their supervisor did. However, for a few staff it was a complete change in both work duties and supervisor. Staff in circulation and interlibrary loan only changed supervisors. This staff member, who had been in periodicals before the reorganization and then had been reassigned to do the cataloging of government documents and serial check-in, moved from reference to cataloging and acquisitions. The staff member had indicated an interest in moving to technical services, so although this was a complete change for her, including reporting to a new supervisor, she was happy with the assignment.

Each staff member was asked not to communicate his or her new assignment or new supervisor to others in the library until everyone had met with the dean. Since the meetings were done all in one day, this did not appear to be a problem, and the staff respected the request. The timing limited rumors and kept staff from speculating about their new assignments.

After the initial meetings, all staff now assigned to technical services met together. The first meeting was a chance for staff members to express their concerns and talk about how the group would now function. It was decided early on in the meeting that calling the department "technical services" no longer seemed appropriate. After a lively discussion, staff members were asked to think about what name seemed more appropriate, so that a new name for the department would be decided at the next meeting. Staff members submitted suggestions for names for the new department, which were then taken to the next departmental meeting. It was important to find a name that reflected the duties of all members and all the functions that now encompassed technical services. At that second technical services meeting, the department was renamed Collection Management. This name change was then announced at the next all-library staff meeting. For clarification purposes, for the rest of this chapter when discussing the original organizational structure, what is usually found in a traditional technical services department will be referred to as cataloging and acquisitions although there are other units in the department as well.

It became clear early in the process that all members of this new department needed to have a clear understanding of what the other members did. The next series of meetings were used as a "show and tell." For "show and tell," each staff member wrote out a list of his or her job duties and then presented this list and talked about the challenges and issues in the position to the rest of the department. It was important that the erroneous assumptions about what each member did be replaced with information about what actually went on in each area. After sharing information about these duties, the commonalities between the positions were evident, and the complexity of each of the jobs was better appreciated by the other members of the department. this process also allowed for discussions on workflow issues and how each member could help others in the department. For example, during this discussion it became clear that circulation staff members were creating brief bibliographic records and other brief records to accommodate the checking out of uncataloged materials and faculty members' personal items being placed on reserve. It was clear that the staff members doing cataloging on a daily basis could assist circulation with these functions, and cataloging took over the task of creating the bibliographic records needed for reserve materials.

Once this series of meetings was completed, the next step was to find ways that the groups could interact with and support each other. Circulation staff began helping cataloging by assigning students working the circulation desk who were trained to handle special projects to cataloging and acquisitions. For example, cataloging had just started a major project that entailed barcoding the entire collection. Where it had been the job of circulation students to barcode materials as they were checked in, once circulation was moved under the newly constituted department of Collection Management, the two areas were able to share the responsibility of barcoding the materials in the stacks. This change did not have to be cleared by a second supervisor, since the same person was now in charge of both areas. It was further facilitated by students who were working in cataloging retrieving books and taking them down to circulation to be barcoded. At the end of the day students from cataloging would take the books that had been barcoded back up to the stacks and place them back on the shelves. Since the completion of this project, circulation students have continued to help with other projects assigned to cataloging and acquisitions. For example, the reclassification of the fiction books to the 800s was a project handled by Collection Management during the summer of 2002. In this case, circulation students would put the new labels on the books once they had been reclassified. Students from cataloging would take the book trucks and labels down to circulation, then take the finished truck up for shelving to the students shifting the shelves.

Cataloging and acquisitions staff began to help circulation and interlibrary loan with the staffing of those areas. Since both circulation and interlibrary loan are public service points, itwas necessary that someone be present at all times. This is especially true with circulation, and it was decided during the strategic planning process that it should be manned by a full-time staff person for as many hours as possible. This decision was made because many of the functions in that area needed to be done by a full-time staff member, not a student. With the reorganization there were now five additional staff members who could be called on for backup. All the staff in cataloging and acquisitions were cross-trained in circulation on how to check materials in and out. In addition, all staff were trained on how to take fines, add patrons to the database, maintain or edit a patron's record, etc. This allowed for the circulation staff member to be gone and for flexibility in the staffing of that area.

Cross-training in cataloging and acquisitions was already in place. Over the previous two years, due to turnover in staff and the implementation of a new system, all staff members in these areas had been trained to back each other up. In other words, the staff member in charge of special projects, database maintenance, and copy cataloging was also trained in acquisitions, and often helped with the processing of orders when needed. The person doing original and copy cataloging was also trained in processing government documents cataloging and serials check-in. This occurred because of the need to create serial check-in records on our new system, therefore requiring the cataloging staff to learn the serials module. The acquisitions staff member had received limited cross-training in serials and cataloging because she had only recently been hired. The second person doing receipt of materials did not have any training in cataloging or serials because she had been transferred from circulation/fines to cataloging and acquisitions at the time of the reorganization. This staff member's expertise and knowledge about circulation/fines did help in serving as a backup for this area until other staff members were fully trained.

The one area that should have received more cross-training and didn't was interlibrary loan. This was because this area had a long-term staff member who seemed to have everything under control and did not require the intensive staffing that was required in circulation. In addition, the staff member in interlibrary loan did not normally indicate when he needed help or that he was behind in meeting the increasing demands of distance education interlibrary loan. Finally, this was one area in which limited changes occurred when the new online system was implemented. This meant that few staff members outside interlibrary loan were involved with the interlibrary loan department before the reorganization. For these reasons, this area did not benefit from the reorganization in the same way that the other units did. This was also due to the fact that early in the reorganization the interlibrary loan area was running smoothly and was completely autonomous. It was decided that cross-training efforts would focus on circulation, because of a pressing need for staffing there. In retrospect, this was a mistake. During the initial cross-training that occurred in circulation, staff should have been immediately cross-trained in interlibrary loan so that it would not be lost in the process and would be done while all staff were focused on new duties.

Staff Reactions

Reactions to the new organization varied among the staff. Those in reference were in general pleased with the reorganization. It has allowed them to focus on reference and instruction. That department had been renamed Information and Instructional Services (I&I Services), and the head of that department had previously been head of Access Services. One outcome for I & I Services has been the collapsing of service points. Since periodicals check-in and periodical claiming were moved to collection management, students are assigned to work in the periodicals department for a limited number of hours each week.

This reorganization has caused a deemphasis in government documents because of the lack of staffing on the floor that houses the government documents. Use of the collection is considered negligible, mainly because without staffing on the floor to verify use, it is difficult to document the use of these materials. It has also placed the responsibility for shelving of government documents and general maintenance on the floor on the students in circulation who are assigned to shelving materials. Training in the SuDoc classification system was given by the government documents librarian when the responsibility for shelving materials on that floor was turned over to Collection Management.

Dividing the work of maintaining the government documents collection between the government documents librarian and Collection Management has also been confusing at times. Although some processes are very straightforward, the staff member involved in processing government documents had to work closely with the government documents librarian to determine what responsibilities they would have in the deselection and weeding of the collection. All of the processes done by the staff member who worked with the government documents librarian, and now assigned to Collection Management, had to be analyzed and split between the staff member and the government documents librarian.

Processing of government documents also became more complex because of the lack of staffing in the area. Although the library has established very specific location codes for materials in the library, they are particularly important on a floor that is arranged by a completely different classification scheme (SuDoc). This means that the location shown in the online public catalog must be clear and well defined and in some cases more specific than would be the case on a floor that has staff readily available.

Reaction of the cataloging and acquisitions staff was in general very positive. There was a greater concern about the upcoming move to a new area than about the addition of two new departments reporting to "their" supervisor. Most assumed there would be minimal, if any, changes to their duties. This actually ended up being one of the biggest hurdles for the new department. It took several months and a lot of discussion to move the staff away from the "us" and "them" mentality. Even after two years, the phrases such as "their department" and "our department" will occasionally make their way into a discussion.

Circulation and interlibrary loan staff were more reserved about the move. They were concerned about the loss of autonomy associated with being absorbed into a larger group. They voiced a concern that their needs and issues would not be given precedence, especially since their new supervisor had no background in either area. This was compounded by the fact that they had just the previous year, under a different director, been reorganized and made into an official department. That department was called Access Services. At the time these two areas were made into a department, the staff voiced excitement and a feeling that they finally had a voice in the organization and an advocate to take their issues and concerns to the library administration. With the assignment to Collection Management, under a supervisor who did not have any experience in either area, they felt that they had been slighted. The main tactic used to address these concerns was for the new supervisor to spend a lot of time down in the two areas learning the daily routine and talking to the staff about their concerns. It also helped that during the implementation of the new online system, their new supervisor had been in charge of the implementation and had worked closely with all staff members during that process. During the early meetings of the new department, staff members from both circulation and interlibrary loan seemed distant, but they became more supportive of the organization after the staff in cataloging and acquisitions began training in circulation.

Another area of concern that had to be addressed early by this newly constituted department was the different staffing requirements of circulation and interlibrary loan. Once the new department was organized, it was decided that all of
Collection Management should share in the staffing of circulation in the evenings. There was one night each week that needed to be staffed by someone
other than the full-time person hired to work nights and weekends. The entire
Collection Management staff met and discussed the staffing needs of circulation. It was finally decided by the group that the fairest resolution to the problem
was that everyone in the department should share responsibility for staffing the
area. Each staff member would have to work six Thursday evenings each year.
The professional librarian in charge of Collection Management was included in
the rotation. Although this may not sound significant, it was a complete change
for staff members who had traditionally never been required to work evenings or
weekends, and reflects how far the group had come toward identifying
themselves as a department.

Management

Managing a traditional technical services department is complex enough;
managing this newly created department had a completely new set of interesting
challenges and dynamics. First, the staff now assigned to Collection Management, as discussed here, are the following: one staff member is responsible for
original and copy cataloging; one staff member is responsible for special projects, database maintenance, and computer support for the library; one staff
member is responsible for the cataloging and processing of government documents, serials check-in, and bindery; one staff member is responsible for
preorder searching, supervising students doing labeling of materials, mail, and
receipt of materials; one staff member is responsible for acquisitions of materials; two staff members are in circulation (one daytime and one nighttime circulation supervisor); and one staff member is in interlibrary loan. The nighttime
circulation supervisor is responsible for overseeing shelving as well as fines and
has general responsibility for the building during the evening and weekend
hours. All of these positions are classified staff positions. The only professional
position in the department is that of department head. The responsibilities of the
first five positions have fluctuated and changed over the past year, as more understanding and knowledge of the workflow has been gained. Many special projects have been assigned to the department over the past two years, and having a
staff person assigned to work on them became mandatory. These projects should
end some time in the next year, so a reorganization of staff will occur once more.

The biggest challenge in supervising this department is that the staff are
physically located on two different floors. A lot of time is spent running back
and forth between the two floors. In addition, since staff are doing such diverse
jobs, it is often necessary to completely change one's focus and thinking. It

becomes necessary to mentally shift between the two floors. It has also been necessary to set hours for the two departments that are given out to all staff in the building, so that the supervisor can be located when needed.

Second, after the initial meetings and training were done, it became clear that staff meetings needed to be focused. Often discussions would become bogged down in details that only affected part of the group. When this happened, it was difficult to keep the rest of the group focused and involved. To counter this problem, a rotating staff schedule was developed. One week the meeting would be with the staff from cataloging and acquisitions, the following week with the staff from circulation and interlibrary loan. When separate staff meetings for the two groups in the department were first tried, the sense of being one department quickly dissolved. To counter this problem, all of the staff in Collection Management meet on the third week. Setting the meeting time was also an issue that had to be worked out. The available meeting times were limited to one afternoon due to the time constraints of the supervisor and the schedule of the evening circulation supervisor. The number of staff meetings being held in the department also doubled, making it difficult at times to keep to the schedule.

Another challenge in supervising the new department came with learning the daily routine and operations of these new areas. Policies and procedures for the area were in place, but any exceptions to the policy had to be approved by the supervisor. This meant that working down in circulation and interlibrary loan and understanding the policies and procedures was essential. It helped that during implementation of a new online system, all of the policies and procedures had been reviewed and updated, a process that the supervisor had participated in and helped translate to the new system. This did take time, however, and the first few months of the transition were hectic as both staff and supervisor learned new duties.

While staff and supervisors learned these two departments' routines and procedures, the process of helping staff members learn their new jobs and move through the uncertainty of the new organization was also taking place. Although some changes were expected from the strategic planning process, many staff members were surprised by the amount of change that was proposed. This meant that once the changes were in place, staff became suspicious of more change. Motivating staff members to continue to learn new duties and to accept change has been an ongoing challenge. It also became important to allow staff to discuss their concerns and to listen actively to their issues. Often changes could not happen because of the organizational structure or the type of request made by the staff member. Allowing staff to voice concerns in a confidential setting with no fear of reprisal became important.

Voicing frustrations over the move, changes in duty, etc., was not considered exhibiting a poor attitude; rather, these concerns were talked through, and in most cases once the feelings had been aired, the staff member was able to move on and focus on his or her new duties. When a staff member was not able to independently resolve an issue, it then went to a more formal meeting structure, where the staff member was given an indication of the specific behavior that was a concern and the desired outcome. Formal meetings between the supervisor and staff member were scheduled until the problem had been resolved. This tactic was necessary in dealing with one staff member who moved from circulation to cataloging and acquisitions. This was a move not requested or foreseen by the staff member. She felt that she was being punished and had no desire to work behind the scenes and not have daily contact with the public. After informal opportunities for venting were given and the staff member's attitude did not change, more formal meetings were held, with the specific goal of improving work performance. After several months of bimonthly meetings, the staff member and supervisor were able to work out the issue, and the staff member is now a productive member of the department. If the original move had been made differently, this situation could probably have been avoided. In addition, limiting the move of a long-time public services employee to technical services without the employee wanting or requesting to make the move would probably also limit this type of problem.

Finally, managing long-time staff who on the one hand are very knowledgeable and on the other hand are very set in their ways was also an issue in the beginning. Staff members had set and preconceived ideas about the other members in the department. In many cases they had been critical of each other. For example, the cataloging staff were critical of the "on the fly" records that were put into the system by circulation. Circulation staff thought that the cataloging staff had no appreciation for demands made on staff when working with the public. Although cross-training helped with some of these prejudices, it still took a lot of time and effort to break down the barriers and get the two groups to interact and recognize each other's strengths; this is an ongoing process.

Conclusion

When making this type of organizational change, there are many unanticipated consequences. Although many of those consequences are unique to the individual library, several outcomes can be generalized to other situations. Since this reorganization happened almost two years ago, it is possible to look back and identify alternative actions that could have made the process smoother and prevented unintended consequences that resulted from the reorganization.

First, as alluded to previously, many staff members were surprised by the proposed changes to the organization. During the initial strategic planning process, the emphasis had been placed on the "big picture" and the goals and directions for the library as a whole. Although staff were asked to identify how they fit into that organization and how they would like to contribute to the organization, most did not realize the breadth of the changes that were planned or the level of reassignment that would occur. It would have been helpful, and would have made the transition smoother, if staff had been given a clearer understanding of the changes planned from the beginning. Following up this discussion with an in-depth look at individual strengths and weaknesses, and how each member could not only benefit the library but also grow personally and professionally, would have helped staff prepare for reassignment. Moving staff toward the idea of change early in the process, and being clear about the scope of the changes being proposed or sought, would have helped them recognize the intentions of and expected outcome being sought by the administration. Discussions about the reorganization and helping staff work through their fear of change before announcing the changes would have made the final outcome smoother, and the reorganization would have not affected staff morale to the same extent.

In terms of cataloging and acquisitions, the new organizational structure has been both positive and negative. On the positive side, an increased influence and understanding of the role and functions of the core responsibilities of cataloging and acquisitions has occurred due to the new structure. The cross-training and the communication that have resulted from bringing together two areas not traditionally associated with each other has provided broader support and a better understanding of behind-the-scenes processes. It has given the cataloging and acquisitions staff a chance to examine and then articulate to others exactly what they do and why they do it.

The reorganization has also allowed better staff coverage in the library by giving personnel not normally assigned to public services duties a chance to work at a public services desk. The cross-training that occurred between circulation and cataloging and acquisitions staff has allowed for more creative staffing patterns in circulation and additional support for special projects for cataloging and acquisitions. When circulation staff need to go to workshops and so forth, it has been relatively easy to assign someone from cataloging or acquisitions to cover the area. This has happened less in interlibrary loan, but if the same cross-training were done, it could benefit interlibrary loan in the same way that it has benefited circulation. It should be emphasized that cross-training does not eliminate the need to have adequate staffing for an area, but it does allow for flexibility in emergencies.

One of the unintended consequences of this structural change has been the loss of representation of staff. In the new organizational structure, the majority of the classified staff are now all in one department under one supervisor. This means that whereas that supervisor has the majority of classified staff working for her, those same staff have only one voice when dealing with the administration. The reorganization has also limited those areas' voice on library committees and has made it difficult for classified staff to take their concerns and issues forward. It has clearly given the classified staff the impression that their importance and ability to influence decisions in the library are now minimal. Examining the current organizational structure emphasizes this problem. In the new organizational structure, Informational and Instructional Services (previously reference) has four professional librarians and one classified staff member; Special Collections/Archives has two professional librarians and one classified staff member; one professional librarian is in charge of collection development, distance services, and media resources and is the Webmaster for the library. Again, by contrast the new Collection Management department has one professional librarian and seven classified staff.

Finally, another unanticipated consequence of this reorganization has been the lack of understanding by the library staff that additional reorganization could and probably would occur. This is in part because the original reorganization was viewed by staff as being very extensive. Preparing staff for continual change and emphasizing that any reorganization is only the first step in an ongoing process is important. Staff should be prepared for and recognize that continual reorganization is likely to occur, and that reorganization can happen for many reasons. At William Allen White Library, reorganization has continued to occur due to staff turnover and budgetary concerns. The work and effort the staff from these three diverse groups put into coming together as a unit has made them less willing to move within the organization, especially in terms of changing their supervisor,or changing the functions that report to Collection Management. Perhaps this is the best sign, in reality, of how well these three distinct areas can work together.

12

Creating Career Paths for Cataloging Support Staff

Karen M. Letarte
Charles Pennell
Shirley Hamlett

Editor's note: The role and importance of cataloging support staff, both in their job duties and in their professional and continuing education development, have been documented in the literature. The authors of this chapter collate, compile, and report on both research and case studies related to the growing reliance on support staff within cataloging departments to undertake job duties that were previously assigned to professional librarians. By examining the literature and documenting current best practices to establish career paths for cataloging support staff, the authors provide an excellent compilation of both past and current examinations of this topic.

Throughout the history of libraries, advances in technology have created opportunities for improved services to library users. Recent innovations in the areas of technical services have presented challenges and opportunities for new workflows and organizational restructuring to take advantage of these new capabilities. All too often, however, plans for innovative redesign of technical services units overlook the most essential component: the library's human resources, and more specifically, the support staff who accomplish the bulk of the day-to-day work in library technical services. This chapter examines the role and function of cataloging support staff in academic libraries in the digital age, and more important, the changes in infrastructure necessary for effective and ethical use of support staff in academic technical services.

Statement of the Problem

Although academic librarians in recent decades have had avenues available to them for career advancement via promotion and tenure, no systems have been in place to recognize the contributions of support staff to academic libraries or to encourage their professional development (Hurt and Sunday 2002). In cataloging units in particular, support staff members have been expected to take on responsibilities formerly considered "professional" without necessarily being given the training, support, and compensation to do the job (Oberg 1992, 106). In 1997, The American Library Association's Library Support Staff Interests Round Table (LSSIRT) conducted a comprehensive national survey of support staff to identify their key issues and concerns, receiving 2,087 responses (American Library Association, Support Staff Interests Round Table 1997). The top three issues that were identified as important to support staff were

- career ladders (few opportunities for promotion),

- compensation (not appropriate to the level of education, experience, and responsibilities), and

- continuing education (access to continuing education and training opportunities).

In May 2003, the Third ALA Congress on Professional Education: Focus on Library Support Staff (COPE 3) was convened to give voice to these and other key issues. Among the desired outcomes articulated by support staff delegates, two of the strongest were 1) the creation of a national certification program that would give recognition to expertise in the support staff ranks, and 2) the creation of career ladders (American Library Association 2003).

The situation library support staff face is quite complex. The issues of career paths, compensation, and continuing education are closely intertwined and not easily separable. An attempt to solve one problem quickly leads to a chicken-and-egg question: Which issue should be addressed first? Support staff deserve higher levels of compensation for taking on greater responsibilities, yet salary reclassifications are generally dependent upon the ability to demonstrate higher levels of responsibility, which in turn requires support in the form of continuing education and training. While acknowledging that these issues are not discrete problems, this chapter focuses on the issue identified as most important in the 1997 LSSIRT survey, that of career ladders.

Although the key issues listed above apply universally to library support staff, cataloging support staff in academic libraries face particular challenges. Many cataloging jobs are at or near the top of job classification systems, so there is little room for this group to advance. Yet a number of factors make it imperative that support staff continue to take on new responsibilities. Cataloging departments are increasingly involved in digital library initiatives, yet traditional responsibilities must still be met. This pressure will demand that support staff continue to assume new roles and responsibilities. As has been true with every new endeavor over the past 50 years, it will be impossible for cataloging units to meet these new challenges without the labor and expertise of highly skilled support staff. Equally important, support staff members desire the opportunity to make contributions and to build their own careers. Benaud notes that "the desire for personal fulfillment and career satisfaction is not limited to professional catalogers but may be viewed as a universal objective. If we keep our present way of thinking, paraprofessional copy catalogers will become bored and frustrated at having to do basically the same work every day" (1992, p. 86).

Before examining possible solutions to these persistent problems, it is necessary to discuss the evolution of library support staff as a unique class of employee. The following literature review first considers the development of the library support staff as a whole and then analyzes problems and trends specific to cataloging support staff in academic libraries.

Librarians have been documenting the role of support staff, including their job responsibilities and satisfaction, status, qualifications, training needs, and salaries, since at least 1923, when Charles Williamson released his report for the Carnegie Corporation on the state of training for library work. In the years since, there have been great changes in the complexity of all library work, in the automation of routine tasks, and in the differentiation of library service roles into separate professional, paraprofessional, and clerical components. Yet in spite of individuals' research efforts and the attention afforded this issue by the library education system, professional organizations, and occasional conferences since that time, conditions of employment have not improved substantively for most support staff.

Definitions

Before proceeding we should first define the terms used in this chapter to describe various levels of library staff. Many terms have been used in the literature to describe personnel who work in libraries but either do not possess a master's degree in library or information science or do not work in positions that require it. These terms include "subprofessionals" (Williamson 1923; Asheim 1968), "paraprofessionals" (Gartner 1971; Evans 1979; Benaud 1992; Younger 1996; Mohr and Schuneman 1997), "support or supportive staff" (Myers 1989; Younger 1996; Anderson and Bullene 1999; Stambaugh 2000; ALA Council 2002), "library assistants" (Asheim 1968, Evans 1979; Thapisa 1989; Kreitz and Ogden 1990; Goulding 1996), and "nonprofessionals" (Coutois and Goetsch 1984; Turner 1992; Froehlich 1998). Younger makes a technical distinction between support staff and paraprofessionals (1996, pp. 28–29). Support staff includes all members of the library staff with positions in the clerical, library media/technical assistant, and library associate classifications. Paraprofessional refers to the subset of support staff that is assigned supportive responsibilities in the library media/technical assistant or library associate classifications, excluding clerical staff. Lester Asheim ascribes a particular understanding of library service to this group, which he calls library assistants: "Such positions conform closely to the meaning of the term paraprofessional—one who works beside or along-side of the professional members of the staff" (1968, p. 1099).

In addition to professional and supportive library employees, the 2002 ALA policy document *Library and Information Studies and Human Resource Utilization* (*LISHRU*) and its predecessor, *Library Education and Personnel Utilization* (*LEPU*), also recognize a class of employee that possesses non-library-related qualifications and encompasses both professional and supportive functions. This is the specialist class, and includes, for example, personnel with expertise or qualifications in such areas as information technology or human resources.

The term "paraprofessional" is now used less commonly because of perceived negative connotations. Some feel that the term does not adequately reflect the complex nature of the tasks performed (Benaud 1992, p. 84). In Greek, "para" means "half," thus implying that the work of paraprofessionals is less than fully professional. Support staff is the term that seems to be preferred currently. For example, the Library Support Staff Interests Round Table (LSSIRT) is the official name of the ALA group advocating for the interests of this class of employee. For the purposes of this chapter, "support staff" is used to mean any non-MLS personnel whose jobs require knowledge of library functions. It will also include employees who may possess the MLS degree but whose positions do not require the degree. Thus clerical workers on the library side are included, but employees in the specialist class are excluded. A professional cataloger is defined as one holding the master's degree in library or information science and working in a position for which that degree is a requirement (Mohr and Schuneman 1997).

Historical Perspectives

The evolution of library support staff positions has been the subject of several excellent publications in recent years, most notably those of Evans (1979), Mugnier (1980), Russell (1985), and Younger (1996). Of these Evans is by far the most historically comprehensive, covering the development of library staffing from the late 1800s until the 1976 revision of the Asheim report, known as *Library Education and Personnel Utilization* (*LEPU*), which is discussed later.

Evans notes that in the nineteenth century only the head of the library was a "librarian," with most real power vested in library boards. Those reporting to him (and the male pronoun may be used exclusively here) were "library assistants," who could only achieve the title of librarian by appointment to that role in another library. Because of the small size of these early collections and the limited number of staff working therein, a great deal of the work done by these professionals was, in reality, clerical in nature. It was not until around 1921 that graduates of library schools began to be in more general charge of libraries, at least in North America. While the American Library Association early on provided a forum for professional librarians to discuss their status and working conditions, a Library Workers' Association was founded during the 1920s to represent those without formal library credentials. Because library school graduates were in good supply prior to World War II, most positions that might be considered to be doing "library work" were occupied by professionals, leaving little but unskilled work for support staff to do. Evans argues that this era, during which librarians were observed by the public performing primarily technical work, contributed to the low status and salaries that continue to plague libraries to this day:

> It also implicitly denied that learning could take place elsewhere than in an academic program—an attitude that is remarkable in a profession that prides itself on being a source of help in independent, self-guided education. (Evans 1979, p. 81)

A number of events in the mid-1960s were cited as being of particular importance in the emergence of modern library staffing, including the rise of library technician programs in junior colleges, ALA's 1965 refusal to support these programs (American Library Association, Library Education Division 1965), the founding of COLT (originally the Council on Library Technology) by the rebuffed junior college programs, and finally the federal government's publication of the "Library Technician Series," GS-1411 in 1966, in which staff members with a bachelor's degree and/or library experience could rise up into the professional job classification without the graduate library degree (United States Office of Personnel Management 2003).

Mugnier's 1980 book, based on her dissertation at Columbia, covers similar historical ground as Evans, concentrating on the rise of the paraprofessional role within public libraries. She notes that during the 1950s the paraprofessional class came largely from the middle class, especially women with college degrees. "Indigenous" paraprofessionals, defined as those from the class they would be serving, became a force in the 1960s. Younger (1996), while primarily interested in positions in cataloging operations, compares the rise of paraprofessionals within libraries to parallel trends in nursing, teaching, and social work, and the profession's failure to fully understand the concept of a permanent paraprofessional workforce.

Russell (1985) provides a British perspective parallel to that of U.S. writers in the literature. Up until 1964, when entrance exams for library schools were dropped, libraries only hired two types of employees: professional librarians and those working toward certification. After this date, "Library authorities saw that

the work done by library assistants did not require the standard of education previously required of recruits who were all potential professional librarians. They
started recruiting at a lower level." (1985, p. 295). Qualifications for support
staff, including the City & Guild's Library Assistant's Certificate and the Library Association's BEC (Business Education Council) Award, met with limited success at the time largely, it would seem, due to librarians' ambivalence
toward this training and indeed the role of support staff in general.

Role Differentiation

Official recognition of distinct roles for librarians and support staff was late
in coming when ALA published its *Descriptive List of Professional and Nonprofessional Duties in Libraries* (American Library Association, Board on Personnel Administration, Subcommittee on Analysis of Library Duties 1948).
Listing duties appropriate to the prescribed two levels of library work, it served
as the basis for role differentiation until Lester Asheim's work some 20 years
later. After describing a brief framework in 1967 (Asheim 1967), Asheim, director of ALA's Office for Library Education in the mid-1960s, published his
groundbreaking article, "Education and Manpower for Librarianship: First
Steps Toward a Statement of Policy" in 1968. In this statement he divided library personnel into two categories, professional and supportive. These in turn
contained subgroups, the former librarians and professional-specialists, the latter library clerks, technical assistants, and library assistants. Professional-specialists were described as library administrative staff, though commentary from
practitioners appearing after the article suggested this might logically include
computer programmers as well. Interestingly, the accompanying table draws a
bold dividing line below the library assistants, not above it, seemingly aligning
this group more with professionals than supportive staff.

By the time Asheim's proposal was developed enough to go before the
ALA Council two years later, the earlier table had been considerably fleshed out
and the specialist class made parallel to positions requiring library-related qualifications. This statement, with its 35 numbered elements, was accepted as ALA
policy in 1970. It was subsequently reissued in 1976 as *Library Education and
Personnel Utilization* and has been more frequently cited simply as LEPU. This
policy at last officially recognized the existence of expertise needed within libraries that did not spring from graduate library education, and indeed created a
new parallel range of both professionals and supportive staff with the title "specialist." Requirements were based squarely on educational level, with the master's degree required for professional appointment in either the library- or
non-library-related series. Supportive categories required progressively more
formal education as responsibilities increased. (See Table 12.1.)

Table 12.1. Categories of Library Personnel

Categories of Library Personnel—Professional		
Title		
Basic requirement		
For positions requiring library-related qualifications	*For positions requiring non-library-related qualifications*	
Senior librarian	Senior specialist	In addition to relevant experience, education beyond the M.A., as post-master's degree; Ph.D.; relevant continuing education in many forms
Librarian	Specialist	Master's degree
Categories of Library Personnel—Supportive		
Library associate	Associate specialist	Bachelor's degree (with or without course work in library science); OR bachelor's degree, plus additional academic work short of the master's degree
Library technical assistant	Technical assistant	At least two years of college-level study; OR A.A. degree, with or without library technical assistant training; OR postsecondary school training in relevant skills
Clerk	Clerk	Business school or commercial courses, supplemented by in-service training or on-the-job experience

Based on Asheim (1970, p. 342).

While the split into just two categories of professionals does not seem to have been widely utilized subsequent to Asheim's report, a three-category split of supportive personnel is fairly common, though not necessarily with the titles or educational requirements called for here, nor the salaries to match. In 2002, ALA's Library Career Paths Task Force reviewed and updated LEPU, introducing a "career lattice" graphically displaying the relationship between delineated levels of library work. The later document encourages a broad academic background for all library workers, something advocated as early as Williamson (1923), accepts support staff as integral to the library professions, and

> draws a distinct difference between the individual responsibility for
> professional development expected of librarians and specialists, and li-
> brary managers' responsibility for providing access to continuous
> learning for support staff contributors. (American Library Association,
> Council 2002, p. 1)

Role differentiation, particularly between professionals and support staff
but also between the various levels of support staff, has engaged much of the discussion on support staff issues in the literature. There are several forces assigned
defining roles in the transformation of library staff positions in the past 20 years.
While historically the supply of library school graduates has always been a determining factor in library role definition, Oberg et al. cited additional factors as
the current driving forces: automation and networking; the creation of new tasks
and changes in the status of older ones; static or declining budgets; recent gains
in faculty status for librarians, with the concomitant demands in teaching, research and governance; the move away from authoritarian administrative models; and the emergence of a new, committed and vocal paraprofessional cadre
(1992, p. 216). In another article issued in the same year, Oberg adds "an increasing emphasis on public service, and their evaluation" (Oberg 1992, p. 100).
These factors are noted on both sides of the Atlantic, although for Russell (1985)
and Goulding (1996) reduced public funding with subsequent staffing cuts
outweighs all other factors.

Articles by Abbott (1998) and Veaner (1982, 1994) contrast academic professional activities, performed by an elite, with the "commodity expertise" of
routine library work, particularly in an age of increasing automation:

> one result of heavy commodification in librarianship is quite likely an
> increased distance between a core professional elite that is concerned
> with maintaining and upgrading the increasingly centralized knowl-
> edge and physical resources of the profession-algorithms, databases,
> indexing systems, repositories-and a larger but peripheral group that
> provides actual client access to those resources. (Abbott 1998, p. 440)

Veaner (1994) refers to this professional expertise as "programmatic responsibility," responsibility for overseeing the "library's program," those activities that provide the vision for what makes the library a socially valued
organization. In Veaner's view, written before the ubiquity of Web access, the
wide availability of computerized information in modern society has eroded
much of the traditional domain of the library and enabled almost anyone with
even limited technical skills to build databases, serve up information content,
and broker their own services to the public. Rather than simplify librarians'
work, automation has left only the most complex work to do, a responsibility
that professionals neglect at their peril: "If we distribute programmatic responsibilities broadcast, we deny our professionalism—and that is tantamount to say-
ing that anyone can do a librarian's work" (Veaner 1994, p. 395).

Defining the appropriateness of different types of library work to various groups of personnel has been a continual problem for librarians. Many place this failure to appropriately assign responsibilities squarely on the shoulders of the library profession:

> The problem of role definition and articulation is at the heart of our predicament. The inability of librarians to define their own role less ambiguously inhibits us from describing paraprofessionals more precisely, from explaining ourselves to clients who fail increasingly to distinguish between the two groups, and from exercising leadership in this important arena. (Oberg 1992, p. 109)

On the whole, the library profession has yet to acknowledge fully the presence of library support staff as a distinct, permanent class of library employee (Younger 1996, p. 33; Oberg 1992, p. 105). Support staff positions have often been viewed as either a temporary response to shortages of professional librarians, who would resume the responsibilities when sufficient numbers were regained, or as a kind of training ground for those preparing to obtain the professional degree, rather than as careers in their own right (Younger 1996, p. 33). Yet there are many library support staff members who choose a career-in-rank and who do not wish to pursue the professional degree. The failure to clearly define the roles and responsibilities of professional librarians versus library support staff members has contributed greatly to the inequities that library support staff currently suffer with regard to compensation and advancement. Oberg argues that this role blurring is detrimental to the future of the profession: "The emergence of the paraprofessional as an active, vital force in our libraries compounds librarians' age-old identity crisis and challenges us to resolve at last the problem of our status" (Oberg et al. 1992, p. 215).

The issue of librarians assuming the work of support staff, rather than the obverse, is one that occupies much of the current literature. Examining the roles of beginning librarians at eight University of California campuses, Edwards (1975) concluded that much work assigned at this level, including descriptive and copy cataloging, order verification, and file revision, was more appropriate to support staff. Kreitz and Ogden, looking at the same library system some 15 years later, found that much of the overlap in responsibilities remained in place, noting that, "Librarians who felt overburdened by clerical duties saw themselves prevented from participating in activities that encouraged professional growth. Library assistants who took on additional responsibilities felt the lack of adequate compensation and recognition" (1990, p. 299).

Patricia A. Eskoz, using survey data on cataloging responsibilities collected in 1983–1984 and again in 1986–1987, concluded that, "Professionals still spend too much time in routine cataloging that could be delegated to well-trained, high-level paraprofessionals *under supervision*" (1990, p. 391). Surprisingly, she noted that cataloging administrators agreed, but complained "that there simply are not enough support positions allotted to their departments to free professionals from routine tasks" (Eskoz 1990, p. 391).

One supportive group that has carved a niche for itself in Canada, Australia, and primarily the western half of the United States is the graduates of library technician programs. Davidson-Arnott and Kay examined the role of library technician programs in Canada and of this category of staff in general in an excellent themed issue of *Library Trends*. They assign much of the blame for role blurring between various library groups on a failure by the profession to regulate itself and the credentials of its practitioners:

> Any employer, librarian or otherwise, can hire anyone to do any information job regardless of training level or, indeed, lack of training. In this misguided and often exploitive [sic] situation, management function, information provision and organization, and client services may be conducted by librarians, library technicians, untrained individuals, or staff moved from any other department in the organization. The quality of the work done may be entirely satisfactory or may be judged without any real understanding of the potential for either error or superb work. (Davidson-Arnott and Kay 1998, p. 559)

Also writing from a Canadian perspective, Howarth (1998) differentiates between two classes of paraprofessionals: library technicians, with a degree from a college of applied arts and science (a community college in the U.S. context), and those with at least a bachelor's degree but no degree in library studies. Interestingly, she describes the latter as more hirable, due to their subject expertise. Each of the technical services is considered in turn to see which tasks are generally considered professional and which paraprofessional. For cataloging, she notes that the split between clerical and "brain work" tasks was more obvious in the card era when librarians performed description and subject analysis with limited outside help, while support staff typed and filed cards. In the present era, the amount of "brain work" has diminished considerably with the general acceptance of all copy in the interest of productivity. Outsourcing is cited as a particular threat to paraprofessionals, as most of this work involves lower level cataloging and because outsource agencies tend to hire professionals.

Support Staff Within Cataloging Operations

The etiology of the current situation facing cataloging support staff in particular is complex. Factors include inadequacy of the current infrastructure for employment, overqualification of the support staff workforce, role blurring and task overlap with professional catalogers, shifting organizational philosophies and structures, and evolving models of librarianship.

Inadequacies of the Current Employment Infrastructure

Although the nature of the work performed by support staff in cataloging units has changed almost beyond recognition in the past 20 years, job titles, descriptions, classification systems, and requirements have not been updated to reflect this. This problem has its roots in century-old policies. Younger (1996) traces the development of the paraprofessional workforce within cataloging operations from the turn of the twentieth century to the 1990s. For the period from 1990 to 1950, the operative model for division of labor was simply that of the professional versus the clerical (Younger 1996, pp. 29–30). Professional catalogers performed the intellectual work of cataloging, supported by cataloging clerks who performed such routine tasks as typing, duplicating, and filing catalog cards. With the advent of machine-readable cataloging records and shared bibliographic utilities, the nature of the work has changed. Such clear-cut distinctions are no longer possible, and cataloging support staff currently participate in a variety of activities that were formerly the exclusive province of professional catalogers, including original cataloging and subject analysis (Mohr and Schuneman 1997; Oberg 1992; Bordeianu and Seiser 1999).

Stambaugh's 2000 article reports that job classification systems remain current and useful for only five to seven years given the rapid pace of change. Yet Stambaugh found that 95 percent of respondents were using a classification system that was at least eight years old (2000, p. 167). This finding would suggest that a majority of cataloging support staff positions have not been analyzed recently enough for them to be ranked appropriately within the institution's job classification system.

Despite the fact that 90 percent of ARL respondents identified the existence of career ladders for support staff within their institutions, these traditional systems have not met the needs of support staff (Oberg et al. 1992, p. 233).

Three key problems with existing classification systems can be identified. First, existing job classification schedules are inflexible. Traditional job classification systems consist of "fairly rigid classification ranges with numerous pay levels that are attained through annual step increases" until the top of the range is reached "through seniority or longevity" (Stambaugh 2000, p. 167). Most cataloging positions are near the top of the schedules, providing little room for advancement. Second, progression through the ranks cannot be achieved on the basis of individual merit but only through seniority or at the mercy of the distribution of vacant positions, which are often heavily weighted toward the entry-level positions (Duke University, Perkins Library, Career Paths Task Force 1999, p. 4). Third, classification systems often fail to recognize properly the complexity of cataloging support staff positions.

Within many job classification systems, library cataloging positions may be classed parallel to clerical positions in the parent institution, a placement that may have been appropriate 40 years ago but that no longer reflects the level of knowledge and skill required to accomplish today's cataloging work. A recent job posting at North Carolina State University for a professional painter's position underscores the inherent inequities in the larger job classification systems within which most academic libraries must operate. The painter's position was classed at the same level and salary grade (61) as a Library Technical Assistant I position in cataloging, yet a grammar school degree was listed as the minimum preferred (not required) educational requirement for the painter position, while the library position preferred a bachelor's degree but required only a high school diploma.

The literature provides widespread evidence of the increased complexity and sophistication of work as cataloging support staff positions have subsumed responsibilities previously considered appropriate for professional catalogers. Such responsibilities range from original cataloging, including subject cataloging, to supervision, to working with emerging metadata standards. Commenting on the results of the 1990 national survey of academic library support staff, Oberg questions "whether librarians have communicated effectively to campus administrators and personnel officers the magnitude of the changes that have occurred in paraprofessional jobs" (Oberg et al. 1992, p. 233). Sadly, outdated job classification and compensation schedules attest that librarians have been poor advocates for their support staff colleagues.

Comparison of salaries and classifications across institutions to address the problem through a coordinated national effort is further hindered by the use of nonstandard job titles, descriptions, and requirements. Although Asheim's staff education and utilization models of the late 1960s (Asheim 1968, 1970) were accepted as policy in ALA Council over 30 years ago, their application for support staff position titles and qualifications has never achieved the widespread support that the graduate library degree has achieved for professional positions. As Andrews and Kelly noted in 1988, "There is no consistent name for this group of library employees in library literature" (p. 55). Table 12.2 illustrates the confusing array of job titles, descriptions, and requirements.

Information in the table was taken from Web pages of the institutions in May 2003. The positions above are similar, all including derivative cataloging of materials without Library of Congress catalog records. Job titles vary, including Library Assistant, Library Specialist, and Library Technician. At some classification levels, positions will require supervisory responsibilities (University of Miami); at others, the duties may include them (State Library of Connecticut, University of Arizona). Educational and experience requirements range from a high school diploma/GED and three years of experience (University of Miami) to a bachelor's degree plus one year of experience (University of Arizona). All institutions shown recognize the importance of experience, with all but the University of Miami allowing some amount of experience to substitute for education.

Table 12.2. Support Staff Job Titles, Duties, and Requirements

Job Title	Description	Sample Responsibilities	Experience/Educational Requirements	Source
Library Technician II	A person in this library position performs advanced technical and other library work involving the maintenance and use of library collection and assisting customers in their search for materials and information. Traditional and computer-dependent collection maintenance and search methods are used. Technician II works under the general supervision of the Associate Senior Librarian or other section head and periodically provides supervision and direction to Technicians I, library assistants and pages.	Manages the library collection by cataloguing books and other materials on all library systems, culling outdated, unused and damaged items from the collection, keeping the collection inventory properly organized and recommending collection purchases in specialized areas based on reader interest and reviews.	Two year or associate's degree as a library technical assistant or a related field from an accredited college or school beyond high school and three years of library work experience. A bachelor's degree in library science or liberal arts from accredited college or university and one or more years of varied library experience including some supervision is preferred	Connecticut State Library
Library Assistant IV	Library work of a highly complex nature requiring much independent judgment based on extensive knowledge of library policies and procedures and/or knowledge of all bibliographic cataloging codes and rules.	Plans, assigns, and directs work. May be responsible for a unit of a department or for a section of a division. May train, assign work, and recommend hiring and firing and responsible for evaluations of LA I, LA II, and LA III. May perform non-supervisory tasks in a subject or language specialty or in a highly specialized library technique, such as cataloging books with many variant editions.	High school diploma or equivalent, 3 years related experience	University of Miami

(Continued)

Table 12.2. Support Staff Job Titles, Duties, and Requirements

Job Title	Description	Sample Responsibilities	Experience/Educational Requirements	Source
Library Assistant VI	Performs a variety of advanced library support tasks common to the library unit following policies and procedures for one or more areas including processing library materials/documents, personal computer operations, records and file maintenance, customer relations, correspondence, and/or others.	Performs specialized office and administrative tasks independently with advanced knowledge of library terminology and procedures and comprehensive knowledge of functional area policies and procedures and follows precedent and identifies problems with suggested solutions in meeting organizational goals and objectives. Uses advanced knowledge of subject matter sufficient to identify, understand and respond to student/customer needs. Uses discretion and sound judgment to resolve difficult problems within assigned area and interprets policies, procedures, and guidelines. Utilizes advanced technology to accomplish goals and objectives; analyzes moderately complex data in order to compile, prepare and distribute necessary information.	High school diploma (or GED) plus passing grades on a basic clerical aptitude test and a basic computer keyboarding test plus a minimum of two years experience in the next lower level (Library Assistant V) or equivalent (HS + 9). In addition, successful completion of appropriate library modules for promotion. A higher-level degree may substitute for one year experience.	Auburn University

(Continued)

Job Title	Description	Sample Responsibilities	Experience/Educational Requirements	Source
Library Specialist	Utilizes a specialized knowledge of a subject, language or discipline that applies to library processing or service within the library or provides specialized knowledge of one library function. This classification primarily utilizes one major automated system to provide access to a library collection and performs the more difficult functions of an automated system. The Library Specialist may manage a specialized service area and may supervise staff employees and student assistants.	Creates and edits complex bibliographic records in all formats using local and national standards; performs complex bibliographic searching and verification; Monitors and analyzes changes in bibliographic records for online systems and software. Performs complex reclassification and copy cataloging in all formats and in all language including roman script; Processes complex monograph and serial added publications; Performs high level authority control; Verifies, reconciles and occasionally assigns call numbers and subject headings for bibliographic records; Searches and interprets complex title relationships and determines new form of entry; Resolves complex conflicts both in a card and online environment for name, series and subject headings.	Bachelor's degree AND one year related library experience; OR, five years related library experience OR, any equivalent combination of experience, training and/or education approved by Human Resources	University of Arizona
Library Technical Assistant I	Work in this class involves the performance of technical duties in library functions including but not limited to cataloging, interlibrary loan, acquisitions, collection development, serials or reference; or the performance of a combination of these functions in a smaller school or departmental library.	Employees are responsible for performing various routine technical functions and may supervise library clerical activities under the general supervision of a professional librarian Employees function with considerable independence in performing duties within their library activity; work is occasionally monitored for adherence to established policies and procedures and administrative or technical assistance is within close range.	Education equivalent to graduation from high school and four years of library experience; or an associate degree in library technology from a two-year technical school or community college; or graduation from a four-year college or university; or an equivalent combination of education and experience.	NCSU Libraries

One area that has not been delineated successfully in many job classification schedules is the effect of supervisory responsibilities on job classification. In some systems, the only way to advance to the associate level positions (as defined by the *LISHRU*) is to take on supervision. Classification systems may not adequately address the specialized knowledge necessary for high-level cataloging tasks. In addition, support staff members willing to take on the burden of supervising their peers may not be adequately compensated for this additional responsibility. This relationship needs to be clearly thought out and reflected in the classification system.

As shown, minimum educational requirements for support staff positions vary widely from institution to institution but often fail to reflect qualifications possessed by incumbent staff or the appropriate educational level necessary for the work. Oberg's 1990 national survey of the working conditions of academic library support staff found that 93 percent of ARL library respondents require a high school degree, 58 percent the associate's degree, 76 percent the bachelor's degree, and 24 percent a graduate degree for support staff positions across the library (Oberg et al. 1992, p. 221). Bordeianu and Seiser's 1998 study of requirements for cataloging support staff positions in ARL libraries revealed great variation, but 44.8 percent of respondents did not require postsecondary education for copy cataloging positions (1999, pp. 536–537). Benaud asserts that in her experience "minimum formal requirements usually are a bachelor's degree, a number of years of general library experience, or both" for paraprofessional cataloging positions, and that it is not uncommon in university libraries for support staff to hold master's degrees as well (1992, p. 86). She further observes that requirements for high-level support staff positions do not vary considerably from those for entry-level librarians (Benaud 1992, p. 87).

Overqualification of Support Staff Workforce

Many cataloging support staff are overqualified for their positions. Oberg's 1990 survey revealed that in 97 percent of ARL libraries, support staff possess educational credentials higher than those required for their positions (Oberg et al. 1992, p. 222). Thus one of the chief benefits that the support staff workforce currently provides for libraries is highly skilled labor at a bargain-basement cost. As many library support staff members have qualifications beyond what is required for their jobs, the library gets more than it pays for. Overqualification of the workforce contributes to another significant problem, that of task blurring between professional librarians and support staff (Oberg et al. 1992, 232).

Role Blurring within Cataloging Units

Oberg states that, "Personnel utilization and role definition have been persistent problems within librarianship. The separation of workplace tasks into categories unambiguously defined by their levels of complexity and consistently

performed by staff with appropriate educational qualifications and training continues to elude the profession" (Oberg et al. 1992, p. 233). Perhaps nowhere has
this been as evident as in academic library cataloging units.

In the model of professional versus clerical work that was in place up until
the 1950s, professional catalogers performed the intellectual work of cataloging
and support staff the routine tasks (Mohr and Schuneman 1997, p. 205). Today
there is considerable overlap of tasks, with increasing numbers of support staff
members performing previously "professional" tasks such as original cataloging. Oberg's 1990 study found that support staff performed original cataloging
in 51 percent of ARL libraries and handled subject analysis and classification in
36 percent (Oberg et al. 1992). By 1997, Mohr and Schuneman's study of ARL
libraries reported a significant increase, with 77.1 percent of respondents reporting support staff involvement in some original cataloging tasks. Bordeianu and
Seiser also studied support staff involvement in cataloging in ARL libraries in
1998, with support staff performing original cataloging in 67 percent of
responding institutions (1999, p. 536).

Such task blurring makes both practical and financial sense for institutions
facing large backlogs and shortages of professional catalogers. Interestingly,
Mohr and Schuneman found that the most common reason cited for support staff
involvement in cataloging was professional development for support staff, followed closely by cost saving and volume of work (1997, p. 212). While professional development opportunities are generally valued by most employees, they
also resent being asked to do work that they previously had been told was above
their classification without additional compensation. Younger argues that for
too long,

> We have defined professional responsibilities by the degree held by the
> incumbent rather than the nature of the activity. Professional responsi-
> bilities are those done by a person with a master's degree in library sci-
> ence. This approach has contributed to the underutilization of librarians
> and support staff, discouraging both from realizing their full potential.
> (1996, p. 38)

Oberg (1992), Rider (1996), Younger (1996), and Howarth (1998) have all
called for the profession clearly to define roles and responsibilities for librarians
and support staff. To some extent this is happening by default in academic library cataloging units, likely due in part to expanded responsibilities for those librarians with faculty status. Buttlar and Garcha's 1998 study examined the
evolution of job activities of professional catalogers over a 10-year period from
1987 to 1997, finding that professional catalogers are increasingly involved in
activities outside of cataloging. In 1997, the top 25 activities included setting local standards, designing cataloging policies and procedures, compiling statistics, and managing workflows. Professional cataloger roles that appear to be
emerging naturally include managers and policymakers (Buttlar and Garcha

1998, p. 320). This view is echoed by others (Mohr and Schuneman 1997; Veaner 1982; Bishoff 1987; Younger 1996; Rider 1996), who see the profession looking toward librarians as "managers, leaders and innovators, less involved than previously in day-to-day operations" (Mohr and Schuneman 1997, p. 206). While the reality is likely that many librarians are already fulfilling these roles, a clear articulation of roles across the field is needed.

In her keynote address to the COPE 3 delegation, Kathleen Weibel (2003) described a model she calls her tribute to the Palmer handwriting method. The model depicts a series of connected loops, which represent the evolution of library work. At the beginning of the loop, librarians are developing work as new services and functions. As the work becomes established and codified, support staff are able to take over responsibility for performing the work. And the cycle continues with the next innovation. Thus task overlap occurs naturally and desirably as part of the cycle. Task overlap is also inevitable because entry-level professional catalogers, who will assume leadership and managerial roles as their careers develop, must learn their craft to become effective managers. As new kinds of services and work are developed, more will be demanded of cataloging support staff. Will they have incentives to assume new responsibilities?

Shifting Organizational Philosophies and Structures and Evolving Models of Librarianship

A glance at both emerging trends within organizational management and innovations in bibliographic control suggests that structures and activities of technical services units in the future will be very different from the traditional models that predominate today. Greater numbers of libraries are abandoning traditional hierarchical organizations for team-based and increasingly cross-functional structures. In view of the rapid pace of change and proliferation of new formats for information, it is not difficult to conceive of a need for highly flexible, cross-functional, project-based teams rather than the hierarchical and segregated structures currently in use. Team-based structures will depend on quality contributions from all team members and will require new skills and competencies, not only for support staff members but for all library employees. New digital initiatives such as institutional repositories will also demand new technical skills for support staff.

In addition to team structures, the competency-centered learning organization is another fast-growing management trend. The University of Nebraska Libraries recently adopted the learning organization model and developed core competencies for all library employees. A learning organization is one "that has an enhanced capacity to learn, adapt and change, and is skilled at creating, acquiring, and transferring knowledge and insights. In these organizations, staff are encouraged to continuously learn new skills" (Giesecke and McNeil 1999, p. 4). ARL SPEC Kit 270, *Core Competencies*, defines core competencies as "the skills, knowledge, abilities and attributes that employees across an organization are expected to have to contribute successfully within a particular organizational context" (McNeil 2002, p. 7). Core competencies are applicable to all library staff, not just support staff. McNeil reports that 25 percent of the 65 respondents, or 17 of the 124 ARL member libraries (13 percent), have already adopted core competencies. Fifty percent of the respondents that do not currently use core competencies are planning to develop them (22 of 44). Fifty-three percent of the respondents that use core competencies tie salary increases to core competency attainment. The establishment of core competencies that are important to the organization's mission and strategic plan allows all employees to be accountable to that vision.

At the University of Nebraska, the list of core competencies established by the Libraries includes analytical skills/problem solving/decision making, communication skills, creativity/innovation, expertise and technical knowledge, flexibility/adaptability, organizational understanding and global thinking, and service attitude/user satisfaction. The Library administration is in the process of incorporating the core competencies into the performance evaluation process. A logical next development would be to include core competencies in position requirements for job postings.

At three institutions that have instituted career path models for support staff, the University of Connecticut, Auburn University, and The University of Arizona, employee eligibility for promotion is dependent upon demonstrated mastery of library-established competencies and commitment to the library's mission (Duke University, Perkins Library, Career Paths Task Force 1999, p. 7). Core competencies are a trend that will likely continue to grow among academic libraries.

Toward Career Paths for Support Staff in Cataloging

A review of the literature has shown that cataloging support staff face particular challenges in role definition; continually increasing responsibilities; and an infrastructure inadequate for supporting career advancement, appropriate compensation, and training and development. The emergence of the career paths or career ladders model seems to hold some promise for offering support staff better opportunities for advancement.

The next section of this chapter examines existing career ladders programs in libraries. In 1998, the Career Paths Task Force at Duke University was charged with studying the problem of lack of opportunity for advancement; it produced an excellent analysis of the career paths model (Duke University, Perkins Library, Career Paths Task Force 1999). The Task Force defined a career path as "a system of ranking employees that recognizes their contributions to the library and the University and allows an upward progress that is to some extent under their own control. . . . [S]taff can advance by meeting a combination of certain clearly defined criteria of length, quantity and quality of service" (1999, p. 1).

Existing Career Ladder Programs

We now examine three examples of career path systems already in place in libraries. Although such a system has been in place for some time at the Library of Congress (Hiatt 1987), Auburn University (Ransell 2002) and the University of Connecticut (Hurt and Sunday 2002) have recently instituted programs incorporating the model.

Auburn University Libraries

At Auburn University, frustration with the traditional classification system and the difficulty of retaining talented staff led to the creation of a new system. The Career Ladders Program instituted at Auburn University Library is based on the University's concept of job families, defined as "a series of progressively higher, related jobs distinguished by levels of knowledge, skills and abilities and other factors, providing promotional opportunities over time" (Ransell 2002). The old classification system did not recognize employees' knowledge, skills, or abilities, and the only way to obtain promotion was by changing jobs.

The Career Ladders Program at Auburn encompasses two job families, the library assistant family and the library associate family, each with its own educational requirements. The library assistant family encompasses six job levels (grades 3–8) and does not require a college degree. The library associate family includes three job levels (grades 10–12) and has a bachelor's degree as the minimum educational requirement. Employees become eligible for promotion through a combination of satisfactory job performance, demonstrated mastery of competencies appropriate to the next highest level, fulfillment of a minimum time requirement in the current position, and completion of required coursework for each level. For example, at the library associate level an employee must have three years of experience, demonstrate competencies, show professional development in the form of writing or presenting work, and participate in professional service to move from Level I to Level II. (Ransell 2002; http://www.lib. auburn.edu/dean/career/guidelines.html).

During the program's first year in 2000, about 35 employees were promoted. The high number was due to the fact that many were long-term employees who had been working significantly above their grade level. There were seven promotions the second year and nine in the third year. The response of the library staff has been very positive. The program's effects on retention are difficult to measure, as many employees tend to stay in their jobs. But Ransell observes: "Morale is so much improved. [Employees] have an avenue for promotion, yet do not have to change jobs or leave the library—and they are recognized for their abilities" (Ransell 2003).

The University of Connecticut

A recent reorganization at the University of Connecticut Library to a team-based structure including area and cross-functional teams was the impetus to create a system to recognize and encourage contributions of library support staff (Hurt and Sunday 2002). The library instituted the Career Ladders Program (CLP) in 2000. CLP provides for advancement either across the four broad job classification levels (in effect, the reclassification of a position) or from tier to tier within each classification. Three tiers have been defined for each job classification. They include developing, accomplished, and mastery levels. At the developing level, employees demonstrate successful performance of basic job responsibilities and an understanding of library work areas tangential to their own. At the accomplished level, employees surpass developing tier requirements and evaluate their own jobs for possible improvement while exemplifying excellent service in their own areas. At the mastery level, requirements for the previous tiers are surpassed and employees demonstrate leadership that promotes quality improvement more broadly within the library, beyond their own units. Tier movement is tied to mastery of defined organizational competencies or criteria. The five criteria include a minimum period of service in each tier, leadership and initiatives, critical-thinking and problem-solving skills, distinctive knowledge and skills, and commitment to service and community. Promotion is based on peer review of a professional portfolio (Hurt and Sunday 2002).

The Library of Congress

The Library of Congress (LC) has long had a career ladder structure in place. Although libraries widely adopt the Library's cataloging policies and practices, its career ladder has not been emulated. LC's career ladder includes two classes of library workers. The library technician series

> includes all positions that primarily require a practical knowledge of the methods and techniques of library or related information work in acquiring, organizing, preserving, accessing, and/or disseminating information. Library technicians provide technical support by performing a wide variety of tasks providing direct services to the public and indirect technical services such as materials acquisition, copy cataloging, support of automated systems, or other similar work in support of library or related information programs and operations. The work requires a practical knowledge of library or related information services, tools, and methods and procedures. (United States Office of Personnel Management 2003)

The librarian series

> includes positions that involve supervision or performance of work that
> requires primarily a full professional knowledge of the theories, objec-
> tives, principles, and techniques of librarianship, to select, organize,
> preserve, access, and disseminate information. This includes determin-
> ing the most cost-effective way to provide information that will best
> meet user needs. Typical functions in librarianship are collection devel-
> opment, acquisitions, cataloging and classification, reference, circula-
> tion, computer system and database management, and preservation.
> Some positions also require knowledge of one or more subject-matter
> specializations or foreign languages. (United States, Office of
> Personnel Management 2003)

A unique feature of LC's model is somewhat controversial with regard to
the profession's insistence that a librarian is defined as one holding the MLS or
equivalent degree. The minimum educational requirement for a technician position is two years of college. A librarian position requires the MLS degree. However, in both series, experience can be substituted for education, making it
possible to classify someone with a bachelor's degree and appropriate experience in the librarian series. On-the-job training for the two series does not differ
substantially. The basis for mastering the requirements for a position, whether
technician or librarian, is one-on-one training with an assigned senior staff
member (Hiatt 1987, p. 126).

Career Ladders for Cataloging Support Staff: Models and Processes

Until now, libraries have been fortunate to attract talented support staff
who are willing to contribute their efforts beyond what is strictly required by
their jobs to further the organizational mission. However, many of the incentives
that attracted these kinds of employees to libraries in the first place have eroded
over time as shrinking resources have reduced fringe benefits and job security.
The wave of coming retirements will result in shortages not only in the professional ranks but among support staff as well.

Organizational changes and changes in technology will only present
greater challenges and demands for new skills in the future for cataloging support staff. As things currently stand, support staff have little incentive to acquire
new skills that are needed to do their jobs right now (Kemp 1995, p. 38). Existing programs demonstrate that career ladder programs hold potential for support
staff to progress and develop careers-in-rank and can both help existing staff to
advance and attract new employees to the ranks. A career ladder structure is a
natural complement to emerging organizational structures and trends such as
teams and competency-centered organizations. A ladder provides a structure

and an incentive for employees to develop the skills and competencies that the organization needs.

Although career ladder models would be implemented to incorporate all library support staff positions, it is useful to consider the benefits offered to cataloging support staff in particular. Based on issues raised in the literature and analyses of existing programs, a model for a career ladder for cataloging support staff could incorporate the following elements:

- Entry points that are flexible and based on a combination of clearly defined criteria, considering an employee's educational credentials, experience, and demonstrated competency in specific areas.

- A promotion process that is employee-initiated (i.e., the employee does not have to wait for the library to conduct a classification study).

- A structure that permits the employee to advance without having to change jobs.

- Promotion based on individual merit and not tied to the position.

- Promotion based on clearly defined, rigorous criteria that take into account performance of job responsibilities, demonstrated mastery of library-wide and position-specific competencies, and demonstrated commitment to the library's mission, goals, and strategic plan.

- A review process that is fair and appropriate, whether based on peer review or other means.

Considerations for Establishing a Career Ladder Program

A number of questions must be examined in the process of establishing a career ladder, including the following:

- Where do cataloging support staff positions fit in the overall structure of the library?

- Are there discernible levels within the work, of difficulty or skill groups?

- What are the appropriate entry-level educational and experience requirements for each level? Where does certification fit into this?

- What are the general skills and competencies needed by all cataloging support staff?

- What are the more specific skills and competencies needed at each level?

- What are the criteria for advancement between each level?

Position Classification and Analysis

As has been discussed, current position classification schedules are often outdated and do not recognize the increased responsibilities of cataloging support staff positions. The question of where cataloging support staff positions belong relative to other positions in the library is an important one. Further, position descriptions and job titles tend to be nonstandard and outdated. Thus an important step is a classification study of existing positions to update classifications, job titles, and position descriptions to bring them in line with the work currently being done.

Many libraries place copy cataloging positions in the library assistant category and original cataloging positions in the library associate category (as defined by the *LISHRU*). Cataloging support staff members now participate in the full spectrum of cataloging activities, from copy cataloging to original subject analysis and foreign language cataloging. It is likely that expectations of support staff will continue to increase, as cataloging units become more involved in metadata and digital library initiatives, and as organizational structures become less hierarchical. All of these developments suggest that most cataloging support staff positions, other than perhaps marking and preparation, increasingly a student activity, fit better into the LIS associate category than the assistant one.

Minimum Educational Requirements

What are the minimum educational requirements needed to do the work in today's academic cataloging units? Increased expectations for support staff may require that the minimum educational qualification be the bachelor's degree, or a combination of college coursework, experience and demonstrated competency in specific areas. The literature shows that a broad general education is the best preparation for cataloging. The literature also appears to support the hypothesis that a majority of support staff members in academic libraries already hold the bachelor's or higher degrees (Oberg et al. 1992). Requiring the bachelor's degree would thus acknowledge what is needed to perform the work and reflect the level of credentials already possessed by most staff. Perhaps this would lead to compensation more appropriate to the level of qualification.

Differentiation of Responsibilities and Functions

More data are needed on the variety and scope of work that support staff are actually doing in cataloging units. As interest in competency-based advancement, certification, and other credentialing continues to grow, so does the need for a comprehensive national survey of work performed. Analyses show that cataloging activities performed by support staff members often include the following:

Copy cataloging tasks

- Searching
- Editing

Original cataloging tasks

- Description
- Formulation of headings
- Subject analysis
- Classification
  - Literature
  - Nonfiction
- Foreign language cataloging
- Cataloging of nonbook formats

Work done by support staff in cataloging units increasingly encompasses a variety of other activities, for example

- database management, including working with holdings formats and standards, link checking, and other kinds of troubleshooting;

- authority work, processing of vendor-generated authority reports;

- batch loading and export of records;

- supervision and training;

- workflow management;

- database creation;

- statistics compilation and analysis; and

- metadata encoding.

Tasks must be differentiated and grouped appropriately. Where in the spectrum do these activities fall? Are there discernible levels of difficulty and skill groups? How will jobs be arrayed along the career ladder?

Role of Certification

At the Third ALA Congress on Professional Education: Focus on Support Staff held in May 2003 (COPE 3), strong interest was expressed by support staff delegates and by LSSIRT for the creation of voluntary certification programs for LIS assistants and associates. ALCTS, in consultation with other relevant groups, should undertake a serious investigation of advantages and disadvantages of a voluntary certification model for cataloging support staff. Further, libraries must determine how certification will be considered as a criterion for entry-level positions and for promotion. ALA/APA and ALCTS should provide guidance on this subject for employers.

Development of Competencies/Criteria for Promotion

Once the structure of ladder and placement of positions within it has been established, it must next be asked what skills and competencies employees will need to do these jobs, and how they will progress through the ranks. As technical services units become increasingly team-based and cross-functional, it may become more useful to think in terms of developing broad skill sets in employees, such as database design, data encoding and representation, etc. Again, this is an area in which a coordinated national effort to develop competencies for technical services activities would be valuable. A comprehensive survey of library career ladder programs would be a useful addition to the literature as well. ALCTS should continue the work begun by the ALA Core Competencies Task Force in 2000.

Contemplation of a career ladder model for the advancement of support staff begs yet another crucial question, that of appropriate roles for effective use of librarians and support staff members. Salary schedules will have to be examined closely, as greater salary overlap between high-level support staff and entry-level librarians may be necessary.

Conclusion

The creation of career ladders for cataloging support staff is not a simple task. Implementing such a structure across a library's support staff positions would be costly and time-consuming. Yet as the literature review has shown, support staff have been facing the same problems of lack of opportunity for advancement, lack of continuing education and training, and inappropriate compensation for the past 30 years without noticeable improvement. Without support staff, our libraries would cease to function. The profession is on the brink of a crisis as record numbers of librarians and support staff prepare for retirement. The ability to recruit and retain a talented pool of support staff is crucial to the future of libraries. The cost of failing to provide support staff with opportunities for advancement is too great. The *LISHRU* asserts that it is the responsibility of the profession to provide career development opportunities for support staff. The profession must recognize its responsibility to our support staff colleagues and act now.

While much work must be done at the local level to implement career ladders for cataloging support staff, there are a number of large-scale design issues to be tackled on a national level by ALA and ALCTS in cooperation with LSSIRT, COLT, ALISE, and other stakeholders:

- The profession must clearly articulate roles for librarians and support staff.

- More research is needed on the variety and scope of work that support staff are actually doing in cataloging/technical services units.

- An investigation of advantages and disadvantages of a voluntary certification model for cataloging support staff should be undertaken.

- Standardized, broadly applicable job titles and descriptions reflecting the sophisticated nature of the work performed by support staff in cataloging units must be created.

- Core competencies should be developed for support staff in cataloging units

- Guidelines and recommendations for differentiating and grouping tasks and skill sets must be developed to aid libraries in creating career ladders.

Support staff members need the same opportunities for advancement, career development, and equitable compensation that are available to librarians. In 1999, the LSSIRT Task Force on Career Ladders concluded that

> Careers will happen when we have a mechanism in place by which we can quantify our qualifications (certification) and progress (career ladders.) We will have careers when our bosses recognize that to do our work well we need more than on-the-job training given second and third hand by someone who attended a workshop and has photocopies of the handouts to share. . . . We will have careers when we care that the standards of our profession are upheld no matter what. We will have a career when we are paid a living wage. (American Library Association, Support Staff Interests Round Table, Task Force on Career Ladders 1999, p. 4)

Support staff members have waited a long time to be recognized for their contributions to libraries. Career path models hold much promise as avenues for long-awaited change.

References

Abbott, Andrew. 1998. "Professionalism and the future of librarianship." *Library Trends* 46 (3): 430–443.

American Library Association. 2003. "COPE delegates define sustainable solutions for support-staff issues." *American Libraries Online* (May 26). Available: http://www.ala.org/al_onlineTemplate.cfm?Section=American_Libraries&template=/ContentManagement/ContentDisplay.cfm&ContentID=32733. (Accessed May 28, 2003).

American Library Association, Board on Personnel Administration, Subcommittee on Analysis of Library Duties. 1948. *Descriptive list of professional and nonprofessional duties.* Chicago: American Library Association.

American Library Association, Council. 1976. *Library education and personnel utilization (LEPU): a statement of policy adopted by the ALA Council, June 30, 1970.* Chicago: American Library Association.

———. 2002. *Library and information studies education and human resource utilization: A statement of policy adopted by the Council of the American Library Association, January 23, 2002.* Chicago: American Library Association.

American Library Association, Library Education Division. 1965. "Statement on junior college library assistant programs." *Newsletter* 53: 21.

American Library Association, Support Staff Interests Round Table. 1997. *Summary of survey to determine top three issues of concern to support staff.* Available: http://www.ala.org/Content/NavigationMenu/Our_Association/Round_Tables/LSSIRT/Strategic_Plan3/Issues_Survey/Results.pdf (Accessed May 28, 2003).

American Library Association, Support Staff Interests Round Table, Task Force on Career Ladders. 1999. *ALA SSIRT Task Force on Career Ladders few opportunities for advancement final report.* Available: http://www.ala.org/Content/NavigationMenu/Our_Association/Round_Tables/LSSIRT/Strategic_Plan3/Task_Force_Reports/career.pdf (Accessed December 12, 2003).

Anderson, Sue, and Kathy Bullene. 1999. "Certification of library support staff: National and state level progress." *Alki* 15 (2): 14–15.

Andrews, Virginia Lee, and Carol Marie Kelley. 1988. "Changing staffing patterns in technical services since the 1970s: A study in change." *Journal of Library Administration* 9 (1): 55–68.

Asheim, Lester. 1968. "Education and manpower for librarianship: First steps toward a statement of policy." *ALA Bulletin* 62 (9): 1096–1106.

———. 1967. "Manpower: A call to action." *Library Journal* 92: 1795–1797.

———. 1970. "Library education and manpower: ALA policy proposal." *American Libraries* 1: 341–344.

Auburn University Library. 2002. *AU Libraries career ladder info: Information about Auburn University Libraries' Career Ladder Program.* Available: http://www.lib.auburn.edu/dean/career/index.html (Accessed May 26, 2003).

Benaud, Claire-Lise. 1992. "The academic paraprofessional cataloger: Underappreciated?" *Cataloging & Classification Quarterly* 15 (3): 81–92.

Bishoff, Lizbeth J. 1987. "Who says we don't need catalogers?" *American Libraries* 18: 694–696.

Bordeianu, Sever, and Virginia Seiser. 1999. "Paraprofessional catalogers in ARL libraries." *College & Research Libraries* 60 (6): 532–540.

Buttlar, Lois, and Rajinder Garcha. 1998. "Catalogers in academic libraries: Their evolving and expanding roles." *College & Research Libraries* 59 (4): 311–321.

Coutois, Martin P., and Lori A. Goetsch. 1984. "Use of nonprofessionals at reference desks." *College and Research Libraries* 45 (5): 385–394.

Davidson-Arnott, Frances, and Deborah Kay. 1998. "Library technician programs: skills-oriented paraprofessional education." *Library Trends* 46 (3): 540–563.

Duke University, Perkins Library, Career Paths Task Force. 1999. *Turning jobs into careers: a preliminary report on career paths for support staff.* Aug. 1999 revision ed. Durham, N.C.: Perkins Library, Duke University.

Edwards, Ralph M. 1975. *The role of the beginning librarian in university libraries.* ACRL Publications in Librarianship, no. 37. Chicago: American Library Association.

Eskoz, Patricia A. 1990. "The catalog librarian—change or status quo? Results of a survey of academic libraries." *Library Resources & Technical Services* 34 (3): 380–392.

Evans, Charles. 1979. "The evolution of paraprofessional library employees." *Advances in Librarianship* 9: 63–101.

Froehlich, Thomas J. 1998. "Ethical considerations regarding library nonprofessionals: Competing perspectives and values." *Library Trends* 46 (3): 444–466.

Gartner, Alan. 1971. *Paraprofessionals and their performance.* New York: Praeger.

Giesecke, Joan, and Beth McNeil. 1999. "Core competencies and the learning organization." *Library Administration & Management* 13 (3): 158–166.

Goulding, Anne. 1996. *Managing change for library support staff.* Aldershot, Hants.; Brookfield, Vt.: Avebury.

Hiatt, Robert M. 1987. "Education and training of cataloging staff at the Library of Congress." *Cataloging and Classification Quarterly* 7 (4): 121–129.

Howarth, Lynne C. 1998. "The role of the paraprofessional in technical services in libraries." *Library Trends* 46 (3): 526–539.

Hurt, Tara Ludlow, and Deborah Stansbury Sunday. 2002. "Career paths for paraprofessionals: Your ladder to success." *Library Administration and Management* 16 (4): 198–202.

Kemp, Jan. 1995. "Reevaluating support staff positions." *Library Administration and Management* 9 (1): 37–43.

Kreitz, Patricia A., and Annegret Ogden. 1990. "Job responsibilities and job satisfaction at the University of California Libraries." *College & Research Libraries* 51 (4): 297–312.

McNeil, Beth, comp. 2002. *Core competencies and the learning organization.* Washington, D.C.: Association of Research Libraries.

Mohr, Deborah A., and Anita Schuneman. 1997. "Changing roles: Original cataloging by paraprofessionals in ARL libraries." *Library Resources & Technical Services* 41 (3): 205–218.

Mugnier, Charlotte. 1980. *The paraprofessional and the professional job structure.* Chicago: American Library Association.

Myers, Margaret. 1989. "Staffing patterns." In *Personnel administration in libraries,* 2nd ed., edited by Sheila Creth and Frederick Duda, 40–63. New York: Neal-Schuman.

Oberg, Larry R. 1992. "The emergence of the paraprofessional in academic libraries: Perceptions and realities." *College & Research Libraries* 53: 99–112.

Oberg, Larry R., Mark E. Mentges, P. N. McDermott, and Vitoon Harusadangkul. 1992. "The role, status, and working conditions of paraprofessionals: A national survey of academic libraries." *College and Research Libraries* 53: 215–238.

Ransell, Kerry A. 2002. *Career ladder opportunities for paraprofessional library staff at Auburn University Library.* Available: http://www.lib.auburn.edu/dean/career/ALA02.ppt (Accessed May 26, 2003).

———. 2003. Personal communication, May 28.

Rider, Mary M. 1996. "Developing new roles for paraprofessionals in cataloging." *Journal of Academic Librarianship* 22 (1): 26–32.

Russell, N. J. 1985. "Professional and non-professional in libraries: The need for a new relationship." *Journal of Librarianship* 17 (4): 293–310.

Stambaugh, Laine. 2000. "Are your library support staff classifications ready for the twenty-first century?" *Library Administration & Management* 14 (3): 167–171.

Thapisa, A. P. N. 1989. "The burden of mundane tasks: Library assistants' perceptions of work." *British Journal of Academic Librarianship* 4 (3): 137–160.

Turner, Brenda G. 1992. "Nonprofessional staff in libraries: A mismanaged resource." *Journal of Library Administration* 16 (4): 57–65.

United States Office of Personnel Management. 2003. *General schedule position classification standards.* Available: http://www.opm.gov/fedclass/html/gsseries.asp (Accessed May 26, 2003).

Veaner, Alan B. 1982. "Continuity or discontinuity—a persistent personnel issue in academic librarianship." *Advances in Library Administration & Organization* 1: 1–20.

———. 1994. "Paradigm lost, paradigm regained? A persistent personnel issue in academic librarianship, II." *College & Research Libraries* 55 (5): 389–402.

Weibel, Kathleen. 2003. "Apples and oranges: Fruits for thought." Keynote address at the 3rd ALA Congress on Professional Education: Focus on Library Support Staff (COPE3), May 16–17, College of DuPage, Glen Ellyn, Illinois.

Williamson, Charles W. 1923. *Training for library service: A report prepared for the Carnegie Corporation of New York.* New York: Updike.

Younger, Jennifer A. 1996. "Support staff and librarians in cataloging." *Cataloging & Classification Quarterly* 23 (1): 27–47.

13

Navigating Toward the Future, Building on Our Strengths: Reorganization and Change at Emory University Libraries

Susan B. Bailey

Editor's note: The author describes how Bibliographic Gateway Services at Emory University Libraries has evolved from a hierarchical to a distributed model, from a division with department heads to one with team leaders. The appendixes document a department that has gone through four organizational iterations in the past six years and is preparing and planning for its next reorganization. The author discusses how change has become a normal part of this department's routine, and how the human factor is so important in the failure or success of any redesign effort. Whether or not the team approach has been successful in this particular organization has yet to be determined, but this chapter is an interesting application of the knowledge access management (KAM) philosophy currently popular in the business community.

In August 1996, the director of Collections and Technical Services (CaTS) in Emory's General Libraries issued a call for staff members to participate in a CaTS Work Redesign Team. She acknowledged that, while incremental changes in work processes had occurred over time, no systematic examination of work processes as a whole had been previously undertaken. In describing the justification for beginning such a process, even as a library-wide reorganization was also underway, she stated that it was necessary because technology was not only changing how we did our work but was also broadening the scope of our work. She cited the need to stop doing some things or streamline existing activities to provide time to take on new activities, such as adding electronic journals to the online catalog. Thus began the process improvement and redesign initiatives that have continued in one way or another to the present. At the time of the appointment of the group that became known as CaTSPIT (Collections and Technical Services Process Improvement Team), most of the group members probably imagined that they would look at processes, design new processes where the old ones were in need of revision, perhaps even describe some potential organizational structure options. They would develop a plan, it would be implemented, and then things would get back to normal. In 1996, it probably had not yet become obvious that ambiguity and ongoing organizational change would become the norm.

The work of CaTSPIT took place in parallel to a library-wide reorganization. There was an expectation that any changes recommended by CaTSPIT would be implemented and in place long enough to generate positive results before the library-wide organizational changes occurred. CaTSPIT members were concerned about recommending structural changes that might be short-lived, but they believed that the changes they were proposing were in keeping with the principles adopted by the Library Design Team (LDT). CaTSPIT members also expected that implementation of their recommendations would facilitate future workflow assessment and change. Although the possibility remained that the structure for CaTS might change again when the library-wide reorganization was implemented, CaTSPIT members were encouraged by the Division director to recommend structural changes if they believed those changes were warranted. Redesigns always seem to take considerably longer than their initiators expect, and both the CaTS redesign and the library-wide reorganization exceeded their original timelines. The CaTS redesigned structure ultimately remained in place for three years, until the April 2001 library-wide reorganization took effect.

Redesign efforts in the General Libraries that began in 1996 were grounded in process improvement and organizational effectiveness approaches, not based on budgetary crises or personnel changes. Some of the previous organizational changes in technical services in the General Libraries had derived from personnel changes (Jasper and Treadwell 1992, pp. 361–366). Data gathering and organizational involvement were hallmarks of both the CaTSPIT and Library Design Team processes. Consultants from ARL and other organizations provided guidance and support for the work of both design teams. Both used interviews, surveys, and focus groups to gather information from members of the staff and library users, and both made site visits to organizations that had successfully managed change processes. The LDT was kept informed of the recommendations and progress of CaTSPIT, though there was no effort to coordinate outcomes. The members of CaTS were effectively in a position to be redesign pioneers within the library, a position that represented both opportunity and challenge. A year into the CaTS redesign implementation, a progress report was prepared that included recommendations to the LDT based on the CaTS experience. The report was viewed as an opportunity to inform the LDT members about some of the changes implemented in CaTS that had proved problematic, in hopes that the LDT could avoid comparable problems.

In 1997, there was some anxiety among CaTSPIT members that their work would be canceled out by the library-wide reorganization. At implementation of the new library structure, much of the CaTS structure did change again. In the move to a flexible and agile organization, the end goal was not a fixed, perfect structure, but rather one that permitted ongoing change as the norm rather than the exception.

Change as Operating Model

Change is complex and sometimes frightening. Although we may intellectually acknowledge that we now live in a world of "permanent white water," that doesn't mean that we truly have internalized it and are comfortable with it. Peter Vaill used the phrase "permanent white water" to describe the complex, turbulent, changing environment in which we find ourselves (1996, p. 4). He noted that our traditional educational systems did not prepare many of us for such an environment. Although it may be debated whether the current environment is truly more unpredictable than that of years past, "permanent white water conditions are regularly taking us all out of our comfort zones and asking things of us that we never imagined would be required. Permanent white water means permanent life outside one's comfort zone" (Vaill 1996, p. 14). The most positive outcomes for dealing with this environment derive from adopting a model of lifelong learning. The problem for many of us who grew up on the institutional model of learning is that "institutional learning assumes that learning begins in confusion and involves considerable inconvenience and pain before it moves to a state of relative competence and comfort" (Vaill 1996, p. 38). This permanent white water environment involves change at such a pace that we have little chance to attain competence or comfort before the next change challenges us to adapt to a new and messy situation that we haven't seen before.

Technical services professionals are certainly no strangers to change or to learning. However, the very nature of much of the work done in technical services, providing access to resources through organization and structure, assumes that it is possible to impose organization on unrelated and disparate resources. We believe that there is an orderly structure into which we can place things and then build upon that structure. So perhaps the world of permanent white water is even more uncomfortable for us than for many of our co-workers.

More than eight years after the appointment of CaTSPIT, there are probably still members of Bibliographic Gateway Services (BGS), the current iteration of technical services at the General Libraries, who believe that the change agents in the library will all either leave or come to their senses and take us back to a traditional, sensible organizational design and traditional, sensible work. "Any major change effort is confusing—alternatively exhilarating and painful for most people in the organization. Some people relish change. For others, the very underpinnings of their work lives are shaken" (Euster et al. 1997, p. 113).

Structural Progression

Organizational change in Emory's technical services has progressed from a very hierarchical model to a more distributed one, from a division with department heads, to a division with team leaders (see Appendixes 13.1–13.4). At each stage along the way, we have created elements that met with success and elements that proved to be problematic or impractical. Each of these lessons helped to inform the next decision, the next iteration. It is likely that the library's organizational structure will to continue to evolve, and it is important for technical services staff to play an important role in whatever the future holds.

The result of the CaTS redesign was a division made up of 13 groups (see Appendix 13.2). While the LDT was working on an organizational structure comprising teams, CaTSPIT was not convinced that the members of the division were ready to move to a team-based model in advance of the library-wide reorganization. There were to be no new staff hired, so moving from a division of six departments to a division of 13 groups meant that at least some staff would find themselves with multiple group assignments. CaTSPIT believed that multiple group assignments would foster an environment that provided staff the opportunity to have greater variety in work assignments, to experience improved communication, and to share information and expertise more broadly. A coordinating group comprising all group leaders and the division director was the new division management group, replacing the previous group composed of the division director and department heads. This group established divisional goals and priorities and discussed workflow and customer service issues. Going from six to thirteen divisional units also meant opportunities for staff members who had not previously occupied supervisory and managerial roles to take on such roles. Most of these new leaders were classified staff rather than librarians. In the new CaTS structure, some groups represented attempts to improve workflow by narrowing the focus to make for a more manageable and coherent work unit. This was the case with the Search-Order-Sort (SOS), Receiving, and FastCat groups. Other groups represented a focus on work not previously singled out for emphasis or importance, such as Database Quality Management, Documentation and Training, Technology, and Liaison. The implementation team for the CaTS redesign had no easy time trying to assign staff to the various groups. Assignments were based on staff expertise and interest, coupled with the divisional need to have a sufficient number of staff hours assigned to make each group viable.

Over the course of its existence, the redesigned CaTS underwent its own series of changes. The Technology and DQM groups merged, because there was significant overlap in membership and a single individual had become group leader for both. The Liaison Group was another casualty, hampered by difficulty in establishing its identity and a significant reduction in membership that rendered it no longer viable. The redesigned CaTS placed an increased focus on internal and external customers, improved productivity in a number of areas, and realized some positive changes in organizational culture. Nevertheless, many staff felt that implementation was uneven among the various groups, that leaders did not clearly articulate expectations, and that communication was no better after implementation than it had been before.

Implementation issues surfaced as General Libraries staff began the process of bringing the proposed library reorganization design to life. In April 2001, a new organizational structure proposal was finally implemented throughout the library. CaTS was effectively split between two new divisions (see Appendix 13.3). Technical Services (now renamed Bibliographic Gateway Services) included teams for MonoCat, FastCat, SerCat (later renamed SCOT, to represent Serials Control), Technical Services for Government Documents, and Database Quality Management. Acquisitions (including Accounting), the Lewis H. Beck Electronic Text Center, Collection Management, and Stacks, made up the new Information Resources Division. The EUCLID Documentation and Training (EUCLID D&T) cross-divisional group was proposed as an organizational construct to maintain a bridge between the two divisions. EUCLID is Emory's name for its integrated library system, and the work of acquisitions, accounting, and cataloging teams all requires training and skills to work effectively within the system. This group would not be a true team but would be a lateral coordinating group with a half-time coordinator. It would also be formed after all the true teams had been formed and were functional. Ultimately, EUCLID D&T was never actually implemented, although both divisions viewed it as an important element to mediate the loss of the technology component of the former DQM Group and the training and documenting components of the former Documentation and Training Group. CaTS staff felt that they had come a long way in taking some control of their technological fate, and the lack of continuity in that area was viewed by many staff members as a major shortcoming in the new organizational structure.

The library-wide reorganization required all team and division leaders to be selected through an application and interview process. All staff members were assured that they could at least remain in a comparable position in the new organization but were encouraged to think of applying for leadership positions or positions that enabled them to take on something new. The CaTS division director applied for and was selected for a new position in the organization outside of technical services, director of the Office of Program Assessment and Planning. Previously the group leader of DQM, I became division leader of Technical Services (BGS), while a member of Collection Management became the division leader of Information Resources. With a number of previous CaTS groups no longer part of the structure, some of the group leaders returned to non-leader roles. The library conducted a significant team start-up process, which helped all leaders and members learn the skills needed to work in a team-based culture. Consultants continued to provide guidance and support to individual teams and the leadership for the first year of implementation. Personnel in all the leader roles in Technical Services (BGS) changed, except in Serials. Some of the leadership changes went smoothly, while others resulted in difficult and strained team start-up and implementation periods. A number of things became clear during implementation. Although there were many staff members who demonstrated a willingness to give the new organizational structure and their new team leaders an opportunity to prove themselves, there were also a number who were very unhappy with the new situation. Some teams were little changed from their initial CaTS make-up, and staff members were comfortable working with each other in much the same way as before. Some, however, objected to having teams and "team-think" imposed on them as part of the team start-up process. Some staff seemed to feel especially annoyed at the ongoing communications and reminders of the expectation that they adopt the behavior and roles of team members, when they believed they had already effectively been behaving as such in the group structure. As time went on, it became evident that much of the resistance and dissatisfaction was associated more with the "team stuff" than with doing the work in a way that was more participative. For staff in multiple teams, some in as many as four, going through the team start-up process multiple times with multiple teams became a major sore point. In an instance of extremely bad timing, the university implemented a phone-in Time and Attendance System (TAS) for nonexempt staff members. As the organization was attempting to focus on teams and teamwork, the rigid timekeeping of an automated system for nonexempt staff clearly pointed out the distinctions among different levels of staff. Baldwin and Migneault (1996, pp. 93–98) provide a good overview of many of the perceived and real differences and potential conflict areas between librarians and nonexempt staff: recruitment (national versus local search), educational requirements (advanced degree versus general degree), average length of the probationary period (years versus months), and performance review processes (more focused on professional activity and research versus primarily focused on job performance). It is frequently the secondary responsibilities that determine the appropriate classification and compensation levels in library positions. Librarians may be perceived as carrying less than their fair share of day-to-day work because of absences to attend conferences and committee meetings and perform other professional responsibilities. The greater latitude in work and workweek schedule for librarians was unfortunately greatly highlighted with the start-up of TAS. The implementation of TAS probably exacerbated other strains being felt during the team start-up process and contributed to additional sensitivity and conflict. As members of a team-based organization, we needed to focus away from our differences and toward the things that made us members of the same teams and division, working to achieve common goals. In spite of the many differences and challenges, it became clear during the implementation period that the library administration expected to see a technical services operation that demonstrated changes even beyond those we originally envisioned. We were to be a technical services staff more actively and openly involved in the life of the library and its operations.

The BGS Coordinating Group (CG), made up of the division leader and the team leaders, was a major strength in attempting to move beyond the challenges that were encountered. Most BGS CG members had worked together closely in CaTS, and the group had great commonality of purpose and determination to work through the problems. The division was the most coherent of the reorganization, composed entirely of cataloging-oriented teams. The other functions often associated with technical services operations had been placed in the Information Resources Division. This commonality of purpose in BGS would provide opportunities to work divisionwide with staff on training and other issues that might aid in developing a more collegial environment among all division members. This could serve as a building block for encouraging staff to develop an identity with the division as a whole, not just with individual teams, which might help to alleviate some of the strains that were being felt.

CORC (Cooperative Online Resource Catalog) Pilot Project

The Serials team leader and I had periodically discussed the need to establish a plan for cataloging of electronic resources within the division. As electronic journals took more and more staff time, it became increasingly difficult for Serials to continue to be the only team cataloging electronic resources. Other BGS Coordinating Group members were also interested in cataloging free Web sites, something that had not been attempted in General Libraries to that time. All viewed the cataloging of Web sites and electronic resources as important and believed it was essential to develop a plan for incorporating this work into BGS workflow. It was also known that staff members already felt that they had more than enough work to do, and that it would probably be difficult to find staff members who felt that they had the time or training to take on the cataloging of these materials.

The BGS Coordinating Group began developing a proposal for a pilot project to catalog Internet resources. CG members discussed ways in which multiple objectives might be accomplished through this project. As team leaders and division leaders, all wanted to develop our own expertise in cataloging Internet resources. As more and more free and paid resources became available via the Web, it was important for all the leaders to have an understanding and appreciation of the issues involved in cataloging and managing them.

OCLC introduced its online training course for cataloging Internet resources at the perfect time, right when CG members were developing the plan for the CORC pilot project. That development enabled the use of the course as a focal point around which to structure the project. Events came together in a way that provided an opportunity to learn about cataloging a new category of materials, to further the goals of developing a sense of identity within the division, and to potentially give staff the opportunity to learn a new skill while also having the opportunity to practice some of the behaviors that they rejected in word but not in action. I extended a call on behalf of the Coordinating Group to all members of the division including the provision that any staff member could express an interest in participating in the project and be considered for inclusion. All Coordinating Group members would be part of the project group. The project group should have members from every team in the division, it should include experienced catalogers but would also be open to staff with no cataloging experience if they were willing to take the course and adhere to the weekly time commitment to the project, and there should be a safe learning environment in which experienced and less experienced staff would work together to help each other learn.

The actual plan for the project evolved somewhat over time, because the division staff members were also heavily involved in a major storage project during the time of group start-up. As things developed, each participant was asked to complete the OCLC Online course before the first discussion meeting. During the project, the CORC project group met monthly in one of the electronic classrooms so all participants could discuss cataloging issues by viewing and analyzing the same record at the same time. Reference staff members also attended some of these meetings, providing valuable public services perspectives and positive cross-divisional interactions. Staff were encouraged to work together, both in taking the online course and in cataloging, and partnerships were particularly encouraged for staff who lacked significant cataloging experience. Participants were asked to set a goal of cataloging five titles per month, after the initial training, and each person was asked to take part in evaluating the project at its conclusion.

In all, 13 staff members, counting the BGS Coordinating Group members, participated in the project. Certainly, conducting the pilot in this way created some difficulties, but most participants had very positive responses when asked about the overall experience. According to staff members who participated, the elements that contributed to the positive experience included clear goals and objectives laid out in the project description; meetings in the electronic classroom; review of cataloging records done as a group; the opportunity to work with a partner; doing new work; engaging in a collaborative approach to their work; working with people from other teams; taking quizzes and tests in the online course; making use of the discussion list created for participants for posting questions, meeting notes, and other information; learning a new format; and experiencing a learning process in which there were no experts and no stupid questions. Participants noted the following elements that they did not view favorably from the project the difficulty of the online cataloging course, with the most difficult material seemingly coming first; the lack of a print manual for the course; difficulty of assessing where the project fell among their other work priorities;

and difficulty of actually allotting five hours per month to the project. In the end, there was a significant interest from all members of the project group in continuing to participate in the ongoing work that would evolve from the pilot.

As the initial planning for the project was done, I shared with other BGS Coordinating Group members an interest in using this project as a kind of experiment to see what lessons might be taken from it to inform other workflow planning. More and more, there were projects that needed participation from a broad section of division staff members, and the cataloging rules and information format trends seemed to be creating more blurred and permeable boundaries in the work. Staff members from BGS and Acquisitions, as well as those from other Emory libraries, were involved in work on the electronic journals database. All staff needed training in using OCLC's Connexion. There were a variety of metadata projects and other initiatives in the library that provided broader organizational collaborative opportunities for catalogers. Teams were still effectively called MonoCat, Serials Control, Government Documents, and Database Quality Management, but many staff in these teams were doing work across boundaries and across the library. It wasn't possible or practical to reorganize every time a new work process or component became important.

Next Steps: Reorganize or Reconceptualize?

Reorganizations on a large scale are costly and take considerable time and resources to implement. They tend to be stressful for many staff, and because events change during the time taken to develop and implement the reorganization, staff, events, and budgets may have changed, thereby creating the need to further adjust the perfectly crafted design! In her paper prepared for the Library of Congress Bicentennial Conference, Karen Calhoun observed:

> [B]ecause we are and will be in a transitional state for some time, librarians must strike an appropriate balance between their everyday work and new ways of doing things. Perhaps in the near term, then, it would be more practical for libraries to avoid radical restructurings and instead make liberal and frequent use of virtual teams. These are cross-functional groups that exist alongside (and sometimes outside) the formal organizational structure. For example, for the purpose of introducing a new electronic resource description process, or providing ongoing support for one, the members of the virtual team would share authority and accountability. At the same time, the members would continue to report to different individuals and departments in the library hierarchy. (2001, p. 372)

This seemed to become an increasingly relevant idea. It was clear that, although the Emory General Libraries had made many efforts to include staff in the organizational redesigns, the work of creating new teams and taking them to the stage of full productivity was a stressful process. I began to wonder if we could somehow meld together the concept of virtual teams with the lessons taken from the CORC Pilot Project and create an ongoing mechanism to address work needs that come and go without the stresses of reorganizing. The permanent white water is a given in today's work environment, so we needed to find a less cumbersome approach to managing the needs that continued to arise for focusing on a topic, addressing the topic, then moving on to the next learning/doing opportunity. In the original call for interested staff, the CORC Pilot Project group was described as the first of many "virtual teams" that staff members might expect to see in the coming years—a group that comes together for a specific purpose and continues or changes as the work changes. The CORC group would be a cross-divisional work group that would assist members of the division in thinking about their work in new and different ways. At the conclusion of the pilot project, based on feedback from participants as well as the divisional need to develop an ongoing workflow for cataloging of Internet resources, the group that began as the project group agreed to continue and evolved into the ECat Working Group.

The BGS Coordinating Group had been engaged in work that was underway throughout the library, that of strategic planning and developing goals and objectives. As budgets had come under increasing pressure, new staff positions were less likely, existing needs often continued, and new needs emerged. Looking at the number of areas that needed attention, CG members hoped to begin using the virtual team concept in the implementation of divisional working groups. The ECat Working Group would be the first, and other potentially valuable working groups were identified. Without question, the nonimplementation of a technology-oriented group that bridged Acquisitions and BGS was viewed as a significant shortfall in the reorganization. There was an additional incentive in the fact that one of the most knowledgeable technology-oriented staff members in the division would be completing her MLS in the near term, and her potential departure at graduation would result in a significant loss of depth in the area of technology within the division unless some of her expertise and skill could be transferred to other staff. The first of the new working groups, therefore, would be Technology.

How were these working groups defined, and what made them different from any other kind of special project or task force group? The goal was to make working groups more formal than ad hoc groups and less formal than teams. There should be some work devoted to establishing group norms and expectations, but it should be minimal compared to that which occurred in formal team start-up. In many ways, the working group concept represented an evolutionary stage. Technical services had been constituted as a division with six departments, then a division with thirteen groups, then a division with five teams (see Appendixes 1–4). While some of the functions of the former CaTS moved as teams into Information Resources, others represented functions that had been valued in the CaTS groups but found no logical formal place in the new structure. In addition, although one of the goals of the new organization had been to be more deliberate about the proliferation of informal groups, monitoring group formation was not a priority during the early days of the reorganization. Organizational experience using groups that were appointed on an ad hoc basis varied greatly. Some of the groups accomplished a specific goal then went away, while others accomplished promising work but then found it difficult to gain acceptance and implementation of recommendations. The deliberate focus of creating a structure to which all newly formed groups had to adhere, while acknowledging the fluidity of the operating environment, seemed like a logical next step.

In October 2002, after developing a more explicit plan for developing the concepts used in the CORC Pilot Project, the BGS CG began the work of chartering working groups. On behalf of the Coordinating Group, I forwarded information to the division staff about the concept, identifying potential work areas that might benefit from creation of a working group, and asking each division staff member to identify areas of expertise and interest. The list of potential groups ranged from technology, to music and media cataloging, to Web documentation. While recognizing that the working group concept was likely to be more successful for some applications than for others, each working group implemented would play a role in contributing to the division's knowledge of how to best approach the work and to incorporate ongoing process improvement. Each group would receive a charge containing specialized information about the group's work and the Coordinating Group's expectations of the group. At least annually, for continuing groups, the charge, direction, and accomplishments of the working group would be reviewed by the CG to determine how well the group was meeting the charge and to get recommendations from the group for the future. Working groups could be proposed and created as needs arose and dissolved, or be redefined as needs changed. Membership in working groups was to be at the discretion of the division leader and the team leaders and could be evaluated on request. Roles that were identified for groups included coordinator, convener, and member. Initially, the coordinator would be a member of the Coordinating Group and would serve as a resource person for the group and a liaison to the CG. While some groups might have individuals who would enjoy a quasi-leadership role, other groups might have no natural take-charge person. So the presence of a BGS leader, either the division leader or one of the team leaders, seemed a necessity to ensure that groups began with an appropriate foundation of support. Aside from these standard elements, the organization, communication, and sharing or assignment of roles were to be determined by each group. To ensure that members held a common understanding of direction, working group members were asked to agree upon several measurable goals each year. Participation in the work of the group and contribution to meeting the goals would be reflected in each member's annual performance review.

Wide participation of staff members was essential if this was to be successful. As with any such call, some staff members were more forthcoming in expressing a willingness to participate than were others. It was also clearly communicated that failure to volunteer didn't guarantee that a staff member might not be called upon to participate in a specific group. It was important to implement working groups gradually, so there could be assessment of what worked and what didn't work before proceeding. It would also be important to demonstrate success with the initial implementations to facilitate future start-ups.

Conclusion

As of this writing, the working groups that have been implemented are still developing. Under the leadership of the experienced technology-oriented staff member, the Technology WG has made the greatest progress. Members of that working group have gained experience in devising and running reports in EUCLID and played a major role in coordinating testing for our next upgrade. Also contributing to its success is the fact that, historically, technology has been a focal point since division members attended an ALCTS Institute on Technical Services Workstations in the spring of 1995 and consequently formed an Expert Users Group. Another group, the previous Backlog Group, has been renamed and reoriented as the In-Process Materials WG. As part of their new role, they have begun monitoring the quantity of materials held in process awaiting cataloging. The Compact Shelving and Storage WG has also been meeting and developing a work plan. Clearly, not all the potential working groups will be implemented, and some are better candidates for success than others. Those that appear to show promise are the ones with a convener who is committed to the work of developing the group and to taking on some leadership in its direction. Some conveners are team leaders, while others are not.

Will this concept prove viable for advancing the work of the division while avoiding the need for full-scale reorganizations? Presently, there isn't enough evidence to assess the question one way or the other. If it does prove successful, it will be a success because of the staff members who choose to engage in the process and collaborate with the BGS Coordinating Group in its efforts. There are staff members who still prefer to distance themselves through either open or passive resistance. While a full range of reasonable measures have been taken to encourage full participation and provide opportunities for staff to take on new roles at a measured pace, these efforts will not succeed with all staff. After reasonable efforts are made to be inclusive and open, the emphasis must reflect back to the work itself and to working with those who are engaged in adapting to the new roles and expectations. Those who do not adapt to new roles will either become increasingly marginalized or will find more comfortable environments to work in.

Will these working groups be a successful bridge among division teams, enabling BGS to address changing work needs without reorganizing? That question can only be answered at a later date. If it does prove to be successful, it will succeed because of the staff members who evaluate their options and choose to be willing participants in the process. Those staff members represent the strength of the division and the organization. Coordinating Group members acknowledge that this is an experimental and evolutionary process. New and unexpected complications are inevitable. Perhaps other library-wide reorganizations are inevitable. In the summer of 2002, the Information Resources division leader left Emory to take a position elsewhere. After a variety of options were examined, the Executive Strategy Group of the General Libraries made the decision to create a Collection Management Division and move other Information Resources teams into different divisions. That decision provided for moving Acquisitions into BGS at the time that the new leader of Collection Management is in place. Will working groups be as logical an option when the work of the teams within BGS is less cohesive? Although the change has not occurred as of this writing, staff members in Acquisitions have been invited to participate in appropriate working groups, and two Acquisitions staff members have joined different working groups. Membership from Acquisitions has proved invaluable in Tech WG testing for the next system upgrade, an upgrade in which a significant number of acquisitions enhancements mirror those that have already occurred in cataloging functions. In some respects, it may not actually matter whether, a year or two from now, there are working groups operating in BGS. The staff members who have chosen to be active participants in the process and have taken advantage of opportunities to work in new and different ways in these groups will have developed skills, strengths, flexibility, and perspectives that can only enable them to work more easily and productively in any organizational model and in navigating the white water to come.

References

Baldwin, David A., and Robert L. Migneault. 1996. *Humanistic management by teamwork.* Englewood, Colo.: Libraries Unlimited.

Calhoun, Karen. 2001. "Redesign of library workflows: Experimental models for electronic resource description." In *Proceedings of the Bicentennial Conference on Bibliographic Control for the New Millennium: Confronting the challenges of networked resources and the Web*, edited by Ann M. Sandberg-Fox. Washington, D.C.: Library of Congress, Cataloging Distribution Service.

Euster, Joanne R., Judith Paquette, Judy Kaufman, and George Soete. 1997. "Reorganizing for a changing world." *Library Administration & Management* 11 (Spring): 103–114.

Jasper, Richard P., and Jane B. Treadwell. 1992. "Reorganizing collections and technical services: Staffing is key." *Library Acquisitions: Practice & Theory* 16: 361–366.

Vaill, Peter. 1996. *Learning as a way of being.* San Francisco: Jossey-Bass.

Appendix 13.1:
Collections and Technical Services Division Prior
to Implementation of CaTSPIT Proposal 1997

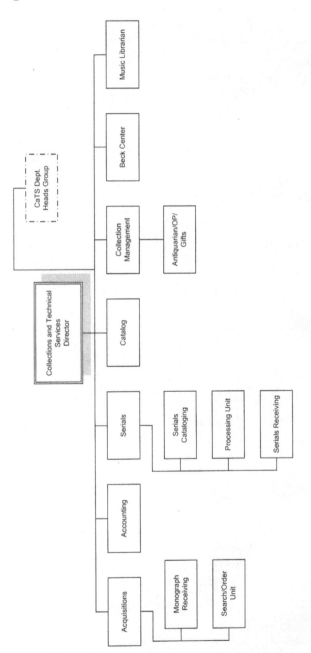

Appendix 13.2:
Collections and Technical Services Division at Implementation of CaTSPIT Proposal 1998

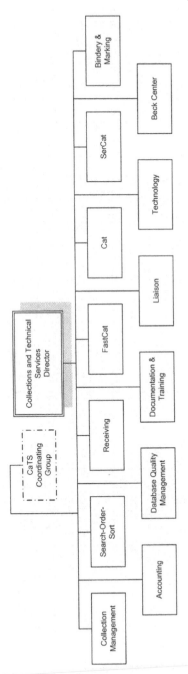

Division made up of 13 groups, each directed by a group leader.
*Indicates separate group with no equivalent in previous structure.

CaTS Coordinating Group (CaTS CG)—Division Director and group leaders.

Accounting—performs accounting functions.

Beck Center—electronic text center, closely aligned with Collection Management.

Collection Management—performs collection management functions, includes Gifts unit.

Bindery & Marking—prepares, sends, receives, and distributes bindery materials and labels and processes new materials for circulation.

Cat (Monographic cataloging)—handles original cataloging and OCLC member-contributed cataloging. Catalogs FastCat exceptions (M, N, BF, BX, P, and analytics)

Collection Management—performs collection management functions, includes Gifts unit.

Database Quality Management (DQM)—* responsible for authority control, recon, transfers, EUCLID corrections and changes.

Documentation & Training (D&T)—* facilitates documentation of procedures and policies within and between groups, coordinates documentation for division. Identifies training needs.

FastCat—* expedites processing of DLC/DLC cataloging.

Liaison—* customer contact persons for specialized internal customers (the Center for Business Information (CBI), Reference, Chemistry) and for other customers. Members field questions, track material in process, solve problems.

Receiving—unpacks, inspects, arranges received materials, both monographs and serials, and distributes materials to appropriate cataloging group. Handles claiming of monographs and serials, creates control records for new serial subscriptions, checks in and routes serials. Represents a change from the previous structure, where the Serials Department included Serials Receiving and Acquisitions handled Monograph Receiving.

Search-Order-Sort—performs pre-order searching, loads initial bibliographic record to EUCLID, the Emory online catalog, creates order records, assigns vendors.

SerCat (Serials cataloging)—catalogs serials in all formats; includes government documents cataloging.

Technology (Tech)—* handles technology support that does not directly require a response from Systems. Consults with Systems Office and provides support for those applications unique to technical services operations.

Notable changes after implementation: 1999—Formation of Government Documents Group; Merger of DQM and Tech; Liaison Group disbanded in favor of Liaison Coordinator.

Appendix 13.3:
Bibliographic Gateway Services at Implementation of New Organization 2001

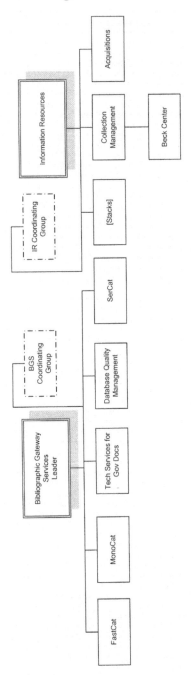

Units of the former CaTS split between two new divisions: Bibliographic Gateway Services (called Technical Services in early days of reorganization) and Information Resources.

BGS Coordinating Group (BGS CG)-Division leader and team leaders.

Remaining BGS teams are mostly comparable to their preceding groups. A computer technical support staff member, previously half-time in Systems and half-time in CaTS, is moved to Systems, and with him, the technical support component from the DQM/Tech merger. Bindery & Marking becomes a sub-group of SerCat. In Information Resources, Collection Management is comparable to its group predecessor, while the former Search-Order-Sort, Receiving, and Accounting are recombined into Acquisitions.

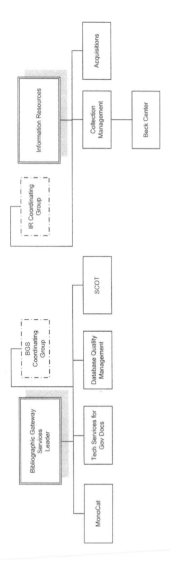

May 2003

2003 organization has evolved as a result of the following:

May 2001—FastCat becomes a subgroup of MonoCat, later evolution into a Working Group.

July 2002—Stacks moves to Access Services.

late 2002—Accounting moves from Acquisitions to Finance & Budget Office.

mid to late 2002—SerCat is renamed SCOT (Serials Control) to represent greater breadth of work (cataloging, binding & marking, electronic journals management)

Appendix 13.4:
Bibliographic Gateway Services at Hiring of Collection Management Division Director, Late 2003?

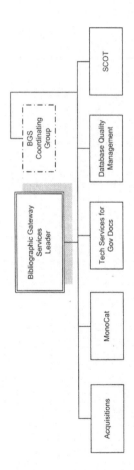

Acquisitions becomes a team in BGS.

Collection Management becomes a division.

14

Technological Change and Technical Services: A Case Study of a Mid-Sized Research Library

Karen M. Ramsay

Editor's note: The author looks at organizational change in the technical services department at the University of Rhode Island. The chapter focuses on how technology has transformed the workflow and work environment of the department. The human factor is always the unforeseen element in any reorganization, and the same holds true for this case study. Change is often assisted (or impeded) by the personnel who decide to leave or stay during the transition. The author concludes by stating how the department is moving toward a proactive rather than a reactive approach to change, thus positioning itself within the organization in the future.

While the library has always faced change, the rate at which changes occur has been accelerating. The image of the University of Rhode Island Libraries had been that of a quiet, sacred temple where the word was protected and materials were paged and viewed on site. Today, the Library has changed into a warmer, friendlier, and more social place, where groups gather to have discussions over coffee, accessing information via wireless systems. The library is being seen differently and sees differently as it moves from a building of volumes (centimeters, linear feet, pages) to a portal providing digital information (electronic resources, bytes, PDF) (Ramsay 2002, pp. 31–38).

The increased speed of technological changes has forced decisions in design and use of space, workflow, procedures, and personnel. "One hundred years later, computers have not only increased productivity, they have led to restructuring in nearly all areas of library operations" (Bordeianu, Lewis, and Wilkinson 1998, p. 261). While some of these changes have been carefully planned, others were motivated by the fear of falling behind. The last decade of change has greatly affected technical services.

The University of Rhode Island Libraries, a mid-sized academic main library with two branches, has seen, reacted to, and continues to plan for change. What follows is an overview of how the Technical Services Department at the University of Rhode Island has evolved over the last 10 years into what it is today and how it is consciously planning for the changes and challenges of the future in terms of personnel, technology, and space.

Technical Services 10 Years Ago

Ten years ago the Technical Services Department consisted of two units, Cataloging and Acquisitions. Cataloging resided on the second floor while Acquisitions was housed in the basement. At that time, the Acquisitions Unit was responsible for both serials and monographs. There were two professional positions: a head of Acquisitions who was responsible for overseeing the operation, including budget, dealing with book vendors, personnel and scheduling; and the assistant acquisitions librarian, who was responsible for supervising serials (subscriptions, renewals, check-in, claims, processing, binding). There were different physical areas within the unit. One area ordered and received monographs, while the other dealt with serials subscriptions and claims. One was responsible for serial check-in and was adjacent to the Reference Desk; the other was a processing area where materials were mended and items were labeled, and bindery where materials were collected and prepared to be sent to the binder and checked in when they were returned.

The Cataloging Unit was organized into two sections, copy cataloging and cataloging. The copy cataloging area consisted of clerical staff supervised by a paraprofessional. The cataloging section was where professionals and paraprofessionals were responsible for original cataloging (both serials and monographs), editing problem records, and handling materials for special collections. New acquisitions were delivered to the copy cataloging area from Acquisitions (from the basement to the second floor). Those bibliographic records that met certain criteria were then cataloged and the books moved to processing for labeling (from the second floor back to the basement). If a record did not meet criteria, then a printout was produced. The books and the printouts were then delivered to Cataloging (down the hall), resolved by the catalogers, and the printouts were returned to the copy cataloging area to edit the records online.

Ten years ago the functions of the Technical Services Department and the procedures employed were very traditional. Although supplemented by automation since the 1970s, the processes and the equipment used were much the same as they had been for decades. There were multiple order forms, form letters, work forms for cataloging, and many, many paper files. Books and paper were moved from office to office and between floors.

The changes that began slowly and carefully 25 years ago picked up speed and firmly took hold within the last 10 years. The next section, which documents these changes, is divided into three parts: technical changes, staff changes, and organizational changes.

A Decade of Change

Technological Changes

Although automation greatly affected the operations of technical services at the University of Rhode Island in the 1970s with the installation of OCLC terminals, the pace at which technology continued to bring change accelerated. The Library hired its first systems librarian in the late 1980s to help plan a course for the technology-driven future. A memo issued in November 1990 announced the creation of a new committee, the Committee to Study the Impact of Automation (CIA) (Cameron 1990).

The committee was charged with studying the effects on staffing and workflow of the new computerized environment. The committee issued a report in June 1991 stating: "[E]xisting automated systems made information more readily accessible to the staff, but it did not reduce the workload or the staff required to make this information available." The report continued, "[T]he transition to full automation will have a more immediate impact on the functions of the Technical Services Department. . . . It seemed reasonable to generalize that Technical Services' positions will experience the major changes in their work patterns" (Report of the Committee to Study the Impact of Automation 1991). There was clear recognition of impending changes in Technical Services.

The pressure to keep up as well as to connect everyone within the community increased. The Library reacted to this pressure with many significant changes in the 1990s: the implementation of an integrated library system; the closing of the card catalog; the opening of a new addition including a student computer facility with 100 computers; and the birth of a statewide, fully integrated, shared database higher education consortium. During this time when changes were made more in reaction to technology rather than by careful planning, systems were put in place but were not well integrated. Many decisions were made without enough experience, such as what information should be included in records and how that information should be displayed. With the OPAC, patrons knew immediately when materials became available, but those items had not yet made it through processing for stamping and theft stripping. Materials could be requested, but Circulation could not locate them because they had not found their way to the shelves. Most of the changes were the result of technology—the opportunities it offered as well as the pressures it exerted.

At the same time, the university was undergoing major reorganization. The two computer centers (Administrative and Academic), Communications (Telephone), Classroom Support (Audio Visual Center), and the Library were combined to form a new entity, the Office of Information Services (OIS). OIS has five divisions, each with a director. The person hired to head this operation holds the dual title of "Vice Provost for Information Services" and "Dean of University Libraries". The first person to hold that position arrived in the fall of 1995.

By the end of the 1990s the Library had changed on the outside (organization) and on the inside (the type and manner of the work). Every staff member had a PC on his or her desk where all communications arrived via e-mail, with access to the Web and the OPAC. Our vocabulary and our tools had changed. During the 1980s the old and the new had coexisted: catalog cards ordered online; typewriters next to printers. The technological changes as well as a commitment to automation took firm hold in the 1990s.

Staffing and Workflow Changes

A decade ago, although the number of units was fewer, the staffing was greater. "Ten years ago, in 1992/1993, the Department had a staff component of 29.5 fte [8.5 fte faculty positions and 21 support positions]. Today [11/02] we have a staff component of 15 fte [4.5 fte faculty and 10.5 fte support positions]" (O'Malley 2002, p. 1). Over the course of the 1990s total numbers in Technical Services were down 49.2 percent: professional positions down 47.1 percent; support staff positions down 50 percent. In 1994 there was a minor reorganization. One professional position in the Acquisitions Unit was transferred to Public Services. The remaining acquisitions librarian became the head of that unit, also serving as the serials librarian. That combined position was left vacant at the close of 1999 as a result of retirement. One person, the head of Technical Services, took over the responsibilities of managing Acquisitions, both serials and monographs. These changes were not the result of planning but rather a reaction to temporary personnel pressures. Combinations of duties were created to solve workflow problems created by vacancies.

At the turn of the century Technical Services looked different and acted differently than it had the decade before. The Acquisitions staff was now preorder searching the OPAC and OCLC, placing orders, checking in and claiming items, generating binding slips and labels electronically, and corresponding with vendors via e-mail. The Cataloging staff was performing all of its work online: editing records, exporting bibliographic records, and contributing records to OCLC, while maintaining records on the shared OPAC. Technical Services was conducting all this work essentially using one tool, the personal computer. The cards, special files, multi-order forms, form letters, typewriters, carbon paper, and white out were no longer needed. Distance to paper files, typewriters, etc., was no longer an issue. The same work was being done, but the manner in which it was executed was very different. It was inevitable that the workflow and possible changes should be examined.

The director of the Library decided that it was time for examination and re-evaluation. In 1999 a consultant was brought in to "have an outsider's view of the technical services operations at URI" (Davidson 1999, p. 8). Among her recommendations were the following:

- Technical services should be encouraged to keep looking toward the future.

- The Technical Services departments should continue to look critically at their own procedures, especially duplication of effort and unnecessary paperwork.

- The library should continue to study space issues, looking toward a possible unification of the technical services departments and an end to the transportation of new books back and forth between them.

The problems enumerated in the report arose, for the most part, from the changes in technology. In the past, books needed to be received where they had been ordered. They were then transported to the location where they would be cataloged and then to the processing area where the labeling machine was located. These back and forth movements between sections of Acquisitions and Cataloging were seen as necessary in the past as each function was handled separately, but now they were seen as inefficient. All functions became integrated with automation, and information could now be transmitted electronically.

Organizational Changes

"Being proactive about change rather than being a Pollyanna is essential for future success" (Diedrichs 1998, p. 120). Concerns about reorganization came from many sources. They had been raised by the director, discussed as a result of the consultant's site report, brought up by the Space Task Force (created in 1999), and addressed in the library managers' meetings. Some referred to the concerns in terms of space issues, others in terms of workflow and organization. There was a general consensus that change was an issue that needed to be addressed.

The chair of Technical Services distributed a memo to the department on June 1, 2000, stating that he had "been giving some attention to how the Dept. is organized. . . . The built-in delay in filling our vacancies has given me an opportunity to work out in some detail how to best fill the vacant management positions" (O'Malley 2000). As much as a state university suffers from the delays of bureaucracy, such delays also afford the organization time to reevaluate its mission and plan for modifications in fulfilling it. This memo announced the chair's plan to change the configuration of Technical Services. Three major changes were outlined. First, a position had been approved and advertised entitled "Head of Monographic Acquisitions and Copy Cataloging". The person hired would be the "monographic acquisitions librarian with combined responsibilities for the copy cataloging routines as well. When this position is filled, we will be shifting existing staff. . . . The physical placement of the staff has yet to be worked out" (O'Malley 2000). Essentially, Acquisitions would now be split into two separate units, one for monographs and one for serials.

The second change would involve the Serials Unit. There would be a delay in filling this position since the state has a "cap," or fixed number, on the total number of positions it allows to be allocated to the university. "The Serials Librarian will be head of serials acquisitions, binding and processing" (O'Malley 2000). This position has become the top priority for the Technical Services Department and as soon as permission can be obtained, it will be advertised. In the meantime, the chair oversees this unit.

The June memo also announced a third, and major, change in the department. The first electronic resources librarian would be "responsible for the acquisitions, continuing access, cataloging and overall supervision of the Library's electronic collections" (O'Malley 2000). Here was recognition that technological changes had affected the Library and the realization that action was needed. With the rapid increase of e-publishing, it had become essential to assign someone to address the issues in this area.

During the last 10 years the library has changed its technology, its workflow, and its organization. Sometimes these changes were made rapidly to keep up with the field, while at other times they were carefully planned. The cumulative effect of these changes and attempted changes has been to produce the library as it is today. The next section describes the implementation of the first part of the chair's planned reorganization within the Technical Services Department: the creation of the Monographic Acquisitions/Copy Cataloging (MACC) Unit.

Technical Services Today

The Changes

The Technical Services Department at the University of Rhode Island Libraries currently consists of four units: the Cataloging Unit, Serials/Bindery, Monographic Acquisitions/Copy Cataloging, and Systems. This latest rendition came into existence in January 2001. The acquisitions librarian, as had been announced, was hired to head the Monographic Acquisitions/Copy Cataloging (MACC) Unit. This unit was designed to handle all monographs in one physical area from request, to receipt, to copy cataloging, to labeling. The goals established for this new unit were to

- relocate staff to the designated location,

- produce written procedures for acquisitions and copy cataloging duties that would serve as manuals/guides for all staff,

- upgrade all staff to the same job title,

- cross-train staff using new procedures, and

- establish workflow patterns within the unit.

The location selected for the MACC Unit was the room in which the ordering, receiving, and standing orders staff was housed. One person was moved up to the second floor, where the copy cataloging stations had been located, along with two staff members who were moved from the current periodicals area. This second floor area would house three support staff to handle serials subscriptions, claims, and check-in. The two copy cataloging stations and staff were relocated from the second floor to the basement. Two staff from Acquisitions remained in the basement. Now there would be four staff members and the head of the MACC Unit in this area.

It was important for people to acclimate to this new situation. Therefore, the staff who had done ordering and receiving continued to do so. The books, once received, were rolled over to the terminals, where they were processed by the staff that had done so previously. Meanwhile, the head of the unit sat with each employee to learn what and how things were done and developed procedures in the form of a working manual.

Three of the support staff of the MACC Unit held the job title "Library Technician". The fourth held the title "Word Processing Typist". Although all staff members were doing the same type of work, strict union interpretations of job titles made it necessary for all employees to have the same job classification before cross-training could be initiated. This short delay was essential to avoid a union grievance. Because the university is a state institution, as well as a unionized campus, instituting a change required many steps and a great deal of paperwork. Special forms and a desk audit had to be completed for the state to determine whether, in fact, the fourth employee was doing the same work as the library technicians. The paperwork was submitted in mid-June, and in August 2001 word was received that the desk audit had determined that the employee should be reclassified to a library technician. At this point all employees were officially responsible for the same duties, the manuals had been developed, and the training could begin.

In theory, during the buying cycle when requests were backed up, duties could be shuffled and everyone could work on ordering or copy cataloging depending on where the need was greater. Cross-training was conducted as a hands-on activity. The employee being trained sat at a terminal and had the manual and a trained employee present. Ordering was done step by step, from preorder searching to sending the electronic order. Copy cataloging training was handled in the same manner. The items went to the workstation, and the trainee handled one book at a time, going through each step using the manual and a trained employee to answer any questions.

At the time of cross-training, the unit was fully staffed. The work was divided as it had been previously: Two staff members worked on the ordering and receipt while two worked on the copy cataloging and labeling of books. It was felt that as a result of the training and the printed instructions, the work could be switched around with little difficulty. Staff continued to switch duties periodically to reinforce the training and skills in performing the different tasks.

Problems and Successes

One of the greatest difficulties to deal with during any change, whether it be a reorganization or changed duties, is the human factor. People are always resistant to change. With the newly created unit came veteran employees who knew their jobs well and were good at them. They were reluctant to learn someone else's job. Explaining the similarities in dealing with bibliographic records and using the systems they were already familiar with helped allay their fears.

As long as staffing remained at 100 percent everything worked well. In June 2002 one staff member, a copy cataloger, transferred to a different unit for evening hours. The loss of a staff member at this time was manageable. The summer in academe is a slow time: Faculty are sparse, the fiscal year is at an end, the new year's budget will not be made available for a couple of months, and there are very few requests and few receipts. In the fall, as ordering and receiving returned to academic levels, working with fewer staff added to the stress level.

Although everyone had been trained in the different processes, there was still resistance. Unless specifically directed, although the work was visibly building in a particular area, staff did not take it upon themselves to move where they were most needed. One of the biggest benefits of cross-training is that it has become much easier to ask staff to switch duties and for staff to feel more comfortable with the tasks. But the stress and strain is evident in the environment when the supervisor has to step in and redirect the workflow. No one will take the initiative to cross the line in terms of duties. A scheduled switch day each week may be instituted. This continues to be the biggest difficulty. It is hoped that this will be alleviated as new software and modules (OCLC Connexion and new Innovative Millennium modules) are introduced and learned. Everyone will be a novice and learning all aspects of the work together at the same time. These new packages and training are now available.

There have been definite successes in the merger process. Participation in the creation of the work procedures aided staff in feeling as though they had some control. Procedures were drafted and then the staff were asked to review them and edit them. Procedures were not drawn up by the supervisor and then handed to them as a fait accompli. This participatory process reinforced staff feelings of competence with the work.

Staff members have commented on their enlightenment now that they understand how others look at bibliographic records, depending upon where in the process they are being viewed. It has become easier for them to understand general concepts rather than merely carry out steps for a certain task, understand the reasons for questions by others, anticipate what questions might be asked, and furnish information as to why certain records were used. One staff member stated that she was ready to learn something new.

One of the key elements of the success of the creation of this unit was due to the cataloging experience of the head of the unit. The knowledge of bibliographic work has been invaluable for the training of staff, writing up procedures, and dealing with both the acquisitions and cataloging aspects of the work. Questions arise and can be handled without having to slow down the work by having to go to other units for advice or resolution.

Future Plans

The Technical Services Department has definite plans for the future. The first is that the entire department be located on the same floor. The administration, as well as various committees, is in full agreement with this idea. An architect has looked at the various units and has designed a floor plan and drawn up a design to unify the department. The delay is due to lack of funds to complete the plan.

Staffing is another area in which planning is important. The required competencies of the staff have changed. Although staffing has decreased, "What we have seen is the elimination of lower level support staffing needs absorbed into fewer higher qualified support staff. . . So, while we require fewer staff, we need higher qualified, higher paid staff" (O'Malley 2002). This trend will continue as there is less paper to bind and process. It will now be essential to have staff that can understand bibliographic records and are familiar with handling e-resources. Renaming and redefining positions, qualifications, and duties have already begun. The importance of training has become evident and has been scheduled as the technology continues to change and new software, modules, and enhancements become available.

The need has also arisen for completely new positions. "In general, libraries have dealt with change reasonably well by retaining traditional value sets and structures. While they have added positions to deal with specific functions like automation, much of the reorganization in most libraries has merely grafted new specializations to old structures" (Williams 2001, p. 37). At the University of Rhode Island Libraries the appearance of the electronic resources librarian is an example of a grafted specialization.

The electronic resources librarian (ERL) is also the collection development manager (see Appendixes 14.1–14.3 for organizational charts of URI Technical Services for 1993, 2003, and 2013). The position appears in the table of organization as a slashed position (one person with a dual title and responsibilities, "Electronic Resources Librarian/Collection Development Manager") . The ERL half falls under the Technical Services Department, while the collection development manager answers directly to the dean of Libraries. The structure is still being scrutinized. The last discussion on departmental staffing in November 2002 brought forth a reconsideration of that one part-time position to expand into a new unit called the Electronic Resources Unit. This unit would consist of a head, a full-time electronic resources librarian, and a full-time support staff member.

Finally, the serials librarian position has become part of the future plan for Technical Services. The Serials Unit exists as a part of the reorganization that took place in 2001. Unfortunately, this part of the plan cannot be completed without permission to fill the vacant position. The constraints on a state institution are a reality as labor unions, budget rescissions, and job freezes present themselves as obstacles to careful planning. Reactive moves can be more opportunistic; as a position opens there is a rush to fill it. The problem with the result of reaction is that the situation is not necessarily desirable or efficient. Having a plan formulated and advancing slowly toward a more desirable goal may take patience and fortitude but will ultimately be more satisfactory.

The Technical Services Department at the University of Rhode Island is consciously planning for change and no longer reacting as it did in the 1990s. The future plan is for Technical Services to be composed of the Database Management Unit (currently Cataloging); MACC Unit; Serials, Processing/Binding; Electronic Resources; and Systems. Larry Marshall explains how reinvention is essential for businesses to become nimble and maintain an edge in a quickly changing environment (1999, p. 20). Delmus Williams (2001) takes that a step further, declaring that libraries need to follow the lead of business and become flexible with our changing environment: "Now, when the gravest risk we face as a profession comes from failure to step into our uncertain environment, libraries must build organizations that can leverage limited resources, build and modify skill sets quickly, and address change intelligently, quickly, and graciously" (2001, p. 45).

The University of Rhode Island Libraries Technical Services Department will continue to examine itself since "things are never going to get back to 'normal.' Unpredictability and change are the norm" (Diedrichs 1998, p. 120). There have been significant changes made within the last three years that have sensitized the Library to continual change. Technical Services has become more aware of how the tasks, the workflow, and diminishing staff might continue to be redefined and reorganized. The evolution will certainly continue in this new millennium, but it will be a carefully thought out plan, not simply a reactive one.

References

Bordeianu, Sever, Linda K. Lewis, and Frances C. Wilkinson. 1998. "Merging the acquisitions and serials department at the University of New Mexico: A case study." *Library Acquisitions Practice & Theory* 22 (3): 259–270.

Cameron, Lucille. 1990. Memo, November 28.

Davidson, Martha W. 1999. "Technical services at the University of Rhode Island Libraries: Report of a site visit, March 3." Unpublished document.

Diedrichs, Carol Pitts. 1998. "Rethinking and transforming acquisitions: the acquisitions librarian's perspective." *Library Resources & Technical Services* 42 (2): 113–125.

Marshall, Larry. 1999. "The art of reinvention." *Electronic Business* 25: 20–21.

O'Malley, William T. 2000. "Report from the chair." Memo, June 1.

———. 2002. "Departmental staffing." Memo, November 12.

Ramsay, Karen M. 2002. "B.D. (before digital)—A.D. (after digital): Rethinking space in a mid-sized academic library." *Technical Services Quarterly* 19 (4): 31–38.

"Report of the Committee to Study the Impact of Automation." 1991, June 24. Unpublished document.

Williams, Delmus E. 2001. "Developing libraries as nimble organizations." *Technical Services Quarterly*, 18 (4): 35–46.

Additional Readings

Branton, Ann, and Tracy Englert. "Mandate for change: Merging acquisitions and cataloging functions into a single workflow." *Library Collections, Acquisitions, and Technical Services* 26, no. 4 (2002): 345–354.

Gorman, Michael. "Innocent pleasures." *The future is now: The changing face of technical services: Proceedings of the OCLC Symposium, ALA Midwinter Conference, February 4, 1994*, 39–42. Dublin, Ohio: OCLC Online Computer Library Center.

Hirshon, Arnold. "The lobster quadrille." *The future is now: The changing face of technical services: Proceedings of the OCLC Symposium, ALA Midwinter Conference, February 4, 1994*, 14–20. Dublin, Ohio: OCLC Online Computer Library Center.

Koh, Gertrude S. "Knowledge access management: the redefinition and renaming of technical services." *Libri*, 50 (2000): 163–173.

Taylor, Arlene G. "The information universe: Will we have chaos or control?" *American Libraries* 25 no. 7 (1994): 629–632.

Thornton, Glenda A. "Renovation of technical services: Physical and philosophical considerations." *Technical Services Quarterly* 15 no. 3 (1998): 49–61.

Wiles-Young, Sharon, Judy McNally, and Jos Anemaet. "Merger, reorganization and technology meet technical services." *The Serials Librarian* 34, nos. 3/4 (1998): 379–384.

Appendix 14.1:
University of Rhode Island Libraries
Technical Services, 1993

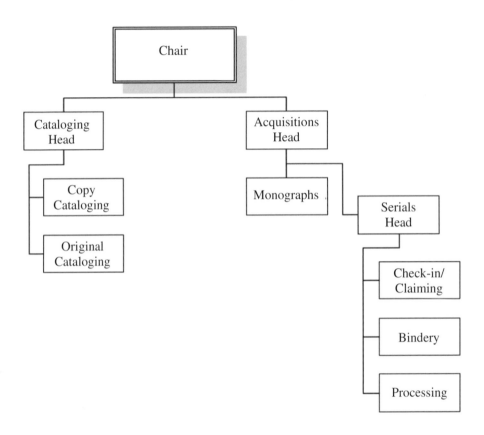

Appendix 14.2:
University of Rhode Island Libraries
Technical Services, 2003

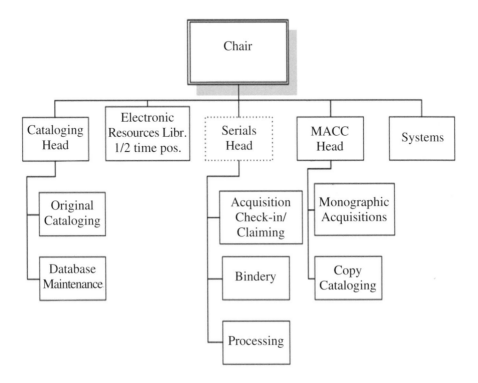

Appendix 14.3:
University of Rhode Island Libraries Technical Services, 2013?

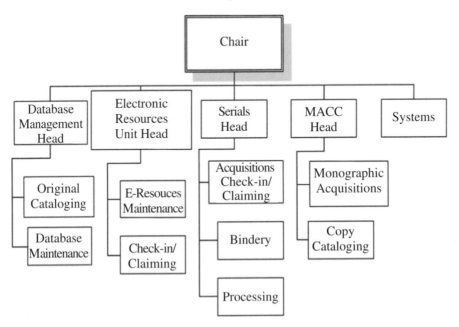

15

Personnel Turnover as Impetus for Change

Martha Ann Bace
Patricia Ratkovich

Editor's note: Personnel turnover as the impetus for change within a department or organization happens more often than is documented. At the University of Alabama Libraries, this has been more of a persistent problem than elsewhere. The authors document the problem of retention of both professional librarians and support staff, as well as their search for a new organizational structure within which to operate. Downsizing, hiring freezes, and low salaries are some of the challenges the authors of this chapter have had to face. Sound familiar?

personnel: 1 b: persons of a particular (as professional or occupational) group—(Webster 1986, p.1687)

turnover: 3: a reorganization with a view to a shift in personnel: shake-up—(Webster 1986, p. 2469)

impetus: 1 a : a driving or impelling force—(Webster 1986, p. 1134)

change: 1: to make different; a: to make different in some particular but short of conversion into something else: alter, modify—(Webster 1986, p. 373)

Personnel turnover provides a constant impetus for change within any organization. The persistent challenge for any institution is to deal with changing workflows with the personnel on hand. This is the course of action that the University of Alabama Libraries Catalog Department has undertaken to meet this challenge.

Overview of Personnel Turnovers

Various factors influenced the redirection of workflow. A factor of great impact was the migration from the NOTIS integrated library system to Endeavor's Voyager system. Prior to the move, the Acquisitions Department had not needed to import a bibliographic record to begin the order process when creating a purchase order. Catalog Department personnel added records upon receipt of the materials. The Voyager Acquisitions module, however, required a bibliographic record before creating a purchase order. It quickly became apparent that the two departments would be duplicating efforts, and that streamlining the process would save considerable time. It was decided, therefore, that the Acquisitions Department would import the appropriate record when ordering materials.

Before the migration, the Catalog Department consisted of four units, two of which were supervised by catalog librarians (see Appendix 15.1). The monographs unit was made up of four librarians and four copy catalogers, and the serials/nonbook unit included three librarians and four copy catalogers. The two other units—the catalog management unit and the shelf preparation unit—were student workstudy units supervised by senior support staff. When the Libraries migrated to Voyager in 1998, the department was reorganized into three units under the department head; a catalog librarian supervised each unit (see Appendix 15.2). In August 2001 the department head transferred to the library school, and the unit heads assumed departmental leadership responsibilities for the next 15 months (see Appendix 15.3).

Throughout these personnel turnovers, each unit head was responsible for hiring new copy catalogers while vacant faculty positions were filled through national, regional, or internal searches. All training was done at the unit level and was supervised by the unit head. Training covered all aspects of the cataloging process, including authority control and using the integrated library system catalog module and the bibliographic utility, OCLC.

A constant victim of the first two organizational structures was communication. Misperceptions and miscommunications within the department led to internal stress and dissatisfaction. Resolving these inter-unit issues took time and effort. Because of the lack of cross training, most had no idea how their work affected the other units or even what their co-workers' responsibilities entailed. The formal organizational structure occasionally hindered the communication of new policies and procedures between the units as well.

One issue that played a major part in determining the need to change was that when personnel left the department, there was often difficulty in replacing them. Over the course of the six years, the Catalog Department saw the support staff turnover rate peak at six individuals leaving in 2001 (see Appendix 15.4). While the faculty turnover rate was not as extreme for the same period, it was just as detrimental. By the spring of 2002, the original complement of eight librarians had been reduced to three and a half and the twelve support staff to ten.

Part of the difficulty in filling open positions lay in the lack of qualified applicants. "The 'increased demand and declining supply' of qualified applicants for library jobs is a major problem facing the profession" (Berry 2003, p. 8). The size of the community in many ways determines the size of the pool of applicants; depending on the current market trends and needs, the pool could be extremely small or fairly large.

Also, once they were hired, training new personnel was time and labor intensive. Even though new support staff with some library background might not take long to become contributing members of the department, all new hires faced a six-month training and probationary period. During this time their work had to be reviewed by a staff member or cataloger before the materials could be processed for shelving. Between 1996 and 2002, the Catalog Department had at least one person in training and on probation at all times. This included several staff members, including the four temporary faculty positions, several of whom left before their probationary period ended.

Under such circumstances, training becomes an issue unto itself. Because so much time and effort were typically expended on instruction and review, backlogs in the regular workflow occurred quite frequently. After the department head's departure in 2000, the catalogers fulfilled the responsibilities of the department head as well as maintaining their own unit head duties. This created backlogs in materials needing original or complex copy cataloging. Authority control was, out of necessity, limited to verification of main subject headings as the materials were cataloged. Name and series headings were dealt with from printed Voyager reports as time allowed.

After 15 months of endeavoring to cover their own primary work responsibilities, supervise three to five support staff members each, and fill in for the department head, the catalog librarians were ready for change. The effort to meet all these needs became too burdensome. Because of the lack of funding for a new department head, however, the concern became how to utilize the talents and expertise already in the department. Careful consideration was given to the myriad possibilities. Eventually, the library administration appointed a department head from an internal pool. This appointment resulted in the loss of one of the two monographic catalogers.

It was eventually decided that although the workflow would still need to be format-driven to take advantage of current staff expertise, removing the day-to-day managerial tasks from most of the librarians would free them to focus on cataloging that required a higher level of expertise than staff could provide. Freeing the librarians from most of their administrative duties allowed them to better evaluate workflow and create new policies and procedures, stay abreast of new standards and trends, and incorporate new assignments such as the addition of catalog records for electronic resources. To release the librarians from supervisory duties, a senior staff member was promoted to staff supervisor for the monograph copy catalogers. This pulled the largest single group of support staff into one unit (see Appendix 15.5). Physically moving the monograph copy catalogers into closer proximity to one another was designed to foster a more cohesive unit. While there are still support staff members reporting to a librarian, eventually these few positions will report to the department head.

Restructuring the department into a new model presented areas for development that had been neglected in the past: authority control, reestablishing NACO participation, special library-wide projects, and opportunities for research. Efforts to streamline the monographic workflow included tightening the shelf-ready profile and moving more subject areas from the approval plan into the shelf-ready process. Once the shelf-ready vendor implemented the changes, the whole procedure was transferred to the Acquisitions Department, allowing the materials to be handled only one time for both check-in and cataloging.

An obvious result of change is the stress it creates within any group. Mosenkis states that, "Change causes stress—even positive change. We cannot 'fix' the world of work to make change go away, however we can change ourselves" (2002, p. 7). Getting the support staff to buy into the changes and claim ownership in them was the single most difficult challenge. Much of the resistance to change was generated by the view that their previous endeavors were being devalued because the levels of scrutiny had been relaxed. Efforts to reduce the time it took to get materials from receipt to the shelf had produced anxiety among the support staff who were accustomed to being meticulous.

The Problem of Retention

In the SOLINET-sponsored workshop, Transforming Libraries: Creating a New Workplace for the Digital World, Maureen Sullivan (2003) introduced the key elements to support retention in libraries. Among these are the broad areas of organizational structure, organizational systems, and human resources systems.

As a department, when looking at the subgroups of these areas, we recognized many of the issues we had been facing for more than six years. Was it possible to create a department that utilized communication and decision making, that held us accountable, and that created a climate and culture for retention?

Sullivan suggests that a climate that encourages staff to stay should include giving staff the freedom to speak their minds without fear of reprisal, that their work is significant, and that it contributes to the whole library's performance. The environment should be one where there is an "overall sense that we are here to make a difference for our customers and the best way to do this is to work together" (2003).

In Sullivan's ideal organization, compensation and benefits support the human resources system. When faculty and staff are compensated adequately for the work they do, the opportunity for loyalty to the institution is created. This has been one of the major challenges for retaining faculty and staff at the UA Libraries.

In looking at the turnover rate in the catalog department, compensation must be counted as a major reason for leaving. Of the 16 support staff hired and terminated between 1996 and 2001 (see Appendix 15.4), 10 left for higher paying positions—several to other departments within the university. Appendix 15.6 shows the minimums and maximums for both the library assistant and library assistant senior positions in 1996 and 2003. While there has been some increase in salaries since 1996 (9.5 percent increase for library assistants and 7.8 percent for library assistant seniors), those increased salaries do not have the same buying power as the earlier salaries.

One of the more frustrating aspects of taking on temporary catalog librarians was the risk of losing them before their contract was completed. Many of our temporary catalogers had been cataloging interns from the School of Library and Information Science on the UA campus. The internship program gave the student an opportunity to get hands-on experience in the cataloging field and, in most instances, it aided the department by helping to move materials out of the department and onto the shelves. Also, when we were able to hire former interns as temporary catalogers, it took much less training for them to become contributing members of the department.

In the case of the temporary faculty (who are appointed on a six-month contract), three of the four resigned before their term ended to take permanent positions—with higher pay—elsewhere. Of the permanent faculty positions, all four left the department for higher pay. Appendix 15.7 shows the UA library faculty minimum salaries for 1996 and 2003. Beginning salaries for librarians at the rank of instructor increased 35.1 percent between 1996 ($23,100) and 2003 ($31,200). This increase, however, was still below the average beginning salary of $33,202.27 for all ARL libraries (Kyrillidou and Maxwell 1995, p. 21; Kyrillidou and Young 2002, p. 29).

The Search for a New Organizational Structure

The need for a new organizational structure was primarily predicated by the loss of staff and the time spent in training their replacements. It became apparent that we could not maintain the same level of confidence in the quality of cataloging we were providing, when each long-term staff member was having to double-check materials processed by newer personnel. And the same was true for the librarians. The frustration level was acute across the board.

In an effort to involve the entire staff in the redesign of the department, the unit supervisors (before the appointment of the new department head) asked their staff to help research different models in similar-size libraries. As a way to prepare for change, the monographs unit head required her staff to attend the UA Human Resources workshop, Who Moved My Cheese? This workshop, based on Dr. Spencer Johnson's bestseller, enabled the copy catalogers to identify how they as individuals adjusted to change and to discuss ways they could help the department adjust more easily to change.

The entire Technical Services department, both the Acquisitions and Catalog Departments, took part in a continuous quality improvement workshop, also provided by UA Human Resources. As the Acquisitions units did the same for their areas, each of the catalog units developed flowcharts of the various types of work performed (cataloging standing orders, curriculum materials, audiovisual, etc.). A side benefit of seeing the flowcharts of both areas was learning what other units were doing and why the processes were structured the way they were; to a certain degree, it helped strengthen communications between the two departments.

While this particular workshop did not directly address the process of redesigning the catalog workflow, it did illustrate overlaps and similar processes between the two departments. This led to the eventual migration of the shelf-ready program from the Catalog Department to Acquisitions. Still to be transferred is the FastCat procedure (all DLC copy). This will happen when Acquisitions becomes more familiar and comfortable with the shelf-ready program.

In all, about five different organizational configurations were presented as possible models for the redesigned department. The final decision on the structure was made and then presented to the department by the new department head. While the new structure incorporated most of the different ideas developed by the staff, it did not exactly follow any one in particular, and there was initial dissatisfaction on the part of the staff.

Where We Are Now

In terms of retaining support staff, 2002 and 2003 have been relatively stable years. With the addition of two copy catalogers in January 2002 and the reconfiguration of the monographs copy cataloging unit in January 2003, the monographs unit has settled into a well-balanced routine. With the monographs staff supervisor dealing with many of the complex copy cataloging issues previously backlogged on librarians' desks, productivity has increased.

Unfortunately, the situation of the librarians has not been as satisfactory. Although the department head position was filled, because it was an internal appointment we lost a monographic catalog librarian. The department also lost one and a half other catalogers—one to the new metadata unit and the half-time music cataloger to information services. Though a national search filled the position of the serials/nonbook catalog librarian in May 2003, the department is still one and a half librarians down from where it was in 2001. A university-wide hiring freeze has made the possibility of filling either of those positions unlikely in the near future. While not the first choice, the best option for the department may be to hire temporary catalog librarians when funding is available.

Conclusion

As the British theologian, Richard Hooker, said, "Change is not made without inconvenience, even from worse to better" (Bartlett 2000), but being flexible and alert allows us to be proactive in forecasting and implementing change. And while recognizing that change takes time and that accepting change is difficult at best, perseverance and dedication to providing quality service to patrons remain the ultimate goals of the University Libraries Catalog Department.

References

Bartlett, John, comp. 2000. *Familiar Quotations.* 10th ed., revised and enlarged by Nathan Haskell Dole. Boston: Little, Brown, 1919. Available: www.bartleby.com/100/ (Accessed June 27, 2003).

Berry, John N. 2003. "Is certification the answer?" *Library Journal* 128 (1): 8.

Kyrillidou, Martha, and Kimberly A. Maxwell. 1995. *ARL annual salary survey 1995–96.* Washington, D.C.: Association of Research Libraries.

Kyrillidou, Martha, and Mark Young. 2002. *ARL annual salary survey 2001–02.* Washington, D.C.: Association of Research Libraries.

Mosenkis, Sharon L. 2002. "Coping with change in the workplace." *Information Outlook* 6 (10): 7–10.

Sullivan, Maureen. 2003. "Creating an organization that supports retention: Key elements." Presented at the SOLINET workshop, Transforming Libraries: Creating a New Workplace for the Digital World, June 16–17, Tuscaloosa, Alabama.

Webster's Third New International Dictionary of the English Language Unabridged. 1986. Springfield, Mass.: Merriam-Webster,.

Appendix 15.1:
Departmental Organizational Structure
prior to September 1997

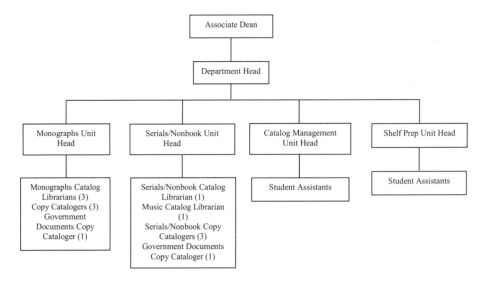

Appendix 15.2:
Departmental Organizational Structure
Between October 1997 and August 2001

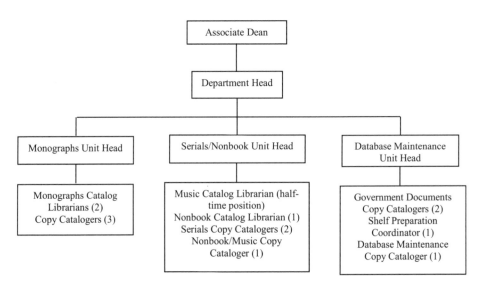

Appendix 15.3:
Departmental Organizational Structure
from August 2001 to October 2002

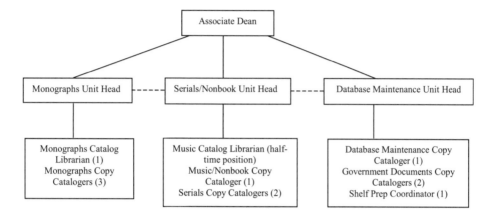

Appendix 15.4:
Staff and Faculty Turnover, 1996–2002

	Start Date	Termination Date	Number of Days in Position	No. of Months in Position	Average No. of Months in Position from 1996-2002
Staff					**14.00**
Staff A	06/17/96	07/30/97	408	13.41	-0.58
Staff B	10/07/96	07/18/97	284	9.34	-4.66
Staff C	10/14/96	09/24/97	345	11.34	-2.65
Staff D	09/02/97	12/19/97	108	3.55	-10.45
Staff E	09/02/97	08/16/99	713	23.44	9.44
Staff F	11/03/97	08/18/00	1,019	33.50	19.50
Staff G	01/20/98	05/31/01	1,227	40.34	26.34
Staff H	09/14/98	04/23/01	952	31.30	17.30
Staff I	08/13/99	08/04/00	357	11.74	-2.26
Staff J	02/28/00	08/01/01	520	17.09	3.10
Staff K	08/21/00	10/01/00	41	1.35	3.61
Staff L	03/19/01	08/01/01	135	4.44	-9.56
Staff M	05/28/01	11/01/01	157	5.16	-8.83
Staff N	06/04/01	08/02/02	424	13.94	-0.06
Staff O	10/01/01	11/01/01	31	1.02	-12.98
Staff P	10/03/01	01/02/02	91	2.99	-11.00
Faculty— Temporary					**3.88**
Faculty A	06/10/01	01/02/02	206	6.77	2.89
Faculty B	08/16/01	11/01/01	77	2.53	-1.35
Faculty C	06/01/02	07/02/02	31	1.02	-2.86
Faculty D	07/29/02	01/03/03	158	5.19	1.31
Faculty— Regular					**24.35**
Faculty E	04/01/96	07/01/98	821	26.99	2.64
Faculty F	12/01/97	06/01/99	547	17.98	-6.37
Faculty G	10/19/98	07/01/01	986	32.41	8.06
Faculty H	02/01/00	10/02/01	609	20.02	-4.33

Appendix 15.5:
Departmental Organizational Structure
since October 2002

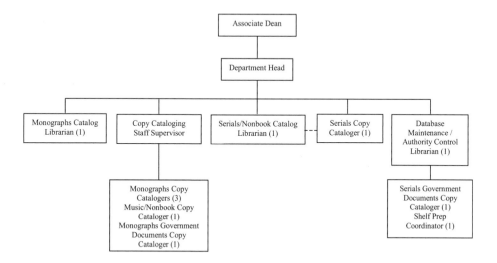

Appendix 15.6:
Support Staff Salaries in 1996 and 2003

	1996		2003		Percent Increase	
	Minimum	Maximum	Minimum	Maximum	Minimum	Maximum
Library Assistant	$15,233.40	$21,560.50	$16,684.20	$25,026.30	9.5	16.1
Library Assistant Senior	$17,651.40	$25,469.60	$19,021.60	$28,512.25	7.8	11.9

Appendix 15.7:
Minimum Librarian Salaries in 1996 and 2003

	1996	2003	Percent Increase
Instructor	$23,100.00	$31,200.00	35.1%
Assistant Professor	$26,600.00	$34,320.00	29.0%

16

Shifting Duties and Responsibilities
of Technical Services Staff

Karen Davis
Constance Demetracopoulos
Daryle McEachern Maroney

Editor's note: The authors describe how a new administration and a new integrated library system were the impetus for reorganization within the Georgia State University Libraries. The results of a committee approach to redesigning technical services duties and responsibilities are documented, and the appendixes illustrate these, as well as the duties of various technical services staff in the new departmental configuration.

Technical services departments periodically undergo reexamination of their organization, policies and procedures, and work. The cycle of reorganization is spurred by new developments in technical services. In this cycle the impetus is usually an outside force influencing the library in some way. Migrating to a new online system or hiring a new university librarian are two of the strongest forces. Starting in the fall of 1997, both these changes occurred in the library at Georgia State University. The new online system had a farther-reaching impact on personnel in the library, because it had been 13 years since the command-driven first only system had been installed. The new online system had a graphical user interface (GUI) to which personnel had little or no exposure. This chapter discusses the broad organizational change in the entire library and specifically the catalog department, as the vision of the new university librarian took shape and the increased use of new technology in the library emerged.

Georgia State University is a state-supported urban research institution in downtown Atlanta. It contains six academic colleges offering courses in fields ranging from business through physics and astronomy and has more than 35,000 students. Faculty and students are served by a Law Library (part of the College of Law), an Instructional Technology Center (part of the College of Education), and the Pullen Library.

The William Russell Pullen Library contains more than 1.3 million volumes, including approximately 5,000 active serials (newspapers, journals, annuals, etc.); 12,000 media materials; and over 250 electronic databases, many of which include full text. In addition, the library is a Federal Document Depository and has more than 800,000 government documents. The library functions as part of a consortium of college and university libraries throughout Georgia.

In the fall of 1997, a new university librarian was hired at William Russell Pullen Library. During the following months and years, she assessed the organizational structure and put in motion a systematic reorganization of all the departments in the library. The library had operated for many years with the same organizational structure, policies and procedures, and online system. There had been little turnover in staff or faculty librarians. With reorganization, the statement "we've always done it that way" was disposed of and critical thinking was engaged to evaluate all aspects of each department.

The first departments to undergo change were those directly affecting the service provided to students, faculty, and the university community. The duties of the retiring associate university librarian (AUL) were split into two sections: Technical Services and Public Services. The new AUL for Public Services shifted responsibility for the Media Center, the Periodicals Service Desk, and the Interlibrary Loan Office from Reference to Circulation (now Access Services). The Collection Development Office was merged into Information Services (formerly Reference), where bibliographers and reference librarians became subject liaisons, with selection, reference, and instructional duties. A Bibliographic Instruction unit was formed to coordinate basic library instruction classes and the liaisons' participation in subject-specific and advanced classes.

The new AUL for Resource Management encouraged the Acquisitions and Cataloging Departments to examine their structures. The Acquisitions Department completed a self-study and shifted positions from their monographs unit to the serials and binding unit, in response to the change in workflows created by the new integrated library system and the approval plan. The acquisitions' monographs unit took over preorder searching for firm orders (materials not on the approval plan) from the Collection Development Office. An additional faculty position, assistant department head/electronic serials librarian, was added to the Acquisitions Department, with duties spanning the acquisition and cataloging of electronic serials.

The intention to form an ad hoc committee to study organizational structure and cataloging responsibilities was announced at a monthly Catalog Department meeting attended by the AUL for Technical Services and the library human resources officer. Together with the Catalog Department head, they stressed, "Everything was on the table." The committee would be given carte blanche to consider whatever administrative models it deemed promising without regard to the department's traditional structure or current personnel.

The department's structure was a conventional hierarchical bureaucracy. Originally, four unit heads (monograph, serials, LC copy, and office manager) reported to the department head. The office manager was in charge of staff and students performing processing and book repair, as well as ordering supplies and keeping up with personnel matters. The LC Copy Unit head was a senior staff member supervising four lower-level staff. The Serials Unit head was a faculty cataloger supervising three staff members, and the Monograph Unit head (a faculty cataloger) supervised two faculty and three staff catalogers.

Change had already started for the department when the experienced LC Unit members (including the unit head) left for higher paying positions within six months of each other and were not replaced. Some of the positions were shifted to the Government Documents Processing Unit, which had been transferred to Cataloging from Reference and reported to the Serials Unit head.

The ad hoc Committee to Review Staffing and Organization of Cataloging was established on February 28, 2001. Its charge was "to prepare a recommendation by March 30, 2001 concerning the staffing needs of the Catalog Department" that would best position the department to meet its part in achieving the goals of the Pullen Library Strategic Plan. The committee was directed to take into account the following:

- The library and university strategic plans;

- Near and mid-term aspects of national cataloging practice;

- The government documents recommendation;

- Current tasks and amount of work;

- Things we should be doing or would like to do;

- Things only we can do;

- Things that could be done by others (outsourcing);

- Responsibilities and roles of faculty and staff; and

- Changes brought on by new ILS, authority control, and Marcive processes.

The Committee consisted of the three unit heads (monograph, serials, and support), one elected faculty librarian, and one elected staff member from each unit. The first order of business for the committee was its own structure. The members quickly agreed to work within a collegial rather than a hierarchical structure. Instead of electing a chair, it was decided to rotate alphabetically the responsibility for facilitating meetings. We also determined that we needed the following documentation as preparatory to our work: library strategic plan, departmental goals, current organizational chart, procedures for YBP cataloging, job descriptions of all staff, backlog report, and production statistics. In addition to these internal documents, the committee also decided that a sampling of how other university libraries had reorganized would be useful. Several members volunteered to conduct a literature search.

The short turnaround period necessitated that the committee meet several times weekly, for two-hour blocks. The review of catalog department tasks was taken up first. The current job descriptions were reviewed and amended to reflect all the tasks actually performed by each staff level. Considerable time was spent determining appropriate duties for each level. The most sensitive discussion centered on the distinction between catalog librarians and classified staff. Over the years, there had been a gradual blurring of roles, causing a marked degree of dissatisfaction on all sides. Staff members had been asked to perform tasks normally associated with librarians, for example original cataloging of theses and dissertations and assigning call numbers and subject headings to member copy. Although some staff members had welcomed the opportunity for more interesting assignments, the committee felt that it was inappropriate to require them of nonlibrarians. At the same time, however, the committee needed to address the issue of staff enrichment by finding challenging tasks appropriate to the existing classified levels.

Because of periodic staffing shortages, catalog librarians had been routinely enlisted in the editing of both LC and other member copy and in performing routine catalog maintenance such as added copies/volumes, transfers, and withdrawals. This practice ran counter to the new university librarian's stress on appropriate use of library faculty. Catalog librarians had faculty status and were expected to participate in service and scholarly activities including publication, presentations at professional conferences, and earning a second master's degree. Two of the catalog librarians were also liaisons to academic departments and were expected to engage in the full range of liaison activities including selection, teaching, Web page development, and consultations. The role of catalog librarians had also changed within the Catalog Department. The administration of special projects had been added to their other duties. One librarian was coordinating Special Collections cataloging; the other was project manager for the Internet cataloging project. In these capacities, catalog librarians were responsible for developing local procedures for the cataloging and processing of materials and coordinating workflow with other library departments.

A thorough examination of the range of duties and responsibilities of cataloging staff resulted in a renewed appreciation of the contributions made by the different administrative levels to the effectiveness of the Catalog Department. It also gave a clearer picture of what needed to be done to meet the goals of the library. Some of what we did could be outsourced. In fact, some of this had already been done with the outsourcing of LC copy and the importing of records for the government documents from MARCIVE. The question of outsourcing was an interesting one. In theory, almost everything could be outsourced. But to what end? Efficiency? Cost-effectiveness? Would outsourcing meet the library's goal of providing the best possible online catalog in support of the university's educational mission? Our recent experience with outsourcing much of our retrospective conversion had alerted us to certain difficulties, especially with nonbook formats such as scores. The committee concluded that although lower-skilled tasks could, and perhaps should, be outsourced, more complex tasks needed to remain in-house. This would have an impact on staffing because it would require higher skills and more extensive training. The cataloging of newer formats like electronic resources, including Internet resources, necessitated documentation such as local procedures and training manuals. These duties would be added to the increasing list of catalog librarian responsibilities.

The other central issue was an appropriate organizational model. The literature search failed to uncover a model that was significantly different from our current one. All of the models were more or less hierarchical. Cataloging tasks seemed to naturally coalesce around a unit structure. The committee concluded that such a structure was the most efficient for our purposes. We did entertain the idea of eliminating the department head position but decided to retain it, along with the unit head positions, as a way of providing stability for ongoing functions, ensuring the orderly flow of information, and facilitating personnel management.

To address the issue of staff enrichment, the committee decided on a pool model for all levels below unit head and catalog librarian. The committee felt that this model would not only provide staff with opportunities for learning new skills and adding greater variety to their work but would also ensure greater flexibility in meeting departmental goals by providing management with a larger pool of equally trained and skilled staff from which to draw as needed. Although each staff member would have a "home unit," he or she would be capable, after proper cross-training, of performing any departmental task appropriate for their classified level and all lower levels. All staff below the library associate level would in effect become floaters among the various units.

The committee also decided to consolidate the various catalog maintenance tasks currently shared between the Monograph and the Serials Units and the physical processing tasks of the Processing Unit into a single new Collection Management Unit. A staff person at the library associate II level (the highest staff position at Pullen Library) would serve as the unit head. The creation of a new unit would rationalize maintenance tasks and afford career advancement opportunity for catalog department staff.

The committee presented its recommendations in the form of a memorandum to the Catalog Department head on April 6, 2001. Following is a list of its recommendations:

Modify the current structure:

- Retain the departmental structure, with unit heads reporting to the department head;
- Retain separate units for monograph and serials cataloging;
- Create a Collection Management Unit incorporating collection maintenance and other physical processing activities;
- Distribute responsibility for administering and managing workflow among faculty and library associates; and
- Pool all staff below the level of library associate.

Increase emphasis on documentation and training.

Regarding staffing:

- Hire a full-time office manager and an administrative assistant to be shared between Acquisitions and Cataloging;
- Hire another faculty cataloger if the combined liaison duties of cataloging faculty exceed 30 hours per week;
- Assign one library associate to be unit head of the new Collection Management Unit;
- Assign two library associates to report to the assistant department head/head, Serials Unit; and
- Upgrade the LAIII positions for Documents, YBP, and End Processing to LTA and fill the three vacant positions.

The Catalog Department head commended the committee for its hard work and expressed general approval of its recommendations, commenting that the "report offers a good framework to use to react to the current situation and move into the future in a constructive way." He did not approve the creation of the administrative assistant position because there already existed a similar position in the library to assist liaison librarians. Although agreeing that the pool model was a good one, the department head did not accept the committee's recommendation for a single pool at the LTA level but proposed instead two separate pools, one of five LTAs and one of three LA IIIs. Documentation of the workings of the committee and various outputs can be found in the appendixes to this chapter.

During the calendar year 2002, we implemented some of the committee's recommendations:

- The departmental reporting structure and separate Monograph and Serials Units were retained.

- A Collection Management Unit was formed and began to take on some catalog maintenance in addition to processing duties.

- Faculty members with no unit head responsibilities were assigned database enhancement projects to manage.

- Though the pool idea was not fully implemented, some cross-training took place, giving the staff members involved a greater depth of knowledge about the workings of the department. We have not been able to evaluate the full impact of this element of the plan because of turnover of cross-trained staff.

- A full-time office manager was hired for Acquisitions and Cataloging.

- Library associates became heads of the new Collection Management and Government Documents Processing Units, and one library associate is assisting the assistant department head in database maintenance.

- No study of cataloging faculty's hourly investment in liaison duties was done, so there is no justification for requesting an additional faculty cataloger.

- Staff vacancies were filled at old position grades, so classified staff levels have not been upgraded. This seriously affects the implementation of the pool model, which was based on interchangeability.

The modified reorganization has been in effect for over a year, but there has been no opportunity to review the recommendations and the manner in which they were implemented. Staff promotions, and resignations, as well as changes in staffing throughout the library, have had an impact on implementation of the pool concept. Some department members feel there is a need to address the discrepancies between the committee's recommendations and subsequent administrative modifications.

Appendix 16.1:
Report of the Ad Hoc Committee to Review Staffing and Organization of Cataloging

Background

Formation of the ad hoc committee: On February 28, 2001, an ad hoc Committee to Review Staffing and Organization of Cataloging was established. Members of the committee are the current unit heads; one faculty member elected from the Monograph Unit; and one staff member elected from each of the current units.

The Associate University Librarian for Resource Management, the Library Human Resources Officer, and the Head, Catalog Department, presented the charge to the committee. It reads as follows:

> In order to position us to meet the changing needs of our students, faculty, and staff, and to better respond to the many changes in information resources, prepare a recommendation by March 30, 2001 that reflects an organizational structure and staffing needs for the Catalog Department, taking into account the following:
>
> ➤ The library and university strategic plans
> ➤ Near and mid-term aspects of national cataloging practice
> ➤ The government documents recommendation
> ➤ Current tasks and amount of work
> ➤ Things we should be doing or would like to do
> ➤ Things only we can do
> ➤ Things that could be done by others (outsourcing)
> ➤ Responsibilities and roles of faculty and staff
> ➤ Changes brought on by new ILS, authority control, and
> ➤ Marcive processes

Deliberations of the ad hoc committee: The committee identified a list of supporting documentation it would need to study in order to complete its charge. These included the library strategic plan, department goals, a current organizational chart of the department, the government documents recommendation, the proposed procedure for YBP cataloging, job descriptions, the latest backlog report, and production statistics. It was agreed to seek additional material on how other libraries have restructured.

Before adjourning, the committee spent some time brainstorming on alternatives to current staffing, structure and workflow. Ideas offered included use of split positions or part-time staffing, and greater use of student assistants; teams or pools vs. units; cross-training; subject/descriptive split vs. whole book cataloging; and merging serial, monograph and non-book cataloging.

The supporting documentation was assembled, including *Spec Kit 215: Library Reorganization & Restructuring*, May 1996. Considerable time was spent in subsequent meetings discussing roles and levels of responsibility of faculty and staff; which tasks are best kept in-house and which can be outsourced; staffing needs for the work to be done in-house; and organizational models.

Roles and responsibilities of faculty and staff: In examining the roles and responsibilities of faculty and staff the committee attempted to define activities appropriate to each level. For example, only faculty are required to participate in activities related to the criteria for promotion (and tenure). All levels have responsibilities relating to management and cataloging. The distinctions lie in the complexity of the tasks performed at each level. See Appendix B for the outline of tasks defined for each level.

Workload: Depending on a stable budget, we anticipate that the number of print titles acquired, especially theses, will hold steady, and that we will see increases in other formats in the coming years. While outsourcing can ease much of the burden of some activities, it must be emphasized that internal personnel will still be needed to monitor and complete the process.

As catalogers are released from the routine cataloging tasks now being outsourced, they can focus on the projects identified in the Catalog Department goals that are based on action items in the Library's strategic plan. Technological changes will continue to generate additional tasks that require new skills. Training and documentation become even more important in this environment. Specialization, while valuable at some levels, needs to be counter-balanced by cross-training, so that the ability to perform a given task is not dependent upon a particular person.

Recommendations

1. Modify the current structure. We searched for different models of organization to consider, but we were unable to locate any library with a genuinely "innovative" structure. A hierarchy similar to our current organization is almost universal. We concluded that the unit structure is still the most effective model for a cataloging department. We recommend retaining that structure with one modification: in considering how to maximize and encourage flexibility while maintaining a structure that will channel energies into meeting the library's goals, we developed the idea of pooling all non-administrative staff at the lower ranks. See Appendix A for a revised organization chart and floor plan.

    a. Retain the departmental structure with Unit Heads reporting to the Department Head. Retaining the Department and Unit Head positions provides stability for ongoing functions, ensures the orderly flow of information, and facilitates personnel management. Members of the LTA and student pools will be assigned to specific unit heads for reporting purposes, but will perform work activities wherever needed.

b.   Retain separate units for Monograph and Serial cataloging. The workflow for new monographic items is linear, while the workflow for serials, database maintenance, and collection maintenance tends to be circular. We agreed that combining monographs with any of these would create unnecessary complications and that it will be more efficient to keep them separate.

c.   Create a Collection Management Unit incorporating collection maintenance and other physical processing activities. Delegating routine collection maintenance activities to the Collection Management Unit will allow other units to focus on cataloging new materials. It will also equalize skill levels among the three units and promote communication, cooperation and cross-training within the pool of LTAs.

d.   Distribute responsibility for administering and managing workflow among faculty and library associates. Administrative tasks expand each time the Catalog Department embraces a new opportunity, such as CORC, authorities processing, or government documents processing. We need to delegate administrative tasks to more of the faculty and staff.

e.   Pool all staff below the level of Library Associate. Rotating non-administrative staff through each unit will provide progressive training in ever more complex tasks. It will also promote improved flexibility in responding to changing priorities, variations in workflow, and personnel changes.

2.   Increase emphasis on documentation and training. Complete documentation of all Catalog Department procedures is essential to support the positioning of personnel to meet shifting priorities. Placing documentation on the Catalog Department web page will further facilitate ease of use and effective time management. The pool concept involving all LTAs in the department will require cross-training in serials, monographs, and collection maintenance. Cross-training will promote new learning opportunities and expand each LTA's competencies and potential within the department. Cross-training at all levels will also promote and encourage a team atmosphere, enhancing cooperation and motivation.

3. Staffing. The kind of work being outsourced reduced the need for lower level staff only. The kind of work being done in-house is stable or increasing and requires higher level skills. We still need at least four faculty catalogers in addition to the Department Head. In addition, we recommend three library associates, eight library technical assistants, student assistants as needed, and two additional staff to support administrative and clerical needs.

   a. Hire a full-time Office Manager and an Administrative Assistant to be shared between Acquisitions and Cataloging. Currently each department has one staff member assigned part-time to handle the tasks of ordering supplies, maintaining office equipment, and so forth. Now that the two departments occupy one office, it will be more efficient to combine the responsibility for these tasks. A full-time office manager will also address the need for someone to monitor the entrance and cover the phones during office hours. This will allow the staff members who currently double as office managers to devote their energy full-time to their primary duties. The Administrative Assistant will provide backup to the Office Manager and will support administrative tasks, committee work, liaison, and research activities for technical services faculty. Such an arrangement will parallel the support enjoyed by faculty in other library departments.

   b. Hire another faculty cataloger if the combined liaison duties of cataloging faculty exceed 30 hours per week. We need four faculty catalogers who each devote at least 30 hours per week to managing and performing cataloging tasks. Committees and other professional activities already consume some of their time. If three faculty catalogers each spend more than ten hours per week on liaison activities, we have lost the equivalent of one faculty cataloger.

   c. Assign one Library Associate to be Unit Head of the new Collection Management Unit. Combining the current Support Unit with related activities transferred from the cataloging units will form the newly created Collection Management Unit. The current Head of the Support Unit will be converted to a Library Associate. Without the office manager duties, this Library Associate can concentrate on collection management activities including end processing, collection maintenance, and preservation.

    d.   Assign two Library Associates to report to the Assistant Department Head/Head, Serials Unit. The Library Associate currently working on enhancement projects will help manage database maintenance and enhancement projects. The Library Associate supervising Government Documents Processing will need to work closely with the serials catalogers.

    e.   Upgrade the LA III positions for Documents, YBP and End Processing to LTA and fill the three vacant positions. The proposals for government documents and YBP cataloging include one LA III each. We also have one vacant LTA position in the Serials Unit. Those three positions with the five currently filled LA III and LTA positions will give us the eight full-time equivalent positions we need for the following activities: in-house monograph cataloging (2); YBP processing (1); government documents processing (1); new serials cataloging (1); added volumes and other collection maintenance (1); end processing (1); and repair (1). The eight staff members will not be assigned to any one activity. They will benefit from having some variety in their workday, and, by sharing responsibility for a variety of tasks they will ensure that we have the flexibility to respond to changes in priorities, workflow, and personnel. For rotating assignments and cross-training to work, all members of the pool must be able to do LTA level tasks. Experienced staff in each area of activity can assist in cross-training others.

4.   *Review the situation again in six months after implementation.* After six months we will be in a better position to estimate the amount and level of staff needed for new activities such as outsourcing follow-up. We will also be able to evaluate the effectiveness of the pool model.

Appendix 16.2:
MEMORANDUM

March 4, 2004
To: Head, Catalog Department
From: The Committee

Subject: Report of the *ad hoc* Committee to Review Staffing and Organization of Cataloging

Attached, please find the report of the *ad hoc* Committee to Review Staffing and Organization of Cataloging. It includes:

- Background

    - Formation of the *ad hoc* committee
    - Deliberations of the *ad hoc* committee
    - Roles and responsibilities of faculty and staff
    - Workload

- Recommendations

    - Modify the current structure
        - Retain the departmental structure with Unit Heads reporting to the Dept. Head
        - Retain a separate unit for Monograph cataloging
        - Create a Collection Management Unit incorporating catalog maintenance and physical processing activities
        - Distribute responsibility for administering and managing workflow to all faculty and library associates
        - Pool all staff below the level of Library Associate

    - Increase emphasis on documentation and training
    - Staffing
        - Hire a full-time Office Manager and an Administrative Assistant to be shared between Acquisitions and Cataloging
        - Hire another faculty cataloger *if* the combined liaison duties of catalog faculty exceed 30 hours per week
        - Assign one Library Associate to be Unit Head of the new Collection Management Unit
        - Assign two Library Associates to report to the Assistant Dept. Head, one for Database Maintenance and Enhancement Projects, and one to Supervise Government Documents processing

– Upgrade the LA III positions for Documents, YBP, and End Processing to LTA and fill the three vacant positions
- Review the situation again in six months

- Appendix A: Structure

  - Organization Chart
  - Floor Plan

- Appendix B: Responsibilities and Roles of Faculty and Staff

- Appendix C: Workload

  - Statistics
  - Discussion
  - Quantity Standards

Appendix 16.3:
Appendix C2: Workload

Over the last five years the Monograph Unit has cataloged an average of 30,000 new titles per year. Approximately 75 percent of these had LC copy. Of the remaining 25 percent or 7500 titles, about 5800 were printed materials, including GSU theses which require original cataloging. In addition to print titles, there were, on average, 400 new scores, 500 audio CDs, 50 other CDs, 600 videos/DVDs, 10 microform titles, and 100 titles in miscellaneous formats such as cassettes, computer files, and maps. Assuming a stable budget, we anticipate that the number of print titles acquired, especially theses, will hold steady, and that we will see increases in other formats in the coming years.

The Serials workload is geared primarily to maintenance activities – added volumes, ceases, cancellations, entry changes, corrections, transfers, lost and withdrawn items, and associated record maintenance. The number of new serial titles in all formats only averages about 1000 per year, when the budget permits. Far from improving efficiency, the implementation of Voyager had a negative effect upon serials throughput, since the migration scrambled the holdings data and the records must be corrected before items can be added or transferred. Few print subscriptions have been canceled as a result of electronic access, due to licensing restrictions and concern over long-term availability. Staffing levels have never been adjusted to address the impact of adding hundreds of new or duplicate titles in electronic format at once, as happens each time we gain access to another aggregated database. The Acquisitions Department is actively recruiting an Electronic Serials Librarian who will assume responsibility for cataloging electronic journals. However, we anticipate that some catalog data entry will be delegated to staff in the Cataloging Serial Unit. This will offset any declines in the numbers of added volumes.

Titles requiring original cataloging average nearly 2 percent. In general, original cataloging takes at least one hour per title and copy cataloging takes at least one half hour per title. Non-periodical added volumes before Voyager could be done at the rate of eight per hour. As holdings records for currently received serials are corrected production should return to that level and may improve, but it will not happen right away. The amount of time required to perform other maintenance activities—reinstatements, lost and withdrawn items, updates, transfers, corrections, book repairs—varies too widely to provide meaningful minimums.

While outsourcing can relieve much of the burden of some activities, it must be emphasized that internal personnel will still be needed to monitor and complete the process. Cataloging and physical processing of browsing books, government documents and YBP cataloging, and authorities matching are now being outsourced. Local monitoring and follow-up for each of these categories of work will still be required. These services are too new to quantify the amount of work that follow-up will necessitate. We are assuming that outsourcing browsing books and YBP will reduce the number of people needed to catalog these titles. However, since the work being done for us by Marcive is a new activity, the necessary in-house follow-up for both government documents and authorities represents an increase in work at a higher skill level.

It is reasonable to anticipate that cataloging and some physical processing of additional new monographic items may be outsourced in the future. Until suitable services become available, these will continue to be done in-house. It is less likely that we will outsource cataloging for new materials already on the premises, such as gifts or the backlog of maps. It is highly unlikely that we will outsource maintenance activities, such as transfers and lost and withdrawn items. We should be particularly cautious about outsourcing serials cataloging and holdings maintenance. The ongoing character of serials requires close supervision to ensure completeness of holdings and accuracy of records. In evaluating any outsourcing opportunities, quality and cost are of equal concern.

As catalogers are relieved of the routine cataloging tasks now being outsourced, they can focus on the projects identified in the Catalog Department goals that are based on action items in the Library's strategic plan. Technological changes will continue to generate additional tasks that require new skills. Training and documentation become even more important in this environment. Specialization, while valuable at some levels, needs to be counterbalanced by cross training, so that the ability to perform a given task is not dependent upon a particular person. The resignation of two experienced serial LTAs has had a catastrophic effect on the production of the Serials Unit. This points up the need for department-wide cross training, which will provide the flexibility to respond more effectively to changing priorities, variations in workflow, and personnel changes.

Appendix 16.4:
Responsibilities and Roles of Faculty and Staff

Cataloging Faculty:

- Management
  - Manage workflow
    - Setting priorities
    - Assigning tasks
    - Tracking progress
  - Develop or revise procedures
  - Supervise full time staff, GRAs, and student assistants
    - Hiring
    - Scheduling
    - Evaluating performance
    - Training and revision
- Non-Routine Cataloging
  - Original Cataloging
  - Subject analysis on copy lacking call numbers or subject headings or original workforms prepared by Library Associates and LTAs
    - Assigning subject headings
    - Assigning new call numbers
  - Complex cataloging
    - Problem solving
    - Foreign languages
    - Developing procedures and workflow for new formats and technologies, e.g. CORC, DVD
    - Complex record relationships such as serial mergers or splits, set records for analytics, boundwiths
    - Complex formats, e.g. recorded music
  - Special projects
- Activities related to inquiry and research
- Service to the University and the Profession
- Cataloging Library Associates
- Management
  - Manage workflow
    - Setting priorities
    - Assigning tasks

- Develop or revise procedures
- Supervise full time staff and student assistants
    Hiring
    Scheduling
    Evaluating performance
    Training and revision
- Subject Authorities work
- Non-Routine Cataloging
    - Descriptive cataloging for originals
    - Complex cataloging
        Problem solving
        Any foreign language they have studied
        All routine formats
        Complex record relationships such as serial mergers or splits, set records for analytics, boundwiths
    - Special maintenance projects
- Library Technical Assistants
- Management
    - Supervision of student assistants
        Hiring
        Scheduling
        Evaluating performance
        Training and revision
- Routine Copy Cataloging (Verification of description, call no., subject headings)
    - All routine formats
    - Any foreign language they have studied
    - Simple record relationships such as straight-forward entry changes, analytics,
- Descriptive cataloging for originals
- Routine Maintenance
    - Added volumes
    - Added copies
    - Lost and withdrawn
    - Ceases and cancels
    - Transfers
    - Holdings cleanup, LDR creation and maintenance
- Bindery preparation
    - Repair, boxing, pambinding

Appendix 16.5:
LA III Pool Duties

End Processing:

- Supervise student assistants
- Revise processing
- Substitute for student assistants as needed (Generating labels, preparing materials for the shelves, repairing materials)

Cataloging

- Verify bibliographic records for YBP LC copy
- Create holdings and item records
- Pass exceptions on to other catalogers

Government Documents

- Perform retrospective cleanup
- Assist with weeding and maintain Needs and Offers list
- Add, edit, and delete item, holdings, and bibliographic records
- Search GIL and other databases to resolve problems

Other duties as assigned

- Assist, at appropriate level, with database cleanup and enhancement projects

Appendix 16.6: Position Description

Position Title: Library Assistant III (pool)
Department: Catalog
Purpose and Scope: This position will be responsible for a combination of activities from the categories listed below. Duties will include coordinating the management of outsourced cataloging, supervising student assistants, cataloging LC copy, assisting with government documents processing, end processing, and other duties as assigned.
Responsible to: Unit Heads in Catalog Department
Supervision of: Student Assistants
Duties:

End Processing

- Supervise student assistants
- Revise processing
- Substitute for student assistants as needed (Generating labels, preparing materials for the shelves, repairing materials)

Cataloging

- Coordinate flow of outsourced cataloging and supervise student assistants
- Verify bibliographic records for YBP LC copy
- Create holdings and item records
- Pass exceptions on to other catalogers

Government Documents

- Perform retrospective cleanup
- Assist with weeding and maintain Needs and Offers list
- Add, edit, and delete item, holdings, and bibliographic records
- Search GIL and other databases to resolve problems

Other duties as assigned

- Assist, at appropriate level, with database cleanup and enhancement projects

Pre-Employment Skills, Training, Education, or Experience.
Required: High school diploma or GED and two years library, customer service, or office experience. Typing 35 wpm.
Preferred: Cataloging experience; some college coursework; typing with excellent accuracy; good English and interpretative skills; ability to do detailed work quickly and accurately.

LTA Pool Duties

Monograph Cataloging

- Catalog books and other materials with contributed copy
- Catalog LC copy for series and other exceptions as passed on by the LA III's

Serials cataloging

- Catalog and classify new serial and periodical titles in both book and non-book form
- Catalog changes in serial and periodical titles in both book and non-book form
- Maintain holdings information in local online catalog and national bibliographic utility
- Update catalog entries for publications as needed
- Handle cataloging problems and requests referred from other departments

Collection Management

- Catalog added volumes and copies to periodicals, other serials, and monographs in both book and non-book form
- Handle insertions in already cataloged volumes
- Adjust records and mark items for lost and withdrawns

Repair

- Perform basic repairs on library materials.
- Create wrappers for materials that are beyond repair.
- Sort damaged library materials to determine appropriate level of treatment.
- Use online equipment to prepare bindery slips and prepare items for the bindery
- Prepare slips for in-house routing of damaged library materials.
- Use online equipment to record locations of library materials in repair process, and load and change item records as needed.
- Manage copying of missing pages and return Interlibrary Loan materials.

Other duties as assigned

- Assist, at appropriate level, with database cleanup and enhancement project

Appendix 16.7:
Position Description

POSITION TITLE: Library Technical Assistant (pool)
DEPARTMENT: Catalog Department
PURPOSE AND SCOPE OF POSITION: This position will be responsible for a combination of activities from the categories listed below. Duties will include: catalog, classify, and maintain monographic and serial titles in both book and non-book form; catalog added volumes and copies in both book and non-book form; and perform repairs on a variety of library materials using a combination of repair treatments.

Successful performance of duties requires a thorough understanding of both present and past cataloging codes, supplemented by Library of Congress rule interpretations and local practices; Library of Congress subject cataloging practices as implemented locally; the OCLC MARC formats; and the Voyager integrated library automation system.
RESPONSIBLE TO: Unit Heads in Catalog Department
SUPERVISION OF: Not applicable
DUTIES:

Monograph Cataloging

- Catalog books and other materials with contributed copy
- Catalog LC copy for series and other exceptions as passed on by the LA III's
- Prepare original descriptive cataloging of books and theses.
- Perform authority work in relation to an online database and other special files.

Serials Cataloging

- Catalog and classify new serial and periodical titles in both book and non-book form
- Catalog changes in serial and periodical titles in both book and non-book form
- Maintain holdings information in local online catalog and national bibliographic utility
- Update catalog entries for publications as needed
- Perform authority work
- Handle cataloging problems and requests referred from other departments

Collection Management

- Catalog added volumes and copies to periodicals, other serials, and monographs in both book and non-book form

- Handle insertions in already cataloged volumes
- Adjust records and mark items for lost and withdrawns

Repair

- Perform basic repairs on library materials.
- Create wrappers for materials that are beyond repair.
- Sort damaged library materials to determine appropriate level of treatment.
- Use online equipment to prepare bindery slips and prepare items for the bindery
- Prepare slips for in-house routing of damaged library materials.
- Use online equipment to record locations of library materials in repair process, and load and change item records as needed.
- Manage copying of missing pages and return Interlibrary Loan materials.

Other duties as assigned

- Assist, at appropriate level, with database cleanup and enhancement projects

PRE-EMPLOYMENT SKILLS, TRAINING, EDUCATION, OR EXPERIENCE:

Required: High school diploma or GED and three years library, customer service, or office experience.

Preferred: Bachelors degree. Knowledge of PC and keyboard. Good English, problem solving skills, and ability to handle a multitude of details accurately. Experience in cataloging and/or work with OCLC and an online automated library system.

Appendix 16.8:
Position Description

POSITION TITLE: Office Manager for Acquisitions and Cataloging
DEPARTMENT: Acquisitions and Cataloging
PURPOSE AND SCOPE OF POSITION: This is an office manager position to support two departments in managing incoming visitors and communications. This position will assist the two department heads and others in the departments with equipment, maintenance, supplies, statistics, file management, and personnel records. This position will help fill in where needed as time is available and will have other duties as assigned.
RESPONSIBLE TO: Head of Acquisitions and Head of Cataloging
SUPERVISION OF: N/A
DUTIES:

- Monitor front door (work 8:30-5:15)
- Answer phone
- Train others in telephone use and voice mail
- Handle departmental mail (for Cataloging)
- Manage and order supplies
- Order equipment
- Handle maintenance and repair requests
- Manage spreadsheet files
  - Departmental statistics
  - Database status files (YBP, GPO, Marcive)
- Update and arrange departmental documentation on the server or web
- Assist with paperwork for hiring, etc.
- Orient new employees to the Technical Services departments and the library. Familiarize them with leave records, etc.
- Maintain attendance and leave records
- Keep up with name plates, keys, faculty business cards
- Keep departmental files and lists, e.g. Emergency phone list
- Manage travel requests
- May maintain departmental web pages
- Assist department heads and Technical Services faculty and staff with other projects

PRE-EMPLOYMENT SKILLS, TRAINING, EDUCATION, OR EXPERIENCE:
REQUIRED: Bachelor's degree; or a high school diploma or GED and four years administrative or office experience; or a combination of training and experience; familiarity with keyboard and commonly used office software.
PREFERRED: Library experience. Computer file management experience. Experience with MS Word, Excel, FrontPage, and other MS Office programs.

17

Technical Services Between Reality and Illusion: Reorganization in Technical Services at the Ohio State University Libraries—Questions and Assessment

Magda El-Sherbini*

Editor's note: The author examines the literature regarding central themes related to change in library technical services in the last 10 years, then proceeds to look at reorganization at the Ohio State University Libraries. Three major reorganizations have happened in the last 10 years, and the process continues to be an ongoing reality. The author concludes by philosophizing on the future of technical services at OSU, as well as the role of continuing education and library administration in the future direction of this department both at OSU and for the profession as a whole.

Introduction

Definition of Terms

Technical services is defined as a "division in a library that is responsible for acquiring, preserving, and cataloging materials" (Garson 2002). Internal organization of a technical services unit in a library is determined by a number of factors, prominent among them the size and type of library. In many academic libraries a technical services unit or department may be divided into smaller units by function. This gives rise to the traditional division into cataloging, acquisitions, and preservation. This is but one example of an organizational model. Another divides technical services by material formats, creating sections that handle monographs, serials and nonbook formats. A combination of these two approaches, as well as other arrangements, is commonly encountered in libraries.

Changes and Challenges

Technical services (TS) have always been considered the backbone of library operations. Library functions traditionally assigned to a technical services unit played a major role in organizing information and knowledge and provided the all-important access points to information. In recent years, libraries in general, and technical services in particular, have been undergoing tremendous changes. These changes can be attributed, in part at least, to the technological revolution that is taking place in the information industry and the impact it is having on libraries. Some of the responses of the library community to these external stimuli have been so extreme that one is sometimes left with an impression that the importance of the library and of technical services and their functions has significantly diminished. In view of some of these changes, the role of technical services seems to be in question.

Changes in library operations and technical services organization are not a new development, and if history is any indication, they are likely to continue into the future. As long as technology is changing, it will have an impact on technical services operations. This, however, does not mean that functions performed by TS units are unimportant or obsolete. The idea here is that technical services functions remain essentially the same, even if the equipment and the processes undergo changes necessitated by technical circumstances. Introduction of electronic resources and their rapid evolution, for example, has had a great impact on technical services organization. Libraries responded to the challenge by looking at the logic behind internal organization and introduced changes that were necessary to satisfy the demand to process new materials and formats. This could mean creating a new division or incorporating the processing of electronic resources within exiting divisions. The need to process and provide access to materials has remained of paramount importance.

This chapter describes patterns of change in technical services during the last 10 years, as well as the causes of these changes. It also presents the case of the Ohio State University Technical Services Department as an example of a large academic library TS unit that is undergoing change.

Literature Review

A survey of library literature of the last decade reveals a wealth of information on technical services organization. A variety of articles, papers, and conference reports cover the technical services organization from many different angles. A brief discussion of the main themes and major ideas under discussion in this literature will help place this study within the context of the ongoing, important debates surrounding the role and the future of technical services in libraries. It may also shed some light on the evolution of the role of technical services and the rationale for some of the changes that have been noted.

In *The Evolving Role of Technical Services in the World of E-journals and the Digital Library* (DeBlois et al. 2000), the authors discuss the evolving role of technical services personnel in providing convenient, user-friendly access to electronic journals at the University of Arizona Health Sciences Library. The technical services staff collaborated with other members of the library's Web Advisory Committee to develop the underlying structure of the Access database, which allows them to create and maintain the ongoing title records in both MS Access and the library's online catalog. In the process, the technical services staff have expanded their traditional knowledge of managing print serials to include computer skills, especially in the area of resolving URL and link issues.

Boissonnas (1995) shares her experiences of changing the organizational structure at Cornell University Libraries, Central Technical Services. She examines the relationship between the organizational changes in the library and the changes in the information delivery landscape. In the section on technical services organization, she analyzes the traditional technical services organizational structure and showed how it did not meet the current needs at her institution. She concludes by presenting what she believes to be the ideal technical services organization model and describes what was done at Cornell University Central Services.

Some authors focused their studies on parts of technical service operations and undertook the task of analyzing individual TS units, such as cataloging or acquisitions. In "Impact of Web Publishing on the Organization of Cataloging Functions," Grenci (2000) selected traditional models of organization of cataloging functions and analyzes how these models work or do not work in the library of today. Her analysis of trends in Web publishing and their effect on the organization of cataloging lead her to the conclusion that the traditional structure of cataloging is not as effective in dealing with the issues of cataloging and processing of materials as it once was. An important aspect of her presentation is the discussion of ideas on how to make various cataloging organizational structures work better to accommodate the challenges and problems presented by Web publishing.

As library technical services units continue to reorganize their operations, library administrators continue to be faced with the issue of justifying existing functions of their TS units. In his discussion of the function of acquisitions, Bloss (1995) tries to address the question, "What does adding value mean to acquisitions librarians?" In acknowledging the added value provided through the acquisitions process, he emphasizes the role that acquisitions librarians play in adding such value.

What libraries must do today to remain relevant in the era of globalization, the World Wide Web, and rapid change in technology is the key component of an important contribution by Spies (2000). In "Libraries, Leadership, and the Future," she addresses issues of the library in general and discusses how libraries must respond to the technological changes. Her line of argumentation is developed on the framework of a series of key questions: How wired is your library? How fast is your library? Is your library harvesting its knowledge? Does your library dare to be open? How good is your library at making friends?, How much does your library weigh?

The changes in technology are not only affecting the organization of technical services but also have an impact on qualification requirements of library staff and technical services librarians. The question of whether cataloging should continue to be performed by professional librarians is being widely debated. The issue of deprofessionalization of cataloging was discussed in an interesting manner by Oliker (1990). In "The Deprofessionalization Story and the Future of Technical Services," he focused on one aspect of the future of technical service, which is the possible deprofessionalization of cataloging, and he asked the question, what story will we tell the future generation of catalogers?

"The Re-professionalization of Cataloging" (Intner 1993) looks at the future of cataloging from the opposite viewpoint. The author raises the important question of what happened to the profession in the 1980s and 1990s and points out that the job of the cataloger is becoming increasingly more demanding and that the requirement of a master's degree in library and information science is more important now than ever. The new catalogers "must meld several different kinds of knowledge into a solid foundation from which to build: standards, management, research, and computing" (Intner 1993, p. 6).

"Managing Cataloging and the Organization of Information: Philosophy, Practices and Challenges at the Onset of the 21st Century" (Carter 2000) is another outstanding account. It is part two of three issues of *Cataloging and Classification Quarterly* (v. 30, nos. 2/3). This part has 14 articles that cover 4 specialized libraries and 10 articles discussing 12 academic libraries. Most of the authors in these articles shared common concerns about technical service operations. Topics covered include streamlining workflow with reorganized and/or reduced staff, implementing first time or replacement library automation system, facing changes in digital era, and whether to include digital resources in the local OPAC system.

Dorner (1999, 2000) examined the library and information science literature of the 1990s to identify the role of catalogers in the twenty-first century. In his first article (1999), the author identifies three issues that affect catalogers: the image of catalogers, the ownership versus access debate, and financial pressures on libraries. In his second article, Dorner (2000) discusses two major themes that affect catalogers: the digitization of information and changes to information standards. The author concludes that catalogers would have an increasingly important role to play in libraries of the future.

Restructuring of technical services that is taking place in academic libraries has been thoroughly documented during the last decade. Stanford University Library is one of the academic libraries that went through several phases of technical services restructuring (Propas 1997). Propas describes major changes in the receiving and processing of materials. Restructuring at Stanford occurred at various levels and included outsourcing (shelf ready), better use of the current technology, and general decentralization of many processes. The plan of restructuring is available at the Stanford Web site (http://www.sul.stanford.edu/depts/ts/redesign/report.html).

Some libraries reorganized their operations by going from the traditional top down division/department structure to a flat organization. By doing this they eliminated redundancy and those elements of their processing workflow that had become unnecessary. the University of Kentucky Libraries' reorganization is based on creating teams to study the three major organizational components: technical services, public services, and management (McLaren 2001). Each team submitted reports that described the process and included recommendations. The report on restructuring of technical services is particularly useful because it describes the implementation and how the staff adapted to the team concept. The University of California San Diego Libraries is another academic library that reorganized as a result of budget constrains and a hiring freeze. The Acquisitions Department was among those directly affected by these changes (Cargille 1995). Cargill describes how the library used downsizing to turn the Acquisitions Department into a better functioning department. As a result of the reorganizing of technical services, they increased productivity and decreased the throughput time for materials in technical services. Individual jobs are becoming more diverse, and cross-training among units increased understanding of various library functions among the staff. In addition, they made better use of technology, and increased staff responsibility by reclassification of some positions.

Technical services management was and continues to be the center of discussion in library literature. An excellent collection of articles was written by experts in the field and collected in a single compilation (Smith and Carter 1996). This book contains 20 chapters covering changes from 1965 to 1996. The authors provide historical background, present current practices, and discuss the future. Chapters focus on trends in technical services for the collection development, catalogs, cataloging, subject access, indexing, preservation, education, and professional development and the future of technical services librarianship.

Technical Services in the Last 10 Years

A survey of library literature allows grouping of central themes that relate to technical services changes. Five areas affected technical services:

- budget reduction,

- shifting technical services functions to staff instead of librarians,

- availability of vendor services (outsourcing, shelf ready, OCLC PromptCat service).

- changes in cataloging standards, and

- Electronic publishing.

Budget Reduction

During the last decade, libraries have been facing severe budget cuts, which are having a profound effect on library operations. Many libraries have been forced to downsize, which in turn has led to decisions that affected their organizational structure. Library literature handled the budget crisis from many different angles. Some authors view the budget reduction as a crisis that has handicapped library services, while others view it as an evolutionary correction. (Boissonnas 1995). Boissonnas makes an interesting observation about library funding: "Throughout the long life of libraries in this country, it is only for a 40-year period that they had what appeared to be unlimited financial resources. Those of us who became librarians during that period became accustomed to a life of ever-increasing budgets, never really imagining that it was going to end someday. Well it has ended, I believe, forever, or at least for the rest of my life" (1995, p. 21).

The current string of budget reductions is having an impact on technical services operations as well as personnel. On the organizational level, it forces libraries to rethink the traditional model of managerial hierarchy. This has resulted in a general flattening of the organizational structures, as some departments have been eliminated or merged with other units, giving rise to new departments with different functions. This less hierarchical model of library administration continues to be considered ideal under the current economic circumstances.

Budget cuts may be having a positive rather than a negative impact on libraries, as libraries seem to be doing more with less. Library literature suggests that libraries now are doing a much better job of processing materials than they did 10 years ago. The backlogs are being reduced, the staff and cataloger roles are being redefined, workflows are not as complicated as they once were, the cost of cataloging is being reduced, and librarians are becoming more involved in technology and metadata initiatives. Libraries today seem to be doing more than before with restricted budgets and resources.

Shifting Technical Services Functions to Staff

A number of important articles on technical services being shifted to staff have appeared in library periodicals recently. Many point to the recent funding problems as a major factor influencing libraries to use nonlibrarians for certain functions previously reserved for professional librarians. This is the case at the Ohio State University Libraries, where for the past decade non-MLS staff have been introduced to technical services functions and tasks once reserved for professional librarians. Original cataloging is an example of a professional assignment that is now fully done by staff of all levels.

Another innovation at the OSU Libraries is the use of graduate student assistants, who are used to help in cataloging foreign language materials, where the library does not have permanent staff with the required language skills. Students who receive thorough training in library procedures and basic cataloging can also assist in doing simple copy cataloging and retrospective conversion. Permanent library staff are cross-trained and prepared to work with students.

Professional librarians at the OSU Libraries are now involved in management, training, and documentation, in addition to problem solving and database maintenance. They also serve as resource staff for the entire library. Successful reorganization of the OSU technical services units can be attributed to a number of factors, including shifting responsibilities for technical processing and cataloging from the professional librarians to the nonprofessional staff and student assistants.

Availability of Vendor Services: Outsourcing, Shelf Ready, and OCLC PromptCat Service

Another factor that affected technical services operations is the appearance of vendor services. Debates about the relative advantages and disadvantages of using vendor services find are ample in the professional literature. There is strong support for the theory that libraries of today can no longer hope to perform all of their former functions in-house, and that some of the more mundane responsibilities must be shifted elsewhere. Vendor services seem to be compatible with what the librarians used to do in the past, and they seem to offer an acceptable alternative. OCLC PromptCat is one example of a service that helps libraries in dealing with the challenge of current material processing.

Outsourcing of materials that libraries cannot handle is a way to avoid backlogs. Outsourcing of authority control is another way to ensure quality control of the local database without devoting a large number of library staff to do the work in-house. Vendor shelf-ready service is an excellent way to buy cataloged and labeled materials that are ready to be shelved. This service will make materials available to the user promptly and at a lower cost.

Vendor services are becoming an extension of technical service operations. They are freeing the library staff to deal more with technology and to devote time to managing and processing of electronic resources and Web information.

Changes in Cataloging Standards

Continuous changes in cataloging rules and standards have a direct impact on staff training in technical services. As the numbers of catalogers actively cataloging continues to decline, the issue of upgrading the skills of professional staff becomes imperative. The task is a challenging one, because many libraries do not have comprehensive continuing education programs in place. Training that does take place at the library usually occurs at the workstation, at the time when the need to train is revealed.

Library literature includes many articles discussing changes that are being introduced to the traditional cataloging standards. These include revisions of the AACR2, harmonization of many of the national variations of the MARC standard, the internationalization of authority files, and many others (Dorner 2000). The latest development in the AACR2 Revised 2002 includes many changes that will affect serials, electronic resources, and monograph cataloging. These changes need to be communicated to the cataloging staff (non-MLS) in a way that will allow for an effective implementation of these changes and integration into current processes. A certain amount of theoretical knowledge of cataloging will have to be provided to facilitate the transition and allow staff to gain a better understanding of the changes.

In addition to introducing changes to the existing standards, the information industry is developing new standards designed for specific types of digital information resources. Creation of new standards such as the Dublin Core (DC), Text Encoding Initiative (TEI) Headers, and Resources Description Framework (RDF) has also affected technical services operations. The library community has had to address the key question of whether to adopt these new standards or create its own standards to accommodate the new electronic formats. These questions have not been answered to date, and the library community is still struggling to find the answer.

Electronic Publishing and Its Impact on Technical Services

With the rapid growth of electronic publishing, technical services have to prepare to make changes in the way they acquire and provide access to electronic resources. Over the last 10 years, technical services have been organizing to accommodate the new formats. Although electronic publishing has had an impact on all technical services, cataloging has been most affected. In some cases, catalogers have been reassigned from cataloging traditional formats (printed monographs, printed serials, microforms, etc.) to cataloging the new electronic formats. In other cases, entire cataloging departments have been restructured to merge and consolidate functions. In one case, Serials Cataloging and Serials Acquisitions were merged to form one department responsible for all serials operations, form acquiring to processing and making materials available to users.

As serials catalogers are assigned responsibility for cataloging electronic resources, they need to receive new training in the application and use of new metadata schemes and the methods of applying these standards to electronic resources. Furthermore, in serials acquisitions, serials librarians find themselves negotiating license agreements for electronic resources and dealing with legal issues. Specialized training is needed in this area to enable librarians to perform new functions.

These changes, along with others, have affected the organization of technical services and forced libraries to think of a functional restructuring to accommodate the acquiring and processing of electronic resources. Library literature provides good examples that could be adapted for reorganizing technical services to accommodate the influx of electronic publishing (e.g., Grenci 2000).

Case Study at the OSUL Cataloging Department: Reorganization Revisited

In the past ten years, the Technical Services Division at the Ohio State University Libraries (OSUL) has been undergoing reorganization that directly affected the Cataloging Department. The next section follows the course of these changes, in chronological order.

The Traditional Model—Pre-1993

Through 1993, the Technical Services Division at the Ohio State University Libraries was composed of two major departments, Cataloging and Acquisitions. Each was managed by a department head, with both heads reporting to the assistant director for technical services. The Cataloging Department consisted of approximately 60 librarians and support staff working in seven sections: search and support staff, copy cataloging, original cataloging, maintenance, authority, special collections, and serials.

At this time the work was based on centralization of processing. Original cataloging was done by librarians, while all copy cataloging was done by experienced staff. There was a great division by function between sections in departments. This separation and division had an adverse effect on communication between staff and librarians and contributed to negative attitudes toward each other's functions and tasks. This contributed to a gradual processing gridlock and the creation of cataloging and processing backlogs, which raised many concerns among public service librarians. This hierarchical management model contributed to the growing dissatisfaction with the overall contribution of tech services to the work of achieving larger goals of the library.

Phase I of the Change—Cataloging Department, 1994–1995 (Cataloging Management Team)

A vacancy in the position of head of the Cataloging Department provided the library administration with an opportunity to review technical services operations and to begin a gradual process of restructuring. A different organizational model based on a team concept was introduced. A new leadership concept was put in place whereby the responsibilities of the former department head were assumed by a team of middle managers. The team consisted of six section heads from the Cataloging Department. At that time, the department consisted of six sections: original cataloging, copy cataloging, search/serials, special collections, catalog maintenance, and authority control. Heads of these sections formed the management team called "The Cataloging Management Team (CMT)." Each member took turns as the team coordinator in charge of setting the agenda, preparing monthly reports, and conducting regular meetings. The team was overseen by the assistant director for Technical Services. The CMT managed the Cataloging Department for a year, from July 1994 to July 1995. The CMT generally succeeded in managing and directing the Cataloging Department. During its tenure, many decisions were made and implemented. Changes in policies and procedures were introduced, OSCAR (the Ohio State Catalog for Automated Retrieval) was implemented for cataloging, retrospective conversion was begun, and other projects were completed. The team functioned well but encountered difficulties, which often impeded its progress.

The most important issue that emerged was the loss of focus and identity of the department. There seemed to be no clear vision for the department. Since the other parts of the Technical Services Division retained their original management models, including the position of department head, an unintended imbalance between Cataloging and other parts of Technical Services began to emerge. This led to a desire on the part of the head of the Special Collections Section to leave Cataloging and create a separate department.

There were other internal issues that caused the library to question the team management concept. The Cataloging Department was losing many faculty librarians due to confusion and insecurity about tenure status and an administrative decision to downsize the Original Cataloging Section, which until then was fully staffed by degreed librarians. Loss of professional staff came at an inopportune time, when management skills that were required to manage the many new initiatives being implemented were in great demand.

Phase II of the Change—Cataloging Department, July 1995–1998 (Single Department Head)

Based on the assessment of the effectiveness of the CMT, a decision was made to dissolve the team in July 1995 and to create Special Collections Cataloging as a separate department. The other sections in Cataloging (Search/Serials/Support,

Copy Cataloging, Monograph, Authority, and Maintenance) continued to manage their respective sections as well as to address, collectively and individually, the ongoing management of the department.

This kind of arrangement was extremely confusing and created many internal difficulties. In the fall of 1995, the assistant director for Technical Services proposed to have a major reorganization in Technical Services. As a result of this, the Copy Cataloging Section was moved with some of its staff to the Acquisitions Department and assigned responsibility for simple copy cataloging upon receipt. Some of the Copy Cataloging staff were reassigned to the Special Collections Department. The remaining four sections formed the Cataloging Department and a department head was appointed. The Cataloging Department was once again headed by a single department head.

Major functions of the Cataloging Department were to perform complex copy and original cataloging for all formats and all languages, retrospective conversion, analytics, cat-as mono, thesis, serials, authority control, and database maintenance. The department consisted of 5 1/2 librarian positions, including the department head; 11 support staff; and 9 graduate student assistants. The department was divided into original and complex copy cataloging for books, non-roman languages (copy and original), serials/thesis and nonook formats, and authority/catalog maintenance. Each of these sections was managed by a librarian.

This model of organization worked well, and the Cataloging Department soon regained its direction and identity and became more focused. The first priorities of the Cataloging Department were to restore confidence and good reputation among other library divisions, 2) unify the staff and the librarians in the department toward common goals, 3) set a sense of direction, and 4) create its mission to reflect the library mission. To begin working together toward these goals, the Cataloging Department organized its first retreat in 1997 (*Cataloging Retreats* n.d.). Although there was some initial resistance to the idea, members of the department were pleasantly surprised with the tone of the retreat and generally agreed that it was very successful.

In 1998 the Cataloging Department followed the direction that was set at the 1997 retreat and succeeded in accomplishing several goals, among which were elimination of the Western language cataloging backlog (about 50,000 titles) and the completion of many retrospective conversion projects. This was accomplished in addition to keeping current with the cataloging of new receipts.

Phase III—Technical Services, 1998–2002 (Smaller Technical Services Departments)

In 1998 the assistant director for Technical Services left the OSU Libraries for a new position, and the head of Acquisitions assumed the responsibilities of the former assistant director. At the same time a decision was made to eliminate the position of head of Acquisitions. This was the beginning of a more comprehensive reorganization of technical services that took place in 1998. Discussions that led to this phase of the reorganization were long and arduous. Several scenarios were presented and discussed. Negotiations were made more difficult by the introduction of individual agendas and partisan bickering.

Consideration of cooperative strategies and larger goals finally prevailed, and a new departmental structure emerged. Five smaller departments replaced the previous two: Monographs, Cataloging, Serials and Electronic Resources, Special Collections, and Technical Services Accounting and Support Services.

A number of internal changes were introduced in each new department. Staffing was increased for electronic resource processing, monographs processing, training, and documentation. Electronic resources and serials cataloging were merged into a single department. A new position was created for the non-roman language coordinator. Monograph acquisitions and cataloging on receipt were merged into a single department (*Technical Service Reorganization Chart* n.d.).

Reorganization of technical services had a great impact on the Cataloging Department. To meet the challenge of managing the electronic collections and digitization, the Serials Section, which was part of the Cataloging Department, was merged with Serials Acquisitions to form a new Serials and Electronic Resources Department. The Cataloging Department gained a new librarian position (coordinator of the Non-Roman Languages Section) and increased one librarian appointment from 50 percent to full time.

After the reorganization in early 1999, the Cataloging Department was staffed by 6 librarians, 12 professional staff, and 11 graduate student assistants. It was divided into five sections: Principal Cataloger, Western Languages/AV/Regional Campus, Authority/Database Maintenance, Special Projects/Thesis, and Non-Roman Languages Section.

Current Changes—2002–

Reorganization of technical services is an ongoing process at OSU, as changes are made each time a position is vacated. With each vacancy, the position is reviewed by the administration and a decision is made about how to fill the position and where the new assignment will be made. Positions are often shifted from one department to another. One example of such a shift is the vacancy created in the position of coordinator of Western Languages Cataloging Section. When the position was filled, it was reassigned from the Cataloging Department to the Serials and Electronic Resources Department to accommodate the workload increases in this area. This was a conscious decision on the part of the administration to divert resources from the department that was processing print materials to the one dealing with electronic formats

Another instance of this type of attrition occurred when the position of co-ordinator of the Non-Roman Language Section became vacated. The position was not filled, due primarily to severe budget restrictions. Following these personnel shifts, the Cataloging Department now consists of 4 librarians including the head of the department, 15 support staff, and 7 graduate student assistants, supplemented by an additional 7,000 student hours.

The department's primary function is original and complex copy catalog-ing for all Western language materials, original and copy cataloging for all for-eign language materials and nonbook formats (except serials), Ohio State University's theses and dissertations (including the electronic thesis and disser-tation), government documents, retrospective conversion activities, database maintenance, training and documentation, and problem solving.

In addition, staff are involved in contributing authority records to the NACO (the name authority program component of the Program for Cooperative Cataloging) and BIBCO (the monographic bibliographic record component of the Program for Cooperative Cataloging) programs. The department is also managing many OCLC TECHPRO contracts cataloging projects for Slavic, He-brew, and Asian language materials. Although the department is understaffed, productivity ranges from about 5,000 to 6,000 records a month (see Cataloging Statistics on the Cataloging Department's Web Page, http://www.lib.ohio-state. edu/catweb/rptmenu.htm).

The Cataloging Department is now more fully integrated with the rest of technical services. Because the department experienced many changes and much restructuring, today there is little fear of reorganizing; staff have become more confident and more adaptable to change. As for the functions of the depart-ment, all staff are very well trained and there is much cross-training among sec-tions. Boundaries that once existed between departments and sections have been largely eliminated, and there is more direct communication between the staff and their supervisors. The Cataloging Department is in the vanguard of change at the OSU Libraries. Departmental retreats and training workshops are held fre-quently, allowing staff to function better and to be part of the decision-making process.

Experiences of the last decade suggest that reorganization has become part of the management landscape. The Cataloging Department will continue to ex-plore new ways to become more effective and more productive. The dynamic nature of the Cataloging Department allows it now to achieve its mission to ac-commodate national trends and user needs.

The recent wave of reorganization was undertaken to meet immediate needs. A new reorganization formula was developed in which semi-permanent reassignment of staff is replacing permanent personnel changes. The OSU Li-brary is able to do this by making job descriptions more generic and including as many tasks as the civil services classification allows. This arrangement allows for more flexibility and assists the department members in becoming more productive.

In July 2003, the assistant director for Technical Services is leaving OSUL for a new position. Once again, this will affect technical services operations, and staff are anticipating the next wave of changes.

What Have We Learned from Reorganizing?

- Changes are inevitable and unavoidable.

- Changes direct us to seek new solutions and make better use of resources.

- Changes do not alter the library mission or value but do affect the way the library functions.

- Changes should not be introduced solely for the purpose of meeting immediate need.

- Reorganization should be constructed toward the future.

- Don't turn planning discussions into negotiations.

- Consider existing staff skills and expertise.

- Make every effort to be objective in decisions that affect personnel

- Communicate changes to the staff and make them feel that they are part of decision making.

- Communicate changes to the entire library and consider how change will affect their work and services

- Implement changes gradually.

- Set goals and objectives and assist staff in achieving them.

- Be prepared to provide cross-training among sections.

The Future of Technical Services: An Assessment Based on a Case Study at OSUL

In discussing the future of technical services, several questions need to be answered:

- What role can technical services play in the era of virtual libraries?

- What kind of education and continuing education should technical services staff undertake to keep up with the changes?

- What level of technical service staff is needed to perform certain functions (MLS versus paraprofessional), and how does this affect the profession as a whole?

- What is the role of library administrators in re-professionalizing technical services?

What Role Can Technical Services Play in the Era of Virtual Libraries?

There are vast amounts of information available through the Internet. Most of this information is not indexed properly, and in many cases it is impossible to access. Considering the growth of digital information, one could venture a guess that over time there will be a decline in the amount of print materials reaching the library, and electronic resources will gain prominence as a form of scholarly communication. Information that is available through the Internet has changed the way in which information is accessed. With the increasing demand to have all information available electronically, libraries face the task of providing not only the bibliographic description for this information (in a form of bibliographic records) but full text, full image, and full database (Jones 1997).

Technical services librarians face the task of organizing Web-based information and providing controlled vocabulary and effective indexing. Catalogers in particular have the knowledge and the expertise in organizing library materials. They should be applying this knowledge to Web resources. Current cataloging tools such as MARC 21 and AACR2 have been modified to accommodate networked resources. Catalogers should take advantage of these existing cataloging tools to organize Web information. In addition, they should be aware of other cataloging tools that could also be applied. Their role in this area is to evaluate these tools (such as Dublin Core) and make good use of them.

Technical services of the future should not only focus on creating a single database, such as the library catalog but should also develop ways of providing client service-based indexes of networked information. Libraries should recognize that they are not the only gateway to information. Neither are the local library catalogs the only means to access resources for information seekers. There is great competition between libraries and commercial information providers, and both should be working side by side to benefit from each other's expertise.

Technical services librarians continue to play an important role in the creation of virtual libraries. Creating a virtual library and diverting significant parts of the materials budget to electronic resources is having a profound impact on technical service organizations in general and cataloging departments in particular. Catalogers have theoretical as well as practical background in organizing information. The term *cataloging* has now been broadened to include concepts such as organization of information and, as Dorner mentioned (2000),"This will entail the creation of any variety of catalogs and information databases and a conceptual understanding of object description, hierarchies, bibliographic relationships, database structure, user needs, and so forth" (2000, p. 73).

Although the emphasis in library literature is on the catalogers' role and what catalogers can do in the era of networked information, one should not lose sight of the fact that catalogers cannot assume this role by themselves. Library administrators have an important role in preparing librarians for the future. They should set up goals and objectives to assist staff in achieving these goals.

At the OSU Libraries, technical service librarians are involved in a variety of projects related to electronic resources. The Serials and Electronic Resources Department is involved in cataloging electronic resources (e-journals as well as Web sites). The Cataloging Department is involved in cataloging electronic theses and dissertations. In both areas, staff and librarians are working side by side to create bibliographic records for these resources.

What Kind of Education and Continuing Education Should Technical Services Staff Undertake ito Keep Pace with the Changes?

For technical services staff to keep pace with constant change, library administration must provide opportunities for continuous training. It is evident that different types of training are required for professional librarians and support staff. Methods of training may vary from institution to institution and may include workshops, attendance at conferences, and seminars. Training in project management skills would benefit professional librarians, while computer-related skills such as system analysis and design and programming are very important for technical services staff.

Library schools have a great role to play in the era of information management. They tend to focus their attention on teaching curriculum to support the traditional functions of libraries, such as management, technical services, and public services. In teaching cataloging, library schools used to stress the importance of the cataloging tools that were used in libraries to organize print and nonprint collections. Now library schools are also supporting the rapid developments in technology and are devising ways in which the new librarian can meet the challenges provided by the diversity of formats served up by the information industry. Schools have to develop courses that will impart the knowledge necessary for organizing information to meet today's information needs.

In a study of academic institutions offering degrees in librarianship, O'Neill (1998) found that there are some American ALA-accredited schools that provide a post-master's degree or certificate. These programs require that librarians be close to a school that offers this degree and have the time and money to return to school for an additional 24 to 30 credit hours. Some schools also provide half- or full-day workshops or conferences on specific topics. In addition, I found that there are a large number of workshops on Web resources, html and Web design, the Internet, new software packages, and automation. There are other workshops related to the information needs of special populations, management and Total Quality Management (TQM), staff training, leadership, and decision making. A few schools provide continuing education for cataloging, collection development, acquisitions, and serials also.

In addition to the traditional methods of delivering instruction, library schools also provide continuing education through distance learning. This method does not require the students to be close to the site. Courses offered through distance learning vary in length and subject matter and are gaining wide acceptance.

Continuing education and training at the OSU Libraries occurs on various levels. Rather limited in-house training is supplemented by a variety of opportunities available regionally and nationally. Library management provides funds for attending workshops that are directly related to professional development for staff and librarians. Central Ohio offers a variety of library training opportunities in the region. A wide variety of workshops and seminars is offered locally by OHIONET, a state network organization that provides products and services to the library community. In addition, librarians can gain up-to-date information about the profession by attending OCLC seminars. These seminars usually focus on unique topics related to trends in libraries and the development of new technologies that affect libraries. Most librarians also attend regional and national conferences held by professional organizations such as ALA. National conferences in particular offer an opportunity for high-level discussions on the changes that face technical services, as well as a chance to share individual experiences.

What Level of Technical Service Staff Is Needed to Perform Certain Functions (MLS versus Paraprofessional), and How Does This Affect the Profession as a Whole?

This brief description of the reorganization of technical services at the OSU Libraries helps to highlight the changing role of professional staff in library operations. It is evident that classified staff are now performing tasks that were once reserved for librarians. Copy cataloging as well as original cataloging are now performed by classified staff. Graduate students and student assistants are performing the same function for non-roman language materials where the library has no resident language expertise. For the most part, quality of records created by trained staff is comparable to that created by librarians. Professional librarians find themselves managing departments or smaller units within departments, or coordinating activities in their departments. In addition, they serve as resource librarians to solve problems or to prepare and conduct training for students and staff.

What Is the Role of Library Administrators in Re-Professionalizing of Technical Services?

There is an entire generation of experienced librarians nearing retirement age. They are the custodians of accumulated knowledge of processes that made up the foundation of library operations. Loss of this expertise is bound to affect libraries in ways that are difficult to anticipate. Many technical services librarians have already left the field to work in the commercial sector, or have changed professions. With this last wave of retirements, libraries face the danger of losing the tradition of maintaining standards that formed the backbone of librarianship for centuries.

Currently, professional librarians are making a big difference in carrying out the responsibility of managing their departments, from problem solving to training new staff and students. Their knowledge and extensive expertise cannot be easily replaced. They know both the history and present practice of library operations. They are experts in online systems and are able to solve problems effectively.

All too often these professional positions fall victim to various reorganization attempts. They are rarely, if ever, filled with staff of equal experience and expertise. Important cataloging and technical services knowledge is lost in the process, as there is little opportunity to pass it on to the new generation entering the marketplace.

Library administrators need to consider the future and keep in mind that technology cannot offer solutions to all problems. Libraries will continue to receive materials in traditional formats that will require full cataloging description and analysis. If libraries do not retain a core group of technical services professional librarians, no one will be able to conduct training or manage these processes in the future.

Professional librarians have the theoretical background of cataloging and a broad perspective. They are adding value to the services that are needed by information seekers. If technical services will not promote catalogers and redefine the role of catalogers in organizing information, the library profession will no longer be able to retain control over this critical function. The task of library administrators is to act quickly to save the profession, by re-professionalizing technical services in general and cataloging in particular.

Conclusion

As this paper demonstrates, libraries in general and technical services in particular have been undergoing major changes. These changes extend to the library profession as a whole, and the traditional view of the role of the professional librarian has been challenged. Recent budget reductions have forced organizational changes that are permanently changing library processes and structures.

Initial evidence suggests that many of these changes are having a positive effect on library operations. Library organizations are maintaining their service levels and trimming down at the same time. Better use is being made of existing resources as libraries train staff to perform more complex tasks. Professional librarians are assuming more responsibility for the management of libraries as professional staff are assuming greater responsibility for technical processing.

This picture would not be complete without a counter point. As libraries rush to restructure and reorganize, they cause instability among the professional ranks. Librarians are leaving the field in great numbers, and there is danger of losing some of the continuity that was once passed from one generation to the next. As libraries make more use of vendor services and nonprofessional staff for cataloging, the question of quality must be addressed, particularly at a time when technology demands high quality of records to make retrieval possible. The old adage "garbage in—garbage out" assumes a new meaning as it is applied to library databases.

Libraries need to reorganize to remain competitive and continue to play the vital role of mediators and organizers of information. Technical services librarians need to be flexible and must be able to work in team environments and display innovation and creativity. As the rampant reorganization and restructuring continues, library administrators should ask themselves whether unchecked change and restructuring will not reorganize their libraries right out of business.

Note

* I would like to acknowledge George Klim, the director of OCLC Services at the OHIONET, for reading the manuscript and making valuable comments and suggestions.

References

Bloss, Alex. 1995. "The value-added acquisitions librarian: Defining our role in time of change." *Library Acquisitions: Practice & Theory* 19 (3): 321–330.

Boissonnas, Chiristian M. 1995. "Darwinism in technical services: Natural selection in an evolving information delivery environment." *Library Acquisitions: Practice & Theory* 19 (1): 21–32.

Cargille, Karen. 1995. "The up side of downsizing." *Library Acquisitions: Practice & Theory* 19, (1): 53–57.

Carter, Ruth C., ed. 2000. "Managing cataloging and organization of information: Philosophies, practices and challenges at the onset of the 21st century. part II: Specialized and academic libraries in the United States." *Cataloging and Classification Quarterly* 30 (2/3).

Cataloging retreats. n.d. Ohio State University Libraries, Cataloging Department. Available: http://www.lib.ohio-state.edu/catweb/retreats.htm (Accessed July 10, 2003).

DeBlois, Lillian, Mary L. Holcomb, and Jeanette C. McCray. 2000. *The evolving role of technical services in the world of e-journals and the digital library.* Available: http://www.mlgsca.mlanet.org/mlg2000/ab_deblois.htm (Accessed July 10, 2003).

Dorner, Dan. 1999. "Cataloging in the 21st century-part 1: Contextual issues." *Library Collection, Acquisitions & Technical Services* 23 (4): 393–399.

———. 2000. "Cataloging in the 21st century-part 2: Digitization and information standards." *Library Collection, Acquisitions & Technical Services* 24: 73–87.

Garson, Ken, ed. 2002. *Glossary of library terms.* Drexel University Libraries. Available: http://www.library.drexel.edu/research/tutorials/glossary.html#TECHNICAL (Accessed July 10, 2003).

Grenci, Mary. 2000. "The impact of web publishing on the organization of cataloging functions." *Library Collections, Acquisitions, and Technical Services* 24 2, Summer): 153–170.

Intner, Shella S. 1993. "The re-professionalization of cataloging." *Technicalities* 13 (5, May): 6–8.

Jones, Neil. 1997. "Network-accessible resources and the redefinition of technical services." *New Library World* 98 (1136): 168–192.

McLaren, Mary. 2001. "Team structure: Establishment and evolution within technical services at the University of Kentucky Libraries." *Library Collection, Acquisitions & Technical Services* 25: 357–369.

Oliker, Michael A. 1990. "The deprofessionalization story and the future of technical services." *Illinois Libraries* 72 (September): 472–478.

O'Neill, Ann L. 1998. "What's for dinner? Continuing education after the MLS." *Library Acquisitions: Practices & Theory* 22 (1): 35–40.

Propas, Sharon. 1997. "Rearranging the universe: Reengineering, reinventing, and recycling." *Library Acquisitions: Practice & Theory* 21 (2): 135–140.

Smith, Linda C., and Ruth C. Carter, ed. 1996. *Technical services management, 1965–1990: A quarter century of change and a look to the future: Festschrift for Kathryn Luther Henderson.* New York: Haworth Press.

Spies, Phyllis B. 2000. "Libraries, leadership, and the future." *Library Management.* 21 (3): 123–127.

Technical service reorganization chart. n.d. The Ohio State University Libraries. Available: http://www.lib.ohio-state.edu/tsweb/reorg.htm (Historical document) or http://www.lib.ohio-state.edu/tsweb/tsorgchart.pdf (Current organization chart) (Accessed July 10, 2003).

18

Shuffling the Deck: Two Reorganizations at the University of Massachusetts Amherst

Patricia S. Banach

Editor's note: Taking advantage of technology, collaborative relation-ships, and new workflows can often be the impetus for reorganization. At the University of Massachusetts Amherst Library, the author discusses how new collaborations, a paper-entrenched workflow, and new technology assisted in the reorganization of interlibrary loan operations and then in collections man-agement procedures. A state-sponsored early retirement incentive program in 2001 caused the Library to lose 20 percent of its library staff at once, thus pre-cipitating more reorganization and realignment of departments and personnel. While one reorganization was fairly relaxed, the second was hurried and driven by circumstances.

In January 1997, a new director of Libraries took the helm at the University of Massachusetts Amherst, filling the position left vacant by the retirement of the previous director, who had served for almost 25 years. The arrival of a new director was the impetus for a library-wide reorganization, which was crafted over a period of almost two years. It involved broad, library-wide input through a series of white papers, and a steering committee that provided input concern-ing library organizational needs at this juncture in the library's history.

Among the changes that occurred in the December 1998 reorganization were staff and departmental realignments in what had been called the Technical Services Division. The recently retired associate director for Technical Services was replaced by a new associate director for Collection Management, the posi-tion being filled by the former head of Cataloging. The former assistant head of Cataloging became head of Cataloging. The position of head of Acquisitions, which had also been vacated through retirement in Fall 1997, was not filled, and the Acquisitions Department was jointly managed by the existing head of the Serials section and the head of the Monographic Section. None of those reassignments was particularly surprising or revolutionary. But one surprising and novel aspect of the reorganization was the transfer of the Interlibrary Loan Department from the Public Services Division to the newly designated Collection Management Cluster, as Technical Services was now named.

There were a number of reasons for the realignment, and it had some beneficial consequences, not all of which were foreseen. There were two major reasons for this administrative change, one of which might best be described as philosophical and the other technical. The philosophical change was based on the view that Interlibrary Loan was no longer an arm of Reference fulfilling only those needs of graduate level research but increasingly, as acquisitions budgets failed to keep pace with inflation, an integral part of the acquisitions picture. Aligning Interlibrary Loan as an alternative to ownership, under the umbrella of Collection Management, was an attempt to reflect organizationally this new paradigm.

The second major reason was a critical need to automate the heavily paper-based workflow that was at that time still deeply entrenched in the Interlibrary Loan Department. For a variety of reasons, including a lack of physical space, Interlibrary Loan staff did not have access to desktop personal computers. This unfortunate restriction was in the process of being remedied concurrent with the reorganization. Interlibrary Loan was scheduled to be moved to a new, custom-designed space wired for PCs but aesthetically much less desirable (underground) than the former picture-window pond-view space. The director of Libraries perceived that an alignment with the fully automated traditional Technical Services departments would bring hardware, software, and workflow expertise to an area in a critical transition.

Although these primary factors influenced the decision and seemed eminently reasonable in the abstract, this reorganizational decision caused what might best be described as an identity crisis in the Interlibrary Loan Department. The six-member staff had long been part of Public Services, and being reassigned to a newly renamed cluster, formerly composed of Technical Services departments, was something of a psychological challenge. Staff were anxious about whether their public service ethic would be honored and valued. They were also physically uprooted from their old space and, most traumatic of all, their long-time (25 years) department head had, just days before the reorganization was announced, made plans to relocate to a new region of the country. The circumstances described above could have derailed prospects for a successful transition were it not for the commitment and dedication of the ILL staff, who pursued their unchanged but expanded mission resolutely.

The associate director for Collection Management, working with a newly designated acting head of Interlibrary Loan, assessed the technical needs of the department. Collection Management already had a successful track record of collaboration with Interlibrary Loan. During the year prior to the reorganization, the technical expertise residing in Collection Management had been brought to bear on Interlibrary Loan workflow. Programming support from Collection Management had obviated the time-consuming practice of manually searching each incoming ILL request in the OPAC. The new workflow resulted in the automated production of pull-slips in call number order to facilitate retrieval of materials from the stacks. After the reorganization, additional workflow changes and efficiencies ensued through these collaborative efforts, and they continued when a new head of the newly named Resource Access (formerly ILL) Department was hired in Spring 1999 after a national search.

Among the initial changes introduced was a full implementation of Ariel software for electronic transmission of journal articles. Existing Ariel stations in the Resource Access Department and in the Physical Sciences & Engineering Library became the primary means of sending and receiving journal articles, cutting days off the time that mail took and improving the quality of transmission over fax technology. Resource Access also purchased and implemented CLIO,[1] an internal ILL management system, which tracked ILL requests electronically and made it possible to eliminate paper files of requests, thus saving the time previously spent filing.

Another initiative undertaken during the early phases of reorganization was an overture to the sister campus medical school library, 50 miles away, to participate in an expedited Interlibrary Loan agreement. Although Interlibrary Loan had long taken place between the Amherst (main) campus and the Worcester Medical School campus, the delivery times were on the order of 7 to 10 days. Since the medical library in Worcester held materials of particular interest to the Nursing and Public Health programs in the Amherst campus, this time lag needed to be reduced. In Spring 1999 an agreement was reached for 24-hour turnaround on requests to the Medical School. This collaboration greatly improved the accessibility of costly scientific, technical, and medical journal literature to the Amherst campus.

The collaboration with the Worcester Medical School also paved the way for a fourth and in many ways more ambitious collaboration, based on a joint application for a university grant to support the purchase of the ILLiad Interlibrary Loan software. At the time of the grant, the Resource Access Department had recently implemented WebZap[2] software to create a highly successful Web-requesting mechanism for ILL requests. The popularity and quick acceptance of the Web-based ILL request form on the part of library users and staff was the impetus for seeking an even more robust and fully integrated software package to support all aspects of Interlibrary Loan. Users were pleased with the ability to make requests 24/7 from home and dorm, and staff were pleased with elimination of the need to read and rekey often illegible paper request forms. The ILLiad software, which retained the best functionality of WebZap and CLIO but offered more statistical integration and patron-initiated tracking features, was costly. A joint grant proposal to the University Information Technology Council resulted in funds being allocated to purchase and implement ILLiad.

While enhancements to Interlibrary Loan workflow were being introduced at a rapid pace, the Resource Access Department had a second prong to their mandate, to introduce a document delivery service. Again, expertise from Collection Management was brought to bear in a collaboration to implement an effective and efficient document delivery service. While Resource Access staff considered which vendor services could best fill commercial document delivery needs, staff from other parts of Collection Management provided technical expertise. Most important in the latter category was the knowledge of patron file data, as well as the ability to create a serials holdings output file to satisfy the requirements of the document delivery vendor's software. The successful creation of the serials holdings output file, from non-MARC holdings data, resulted in the important ability to block patron borrowing of owned materials at the volume level instead of at the title level. Without volume level blocking, one of the primary goals of the document delivery service would not have been fulfilled. The library was forced in Fall 2001 to undertake a massive, unanticipated serials cancellation project. Blocking document delivery specific to the volume requested allowed the library to offer document delivery on owned titles that had recently been canceled but prevented costly requests for volumes of those same titles which were already owned. Shared expertise from other Collection Management staff was essential to the success of this venture.

Concurrent with the other initiatives occurring in the Resource Access Department during 1999 and 2000 was the decision to participate as an original member of the fledgling RAPID interlibrary loan cooperative organized by Colorado State University. The Resource Access Department had been one of a small number of partners with CSU in a subsidized project to help rebuild their flood-devastated collection. From February to December 2000, the University of Massachusetts (UMass) Amherst Library copied and supplied to CSU over 348,117 pages to restore damaged volumes. When this project concluded, UMass Amherst agreed to participate in an expedited ILL service called RAPID. This service has arguably the fastest ILL turnarounds known, based on technology that searches a combined database extracted from the members' OPACS of items known to be owned and available. Fill rates for RAPID requests are often as high as 90 percent, far exceeding ARL standards of 59 percent.

While much of the foregoing description of synergies supported by Resource Access alignment with Collection Management is technology-based, three aspects of reorganization are more broadly rooted and are staff focused. One of the perhaps unforeseen benefits of alignment with Collection Management was the inclusion of the head of Resource Access in the regular weekly department head meetings with the associate director for Collection Management. The head of Resource Access came from a public service background. Topics under discussion in Collection Management were ultimately aimed at providing better public service but heretofore did not frequently benefit from a public services perspective. The addition of the head of Resource Access to the mix resulted in a ready-made public services viewpoint at the table. This perspective contributed to a more focused discussion and likely long-term better outcomes. One particular example of "enlightenment" occurred when the then-acting head of Interlibrary Loan explained the impact of the availability of detailed serials holdings statements on ILL lending fill rates. This connection, obvious as it may seem, was not fully appreciated in Collection Management prior to the elucidation of OCLC ILL workflow provided by the acting head of ILL. As a result of the input, Collection Management has embarked on an as yet unfulfilled promise to batch load serials holdings to OCLC as soon as the technical requirements can be satisfied.

Another unanticipated benefit from the Resource Access alliance with Collection Management was the ability of the associate director for Collection Management to flexibly support the increasing staffing needs of the Resource Access Department. As library resources shrank, particularly after the 40 percent acquisitions cut in November 2001, the need to rely on Interlibrary Loan increased. The Resource Access Department was also a victim of its own success. As streamlined workflow, improved technology, unmet local need, and Web-based requesting coalesced, demand for ILL services skyrocketed. From FY 1999 to FY 2002 borrowing increased 79 percent and lending increased 49 percent. To meet the need, the associate director for Collection Management transferred staff from cataloging and processing functions to support the ILL functions. The ability to make these staffing adjustments was facilitated by awareness of the need and by staff receptivity to helping out in another part of the same cluster.

One other aspect of the December 1998 reorganization laid the groundwork for the next round of reorganization that occurred in June 2002. In December 1998, a cross-functional team called the Collection Access Team was established. The Collection Access Team was composed of the coordinator of Collection Development (who reported to the Research and Instructional Services Cluster) and the heads of Resource Access and Acquisitions.[3] The role of this group was to monitor the acquisitions budget and collaborate on which information needs would be filled though ownership and which through commercial document delivery or interlibrary loan. This collaboration proved highly effective and indeed critical when the major budget cuts of November 2001 ensued.[4] This group met regularly and eventually provided the model for one aspect of the July 2002 reorganization.

As successful as the alignment of Resource Access with Collection Management was in the December 1998 reorganization, no progressive library is a static organization (see Appendix 18.1). In early 2002 it became obvious that external and internal factors would require another reorganization. While the first reorganization was based on a fairly lengthy reflective process, the second reorganization in July 2002 was more crisis-based.

As previously noted, the Library suffered a catastrophic budget cut in No-vember 2001 due to budgetary problems in the Commonwealth of Massachu-setts. The second shoe to drop in the budget climate was a state-sponsored early retirement incentive program. As a result of this incentive, approximately 20 percent of the library staff retired. The concomitant loss of acquisitions funding and staff retirements had a ripple effect that could not be sustained by the status quo. In collaboration with her senior staff, the director of Libraries crafted a new organizational structure. The collaborative experiment that had been the Collec-tion Access Team was made permanent in the new organization when the former coordinator of Collection Development was named to the newly created position of associate director for Content, Acquisitions, and Access. Acquisitions, Re-source Access, Collection Development, Circulation, Reserve, and Digital Ini-tiatives were consolidated under this new leadership. Collection Management took on responsibility for a combined and downsized Cataloging and Processing Department. This department was formed through the merger of the former Cat-aloging Department, whose department head had retired, and the Information Processing Department, a number of whose members had been transferred to sustain other critical functions depleted through retirement. Two other newly formed departments were assigned to the reorganized Collection Management Division. The Serials and Microforms Department encompassed serials catalog-ing, periodical check-in, binding, microforms, and the current periodicals room. The latter two units of the Serials and Microforms Department had previously been public services units in two different divisions of the library. The third department formed was Stacks Management, a split of a function formerly associated with Circulation.

Although no one associated with the second reorganization would character-ize it as an upbeat time in the life of the organization, it did provide another oppor-tunity to leverage technical services expertise for the greater good. Budget cuts, staff losses, and involuntary staff transfers were traumatic. But looking back from the vantage point of nine months (as of this writing), the organization continues to fulfill its critical role meeting the research and information needs of the campus. The combined Cataloging and Processing Department was the easiest of the three departments to create and absorb because the two former departments had traditionally been closely allied. In some respects merging these two depart-ments enabled slightly divergent policies and practices to be synchronized.

The formation of the Serials and Microforms Department was a solution recommended by a staff "swat team" charged with analyzing related functions. Whereas in the past the current periodical room had been an arm of Circulation, in the new organization the close alliance with periodical check-in and binding could be fully exploited. Staff could readily see the connection between daily check-in of periodical issues, timely claiming of missing issues, and efficient binding strategies. The introduction of Microforms into this mix was less orga-nizationally driven and more dictated by the need to consolidate public service points. Whereas the current periodicals collection had resided physically on the second floor and microforms on the main floor, the two service points were now consolidated in one area on the main floor. This move made the current periodical collection more accessible to the public and also enabled both collections to be serviced by the same staff. This arrangement has resulted in a staff that is cross-trained in both workflows and can flexibly back up the service point as needed. It has also created a greater awareness in all of the staff of how their reciprocal parts of the workflow affect the whole. The tension that existed in the past between the Current Periodical Room's function to meet public service need and the Bindery Unit's need to bind on a regular schedule has been finessed to adjust the binding schedule to a more user-friendly timetable.

Perhaps the greatest impact of traditional technical services expertise has been felt in the transfer of Stacks Management to the Collection Management Division. While a large part of the impetus was necessity driven by retirement, there have been several advantages to the alignment. Preservation functions, though underfunded, have long been the responsibility of Collection Management. But the shelving and most of the physical handling of the collection was a Circulation function. In the new arrangement, a senior paraprofessional from the Cataloging and Processing area was assigned to the position of head of Stacks Management. Within a few weeks of the organizational change, book shelving techniques were revised and all shelvers were apprised of the new, more preservation-appropriate shelving plan. (No more fore edge shelving of oversized books!) Likewise, laborious relabeling routines, which had been going on in the stacks area unbeknownst to Collection Management, were streamlined. A new labeling station was created in the Stacks distribution area and existing OPAC-driven label printing replaced manual routines. To further improve the tie between shelving and the preservation unit, all student staff in Stacks Management (over 40 students) were given a mandatory, specially designed preservation training workshop. It is expected that these ongoing efforts will yield benefits in the long term as students and Stacks Management staff learn how a few simple changes can extend the life of the collection.

One initially unanticipated but highly beneficial synergy in the new organizational alignment of Stacks Management with Collection Management is the impact on the recently initiated effort to transfer volumes from the overcrowded stacks to the newly opened Five College Depository. The UMass Library System on the Amherst campus consists of a main library, Du Bois, housed in a 26-story building with alternating stack and study carrel floors (two stack floors, one carrel floor). There are also two branch libraries: the Biological Sciences Library and the Physical Sciences and Engineering Library. (A small music listening and reserve satellite also exists.) The Du Bois Library houses approximately 2.65 million volumes and the combined branch libraries another 350,000 volumes. All facilities are at or over functional capacity of 85 percent.

Shelving in all facilities was becoming increasingly difficult. Indeed, Stacks Management in the Du Bois Library had "overflow" shelves in the distribution area where books that could not fit on their appointed shelves in the stacks were returned and left in limbo. No clue existed in the OPAC that these volumes, whose status displayed as "check shelf," were actually waiting in distribution. One of the first improvements in workflow after the reorganization was that staff in Collection Management created a new OPAC status for these books advising users to request them from Circulation.[5] Stacks Management staff now routinely update the status of overflow books so that they can be found during the weeks (or more) that it might take to shift the stacks to make room for them where they belong.

Although the short-term solution to overcrowded stacks was the creation of the overflow shelves, the long-term solution was to identify and send low-use books to the Five College Depository. The Depository is a shared facility among the Five Colleges[6] in the Amherst/Northampton area and is located about six miles from the Amherst campus in a former Strategic Air Command bunker.

The Five College Depository opened on November 4, 2002, just in the nick of time from the point of view of UMass Amherst. A major stack-shifting project was already in progress in Du Bois as a result of the need to integrate a portion of the recent bound periodical collection into the general stack collection. In anticipation of the opening of the Depository, the newly organized Stacks Management Department started pulling and boxing volumes from most stack floors. This effort was greatly expedited by expertise in Collection Management that was brought to bear in creating lists from the OPAC of designated call number ranges for review by Collection Development staff and subsequent pulling and boxing by Stacks Management staff. Collection Management also understood and supported the database changes needed to accurately reflect the location of boxed materials prior to accessioning in the Depository. Further, they assisted with the orientation of the newly hired Five College Depository manager and have worked closely with him and his new staff to update records efficiently and expeditiously. The cataloging and record coding expertise of the Collection Management staff has been of tremendous help in keeping track of this large transfer of materials. Moreover, as transfers begin to come from the branch libraries as well as the main library, a Stacks Management Task Force including staff from the branch, Collection Development, and Stacks Management has been working to carefully coordinate future shipments to the Depository.

As this chapter is being written, the second reorganization of Collection Management at the University of Massachusetts Amherst is only nine months into implementation (see Appendix 18.2). Unlike the December 1998 reorganization, which was the result of a fairly leisurely process aimed at an innovative redesign, the second reorganization was hurried and driven by dire circumstances. However, it is increasingly clear that leveraging the expertise of technical services, known as Collection Management at UMass, has had a positive impact on the organization. Expertise that sometimes is not fully appreciated can have a very powerful impact for good when it is effectively channeled. The reduced circumstances of the University of Massachusetts Amherst Library System in July 2002 required that each staff member be assigned in a manner that would enable the Library to continue to meet its mission. The skills and knowledge of technical services have been an important part of the success of the library at this juncture and likely will be again in some new round of reorganization in the future. But none of this would have been possible without staff committed to contributing to the organization to their maximum potential regardless of where in the organizational structure their talents are assigned.

Notes

1. CLIO (http://www.cliosoftware.com/public/).

2. WebZap is Web-based electronic interlibrary loan software developed at Colorado State University Libraries (http://www.webzap.org/).

3. The position of head of Acquisitions was filled by internal designation in October 1999.

4. In November 2001 the library suffered a mid-year cut of 40 percent of the acquisitions budget.

5. Although organizationally Stacks Management is not part of Circulation, patrons are directed to "ask at Circulation" for these overflow books because Circulation is perceived to be a library function that patrons can recognize.

6. University of Massachusetts Amherst, Amherst College, Hampshire College, Mount Holyoke College, and Smith College.

Appendix 18.1:
University of Massachusetts Amherst Library System Organization Chart, January 1999

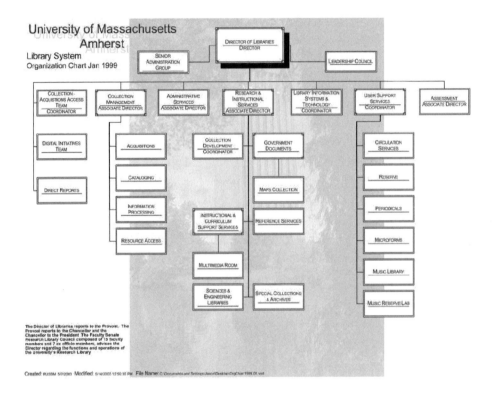

University of Massachusetts Amherst
Library System
Organization Chart Jan 1999

The Director of Libraries reports to the Provost. The Provost reports to the Chancellor and the Chancellor to the President. The Faculty Senate Research Library Council composed of 15 faculty members and 7 ex officio members, advises the Director regarding the functions and operations of the University's Research Library

Created: RUSSM 5/7/2003   Modified: 5/14/2003 12:50:10 PM   File Name: C:\Documents and Settings\Jason\Desktop\OrgChart1999.01.vsd

Appendix 18.2:
University of Massachusetts Amherst Library
System Organization Chart, July 2002

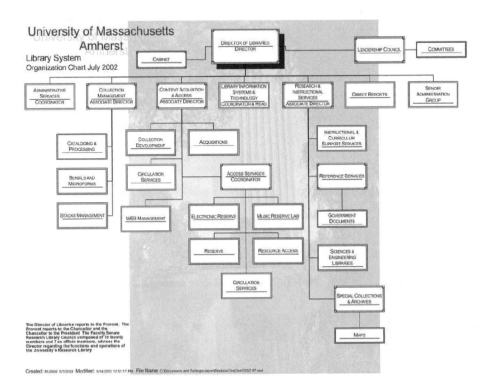

19

Redesigning Technical Services in an Academic Law Library

Andrea Rabbia

Editor's note: The author discusses how workflow can sometimes impede access, budgets, and customer satisfaction, when it is not sufficiently documented or examined for efficiency. At the H. Douglas Barclay Law Library within the Syracuse University College of Law, many "cracks" in the current system of acquiring, processing, and shelving materials resulted in inefficient time spent by staff and reordering/repurchasing of lost or misappropriated materials. The author provides detailed information on various processes and workflows that were redesigned and personnel who were cross-trained to become a more efficient and effective department. The importance of designing workflows that take advantage of current staff and their expertise and experience again points to the knowledge access management (KAM) philosophy.

In the summer of 1999 I was concerned by the lack of operational efficiency and accuracy in the Technical Services Department at H. Douglas Barclay Law Library. I had been supervising Technical Services since 1995, and although I thought I had been continuously streamlining the operation, it was clear that many aspects of the department's operation were "falling through the cracks." Each day in Technical Services presented me with new, if not unique, opportunities to use problem-solving skills. One such opportunity was discovering that we needed to repurchase *two* loose-leaf treatises as a result of Technical Services having consistently misidentified and written the wrong call number on one treatise. Forcing months of loose-leaf releases into the wrong title resulted in the two titles lacking integrity. Another such opportunity was uncovering that

411

the department had processed a pile of errata sheets without noting the call number on each. Unfortunately, the sheets also lacked headers or footers indicating the title of the work being corrected. The errata sheets were never positively identified or added to the appropriate titles, and to this day some portion of our treatise collection, which the publisher attempted to correct, is still in error.

Although I valued the problem-solving exercises, it was clear that day-to-day tasks were not accomplished in a timely or accurate manner, and that many areas of the operation were simply being neglected or ignored. The cumulative effect of the inaccuracies, neglect, and disregard of tasks indicated a workflow laden with structural "cracks" that needed to be fixed. Moreover, since we were struggling to keep up with the daily routine, the thought of providing any new services made me want to reach my hand up from under the pile of work on my desk and grab the drop-down oxygen mask so I could breathe.

Desperation was looming. *How* could we keep up, or better yet, provide such new services? By focusing on the how, rather than being overwhelmed by the what, I began to realize that we could seal the "cracks" in the system and emerge from underneath the swelling workload. Solving the workflow problems would necessitate an assessment of our mission, an evaluation of the department, and then the streamlining of operations to conform to that mission. More important, as a by-product of this process the department would position itself to provide new services. This case study describes how our problems, or "cracks," in an academic law library Technical Services system were resolved by redesigning the department, organization, and workflows to close the crevices and allow Technical Services to provide new services that "add value" to the library and the College of Law.

Law Library Structure

The Syracuse University College of Law Library is a medium-sized academic law library. As one of 182 American Bar Association-accredited law schools in the 1998–1999 academic year, the year we redesigned Technical Services, we ranked 104th in total budget, 112th in titles held, 79th in volume equivalents held, and 104th in FTE library staff. The Law Library had a total of 16 FTE staff members: 8 1/2 librarian positions (including an acting director) and 8 1/2 support staff positions. The Technical Services department had 1 1/2 FTE librarian positions and 6 FTE support staff positions.

Due to the relatively small size of the staff, each Technical Services staff member performed a distinct and separate job function. Technical Services did not have enough resources to allocate additional staff to any particular job function when needed, nor did we have enough staff resources to keep that part of the operation running if a staff member was absent. In addition, the small staff size resulted in some job functions not being performed at all. To compound the problem, Technical Services had significant staff turnover. Consequently we were continually training staff or supervisors were "filling in" to cover such vacancies.

In addition to the limitations of staff size, Technical Services also underwent some monumental changes that affected its productivity. Two years earlier, in May 1997, the Law Library had migrated to Voyager, a new integrated library system (ILS), and for the first time began using an automated serials check-in system. One year earlier, in the summer of 1998, Technical Services had physically moved outside of the library proper, taking over the fifth floor of the College. Overall, Technical Services was not resistant to change; however, at this point in time staff were *weary* from the last two major changes. At the same time, the department was also attempting to integrate new services into the workload. As a result, many things were "falling through the cracks."

"Cracks" in the Technical Services System

To the outside observer Technical Services appeared to be functioning normally, that is, ordering, receiving, paying for, and cataloging materials; however, the day-to-day tasks were not being accomplished in a timely or precise manner. For instance, we were not processing the day's mail receipts, mostly serial continuations, within 24 hours. When the next day's mail was delivered we were already half a day behind. Often we never caught up with that half-day and subsequently many items did not get checked-in until months later. For those items that we did check in, the latest serials receipts were not correctly displayed in the public catalog, often because they had been checked-in on the wrong record or incorrectly coded for display in the public catalog. These cracks were most evident to our patrons.

As a courtesy we had been sending research materials, such as time-sensitive "highlights" from loose-leaf services, advance sheets from consolidated law services, or legal newspapers, to our faculty via campus mail with the understanding that they would return them to be shelved in the collection. Since migrating to an automated serials check-in system we had been unable to consistently get these materials to our faculty. Moreover, we had difficulty tracking these materials to ensure we got them into the collection. This crack was most evident to our faculty.

Collection developers were making duplicate order requests because they saw no evidence that their previous requests were ordered. Our acquisitions clerk was having difficulty keeping on top of the acquisitions process, mostly due to the new ILS. Since collection developers would search the public catalog to see if a particular title was in the collection or on order, it was essential that the acquisitions staff member place orders in a timely fashion. Unfortunately the new ILS required far more steps to create an order than our previous online system. Collection developers, who might have received multiple advertisements for a particular title, would submit repeated acquisitions requests for the same item. This resulted in a greater workload for an already overburdened acquisitions clerk. This crack was most evident to our collection development team.

More astonishingly, functions that were not as visible to patrons were simply being ignored. In addition to the cracks where processes disintegrated, we had gaping "holes" in the operation as a result of this neglect. One of the holes was serial issues that we should have claimed but did not. Subscription maintenance had never been mastered, whether in the new ILS or in the manual Kardex system, which we abandoned in 1997. Without the appropriate knowledge to transfer to the new ILS system or the resources to devote to learning and staying on top of claiming, we neglected it, except when prompted by faculty, patrons, or our loose-leaf filers. In fact, we did not even notice when a certain publisher, as a result of computer error, lost our subscriptions to several titles, including a prominent legal encyclopedia. Neither did we take action when, during the course of the serials check-in process, we skipped an issue of a periodical. Both resulted in holes in our collection. When it came time to bind periodicals, we often had missed the statute of limitations on claiming and then had to repurchase the issue. This crack was evident not only in our collection but also in our acquisitions budget.

Another area where neglect reined was in government documents processing. This crack was evident in our July 1999 Federal Depository Library Inspection. With the migration to a new ILS and the diversion of staff resources to implementation, we continued using a Kardex system to track depository receipts; we were not prepared to convert government documents serials check-in to the ILS at that time. Before moving Technical Services, we stacked boxes of unprocessed government documents out of sight. After moving, we placed the entire unprocessed government documents collection in a common workroom to make them a visible eyesore. Although I would like to think that uncovering the problem was half the battle, this was not the case. These boxes were still piled high in the summer of 1999. We needed an adequate system for handling the whole depository process, including the backlog.

New Requests to "Add Value"

Amidst this gradual decline in the quality and quantity of our Technical Services productivity, we were asked to "add value" to the library by managing new services, such as "collection management." In February 1997 the law library transformed a Collection Management supervisor position into a reference librarian. With this change, Technical Services inherited a large share of collection management responsibilities. Since Technical Services was already shelving all new materials, shifting the collection when necessary, shelf-reading the collection at the semester's end, resolving subscription questions, and correcting call number mistakes, we were the natural choice to manage the collection more effectively. The library needed the assistance and expertise of Technical Services. We were not prepared, however, to invest our limited resources in this endeavor, despite the need. Instead, we chose to depend heavily on student workers and a minimum amount of oversight rather than be proactive in managing the collection. Our dependence on student shelvers often meant that supplements, which should have been pulled from the collection, were not. The result was that our limited library materials space was being wasted.

By the summer of 1999 it was evident that Technical Services was contributing to some problems in the collection. For instance, as a result of the inaccurate check-in of materials, Technical Services was sending loose-leaf supplements to the circulation desk student filers labeled with the wrong call numbers. Unfortunately the students often didn't notice the wrong call number on the filing because the title was similar, a very common occurrence for legal materials. This resulted in two loose-leaf services that were no longer "good law." At this point the cost of labor hours to refile the two services was more than repurchasing both loose-leaf services.

Another request for Technical Services to "add value" came from the dean, who suggested that the library enhance its service to the faculty by further rushing their new material requests. At that time we were offering a rush service for items faculty requested the library to purchase. When the request came in, we would place the order with the vendor within 24 hours. After the material was received and sent to cataloging, we offered another 24-hour service to catalog it and notify the faculty member it was available. The dean thought the overall process took a long time, in particular because the faculty had been utilizing amazon.com for their personal purchases. The faculty could not understand why this process was taking the library so long, and the dean wanted Technical Services to shorten the process as much as possible. Although we could not control the timeliness of vendors in filling our order requests, we could investigate ways to expedite the ordering process and further expedite the items through Technical Services once they were received.

Reevaluation

Facing new requests to add additional value to the library, the cracks in our current system, the impact on our productivity caused by our two-year-old ILS, and our move one year prior, I knew that to move forward, that is, "add more value," we had to refocus our efforts. Thankfully the previous two years of "getting adjusted" meant we were ripe for change. It also meant that we were well-positioned to realistically assess the department, its new location, and the new ILS. We had the perspective needed to assess how these changes affected our interaction and workflow. The time had come to reevaluate our department: our mission, goals, strengths, weaknesses, what we were doing, what we were neglecting, and why.

As I began evaluating the department, which included Acquisitions, Accounts Payable, Cataloging, Government Documents, Physical Processing, and Serials, I realized that a redesign of Technical Services would benefit the entire library. When I spoke with the acting director, herself from Technical Services, she agreed that it was a good time to change. We both had ideas of changes that *we* wanted to see made, none of which included decreasing staff positions. In fact, we had added a staff position when we migrated to the new ILS. What we wanted to see changed included

- distributing the workload evenly across Technical Services,

- increasing the accuracy and integrity of the ILS database and subsequently the library catalog,

- making processes more linear and eliminating unnecessary "loop-backs,"

- giving staff the training and skills that they desired to learn by cross-training,

- reducing the amount of time materials sat in Technical Services, unavailable to patrons,

- improving government documents processes, and

- eliminating cracks where materials or processes might disintegrate.

Our primary objectives were to ensure that mission-critical tasks were accomplished (both department-wide and job-specific tasks) and to be flexible as to how tasks were performed and by whom. Managers should have a clearly defined purpose before beginning any "redesigning" or "reengineering" process; we had many. Although we had purposes, as well as ideas for implementing them, we did not want to dictate or impose them on the staff. Our hope was that staff would see the cracks in the system and offer creative solutions to resolve the issues. Most of our Technical Services staff members were MLS students at Syracuse University, so they were an ongoing source of creative ideas.

Priorities in Practice

Starting with a firmly established purpose to ensure that mission-critical Technical Services were accomplished, and the blessings of our acting director, we were ready to begin the redesigning process. In July 1999 the acting director and I called together all of the Technical Services staff to discuss the purpose and goals of redesigning Technical Services and to solicit their input. The acting director described the "big picture" of the library's role at the College and the university, reiterated the library's mission and goals, and identified some of our objectives during this process.

After this introduction and a brief discussion we asked each staff member the following five questions designed to identify what Technical Services staff were actually spending time doing; that is, what were the core activities of Technical Services, and what was the value of these core activities?

1. In your estimation, what is the most important thing you do?

2. In your estimation, what is the least important thing you do?

3. What would you rather be doing (work-related)?

4. Does everything you do contribute to accomplishing our library-wide mission and goals?

5. If we didn't have student workers, what tasks would not get done?

The questions did not originate from an academic search of the literature but rather from a belief that staff knew more about their jobs and department than anyone else. In fact, question 5 was designed to acknowledge that staff should do critical functions, and things that could wait—or were periodic—should be delegated to students. For example, prior to automated serials check-in, students recorded serial receipts in a Kardex, where errors did not display in the public catalog. After migrating to the automated check-in system, these errors became visible to the user. After two years on the ILS we saw that this was not acceptable; we needed to rethink the role of students in the department. By asking these questions we determined and established the priorities of the department and of each individual job and diagnosed the underlying problems that were resulting in a declining level of service with the new ILS.

Questions 1 through 3 are discussed below.

The Most Important

We spent the majority of our first meeting focusing on the first two questions. Staff easily identified the core activities of Technical Services, which are arranged below by service area.

Core Activities for All Technical Service Areas

• Getting everything into the new ILS; guaranteeing that a record exists in the catalog to represent all titles in the collection and that all holdings and current serials receipts are accurately and completely reflected on those records.

• Supporting Public Services both internally, by helping to resolve problems, and externally by assisting the public.

Core Activities for Acquisitions

- Ordering materials, both new items and replacing missing, lost, or damaged items; claiming items that have not yet been received.

Core Activities for Accounts Payable

- Paying the library's bills for items and services purchased, managing aspects of the library's fund accounting to ensure that bills are paid on time, and resolving account discrepancies with vendors.

Core Activities for Cataloging

- Adding records to the library catalog, including copy cataloging; processing and shipping materials to and from an outsource vendor; retrospective conversion; adding and updating records to manage title changes; and expediting cataloging of faculty-requested items.

- Maintaining the library's shelflist, particularly since 13 percent of the collection was yet to be retrospectively cataloged.

- Withdrawing records from the library catalog and either withdrawing our holdings from OCLC or closing our holdings in the local library catalog if we were retaining canceled, ceased, discontinued, or merged titles.

Core Activities for Collection Maintenance

- Physically processing materials, both continuation/serials items and new items, for circulation and use.

- Shelving new materials and continuation items from serials and distributing loose-leaf filings to the circulation department.

- Pulling, processing, and preparing serials, periodicals, and law reviews for binding.

Core Activities for Serials

- Opening and sorting the daily mail, creating serials check-in records (as we were still in the process of converting the Kardex system to the new ILS), maintaining serials check-in records in the new ILS, performing serials check-in, claiming missing items, and maintaining subscriptions with vendors.

The Least Important

Staff members had some difficulty identifying any activities as "least important." After systematic consideration, they did identify the following activities as being least important:

- Filing publisher catalogs

- Organizing faculty order files

- Searching bibliographies/catalogs (bulk searching)

- Cleaning up cataloging backlog

- Cleaning up the cataloging "problem" shelf

- Updating manuals (with the exception of Cataloging staff, who viewed this as a higher priority)

- Writing procedures

- Educating each other about their specific jobs

The topic of educating each other about their specific roles in the department generated considerable discussion from the staff. They discussed how gaining expertise, but not becoming "experts," in other areas of Technical Services, would assist them in doing their jobs better. Staff suggested doing this by following the process in place for student interns; have new employees spend some time shadowing each staff member in Technical Services to see what each person does on a day-to-day basis. One of the newer staff members recommended that this shadowing should occur only after new employees had passed their 45-workday probationary period.

The staff also advocated having a centralized procedure manual rather than individual manuals for each position. Staff remarked that this would make updating manuals and procedures easier. It would also ensure that all employees have a common reference for learning about what and how others did their job. It would enable staff to know what their co-workers did and would then help eliminate the "ping-pong" workflow that was happening in Technical Services. For example, a title would get passed around to multiple staff members, sometimes to the same staff person, more than once in an effort to get a problem solved. As a manager, I liked their reasoning about the procedures manual because I knew the importance of having updated procedures. Their proposal would in effect move "updating manuals" higher in the priority list by their willingness to commit to getting them into a centralized format.

The Middle of the Road

I found it telling that few tasks made it to the "least important" list. As a result, it became necessary to create a new priority category called "the middle of the road." "Middle of the road" activities take time and are important but are often neglected, as neither the public or library administrators see the evidence of neglecting them. Staff identified the following activities for this new category:

- Recording title and volume count statistics
- Updating the cataloging manual
- "Cleaning up" records in the ILS, that is, database management
- Ordering supplies to process items for the collection
- Returning unwanted items to vendors
- Government documents check-in
- Verifying the validity and accuracy of claims before sending
- Maintaining duplicate vendor records in the library's ILS and the university's accounting system
- Pulling catalog cards for the items that are either in the ILS or have been withdrawn

The result of this question and answer process was three priority lists based on what staff *actually did*. As I mentioned, these questions did not originate from an academic search of the literature but rather from our belief that staff knew more about their jobs and department than anyone else did. These priority lists were the evidence that supported this assumption for our department.

After establishing these priority lists, we asked the staff to think about the following question: "What would I rather be doing, within the parameters of Technical Services work?" Here staff identified the areas where they would like to devote their time. For instance, the catalogers had a strong desire to clean up the catalog and resolve "problematic" material cataloging. They felt this was an important activity—one that was consistent with the library's goals—but acknowledged that they were not able to devote enough time to it.

Management's Priorities

After having the staff identify what their practice had determined were the priorities of the department, the acting director and I presented to the staff what we believed should be the priorities for Technical Services. We included the Law Library's annual calendar of activities, such as the Law School's budget cycle and our vendors' annual subscription renewals, to facilitate fitting these cyclical activities into the planning. We then identified the following priorities for Technical Services:

- Creating a complete and accurate ILS database and catalog. We needed to have our library holdings correctly and comprehensively reflected in the public catalog. This included retrospective conversion and comprehensive serial holdings. Accomplishing this would assist the different user populations, including interlibrary loan staff, faculty, students, and the local bar. Accomplishing this was even more important at that time since our director, who had been the library's sole collection development librarian for 17 years, had resigned, and no one person "knew" the collection completely. The database also needed to be comprehensive and accurate so that data extracted from it would be meaningful and useful to us. The information in the database could be used for a multitude of purposes, including providing accurate statistics for the ABA Annual Report and in supporting collection and budgetary decisions.

- We needed to make the entire Technical Services processes as linear as possible. Linearization would eliminate the circularity of processes and cut down on the amount of time staff spent with an item, from ordering through shelving. Linearization would eliminate the amount of time the item spent in Technical Services, unavailable to patrons. Linearization might result in one staff member ordering, receiving, cataloging, and processing an item. Ideally, any loops that we still had would be necessary loops. A linear nature to the process would also assist in training new employees. Obviously there would be cross-training involved, thereby increasing the skill set of the staff. Moreover, knowledge of procedural duties would be spread to other staff in the organization and not totally lost when a staff member left the organization. The library would be a better organization because work could continue without interruptions.

- Writing and revising procedural documentation. The constant review of procedural documentation would help eliminate redundancy in the procedures, thereby aiding in linearizing Technical Services activities. Updated procedures would be useful teaching aids for new employees to learn procedures that were consistent with the practices of the overall department, particularly those practices that affected other staff.

Common Priorities and Diagnosis

The staff listened graciously as the acting director and I described where management wanted to see Technical Service staff efforts spent. Together management and staff analyzed management's list against the staff's initial priorities to find commonalities. We identified the goals of Technical Services: getting everything in the public catalog (e.g., retrospective cataloging, correct holdings, current serials check-in); making the public catalog accurate; and ensuring that it reflected a timely and accurate collection. We had a surprising consensus that mail check-in was one of the most important things the department did. In fact, staff were adamant that the day's serial receipts be checked-in on the day they arrived, on the correct record, and with the correct treatment; they may have been tired of cleaning up the mistakes that Public Services was sending back due to our students' errors. Obviously we had diagnosed the problem: We were not spending time where our priorities lie. We needed to determine what course of action to take and how to redesign each service area.

Impact of the New ILS

At the next meeting, discussion turned toward assessing the impact of the new ILS on the workflow of Technical Services. We discussed the library catalog, specifically where the emphasis of the library catalog was currently and where the emphasis would be in the future. We noted that the library catalog was currently a representation of the library's holdings. In the future, however, the consensus was that the library catalog would become the library. Fewer patrons would need to visit the physical library, due to the extent of what would be available through the public catalog. This is especially true in an academic law library, where students are provided unlimited access to both of law's primary legal databases, Lexis and Westlaw. Therefore, we had to improve the library catalog to include resources that were electronically available as well as the related electronic resources *about* our physical collection. Doing so would provide users a preview of what they were getting. In essence, the public catalog would become the collection, through having both electronic resources and related information about physical resources, such as tables of contents and reviews, in one place. Our role would be to tie these materials together in the public catalog.

We discussed the dual impact of an ILS that serves this purpose. One impact was in database management, requiring a higher level of accuracy and scope to manage the collection. The other impact was in print resources being represented alongside electronic resources to form this collection. Therefore both electronic and physical resources must have representation in the public catalog. We discussed the amount of effort that must be expended to accomplish this, as well as the potential payoff.

In addition to the public catalog view of the ILS, we acknowledged that the ILS should also represent *how* we manage the resources. For instance, we wanted to record why certain decisions were made, the history of our treatment of any given resource including cancellations, reinstatements, or changes in format, etc. To some extent we were using the purchase order and the holdings records to track this information. Ideally, we also wanted to be able to extract this information on demand from the ILS, which was not possible at that time due to the ILS database being governed by an outside entity.

There were also other functions that we were not using in the ILS because they were beyond our control: authority control, automated inventory control, EDI, currency conversion, customized reporting, indicating "circulates" and "does not circulate" in the public catalog, and self check-out. All of this functionality was something that we wished to investigate, to see if it could improve the level of service we offered. There were also functions that we were not utilizing in the ILS because we had a better alternative method for accomplishing them, such as serials routing and holdings compression. We also acknowledged one function that we were doing in the ILS, but not very well—claiming.

Linearizing Workflow

After identification, diagnosis, and setting goals, we focused on different ways to structure the department and to divide the workload. Our goal was to linearize the workflow. To linearize the workflow we meant to cut down on the amount of time each staff person spent with an item, from ordering through shelving, and to eliminate the circularity of processes, such as occurs when staff see the same item at multiple points in the process. Linearization eliminates the amount of time an item spends in Technical Services unavailable to patrons. To most effectively linearize the workflow in Technical Services, I polled each staff member and asked: "If you were the only staff person here, in what order would you work?" Various views were expressed, but most agreed that since the mail was delivered early in the morning each day, they would begin there. So we began the process with how the materials flowed, starting with the arrival of the mail each morning.

Serials

Staff discussed dividing mail responsibilities among each library assistant, making the mail sorting and check-in everyone's responsibility. Staff proposed that each staff member would be responsible for checking in one "part" of the mail and for claiming any of the pieces for which he or she was responsible. Staff estimated that they could effectively deal with about 80 to 90 percent of the titles, leaving only 10 to 20 percent of problematic materials for the Serials staff member to resolve. Staff seemed to like the idea of dividing the mail alphabetically by title; for example, one staff member would process items in the A–E title ranges, such as *ABA Journal, Bankruptcy Law Reporter, California Reporter,* etc. Staff noted that if divided by title, the staff member responsible for the title would also handle any title changes.

As appealing as dividing the mail by title was, we also discussed other approaches such as dividing serials check-in by format. This approach would result in staff specializing in particular formats, such as newspapers, which require immediate action each morning, in addition to the particular titles that are issued in such formats. In practice this was how the daily mail was getting processed. Staff opened and sorted the mail by format or item type, for example loose-leafs; law reviews/journals; reporters, including advance sheets and bound volumes; government documents; microforms; periodicals and miscellaneous formats; hardbound-monographs and monographic series; replacement volumes; and pocket parts.

Cataloging

After the proposal to divide serials check-in by format, discussions turned to the cataloging process. In an effort to get new materials to the patrons more expeditiously, I introduced the concept of "fast cataloging" whereby the same staff person would both receive and catalog an item. Staff were interested in learning how to catalog, and we noted that the process could be quite linear: receive the new acquisition item, receive Collection Development approval to add it to the collection, pay for it, then catalog it. Staff noted that any cataloging problems could be sent to the Cataloging staff member for resolution. We noted that this would continue to duplicate the exporting of MARC records – both during the ordering and the cataloging processes. We next determined that updating MARC format holdings records could be more efficiently handled as part of the serials process rather than being sent to cataloging.

By the end of this meeting we had decided to have three staff members responsible for serials check-in and two staff members who would be responsible for receiving and cataloging new monographs. We suggested, and the staff agreed to, experimenting with the new workflow over the next few weeks. Further, the three staff members who were to be responsible for serials check-in agreed to be trained, check items in, and divide up the work in different ways (format versus titles) to evaluate what worked best.

Acquisitions and Accounts Payable

During this same meeting we also identified an area that presented a real problem—the payment process, particularly in regard to university auditing. We were without an Acquisitions assistant while reengineering the acquisitions portion of Technical Services. To acquire the expertise needed to evaluate the acquisitions process, we needed to obtain input from our former Acquisitions assistant on the relationship between the receipt and payment processes, specifically the importance of and interaction between the receipt process and the Collection Development approval process.

When we spoke with the former Acquisitions assistant, she confirmed that it would be okay for other staff members to receive new items, provided staff documented what they did. She also noted that the training issues involved would be related to the complexities of the purchase orders for new serials and separating new acquisition items from the standard serials check-in items to ensure that the new acquisitions receive Collection Development Committee approval in a timely manner.

By the next meeting, the acting director had received clarification about the university's internal auditing rules. She reported that as long as a separate person approves invoices, it is acceptable for the staff member who creates the purchase order to also create the invoice to pay for the item. Therefore, it is acceptable for both the Accounts Payable staff member and the Acquisitions staff member to create purchase orders and invoices because it is the Technical Services supervisor who *approves* all invoices. This information allowed us to rethink who and how payment of items could be integrated into a streamlined workflow. Even after this clarification, staff and management still leaned toward having one staff member responsible for accounts payable. We all acknowledged that having only one staff member responsible for creating invoices would make things easier if problems were to arise. The acting director also noted that the payment process is where a problem *really* counts.

We next discussed whether to pay for new books before or after they received approval to be added to the collection by the Collection Development Committee. The problem of paying for items before receiving committee approval was in getting the library's money back from the vendor if we returned an item. In the end staff felt that it was most logical to have the Accounts Payable staff member receive and build a "new books truck," that is, the truck that Collection Development reviews for approval, for all new items and create all of the invoices, whether paying before or after receiving the committee's approval.

New Models for Technical Services

We now had a conceptual model of how the workflow could be divided. We then spent a week drawing several diagrams to illustrate how to practically divide the work, combine tasks, and make processes more linear, and finally we created "pairings of duties." The "pairings of duties" were fashioned to cross-train staff so that each position would have a back-up to accommodate absences, staff turnover, etc. The pairings also allowed staff to learn skills of interest to them, for instance how to copy catalog or have control over ordering replacement journals to complete bindery operations. Staff members would have one area of expertise, plus a basic understanding of another's duties, so that critical tasks would be accomplished when necessary.

The three staff members who had experimented with serials check-in over the previous week reported that they found serials check-in benefiting them by showing them how what they did in their "area of expertise" affected other areas of Technical Services. It also helped them to understand the integrated relationships of the new ILS. They proposed that serials check-in responsibilities be broadened to allow each staff member to participate. From my management perspective, I agreed that this would also improve the level of service to our patrons. The added hands would allow for the day's mail receipts to be processed within a 24-hour period without placing an extraordinary burden on other areas of Technical Services.

Since the migration to the new ILS and implementation of automated serials check-in, our old practice for serials check-in was no longer sufficient. In the days of Kardex we had one student checking in the day's mail receipts during a four-hour period each morning. When we converted to an automated check-in system, this four-hour stretch was no longer sufficient, and mail sat for days before being processed. It was evident that having all five staff members, with their knowledge of the materials and the appropriate treatment for such materials, would help to spread out the burden and accomplish a single day's serial check-in with each staff person participating for approximately one hour each morning.

With all staff sharing responsibility for serials check-in, we shifted the "pairings" around until we were able to "pair" the duties to balance workload and interests. Our new model for Technical Services appears in the Figure 19.1. Notice how all areas overlap serials, which includes two staff members. All areas also overlap each other to some extent, with the exception that accounts payable and cataloging do not overlap.

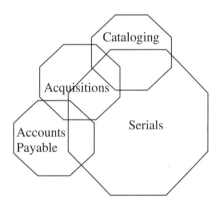

Figure 19.1. New Technical Services Model.

Pairing of Duties

With all of the staff participating in the daily serials check-in, we looked at various possible pairings of duties. Throughout the discussions staff saw that there were certain pairings that could be logically developed. They also saw opportunities to pair duties to enhance their skills. Following are the pairings that we finally decided on; the boldface text indicates the primary area of expertise:

- *Accounts Payable* + *Serials Management Position*—Including accounts payable, vendor maintenance, returns to vendors, cancellations and associated database management, updating MARC format holdings records, and purchase order management (ensuring good rollover).

- *Acquisitions* + *Rush Cataloging* + *"Liaison" Position*—Including acting as "liaison" to Collection Development Committee and some faculty, order research, vendor maintenance, placing orders (via Web, e-mail, fax, mail, phone), purchase order management (ensuring good rollover), and rush cataloging (i.e. expedited cataloging of faculty-requested materials).

- *Cataloging* + *Government Documents Position*—Including "non-continuing" cataloging, such as "write-to-orders" (serials that we do not have on standing order) and monographic serials from check-in; audio/visual cataloging; processing and shipping materials to and from an outsource vendor; retrospective conversion cataloging; withdrawing records; database management; backup government documents receiving; government documents cataloging; government documents serials set-up; and recording statistics of titles and volumes added and discarded.

- *Serials Management* + *Acquisitions Position*—Including claims management (for serials and new orders), bindery management (including binding, ordering replacements, implementing appropriate public catalog displays, and updating MARC format holdings records), subscriptions management (claiming, ordering replacements, compiling the duplicate journal sell list), and recording statistics for volumes added or withdrawn and microforms added to the collection.

- *Serials Records Management* + *Cataloging Position*—Including continuation cataloging (including microforms), setting up new continuation serials check-in records, serials check-in record clean-up (such as repatterning of problematic subscriptions; the simple repatterning would be done as part of the normal check-in process), MARC format holdings records maintenance (creating holdings and updating information), primary government documents receiving and processing, government documents cataloging, government documents serials set-up, and recording statistics for volumes and titles added or withdrawn from the collection.

  This position would also process the "To Be Determined Kardex," that is, old Kardex cards that last had receipts in 1997 or prior. Including investigating the validity of title (identifying title changes, ceased publications, etc.), sending the title to the Collection Development Committee to decide retention (keep, withdraw, or reinstate), and carrying out the Committee's retention decision. For instance, if the Committee decided to keep the title, this staff member would update the MARC format holdings record and add a 948 field to the bibliographic record to indicate the acquisitions status. If the Committee decided to withdraw the title and our holdings, then this staff member would withdraw the title from the local catalog and from OCLC. If the Committee decided to reinstate the title, then this staff member would create a purchase order and set up serials check-in.

Implementation and Evaluation

We implemented this paired-duties model in September 1999. Most of the changes began immediately, with a few exceptions that will be noted later. Staff readily began learning the new aspects of their duties, as well as sharing their expertise with their paired counterparts. After a few months we met again to evaluate how the new model was working.

Overall, the staff appreciated sharing in serials check-in responsibilities and they successfully integrated this duty into their normal workday. Staff were able to make this aspect of their revised duties beneficial to their overall job responsibilities. Not all new workflows were as easily or seamlessly integrated. For instance, a few weeks after implementing the pairings, the Serials Management + Acquisitions staff member brought to my attention that being responsible for all claims management was not effective. The staff member had determined that her knowledge of new orders was insufficient to effectively manage claiming items that did not arrive in a timely manner. The Serials Management + Acquisitions staff member did not know what to expect from the monographic vendors, as opposed to having a thorough knowledge of how the serials vendors and jobbers operated. The staff member would have had to reinvent the acquisitions process to understand what had been ordered and what to expect from the vendor. This staff member rightly proposed that new order claiming be returned to the Acquisitions + Rush Cataloging + "Liaison" position.

By the end of December 1999 we had found one pairing that was no longer necessary. We had originally paired cataloging with serials record set-up to manage government documents. Our rationale was that we had a tremendous backlog of unprocessed government documents that needed to be physically opened, cataloged, have serials check-in records created, then be checked in and processed. After a few months, we discovered that most of the depository titles that we had added, or had intended to add, to the collection were already cataloged and simply needed a purchase order and serials component created to allow check-in and serials management to occur.

Soon the Cataloging + Government Documents position was needed less for government documents. The Serials Records Management + Cataloging person, who was fully trained in setting up serials records, had easily integrated setting up these serials into the normal workload and began checking-in the government documents. I should note that this easy integration was possible because we are a limited depository library, selecting only 3 percent of items in the 1999–2000 academic year. Hence, once the paired team had eliminated the backlog of government documents, there was no longer a need for the team because staff were able to integrate the cataloging and serials management work into their normal workloads.

One aspect of the pairing of duties that we never implemented was the pairing of acquisitions with "rush" cataloging. The first month of implementation we focused on Technical Services reclaiming our role in serials check-in responsibilities and providing an effective interface for the public to view our collections. This focus consumed much of the Acquisitions + Rush Cataloging + "Liaison" staff member's time. In addition, by the end of the first month, the Cataloging + Government Documents staff member had finished processing the backlog of work in government documents and needed less support in "rush" cataloging.

The Suffering Silent

The Acquisitions + Rush Cataloging + "Liaison" staff member, whom the library hired during the initial redesign process, resigned nine months after we implemented the paired duties. After his departure, it was evident that he had been a "suffering silent" type. The staff member had inherited months of unfilled acquisition requests and had been led to believe by the former acquisitions assistant that he "need not worry about them." This staff member was also struggling to keep up with the current workload. This was partly due to a new Collection Development Committee that had been created a few months prior to the beginning of the initial redesign process. This staff person was encountering obstacles from every direction and was not yet comfortable enough with the job responsibilities to communicate the problems with the position.

When he left we were confronted with 300 unfilled acquisitions requests. I first questioned whether this situation was the result of a lack of ability on the employee's part, until I saw that many of these unfilled orders were from his predecessor! At the same time, I was confronted by an anxious Collection Development Committee that wanted to know the status of the outstanding orders they had submitted months previously; by faculty who wanted to know if the items they had requested for the next semester were available; and by a backlog of orders that seemed insurmountable given the timeframe offered. Granted, the Serials Management + Acquisitions staff member had the skills to place these orders, but the workload could not be effectively delegated.

I first attempted to sit down and create all of the necessary purchase orders myself. This attempt was a very eye-opening experience. I learned just how cumbersome the acquisitions process was in the new ILS. It would have taken me at least 12 months to process the backlog. It was no wonder the acquisitions process had been struggling since the migration to the new ILS. Realizing that I could not process more than 300 orders in the last month before the new semester began, I appealed to our acting director for immediate assistance. My immediate alarm, stress, and shock were in such contrast to my normal resiliency that she quickly assessed the situation, weeded the duplicate acquisitions requests, performed the collection development approval step prior to placing orders, and developed strategies to process the backlog.

Changes to Redesign Acquisitions

With the acquisitions position vacant, management was responsible for redesigning the acquisitions position and process. The acting director suggested two immediate changes that were to save hundreds of hours of labor. First, the library would no longer create individual purchase orders to be printed and mailed to vendors. Management suspected that the process involved in creating, printing, and mailing purchase orders to vendors, who then had to enter the order information into their systems, was a major cause of the delay in fulfilling orders. By eliminating individual purchase orders and conveying orders electronically we would save time. Second, as much as possible we would use the library's credit card to order and purchase materials, thereby expediting payment and shipping. Frequently our faculty had inquired why they could order a book from amazon.com and receive it in one-two weeks, when it often took the library much longer. That was a good question. It led us to follow a more consumer-oriented acquisitions process.

Eliminating the need for an individual purchase order eliminated the need to import an OCLC bibliographic record to create that purchase order. However, eliminating this step also sacrificed having full access (author, title, series, and subject) to the item on order. The acting director suggested an alternative ordering process that would provide title access only to items on order. This ordering process would apply to monographic orders only, since monographs would never require a purchase order for serials control. This alternative ordering process would get the items into the library at a much faster rate and retain a sufficient audit trail.

The alternative ordering process required creating a generic bibliographic record with a MARC tag 245 title of [month year] monograph orders/[vendor]. For example:

*245 00 $a **January 2004** monograph orders / **Amazon***

We opted not to put the vendor in MARC tag 245$c, as $c would not always display in the ILS search results set, especially in staff searches. When the Collection Development Committee submitted an order request, the monograph title would be added as a MARC tag 740 in the appropriate bibliographic record (i.e., the generic bibliographic record for that particular vendor, for the month ordered), using the following construct:

740 02 $a Title $n edition notes $5 order notes.

For example:

> **740 02 $a Double fold: libraries and the assault on paper**
> **$5 requested by Andrea**

If the vendor provided any order updates (e.g., on backorder, not yet published, etc.), the Acquisitions staff member would annotate the bibliographic record with such order status updates using the 740 $5 of the title, for example:

> *740 02 $a Double fold: libraries and the assault on paper $5*
> *requested by Andrea,* **Publication expected 10/00**

Upon arrival, the Acquisitions staff member would "receive" the monograph on the generic bibliographic record by adding an "R" along with the receipt date to $5 of the title's 740 field, following this construct:

> $5 R [date].

For example:

> *740 02 $a Double fold: libraries and the assault on paper*
> *$5 requested by Andrea,* ***R 10/10/01***

Then the item would be sent with the initial order request to the Accounts Payable staff member to reconcile the budget, that is, to create an invoice to deduct the amount charged to our credit card from the acquisitions ledger.

Speeding up the acquisitions process revealed yet another area where the workflow got bogged down—the Collection Development process of reviewing and approving all items considered for the collection. With the shift from a single Collection Development librarian to a Committee structure, review of newly acquired items had become a committee responsibility. We realized that all orders were being reviewed twice: once by the Collection Development Committee chair prior to placing the order, and again by the Collection Development Committee after arrival. We eliminated the latter review and the backlog created by the committee not being able to review the "new book truck" in a timely manner. Consequently, titles flowed from receipt to payment then to cataloging all in the same day.

The next step in the process was for the Cataloging staff member to import an OCLC bibliographic record for the title into the ILS, create a MARC format holding record, and create an item record with a barcode for circulation. Once the item's specific OCLC bibliographic record had been added to the ILS catalog, the Cataloging staff member would add an "R " as the first character in the title's 740 field on the generic bibliographic record to prevent title retrieval when searching for the title in the public catalog. For example:

> *740 02 $a* ***R*** *Double fold: libraries and the assault on paper*
> *$5 requested by Andrea, R 10/10/01*

After all of the titles on the generic bibliographic record had been received and cataloged, the generic bibliographic record and its MARC format holdings record would be suppressed from the public catalog.

Other Redesigns

With contributions from all of the Technical Services staff, we also implemented the following redesigns:

- Revised work forms for recording the various pieces of information needed during the process of getting materials from acquisitions to the shelf.

- Changed the initial acquisition request form to allow the Collection Development Committee to contribute additional information prior to ordering, such as retention decisions for previous editions and location decisions, and incorporated an area for the committee's approval for order and payment.

- Implemented EDI (electronic data interchange) to automatically create invoices from one of our larger acquisitions jobbers.

Another redesign occurred in April 2002, when we delegated accounts payable responsibilities for one of the major legal vendors to a staff member who had been with us in the Accounts Payable + Serials Management position during the initial redesign in 1999. When the staff member was rehired for the Serials Records Management + Cataloging position, we capitalized on her previous training and skills to help distribute the workload in accounts payable, thereby creating a new pairing: Serials Records Management + Cataloging + Accounts Payable. The need to distribute the workload evenly in Accounts Payable prompted us to rethink our prior hesitation about having more than one staff person responsible for creating invoices. Being able to limit the task delegation to one vendor, plus being able to capitalize on the previous training we had given this staff member, made this a viable option with controllable risks.

Looking Back . . .

During the first major overhaul of Technical Services operations we had trained ourselves to continually evaluate the department and its services, focused on providing the most important service to patrons at any given point—even if this "most important service" fluctuated day-by-day or hour-by-hour. Department managers continually reinforced this approach to make it part of the culture, following through with designing, or redesigning, workflows to meet those "most important" needs. Having created an environment conducive to change, it was evident that we needed to redesign the entire acquisitions process, which we did the following year.

The improvements that we made as a result of redesigning Technical Services included redistributing the workload evenly; increasing the accuracy, comprehensiveness, currency, and integrity of the ILS database and library catalog; making processes more linear; reducing the length of time materials sat in Technical Services; improving government documents processing; proactively undertaking collection management; and shortening the amount of time required to fill order requests.

One reason this process to redesign Technical Services was successful for us was because most of the staff had been working at the law library for less than three years. The only "old-timers" were managers—the acting director; the Technical Services supervisor; and me, the Technical Services librarian—and we were desperate for change. Obviously, if you have staff who have been at your organization for a longer time, then more time will be needed to get them to buy in to the process. The initial questions we asked the staff can be a critical key to setting the stage for the discussion of change and for building a vested interest among the "old-timers" in the process.

Throughout all redesign processes management and staff thoroughly enjoyed the exchange of ideas and the open communication. Together creative solutions to problems were implemented, neglected areas corrected, and most important, we "added value" to the library through the public catalog. If you don't look forward to the day when your director stops in your office to discuss how the Technical Services department can further "add value" to the library while you struggle to find the time to keep up with the daily routine, then it's definitely time to rethink the way you are doing things and redesign.

How we redesigned our workflow may not necessarily be suitable for your library, but the process outlined above can be adapted to any technical services department. Based on our experience redesigning, I assert that redesigning technical services is not something that should be implemented from the top-down or be delegated to a consultant. It is important to retain the intimate knowledge of *why* you are redesigning; the staff have the knowledge that defines the purpose. Without such knowledge, success will be far more difficult. If you start with a clearly defined purpose and explain it to your staff they, too, will welcome the opportunity to help create solutions. Ultimately, the process will impart to everyone the ability to continually evaluate and adapt operations to meet the *immediate* needs of all your users.

20

National Cataloging and Indexing Program for United States Government Publications: Innovative Responses to Challenges Created by Online Publishing

Thomas A. Downing

Editor's note: The author documents the challenges of managing and directing the cataloging operations of the United States Government Printing Office. How does or can one supposedly catalog everything published by the U.S. government, whether it is in print or online? This is the challenge of the author, and he provides interesting commentary on the operations of his department, the staffing issues, some of the procedures and processes incorporated by staff members to locate and catalog online government publications, and concerns and initiatives for the future.

The Challenges

How does an institution that is required, by law, to catalog all U.S. government publications manage such an open-ended task, and do so without even being notified by most agencies of the many online and tangible titles they are publishing? This mandate to catalog all titles published by U.S. government agencies sharply contrasts with the practices of most libraries, which selectively identify, acquire, and catalog only those titles that conform to well-defined collection interests. The ease of publishing online publications directly from federal agency servers allows agencies to bypass traditional printing procurement for print publications offered by the U.S. Government Printing Office (GPO), thereby depriving GPO of the opportunity to learn of new publications for classification and cataloging.

In 1997 "fugitive documents," or documents that escape detection and hence cataloging, were estimated to make up as much as 50 percent of all published documents.[1] Eight years before this percentage was determined, a conservative estimate as to the actual number of publications that were never cataloged varied from approximately 30,000 to 50,000 titles per year.[2] This estimate was made before online publishing became prevalent. Without doubt, the ease of online publishing has created more fugitive documents than ever before. This chapter identifies and examines initiatives to compensate for the loss of publishing information that had been routinely provided to GPO by many agencies and to address those challenges that are associated with making permanent public access (PPA) to online information a reality.

The National Cataloging and Indexing Program

Grounded in Section 1711 of Title 44 of the United States Code, the National Cataloging and Indexing Program for United States Government (C&I Program) publications was created and is sustained by the need to " prepare a catalog of Government publications which shall show the documents printed during the preceding month." The scope of titles to be included in this catalog, the *Monthly Catalog of United States Government Publications,* is defined in broad terms that encompass all titles published by U.S. government agencies, "except those determined by their issuing components to be required for official use only or for strictly administrative or operational purposes which have no public interest or educational value and publications classified for reasons of national security" (44 U.S.C. 1902). This cataloging mandate is not restricted to only those titles that may be distributed to approximately 1,200 Federal Depository libraries located throughout the United States. Titles not distributed by any agency that meet the definition of being within the Federal Depository Library Program (FLDP) are required, by statute, to be cataloged.

In 1993 the scope of responsibilities was increased in the context of electronic publishing by Public Law 103-40, The Government Printing Office Electronic Information Access Enhancement Act of 1993, which requires the Superintendent of Documents to, among other responsibilities, "maintain an electronic directory of Federal electronic information." This electronic directory, *The Catalog of United States Government Publications* (http://www.gpoaccess.gov/cgp/index.html) is the online version of the *Monthly Catalog of United States Government Publications* and presently offers online access through bibliographic records to more than 32,000 online titles published by U.S. government agencies, as well as bibliographic records and location information for more than 210,000 titles maintained at more than 1,200 Federal Depository libraries located throughout the United States.

Cataloging and Indexing Program Objectives

The program's objectives are to

- Create a "national bibliography of United States Government publications" that represents, in suitable bibliographic formats, all U.S. government publications.

- Expand the cataloging of online and tangible resources from cataloging only those resources that have been distributed to FDLP libraries to be inclusive of all titles whether distributed or not. Although the practice of "cataloging only" (of titles not distributed) has been part of the C&I Program for decades, in recent years this aspect of the program has suffered from dwindling personnel resources and the increased challenges of identifying and cataloging online resources.

- Build the FDLP Electronic Collection by promptly identifying, evaluating, classifying, cataloging, archiving, and assigning PURLs (Persistent Uniform Resource Locators) to as many agency online resources as possible.

Cataloging Standards and the Dissemination of Bibliographic Records

To ensure the widest possible dissemination of bibliographic records among FDLP and other libraries, the Government Printing Office (GPO) produces cataloging records in accordance with the *Anglo-American Cataloging Rules Second Edition 2002 Revision* (AACR2/2002) and *Library of Congress Rule Interpretations* (LCRIs). *GPO Cataloging Guidelines* provide additional guidance specific to the needs of GPO cataloging operations. Over the years GPO has also promptly joined, as a full member, all national cooperative cataloging programs, including CONSER, NACO, SACO, BIBCO, and PCC. As a member of CONSER, GPO makes full use of the *CONSER Cataloging Manual* and the *CONSER Editing Guide*. These efforts ensure that GPO-produced records are welcomed in the nation's libraries and that they are widely disseminated both within the United States and in many foreign countries. Because so much effort is directed at promptly cataloging as many online and tangible resources as possible, more than 90 percent of GPO's cataloging is original.

At the present time, records are produced in OCLC and then loaded to the CGP application on a daily basis for public access at http://www.gpo/catalog. Records are widely disseminated by the Cataloging Distribution Service of the Library of Congress and commercial vendors.

Evolving Challenges

How then does one manage cataloging operations that are limited only by the number of titles that are published by U.S. government agencies rather than publications that have been carefully chosen according to collection development guidelines? Government publications are broadly defined and encompass everything, except as stipulated as follows: "Government publications, except those determined by their issuing components to be required for official use only or for strictly administrative or operational purposes which have no public interest or educational value and publications classified for reasons of national security, shall be made available through the facilities of the Superintendent of Documents for public information."[3] These guidelines still leave a universe of titles to be cataloged, from all U.S. government agencies, in both tangible and intangible formats. Collection development guidelines normally applied by most libraries are of no value in limiting the scope of what must be cataloged—the scope of titles requiring cataloging is determined by law and by agencies, not by GPO.

Past Organizational Responses

As recently as several years ago, a division of labor, based on physical processing, was maintained between components of the Library Programs Service (LPS). Personnel of one part of the Service were responsible for "riding" print orders for GPO printing placed by federal agencies. Their review of print orders provided LPS with advance information that allowed the Service to order paper or CD ROM publications at agency expense for distribution to FDLP libraries and for cataloging purposes.

When publications arrived at GPO, personnel would classify the documents in accordance with the SuDocs Classification system (organized by publishing agencies, not by subject) and would also assign item numbers (for selection of bibliographic records and tangible resources) and shipping list numbers to the physical piece and would then forward publications to Cataloging Branch (CB) personnel for AACR2 descriptive cataloging, assignment of Library of Congress Subject Headings (LCSH), and production of records in OCLC for dissemination to libraries and access via the online *Catalog of Government Publications.* During or prior to cataloging, publications were distributed to FDLP libraries. Although GPO has not maintained a physical collection of publications for several decades, work was organized around the physical processing of tangible publications from receipt to distribution of copies to depository libraries.

Impact of the World Wide Web

The Web has profoundly changed the environment in which libraries function, but none more so than that of GPO. As previously indicated, in the days of ink on paper "fugitive" publications were estimated to be 50 percent of known titles. While the problems of tangible fugitives remain even today, the challenges of online fugitives, those many tens of thousands of electronic publications that are never "printed" through GPO, are far greater. Most agencies publish directly at their Web sites and no longer procure most of their printing through GPO.

The model used for physical processing continues to be valid for those relatively few titles that come through GPO (current estimates are that about 60 percent of FDLP titles are electronic only) but is of little value in processing online titles. In recent years, various approaches have been used in melding personnel of LPS organizations into work teams, and such approaches will continue to be refined in the future. For the present, however, several significant initiatives have been taken to improve the responsiveness of CB personnel to the challenges of cataloging Internet resources.

Evolving Operational Initiatives

GPO's extremely broad cataloging mandate requires a multifaceted approach to ensuring that online titles are identified and cataloged. Components of this response include the following:

- Recruitment: Continuing extensive nationwide efforts to recruit people to discover, evaluate, catalog, archive, and maintain access to online resources.

- Expansion of cataloger duties: Expanding duties from cataloging tangible and online titles to include resource discovery, evaluation, classification, cataloging, archiving, and assigning PURLs (Persistent Uniform Resource Locators) to help ensure continued online access.

- Increased use of collection-level records: Now considered "integrating resources," as prescribed by chapter 12 (continuing resources) of AACR2/2002, increased use will be made of this option to identify and provide public access to as many agency Web sites as possible for self-directed discovery of title-level resources.

- Continued use, when appropriate, of the "single record" approach to describing two or more formats of the same title.

- Continued use of OCLC's "k" level (less than full) cataloging to supplement the creation of full-level records (most GPO cataloging is full level).

- Creation of ad hoc experimental work teams composed of product management specialist catalogers (serials/monographs) to identify, evaluate, classify, catalog, archive, and PURL online resources.

- Partnerships with groups such as the Association of American Law Librarians' (AALL) "fugitive documents" group and the American Library Association Government Documents Round Table's "fugitives" group to quickly catalog, classify, archive, and PURL online resources that members have identified, evaluated, and referred to LPS personnel as candidates for inclusion in the FDLP Electronic Collection.

- Partnership with staff of the University of Arizona who are identifying significant numbers of tangible titles in their depository collection with online equivalents for cataloging.

- Partnership with staff of the University of North Texas ("Cyber-Cemetery") to catalog online titles that have been captured in the Cyber-Cemetery archive.

- Use of the "LostDocs" email application (lostdocs@gpo.gov) as a source for titles to be cataloged and to promptly respond to individuals who have used this address to identify online titles as candidates for cataloging and inclusion in the FDLP Electronic Collection.

Evolving Results

When combined, these initiatives contribute to the building of the FDLP Electronic Collection through increased discovery, classification, cataloging, and archiving of online resources. No single initiative, not even the hiring of many additional catalogers, is a "magic bullet" that can solve the challenges facing the C&I Program. Given online environments, we do not have the satisfaction of measuring success by visibly eliminating tangible publications from physical backlogs.

The validation of our efforts to catalog the universe of U.S. government publications is difficult, and an absolute measurement of success is illusive because having the universe to catalog is impossible to define, and the life of some of these resources (how long they will be on servers before capture) varies widely, as does the number of available human resources to discover and catalog them. This universe and its major components, titles to be discovered and the resources to discover and catalog them, are shifting on a nearly continuous basis.

Although measurement of titles cataloged against a known quantity of titles to be cataloged is not possible, it is possible to determine some rate of relative success. At the present time, many recently hired catalogers (defined as hired within the past 18 months) have successfully passed through successive stages of training and are beginning to meet production standards. No matter the training, however, catalogers average only about 80 percent of their time cataloging, with approximately 20 percent devoted to research and evaluation-related tasks. Even with the same number of catalogers and the same people working from one year to another, cataloging production varies year by year.

For planning purposes, we assume serials record maintenance and production to be approximately 600 serial records (produced/modified) per serials cataloger and approximately 1,500 records produced per monograph and map cataloger per year (mix of full and abridged cataloging). We also assume that approximately 50,000 publications (approximately 60 percent online) are published each year. This planned rate of annual production (approximately 24,000 records) with 22 catalogers is insufficient, even with more catalogers to be hired, to catalog all titles that are published in a year.

The reality, however, is that as of mid-year 2003, approximately 22 catalogers have produced almost 16,000 records for an annualized production that could approximate 32,000 by year's end. This is not enough to meet the assumed 50,000 titles published each year, but it is a significant effort considering the expansion of noncataloging duties and the difficulties of cataloging many online resources.

Cataloging production has, in fact, increased even as the scope of cataloger duties has increased, with fewer hours for cataloging and more hours devoted to "discovery" and evaluation of online titles for the Electronic Collection. In the past, tangible publications arrived at GPO and were classified by specialists who then forwarded publications with classification information to catalogers for cataloging. This division of labor between elements of LPS had freed catalogers to spend more, rather than less, time on cataloging.

The movement from print to online has required that catalogers do the work that had been done by others to rapidly make decisions "up front" to ensure uniform identification and treatment of serials, for example. Gone are the days when catalogers only cataloged and cataloged only what was on the book cart. They continue to catalog but, in an electronic publishing environment, catalogers do much more: They discover their own work, evaluate it, classify it, ensure proper and persistent public access through assigning PURLs, and, in many cases, also archive titles that they catalog.

GPO and OMB New Compact for Government Printing and the Future of the C&I Program

Internal GPO operational initiatives are having a positive impact on the discovery, evaluation, classification, cataloging, and acquisition of many important online publications for the FDLP Electronic Collection. Nevertheless, internal initiatives alone are insufficient to compensate for the significant problems created by fugitive online titles that escape detection before they are removed from agency servers.

During recent years several presidential administrations have expressed their intent, through the Office of Management and Budget (OMB), to exempt executive branch publishing agencies from the requirements of Title 44 U.S.C., which requires all agencies to procure printing services through GPO. In an historic example of agreement between OMB and GPO, both agencies have agreed to an initiative that should significantly reduce the fugitive documents problem. This agreement promotes the use of GPO as a clearinghouse through which agencies may choose their own printing contractors based on either "best value" or lowest cost via a "front end" Web-based print ordering and invoicing system. GPO, in turn, is to receive an electronic version and two paper copies of each publication to ensure that such titles are cataloged and indexed.[4] GPO will also have the opportunity to obtain print copies for distribution to depository libraries.

Although it is much too soon to measure the long-term positive effects of this agreement, it holds much promise for reducing the fugitive documents problem, at least as it pertains to printing that is now procured without the assistance of GPO. In the context of cataloging, no matter what the actual number of additional titles that "enter the program" may be, current workloads, current personnel resources, and cataloging production data suggest that GPO must employ new approaches to meet the full objective of creating a national bibliography.

A combination of initiatives is needed to ensure a successful effort to reach the goal of establishing a national bibliography and creating a comprehensive FDLP Electronic Collection. Proposed initiatives may include the following:

- Continued efforts to recruit, train, and retain additional catalogers.

- Potential cataloging contract services for selected categories of publications to supplement cataloging performed by GPO catalogers.

- Continued GPO full-level cataloging supplemented by continued k-level cataloging that fully conforms to national standards for those titles judged to be of the greatest public interest. This ensures dissemination of GPO records.

- Cooperative cataloging agreements with selected publishing agency libraries for them to catalog all titles published by their respective agencies and to incorporate these records into the national bibliography. Both GPO- and agency-produced cataloging records would be distributed to library OPACs.

- Employment of harvesting software to pull in metadata for as many publications as possible for creation of Dublin Core level records for those titles not judged to be of significant public interest. These records, combined with all those that meet national standards, would form the National Bibliography of U.S. government publications and would be available for public use at the GPO Access Web site.

- Continued full-level cataloging of selected U.S. government Web sites (DOE Information Bridge, etc.) to provide public access to major bibliographic databases that provide self-directed discovery of online resources as a supplement to title-level records that conform to AACR2 and Dublin Core standards.

These initiatives, combined with the GPO-OMB Compact for Government Printing, should strengthen efforts to provide the public with a national bibliography that, while containing records that meet varying standards, would nonetheless meet the requirements of a national bibliography for a one-stop resource for locating all known U.S. government publications.

Do Internal GPO Initiatives Have Applications Elsewhere?

Two initiatives in particular may have potential applications to other institutions. One is the expansion of cataloger duties to include discovery, evaluation, cataloging, and archiving of selected online resources; these duties readily fit with cataloging online resources. Early involvement in a decision-making process that melds evaluation of online resources and acquisition of resources (through archiving) with cataloging is an efficient and effective way of simultaneously building online collections and cataloging them.

The second initiative concerns partnerships with institutions. Cataloging sufficient numbers of online and tangible publications to support the information needs of any community requires more in the way of personnel and funding than can likely be obtained, no matter the library.

Now, more than ever, cooperative ventures in which libraries identify specific Web sites or online resources of mutual interest and agree to cooperatively catalog parts of the whole for one another are essential. The national cooperative cataloging programs such as CONSER and the Program for Cooperative Cataloging do much to ensure that records are widely shared among libraries. Useful as this is, these cooperative cataloging programs do not bring participants together to predetermine the segments of publishing activities that partners agree, in advance, to systematically bring under bibliographic control.

More will be learned as GPO works with other libraries to develop models for cataloging and archiving partnerships. Activities that support the development of a national bibliography of U.S. government publications should also be effective in creating consortia for acquisition and cataloging of non-U.S. government online resources.

Although specific operations may differ from one institution to another, the common challenges faced by libraries for building and cataloging online collections require collaborative efforts to expand and provide access to collections with limited personnel and other resources. Innovation, communication, and collaboration are critical activities for meeting the continuing challenges of evaluating, acquiring, classifying, and cataloging the ever-increasing numbers of online resources.

Notes

1. [Entered into the record of the Senate Rules Committee hearing on Title 44 revision and compliance, held 5/22/97. Printed in the Congressional Records 5/22/97 by Representative Hoyer, p. E1045-1046.] Administrative Notes (Vol. 18, no. 09, June 15, 1997).

2. Cynthia Bower, "Federal Fugitives, DNDs and Other Aberrants: A Cosmology." *Documents to the People* 17, no. 3 (September 1989): 121.

3. Section 1902, Title 44 United States Code, p. 53 (1988 Edition).

4. Compact between the Office of Management and Budge and the U.S. Government Printing Office, included as an attachment to a GPO news release dated June 6, 2003.

21

A Vision for the Future: Cornell University's Geospatial Information Repository (CUGIR)

Elaine L. Westbrooks*

Editor's note: The author shares her experience with the Cornell University Geospatial Information Repository (CUGIR). Although library technical services departments are increasingly in the position to create and maintain non-MARC metadata, sharing non-MARC resources is largely uncharted territory. The hybrid concept of heterogeneous metadata is championed by the author, especially when dealing with the delivery, access, and sharing of geospatial metadata. CUGIR metadata management exemplifies what technical services needs to be in a digital age: poised to introduce new technologies and standards to efficiently handle the onslaught of metadata being produced by a growing collection of digital objects that may be owned or accessed by others.

In 1998, Albert R. Mann Library created the Cornell University Geospatial Information Repository (CUGIR) (http://cugir.mannlib.cornell.edu), a Web-based repository providing free access to geospatial data and metadata for New York State. CUGIR possesses a number of characteristics that pose unique challenges for academic libraries. First, most academic libraries are not in a position to handle the creation, support, and subsequent development of a GIS repository. Because CUGIR is considered to be a first-rate resource by the university, the library has secured a knowledgeable team that can successfully manage and continue to innovate CUGIR. Second, most GIS repositories manually distribute data and metadata via CD-ROM, whereas CUGIR freely distributes data and metadata via the World Wide Web. In contrast, GIS repositories or units in the academy are almost always under the jurisdiction of urban planning, architecture, or geography departments. CUGIR is positioned in a library environment that embraces standards and practices associated with the preservation, retrieval, acquisition, and organization of information. Furthermore, the library community has always been concerned with the archiving and version control of information. It is assumed that consistent application of standards will increase interoperability, and that metadata, though costly and difficult, adds value to whatever it describes. While metadata is integral to the administration of CUGIR, the GIS community is most concerned with creating data efficiently, lifting the intense burden of metadata, and distributing data according to user requests. In short, CUGIR reserves a position in the library and GIS that requires the CUGIR team to embrace the standards of both communities. The vast majority of standards from these communities directly affect metadata and its management. This begs the following questions: If one were to create a perfect and heterogeneous metadata management system for a digital library, namely, CUGIR, what characteristics would it possess? How would it behave? What problems would it solve?

The CUGIR team sets out to create a system characterized by automatic metadata updating and digital object permanence. The system would reduce the costs associated with metadata creation while reducing the workload of the CUGIR team. Most important, the system would enhance and possibly increase access to CUGIR. Although the CUGIR metadata model is not a perfect metadata management system, it is efficient. This is largely because it is a system that embraces the standards of the library community while adopting GIS software's most attractive features. In striving for metadata management perfection, the CUGIR team became keenly aware of the shortcomings, that is, the lack of version control and preservation, in the way GIS software handles digital objects. The weaknesses of the digital library metadata model were addressed in two ways. First, the storage of surrogate records for multiple *manifestations* of the same *expression* was eliminated (IFLA Study Group on the Functional Requirements for Bibliographic Records 2003, pp. 16–22). Second, the automatic metadata creation tools unique to GIS software applications were used to our advantage. With the weaknesses of both approaches exposed, the team exploited their strengths to create more powerful tools. Based on the team's experiences implementing a metadatabase system, I contend that the CUGIR model is a step in the right direction toward improved management of heterogeneous metadata.

This chapter introduces a new metadata management model to technical services that specifically attempts to address the following problems:

a. Management of multiple metadata schemas in multiple manifestations and expressions in digital libraries;

b. The lack or absence of centrality and persistence/permanence of objects in digital libraries;

c. The creation and maintenance of metadata that is almost always difficult, costly, and time consuming; and,

d. The lack of metadata synchronization tools in traditional and digital libraries.

The goal of the CUGIR team is to take the best of what is found in digital libraries and GIS applications and merge them to make a powerful system from which both communities could benefit. This system, which includes a metadata management model, is collectively known as the CUGIR Metadata Framework. Before this model is presented, it is important to review the literature regarding the use and distribution of non-MARC metadata in libraries as well as the literature behind the management of spatial data and metadata.

Literature Review

Since the advent of MARC, libraries have been generating, sharing, and storing millions of records for bibliographic description and control. Over 30 years later, there are some who consider AACR2 and MARC the only credible instruments of bibliographic description (Chandler and Westbrooks 2002, p. 208). MARC is certainly rich and ubiquitous; however, the traditionalists tend to minimize the fact that it is costly and labor-intensive and requires special technical knowledge about AACR2 rules and MARC encoding. Although the addition of bibliographic description fields such as Electronic Location and Access (MARC 856) describe networked information, there is continuing dissatisfaction with the flat structure of MARC and the limitations that the flatness puts on handling versioning and hierarchical relationships in documents.

Since the Web became prominent in 1995, it has become necessary to use alternative metadata schemas that could efficiently and economically describe electronic resources to aid resource discovery (Lagoze 2001). Library literature is filled with definitions and case studies about such metadata standards used in libraries today (Darzentas 1999; Hwey Jeng 1996; Lange and Winkler 1997; Lee-Smeltzer 2000; Medeiros 2001; Szunejko 2001). Two of the best and earliest articles of this type are Stuart Weibel's "Metadata: The Foundations of Resource Description" (1995), and "Resource Description in the Digital Age," by Jennifer Younger (1997). Another noteworthy contribution is Lorcan Dempsey and Rachel Heery's article, "Metadata: A Current View of Practice and Issues" (1998), which lists various metadata standards and categorizes them according to a typology. Ohio State's Magda El-Sherbini reports on her literature search, e-mail survey, and the challenges of mapping Government Information Locator Service, Dublin Core, Colorado Digital Library Project, and the Content Standard for Digital Geospatial Metadata to MARC 21 (El-Sherbini 2001). The hybrid system of heterogeneous metadata deserves more emphasis in libraries than

"MARC only" traditionalists and DC metadata proponents, who tend to be extreme. While each faction has some convincing arguments to offer, the variety of metadata types in use today all have a role to play. This hybrid system, which acknowledges the simplicity of DC as well as the reliability of MARC, is documented in the Chandler and Westbrooks article, "Distributing Non-MARC Metadata: The CUGIR Metadata Sharing Project" (2002). Chandler and Westbrooks state that "Dublin Core is a standard to aid resource discovery, not to replace rich, complex, and reliable standards such as MARC or CSDGM" (2002, p. 207). Similarly, Sherry Vellucci (1997), from the School of Library and Information Science at St. John's University, encourages libraries to embrace a world of heterogeneous standards.

Research in the areas of spatial metadata management does not exist other than in Kacmar, Jue, Stage, and Koontz's article, "The Automatic Creation and Maintenance of an Organizational Spatial Metadata and Document Digital Library" (1995). Other research in this area is limited to gray literature. Many international governmental and private agencies such as the Intra-governmental Group on Geographic Information have published gray literature regarding the principles of good metadata management, but principles do not constitute methods or even best practices (Intra-governmental Group on Geographic Information Working Group on Metadata Implementation 2002; Westcott 2002).

Many librarians are already aware of the use of non-MARC metadata in libraries today. As digital library departments in libraries use multiple metadata schemas such as Text Encoded Initiative (TEI), and DC for self-contained and independent digital libraries (e.g., Making of America), technical services departments should also get proactively involved in, not only creating and maintaining non-MARC metadata, but more important, developing the means for widely sharing metadata with libraries that need it for resource discovery and access. Before we can fully understand CUGIR metadata management, we need to view CUGIR in context, beginning with its history.

CUGIR History

CUGIR is a clearinghouse and repository that provides unrestricted access to geospatial data and metadata, with special emphasis on those natural features relevant to agriculture, ecology, natural resources, and human–environment interactions in New York State. Albert R. Mann Library staff at Cornell University began looking at ways to disseminate geospatial data from Mann's collections via the WWW in 1995 and, in 1998, and established a Web-based clearinghouse for New York State geospatial data and metadata. According to CUGIR's founders, "Building a clearinghouse entailed creating partnerships with local, state and federal agencies, understanding how to interpret and apply the Federal Geographic Data Committee (FGDC) Content Standard for Geospatial Metadata

(CSDGM), and designing a search and retrieval interface, as well as a flexible and scaleable data storage system" (Herold, Gale, and Turner, 1999 pp. 1–2).

The development of CUGIR has been accomplished through a team-based model of work and cooperation. CUGIR team members were identified and selected from departments within Mann Library: Public Services, Technical Services, Collection Development, and Information Technology. This team provides for the management, preservation, organization, and storage needs of data sets that are distributed in CUGIR but owned by various departments in New York State governmental agencies as well as Cornell-affiliated departments, agencies, and researchers (Herold, Turner, and Gale 1999, p. 3). The CUGIR team consists of five regular members, each coordinating work within his or her areas of specialty. Other library staff participate on an as-needed basis. Primary responsibilities for the overall coordination of clearinghouse development are carried out by the GIS librarian. CUGIR is one of 250 international nodes within the Geospatial Data Clearinghouse that contains searchable metadata records describing geospatial data sets. All nodes are located on data servers using the Z39.50 information retrieval protocol. As a result, nodes can be linked to a single search interface where the metadata contents of all nodes, or any subset in combination, can be searched simultaneously. CUGIR, like most clearinghouse nodes, has its own Web site with customized browsing and searching interfaces. Statistics indicate that CUGIR's utility and popularity continue to grow. Since 1998, CUGIR data requests have increased by at least 40 percent each year. In fact, it is projected that CUGIR will record over 100,000 requests in 2003, the most for any single year since the repository was established in 1998 (Cornell University Geospatial Information Repository 2003).

CUGIR Data

Currently CUGIR freely distributes online over 7,000 data sets produced by 10 data producers or partners. CUGIR data come in seven unique proprietary and nonproprietary formats. In many cases, one data set is produced in multiple formats. For example, the data set "Minor Civil Divisions, Albany County" is available in ArcExport as well as shapefile format. Each format has unique characteristics that make it more or less desirable for certain uses and purposes. CUGIR data are actively maintained according to the needs of the data producers. Unlike most digital library files, which require little more than Internet connectivity and Web browser software, geospatial data require technical expertise in the use of sophisticated and powerful GIS software applications. In addition, users must also understand cartographic and geographic concepts related to GIS.

CUGIR Metadata

In 1994 the FGDC established the CSDGM for describing the content and function of geospatial data. According to the FGDC,

> The standard was developed . . . to determine the availability of a set of geospatial data, to determine the fitness of a set of geospatial data for an intended use, to determine the means of accessing the set of geospatial data . . . . As such, the standard established the names of data elements and compound elements to be used for these purposes, the definition of these data elements and compound elements to be used for these purposes. (Federal Geographic Data Committee, 1998, p. iv)

All data producers should provide up-to-date and accurate information about what data are available and their characteristics. The collection, management, and distribution of *good* metadata can help achieve this goal. A high percentage of CUGIR metadata is produced by the data producer, and all of it is summarily reviewed and enhanced by the metadata librarian.

There are 334 different elements in FGDC's CSDGM, 119 of which exist only to contain other elements (Schweitzer 2002, p. 3). These elements are organized within seven main sections and three supporting sections that describe different aspects of data that potential users might need to know: Identification Information, Data Quality Information, Spatial Data Organization Information, Spatial Reference Information, Entity and Attribute Information, Distribution Information, and Metadata Reference Information. Of these areas, only Identification Information and Metadata Reference Information are defined as being mandatory for all records. All other areas of the standard are mandatory if applicable. Within each section are subfields that can be defined as mandatory, mandatory if applicable, or optional. This flexibility allows metadata creators to determine the level of detail that they can provide or support based on perceived user needs. It also guarantees that at least basic metadata will be recorded about each data set. For more extensive information about FGDC metadata creation, see Hart and Phillips's *Metadata Primer* (2001).

Content Standard for Digital Geospatial Metadata is extremely detailed, hierarchical, and complex, which explains why many organizations fear it. In the case of CUGIR, the management and quality control of metadata falls to the technical services department, where the team's metadata librarian enhances and edits the metadata to make it FGDC-compliant. A combination of free tools such as Metadata Parser and proprietary tools, such as ArcCatalog, are readily available and heavily used by the metadata librarian to create standard metadata. A comprehensive list of tools used for geospatial metadata can be found online at *Metadata Tools for Geospatial Data* (Phillips 2003). Figure 21.1 is an example of an FGDC record in CUGIR entitled, "Minor Civil Divisions, Albany County." The "Online_Linkage" element directs users to the Dublin Core record where the data can be downloaded.

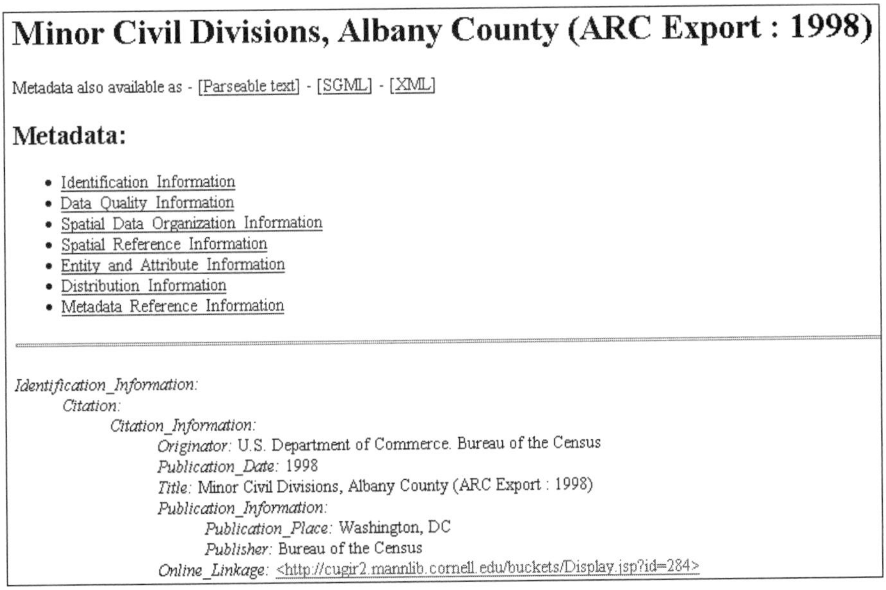

Minor Civil Divisions, Albany County (ARC Export : 1998)

Metadata also available as - [Parseable text] - [SGML] - [XML]

Metadata:

- Identification Information
- Data Quality Information
- Spatial Data Organization Information
- Spatial Reference Information
- Entity and Attribute Information
- Distribution Information
- Metadata Reference Information

Identification_Information:
> *Citation:*
>> *Citation_Information:*
>>> *Originator:* U.S. Department of Commerce. Bureau of the Census
>>> *Publication_Date:* 1998
>>> *Title:* Minor Civil Divisions, Albany County (ARC Export : 1998)
>>> *Publication_Information:*
>>>> *Publication_Place:* Washington, DC
>>>> *Publisher:* Bureau of the Census
>>>> *Online_Linkage:* <http://cugir2.mannlib.cornell.edu/buckets/Display.jsp?id=284>

Figure 21.1. Geospatial/FGDC Metadata Record in CUGIR.
From this record, one may download the data set from the Online Linkage.

Of the 7,117 data sets in CUGIR, 99 percent are accompanied by FGDC-compliant metadata. CUGIR metadata are created and stored as ASCII text, HTML, SGML, and XML, and online users may view any metadata record in the format of their choice.

Libraries are accustomed to adhering to standards, yet the vast majority of GIS repositories are not managed in libraries. As a consequence, there are few digital libraries that take geospatial metadata into consideration. This lack of development and research in geospatial digital libraries has made geospatial research and metadata development forever challenging and frequently groundbreaking. Moreover, it is this reality that has forced the CUGIR team to strive for a framework that not only enhances access and shares heterogeneous metadata but also fosters digital object permanence and centrality in a way that makes the metadata management more efficient, cost-effective, and interoperable.

Now that the background and esoteric characteristics of CUGIR have been documented in great detail, we must turn to the key subset of the CUGIR metadata framework, the metadata management system, to address access, heterogeneous metadata, and object permanence.

CUGIR Metadata Management

Metadata management by definition implies the implementation of a metadata policy (i.e., principles that form the guiding framework within which metadata exists) and adherence to metadata standards (Intra-governmental Group on Geographic Information Working Group on Metadata Implementation 2002, p. 10). Furthermore, metadata management is the process of acquiring and maintaining a controlled set of metadata to describe, discover, retrieve, and access the data to which it refers. If the CUGIR team was going to solve the problems affecting CUGIR and make it successful, the metadata must be managed efficiently.

The CUGIR team identified one major area essential to CUGIR's success: access. Cornell University's core constituency of faculty, students, and staff were clearly not utilizing CUGIR's geospatial resources. Metadata records were not fully accessible, residing inside the CUGIR Web site and the NSDI, which both occupy the "Deep Web" (Bergman 2001). For the team, the question became: How do we make geospatial information resources more accessible to users who might not otherwise encounter them? Because complex metadata schemas like MARC 21 and FGDC are not the "languages" of the WWW, it became clear that more accessible metadata standards must be used to increase CUGIR's Web presence in spite of the deep Web. At the same time MARC, which is not a language for the WWW, remains the most prominent and reliable metadata schema for libraries today, and potentially tomorrow.

Another identified problem was the prevalence of redundant metadata records that differ only in format. The storage of metadata in HTML, XML, SGML, and ASCII text was difficult to manage when changes were necessary. Similarly, the repetition of metadata elements or fields in those metadata also demonstrated inefficient use of storage space. To address these problems, the CUGIR team set out to introduce a more accessible and efficient management system, centered on one metadata work in particular, the canonical record.

Canonical CUGIR Metadata

To minimize the amount of data lost as a result of crosswalking among multiple schemas, the metadata schema conversion process began with the core, or canonical FGDC record that is assembled on-the-fly. The FGDC record is considered the "native" and most complete source of information in one of the most flexible exchange formats, XML. With no existing tools to convert FGDC XML to MARC XML, this was quite a challenge. Elizabeth Mangan of the Library of Congress (LC) created a FGDC to MARC 21 crosswalk that was useful, but a new and customized FGDC XML to MARC XML crosswalk had to be created to suit our purposes (Mangan 1997; Westbrooks 2003). The MARC XML is also derived from the canonical form and produced on-the-fly.

What makes the use of the canonical record even more important is the upcoming introduction of International Standards Organization (ISO) geospatial metadata. ISO metadata when implemented will harmonize the FGDC Metadata Standard (FGDC-STD-001-1998) with ISO's Geographic Information/ Geomatics Technical Committee (TC) 211 Metadata Standard 19115. The standard will be a multilingual XML schema designed to be extensible (profile and extension friendly), multilayered (supporting relational hierarchy of metadata), and modeled in Unified Modeling Language (UML). In addition, it will be integrated with other ISO standards such as DC (ISO 15836) and Codes for the Representation Languages Names (ISO639-2). This harmonization process is a powerful step in the right direction because it not only addresses many known deficiencies in FGDC CSDGM but also enables interoperability while providing additional support for the functions of metadata. Embracing XML-encoded FGDC is the CUGIR team's way of dealing with the upcoming changes. Given the metadata tools and practices we have in place, we expect a predictable and effortless transition from FGDC to ISO. Thus, CUGIR will be poised to make the transition, instead of waiting for proprietary metadata tools to emerge.

To minimize the storage of redundant information, the canonical record is stored in a database and produced on-the-fly. For example, each data partner has standard contact information (e.g., address, telephone number) that is recorded in every metadata record. Instead of repeating such information in each and every metadata record, it is stored once and produced on-the-fly. Figure 21.2 illustrates the CUGIR metadata conversion process.

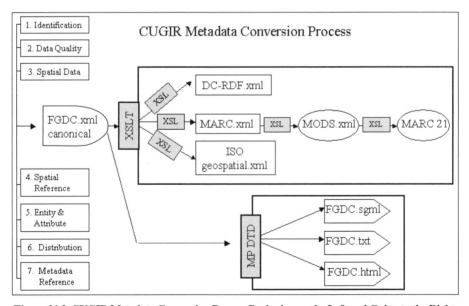

Figure 21.2. CUGIR Metadata Conversion Process Beginning on the Left and Going to the Right.

Metadata Management: MARC 21

All FGDC records were converted to MARC 21 for the online catalog (OPAC), as well as other metadata schemas for sharing and distribution throughout a number of metadata management systems. The contribution of MARC 21 records to OCLC makes CUGIR data internationally accessible to WorldCat users. In addition, other libraries on the OCLC network get the opportunity to utilize full level MARC records. The integration of CUGIR data into the OPAC made it possible for library users to discover geospatial resources as they typically discover journals, books, and online databases. In sum, the transformation from FGDC to MARC 21 enabled the CUGIR team to:

    a.   gain bibliographic control over CUGIR records,

    b.   enhance access to geospatial records via the OPAC, and

    c.   share MARC 21 records with libraries worldwide via WorldCat.

The coexistence of geospatial metadata with traditional resources in the OPAC is essential to making geospatial data sets known and accessible beyond the narrow world of GIS. MARC 21 is based on the XML-encoded FGDC records and transformed on-the-fly using XSLT. Concurrently, the MARC 21 records are added to the OPAC in a batch process. See Figure 21.3 for an example of a MARC 21 record based on the FGDC record shown in Figure 21.1 (page 453).

Minor Civil Divisions, Albany County

Database: Cornell University Library

Title: Minor Civil Divisions, Albany County [electronic resource].

Published: Washington, DC : Bureau of the Census, 1998.

Description: Scale not given.

Electronic Access: http://cugir2.mannlib.cornell.edu/buckets/Display.jsp?id=284

Summary: These files are an extract of selected geographic and cartographic information from the 1995 TIGER/Line files detailing county subdivisions. This dataset includes minor civil divisions and other statistical entities.

Notes: Mode of Access: World Wide Web.
System Requirements: Some files require desktop Geographic information Systems (GIS) software such as MAPInfo, ARC/Info, ArcView, or Adobe Acrobat Reader, for storing, modifying, querying, analyzing, and displaying various forms of geospatial data on Windows, MAC or UNIX platforms. Additionally, some files require desktop extraction utilities such as Winzip to handle compressed or archived files.

Restrictions: Access Constraints: None.
Rights Access: None. Acknowledgement of the U.S. Bureau of the Census would be appreciated for products derived from these files. TIGER, TIGER/Line and Census TIGER are trademarks of the Bureau of the Census.

Figure 21.3. MARC Record in Cornell University Library Online Catalog.
Notice how the "Electronic Access" (MARC 856) field is identical to the link, no. 284,
found in Figure 21.1.

While we are already creating multiple metadata schemas on-the-fly, it seems only natural that we include some of the latest developments in metadata. Though not thoroughly tested, they display great potential and innovation. The Metadata Object Description Schema (MODS) is a subset of MARC 21 and one of the latest developments worthy of investigation. According to its official Web site, "As an XML schema, MODS, is intended to be able to carry selected data from existing MARC 21 records as well as to enable the creation of original re-source description records (Library of Congress, Network Development and MARC Standards Office n.d., p. 1). It includes a subset of MARC fields and uses language-based tags rather than numeric ones, in some cases regrouping elements from the MARC 21 bibliographic format. The Web page also indicates that "MODS is expressed using the XML schema language of the World Wide Web Consortium" (p. 1). Rebecca Guenther, LC Senior Networking and Standards Specialist, adds: "MODS is intended to complement other metadata formats and to provide an alternative between a very simple metadata format with a minimum of fields and no or little substructure such as Dublin Core and a very detailed format with many data elements having various structural complexities such as MARC" (Guenther and McCallum 2002, p. 1).

The adoption of MODS into the metadata framework required the metadata librarian to build a FGDC to MODS crosswalk, stylesheet, and transformation, since none existed (Westbrooks 2003). There are a few institutions other than LC and the California Digital Library that are currently producing MODS records. It is safe to assume that MODS will become one of the sanctioned metadata schemas of the OAI MHP in the near future. MODS is an attractive XML descriptive standard, particularly in the way that it provides flexibility and can be combined with other XML-based standards, including the Metadata Encoding Transmission Schema (METS). The METS schema is a standard for encoding descriptive, administrative, and structural metadata regarding objects within a digital library and is expressed using the XML schema language of the World Wide Web Consortium (2002). To quote Guenther and McCallum, "An additional use of MODS is as an extension schema for descriptive metadata for a METS object" (2002, p. 13). Since any descriptive metadata that is part of CUGIR can be part of METS objects, we anticipate that our next step will be to investigate how well METS can handle geospatial information. Presumably, if we are satisfied, the presence of MODS will help CUGIR transition gracefully into METS.

DC-RDF for OAI and the Semantic Web

The online repository, other than CUGIR and NSDI, chosen to increase access to CUGIR is the Open Archives Initiative (OAI) Community. OAI develops and promotes interoperability standards that aim to facilitate the efficient dissemination of content (Lagoze, Van de Sompel, Nelson, and Warner 2002a, p. 2). In addition, the Open Archives Initiative Protocol for Metadata Harvesting (OAI-PMH) provides an application-independent interoperability framework based on metadata harvesting (Lagoze, Van de Sompel, Nelson, and Warner 2002b). The recommended, but not required, metadata schema for the OAI is Dublin Core. The CUGIR team chose to use DC and the Resource Description Framework, collectively known as DC-RDF, for a number of reasons, the first being the convenient use of OCLC's Connexion to export OAI-ready DC-RDF with little effort. As the metadata project progressed, we favored a less OCLC-centric approach to metadata creation. Moreover, we discovered that DC-RDF metadata records (in XML) could be easily created with XML stylesheets (XSL) coupled with extensible stylesheet language transformations (XSLT). XSL defines how data are presented, whereas XSLTs are designed for use as part of XSL. DC-RDF is naturally encoded in XML, an exchange format through which data providers harvest and share metadata. Another attractive feature of the OAI-PMH is its use of HyperText Transfer Protocol (HTTP) over the complex information retrieval protocol Z39.50. Although Z39.50 has served the library community well, the simplicity of having servers provide CUGIR metadata in bulk for harvesting services by way of HTTP is a viable alternative to National Spatial Data Infrastructure (NSDI) currently in place for GIS repositories across the globe.

Chandler and Foley's 2000 study documents the problems inherent in gaining access to spatial data via the NSDI (pp. 1–2). NSDI nodes are inconsistently available, searches are inaccurate, and the wait time is excessive. In "Metadata Harvesting and the Open Archives Initiative," Clifford Lynch, the executive director of the Coalition for Networked Information (CNI), also documents the strengths and weaknesses of Z39.50, in the context of OAI (2001, pp. 2–4). The use of RDF can be easily justified when one considers the integral role it performs in the Semantic Web. According to Tim Berners-Lee, "The Semantic Web is not a separate Web but an extension of the current one, in which information is given well-defined meaning, better enabling computers and people to work in cooperation. It is based on the RDF, which integrates a variety of applications using XML for syntax" (Berners-Lee et al. 2001, p. 2). Eric Miller and Ralph Swick of the World Wide Web Consortium report, "for the Web to reach its full potential, it must grow and incorporate a semantic Web vision, providing a universally accessible platform that allows data to be shared and processed by people and machines" (2003, p.11). By embracing RDF, the CUGIR team aims to situate CUGIR metadata schemas in a position to flourish within the semantic Web. Finally, up and coming information management systems such as D-Space, Open Archival Information Systems (OAIS), EnCompass, and ExLibris use some form of DC encoded in XML as the lingua franca. It is assumed that CUGIR will be distributed in such systems in the near future.

Achieving Object Permanence

Creating multiple schemas on-the-fly from XML encoded FGDC was one of the easiest steps in the metadata project. Adopting a simple method to create, maintain, and centralize the persistent/permanent hyperlinks in metadata, however, proved to be a formidable challenge. John Kunze, researcher at the University of California at San Francisco Library Center for Knowledge Management, articulates the problem: "Permanence of electronic information, namely, the extent to which structured digital data remains predictably available through known channels, is a central concern for most organizations whose mission includes an archival function" (2001, p. 177). The difficulty in carrying out the aim of permanence, and indeed, centrality in the CUGIR digital library system is in identifying existing solutions that are more simple, flexible, and dynamic than Universal Resource Locators (URL) or Persistent Uniform Resource Locators (PURL) heavily used in libraries today. Given the inadequacies of URLs, it became apparent to the CUGIR team that an identifier resolver was needed to de-couple the identity of the object from the location of the object. There are numerous methods, some of which have been around since the early nineties, that have attempted to achieve this goal. Some of these methods include: Uniform Resource Names (URNs), handle systems, Digital Object Identifiers (DOIs), buckets, and archival resource key schemas. For the goals of the project, we opted for Michael Nelson's bucket architecture, which is a simple component of the Smart Object Dumb Archive Model, known as SODA. This chapter does not discuss intricate details of this component; however, the benefits of the system are noteworthy. What is most valuable about the bucket framework is that information in thousands of metadata records can be easily changed. For example, if CUGIR were moved to another server, all of the URLs would no longer work. Presumably, the buckets, which constitute the 856 field of the MARC record and the "Online_Linkage" field of the FGDC record, would have to be changed in the metadata residing in the OPAC, OCLC, and OAI as well as the canonical FGDC record in CUGIR. In CUGIR's SODA system, however, only the bucket requires changing, as opposed to all of the records in the OPAC, OCLC, and OAI. This model is efficient for the CUGIR team and eliminates the need to update metadata records every time CUGIR metadata is moved.

Building the CUGIR Metadata Framework: Skills and Costs

Thus far, the history of the repository and the components and concepts behind the CUGIR Metadata Framework have been presented primarily in technical terms. Now I discuss how this project was made possible. First, the position of metadata librarian increasingly requires a familiarity and expertise in areas "outside" metadata schemas, authority control, and cataloging. These areas include XML schemas, PERL, XSLT, Web page development, and relational database design. The metadata librarian's knowledge in these areas meant that she had a common language with which to collaborate with CUGIR's programmer. Furthermore, since CUGIR's beginnings, the collaborative and interdisciplinary makeup of the team made innovative work simple.

In terms of costs, Adam Chandler and I were awarded approximately $3,000 by the Cornell University Libraries Internal Grant Competition,

2000/2001 to implement the "Enhancing Access to Cornell University Geospatial Information Repository: FGDC to MARC/Dublin Core Conversion Project." One part-time student worker was hired to do the metadata conversion, and another was hired to set up the OAI Service and SODA infrastructure. The costs associated with maintaining SODA and multiple metadata schemas have been absorbed by the library in the CUGIR metadata workflow. Although the metadata librarian is responsible for creating the original geospatial metadata record, one part-time student in Technical Services performs the majority of tasks associated with the creation and maintenance of the metadata records.

Outcomes of the CUGIR Metadata Framework

The CUGIR metadata framework proved successful in reaching its primary goals: increasing access and implementing an efficient metadata management system. But what impact did all of this work have on CUGIR's users? In other words, did more Cornell constituents discover CUGIR as a result of the metadata framework? The answer to this question is "yes."

When the framework was implemented, referrer data were captured. The referrer data record the Internet Protocol (IP) address of the Web page that a user visited to access the bucket. The IP addresses of the hosts were also collected. To preserve the privacy of users, the IP addresses have been encrypted, and the subnets were dropped from the statistics database. As a result, the domain name rather than the unique address of the computer has been stored. These data confirm when users encountered a bucket from OAI, the OPAC, or FirstSearch. We established a tracking method that observes use patterns and indicates the manner and frequency with which patrons access buckets. Unfortunately, we do not have enough data about the OAI user's harvesting of CUGIR DC-RDF records. Since the metadata framework has been in place, approximately 12,000 buckets have been accessed from a variety of locations. The results indicate that less than 5 percent of our users discover CUGIR metadata via the OPAC. Less than 1 percent of our users discover CUGIR metadata via FirstSearch. Almost 95 percent of our users discover CUGIR metadata from CUGIR's home page.

If only 5 percent of our users discovered CUGIR as a result of this metadata framework, was it worthwhile? Although the statistics do not indicate "success" in regard to access, the work and process of formulating the metadata sharing framework forced us to document all metadata processes, streamline workflows, and create more metadata with less effort. In terms of data management, the metadata framework reduced the number of metadata files that had to be managed and stored. CUGIR no longer stores each metadata schema in multiple formats. In the past, we stored nine metadata files per data set. Now we only store one.

Conclusion

We are confident that our work to make CUGIR more accessible will pay off in the long run. CUGIR geospatial metadata now exists beyond the confines of bits residing on servers in Ithaca, New York, and even beyond the world of geospatial information systems. By implementing the CUGIR metadata framework, we have been able to share, reuse, and repurpose the geospatial metadata in information systems based on MARC/AACR2, DC, and OAI protocols. The way forward is to build open systems and methods that embed the ability to link between different types of metadata. The CUGIR Metadata Sharing Project is an example of a working system utilizing a heterogeneous linking methodology to enhance resource discovery and to share both MARC and non-MARC metadata in a variety of information systems.

The data analysis of the use of the CUGIR metadata management system yielded some interesting insights:

   a.   In spite of the vast efforts to make CUGIR data accessible across metadata schemas and information systems, users who know about CUGIR overwhelmingly prefer to acquire data from the FGDC metadata records on the CUGIR home page. This will always be the case no matter how much metadata sharing persists.

   b.   The OPAC provides minimal means for access for a set of users who might not otherwise discover geospatial data.

   c.   If the SODA system and the metadata framework did not make metadata records so easy to create and maintain, then we would not make the effort to contribute data to OCLC's FirstSearch. The addition of MARC 21 records in OCLC has not significantly increased access to CUGIR. On the other hand, other libraries in the OCLC network have access to full level MARC records and may find them useful.

The fundamental value of the library is the organization of information as the foundation through which information resources can be utilized. Centuries of library research support this claim. The CUGIR team embraces metadata as the first-order prerequisite to establishing a complete spatial repository or clearinghouse as well as the Semantic Web. Furthermore, it should be clear that library standards and theory, as well as GIS standards, must be applied in concert to produce open, interoperable, efficient, and robust digital libraries.

Notes

* I would like to express my gratitude to Adam Chandler, whose groundwork and collaboration led to the CUGIR metadata framework as we know it. A special thanks to Petrina Jackson, for her valuable feedback.

Acronyms:

CSDGM—Content Standard for Digital Geospatial Metadata

CUGIR—Cornell University Geospatial Information Repository

DC—Dublin Core

DC-RDF—Dublin Core Resource Description Framework

DEM—Digital Elevation Models

EPA—Environmental Protection Agency

ESRI—Environmental Systems Research Institute

FGDC—Federal Geographic Data Committee

GIS—Geographic Information System

HTML—Hypertext Markup Language

HTTP—HyperText Transfer Protocol

IP—Internet Protocol

ISO—International Standards Organization

ISO 15836—International Standards Organization Dublin Core Metadata Element Set Number

ISO 19115:2003—International Standards Organization Metadata Schema for Geospatial Metadata Number

ISO TC211—International Standards Organization Technical Committee for Geographic Information/Geomatics

MARC21—Machine Readable Cataloging

METS—Metadata Encoding & Transmission Schema

MODS—Metadata Object Description Schema

NSDI—National Spatial Data Infrastructure

NY—New York

OAI—Open Archives Initiative

OAI-PMH—Open Archives Initiative Protocol for Metadata Harvesting

OAIS—Open Archival Information System

OCLC—Online Computing Library Center

OPAC—Online Public Access Catalog

PDF—Portable Document Format

SGML—Standard Generalized Markup Language

SODA—Smart Object Dumb Archive

URL—Uniform Resource Locator

USDA—United States Department of Agriculture

USGS—United States Geological Survey

XML—eXtensible Markup Language

XSL—eXtensible Stylesheet Language

XSLT—eXtensible Stylesheet Language Transformation

Z39.50—Application Service Definition and Protocol Specification for Information Retrieval

References

Bergman, M. K. 2001. "The deep web: Surfacing hidden value." *Journal of electronic publishing*, 7 (1). Available: http://www.press.umich.edu/jep/07–01/bergman.html (Accessed April 5, 2002).

Berners-Lee, T., J. Hendler, and O. Lassila. 2001. "The Semantic Web." *Scientific American* (May).Available: http://www.scientificamerican.com/article.cfm?articleID=00048144–10D2–1C70–84A9809EC588EF21 &catID=2 (Accessed February 12, 2003).

Chandler, A., and D. Foley. 2000. "Mapping and converting essential Federal Geographic Data Committee (FGDC) metadata into MARC21 and Dublin Core: Towards an alternative to the FGDC Clearinghouse." *D-Lib Magazine* 6, no. 1. Available: http://www.dlib.org/dlib/january00/chandler/01chandler.html (Accessed December 7, 2000).

Chandler, A., and E. L. Westbrooks. 2002. "Distributing non-MARC metadata: The CUGIR Metadata Sharing Project." *Library Collections, Acquisitions, & Technical Services* 26 (3): 207–217.

Cornell University Geospatial Information Repository. 2003. *CUGIR statistics database.* Available: http://rikert.mannlib.cornell.edu/cugir/jsp/downloads.jsp (Accessed May 1, 2003).

Darzentas, J. 1999. "Sharing metadata: Enabling online information provision." *OCLC Sytems & Services*, 15 (4): 172–179.

Dempsey, L., and R. Heery. 1998. "Metadata: A current view of practice and issues." *Journal of Documentation* 54 (2): 145–172.

El-Sherbini, M. 2001. "Metadata and the future of cataloging." *Library Review* 50 (1): 16–27.

Federal Geographic Data Committee. 1998. *Content standard for digital geospatial metadata.* Available: http://www.fgdc.gov/standards/documents/standards/metadata/v2_0698.pdf (Accessed March 15, 2001).

Guenther, R., and S. McCallum. 2002. "New metadata standards for digital re-sources: MODS and METS." *Bulletin of the American Society for Information Science and Technology* 29 (2): 12–15.

Hart, D., and H. Phillips. 2001. *Metadata primer—a "how to" guide on metadata implementation.* Available: http://www.lic.wisc.edu/metadata/metaprim.htm (Accessed August 10, 2001).

Herold, P., T. D. Gale, and T. P. Turner. 1999. "Optimizing web access to geospatial data: The Cornell University Geospatial Information Repository (CUGIR)." Unpublished report.

Herold, P., T. P. Turner, and T. D. Gale. 1999. "Final Project Report: Cornell University Geospatial Information Repository (CUGIR)." Unpublished report.

Hwey Jeng, L. 1996. "A converging vision of cataloging in the electronic world." *Information Technology and Librarianship* 15 (4, December): 222–230.

IFLA Study Group on the Functional Requirements for Bibliographic Records. 2003. *Functional requirements for bibliographic records: final report.* München: K. G. Saur. Available: http://www.ifla.org/VII/s13/frbr/frbr.pdf (Accessed January 15, 2003).

Intra-governmental Group on Geographic Information Working Group on Metadata Implementation. 2002. *Principles of good metadata management.* Available: http://www.iggi.gov.uk/achievements_deliverables/pdf/Guide.pdf (Accessed December 8, 2002).

Issues in science and technology librarianship. Available: http://www.library.ucsb.edu/istl/99–winter/article2.html (Accessed January 24, 3003).

Kacmar, C., D. Jue, D. Stage, and C. Koontz. 1995. *Automatic creation and maintenance of an organizational spatial metadata and document digital library.* The Second Annual Conference on the Theory and Practice of Digital Libraries, June 11–13, Austin, Texas. Available: http://www.csdl.tamu.edu/DL95/papers/kacmar/kacmar.html (Accessed May 3, 2002).

Kunze, J. A. 2001. *A metadata kernel for electronic permanence.* Proceedings of the International Conference on Dublin Core and Metadata Applications, Tokyo, Japan. Available: http://www.nii.ac.jp/dc2001/proceedings/product/paper-27.pdf (Accessed March 15, 2001).

Lagoze, C. (2001). "Keeping Dublin Core simple: Cross-domain discovery or resource description?" *D-Lib Magazine* 7 (1). Available: http://www.dlib.org/dlib/january01/lagoze/01lagoze.html (Accessed February 2, 2003).

Lagoze, C., H. Van de Sompel, M. Nelson, and S. Warner. 2002a. *Open Archives Initiative protocol for metadata harvesting.* Available: http://www.openarchives.org/OAI/openarchivesprotocol.html (Accessed February 1, 2002).

———. 2002b. *Open Archives Initiative frequently asked questions (FAQ).* Open Archives Initiative. Available: http://www.openarchives.org/documents/ FAQ.html (Accessed March 1, 2003).

Lange, H. R., and B. J. Winkler. 1997. "Taming the Internet: Metadata a work in progress." *Advances in Librarianship* 21: 47–72.

Lee-Smeltzer, J. K. H. 2000. "Finding the needle: Controlled vocabularies, resource discovery, and Dublin Core." *Library Collections, Acquisitions & Technical Services* 24: 205–215.

Library of Congress Network Development and MARC Standards Office. n.d. *MODS The Metadata Object Description Schema: The official website.* Available: http://www.loc.gov/standards/mods/ (Accessed February 12, 2003).

Lynch, C. 2001. "Metadata harvesting and the Open Archives Initiative." *Association of Research Library Bimonthly Report* 217 (August): entire issue.

Mangan, E. 1997. *Crosswalk: FGDC content standards for digital geospatial metadata to USMARC.* Alexandria Digital Library. Available: http:// alexandria.sdc.ucsb.edu/public-documents/metadata/fgdc2marc.html (Accessed December 12, 2000).

Medeiros, N. 2001. "On the Dublin Core front: report from the trenches—the 8th Intl Dublin Core Metadata Initiative Workshop." *OCLC Systems & Services* 17 (1): 15–18.

METS Metadata Encoding Transmission Standard: Official Web Site. n.d. Available: http://www.loc.gov/standards/mets/ (Accessed February 12, 2003).

Miller, E., and R. Swick. 2003. "An overview of W3C Semantic Web activity." *Bulletin of the American Society for Information Science and Technology* 9, no. 4. Available: http://www.asis.org/Bulletin/Apr-03/BulletinAprMay03 .pdf (Accessed July 2002).

Phillips, H. 2003. *Metadata tools for geospatial data.* Available: http:// badger.state.wi.us/agencies/wlib/sco/metatool/mtools.htm (Accessed July 22, 2003).

Schweitzer, P. 2002. *Frequently-asked questions on FGDC metadata.* FGDC. Available: http://geology.usgs.gov/tools/metadata/tools/doc/faq.html (Accessed February 2, 2003).

Szunejko, M. H. 2001. "Description of Internet resources: A consideration of the relationship between MARC and other metadata schemes." *Technical Services Quarterly* 18 (3): 1–10.

Vellucci, S. L. 1997. *Options for organizing electronic resources: the coexistence of metadata.* ASIS. Available: http://www.asis.org/Bulletin/Oct-97/vellucci.htm (Accessed January 21, 2002).

Weibel, S. 1995. "Metadata: The foundations of resource description." *D-Lib Magazine*, July (1).

Westbrooks, E. L. 2003. *FGDC to MODS crosswalk* . Available: http://metadata-g.mannlib.cornell.edu/elaine/fgdc/ (Accessed April 30, 2003).

Westcott, B. 2002. *Spatial metadata for management—increasing the value of your data investment.* FGDC. . Available: http://tsc.wes.army.mil/tsc2/symposium/2002/276.pdf (Accessed December 1, 2002).

Younger, J. A. 1997. "Resource description in the digital age." *Library Trends* 45 (3): 462–481.

Index

About the Editor and Contributors

About the Editor

Bradford Lee Eden, Ph.D., is Head, Web and Digitization Services, for the University of Nevada, Las Vegas Libraries. He has recently been appointed editor of *OCLC Systems & Services*, is associate editor of *Library Hi Tech* and *The Journal of Film Music*, and is series editor of the *Routledge Music Bibliographies*. He has master's and Ph.D. degrees in musicology, as well as an MSLS from the University of North Texas. He publishes in the areas of metadata, librarianship, medieval music and liturgy, and J. R. R. Tolkien. He is the author of *Metadata and Its Applications* (ALA TechSource, 2002).

About the Contributors

Martha Ann Bace is Head of the Catalog Department for the University of Alabama at Tuscaloosa Libraries. She received her MLS from George Peabody College for Teachers of Vanderbilt University. She spent six years at the University of Montevallo and seventeen years at Southern Arkansas University prior to her current appointment.

Susan B. Bailey is Division Leader of Bibliographic Gateway Services in the General Libraries of Emory University. Prior to that time, she was involved primarily in database quality, authority control, and media cataloging, as Assistant Head of the Catalog Department at Emory.

Patricia S. Banach is Director of Library Services at Eastern Connecticut State University in Willimantic, Connecticut. Prior to going to Eastern, she worked for 31 years at the University of Massachusetts Amherst in a variety of positions, most recently as Associate Director for Collection Management.

Ruth A. Bogan is Head of Database and Catalog Portal Management Section at Rutgers University Libraries, where she manages a team of dedicated library paraprofessionals in metadata conversion, authority control, and general bibliographic troubleshooting. Over the course of her career she has held positions as cataloger, authorities librarian, and head of several library technical services departments.

Ann Branton is Head of Bibliographic Services for the University of Southern Mississippi Libraries. She received her MLS from the University of North Texas and is an active member of the state professional organization in Mississippi and a regular guest lecturer speaking on topics related to cataloging and the management of technical services for the School of Library and Information Science at USM.

Karen J. Davis is Assistant Professor/Head of Monographic Cataloging and a Liaison Librarian at The University Library, Georgia State University. She previously held positions at Syracuse University Libraries as Special Projects Librarian and Catalog Librarian. She also serves on the editorial board of *OCLC Systems & Services.*

Constance Demetracopoulos is Librarian/Assistant Professor at The University Library, Georgia State University. In addition to her cataloging responsibilities, primarily music and visual materials, she is Coordinator of the Non-Subscription Internet Resources Cataloging Project. She also serves as Liaison for Philosophy and Religious Studies. She will receive a master's degree in philosophy in May 2004.

Thomas A. Downing is Chief, Cataloging Branch, U.S. Government Printing Office. He manages the National Cataloging and Indexing Program for United States Government Publications. He holds a master's degree in library and information science from Simmons College and a master's degree in Hebrew literature and cognate studies from Hebrew Union College.

Nadine P. Ellero is Head of Intellectual Access at The Claude Moore Health Sciences Library at the University of Virginia, which encompasses traditional cataloging and special projects utilizing multiple types of metadata. She obtained her MLS from The State University of New York at Buffalo and is a member of her library's Digital Library Infrastructure Team.

Magda El-Sherbini is Head of the Cataloging Department for the Ohio State University Libraries. She received her MLIS from The Catholic University of America and has been a cataloger most of her professional career.

Kathryn Etcheverria is acting Basque Studies Librarian at the University of Nevada, Reno. She was formerly a Catalog Librarian at the University of Nevada, Reno, and has written several articles on technical services issues.

Jack D. Glazier, Dr., is currently on the faculty at Texas Woman's University in Denton, Texas.

Rhonda R. Glazier is Head of Collection Management at Emporia State University, Emporia, Kansas.

Shirley Hamlett is an original and authorities cataloger (Library Technical Assistant II) in the Cataloging Department of the North Carolina State University Libraries.

Pamela Cline Howley is Catalog Librarian in the Bibliographic Control Services Division of Memorial University of Newfoundland's Queen Elizabeth II Library. She has an MLS from McGill University and 27 years' experience in cataloging and other technical services operations.

Pat Lawton is Visiting Lecturer at the Graduate School of Library and Information Science (GSLIS), University of Illinois at Urbana-Champaign. Her research interests include education for library and information science, online pedagogy, and the impact of new technologies on cataloging and classification theory and practice. She holds an MLS from Indiana University and is a doctoral candidate in the School of Library and Information Science at the University of Wisconsin- Madison.

Annette M. LeClair is Head of Technical Services at Schaffer Library, Union College, in Schenectady, New York. She has an MSLS from the University of North Carolina at Chapel Hill and a master's degree in English from the University of Virginia. She has also taught as an adjunct professor at the School of Information Science and Policy at the University at Albany.

Karen M. Letarte is Assistant Head of Cataloging and Head of Database Development at North Carolina State University Libraries.

Laurie Lopatin is Catalog Librarian at Hofstra University, Hempstead, New York. She has an MLS from Drexel University and a master's degree in information science from Long Island University.

Cheryl Martin most recently served as Director of Bibliographic Services at McMaster University in Hamilton, Ontario. She has a master's degree in musicology and an MLIS, both from the University of Western Ontario. In 2003 she made a career change to the financial services field and presently works in personal banking for Canada's largest financial institution.

Daryle McEachern Maroney is Monographic Cataloger at The University Library, Georgia State University. She has previously worked at the New York Public Library in the Circulation Department, the Law

Library of the New York Telephone Co., the State Archives of Georgia, and Columbia Theological Seminary.

Mary L. Mastraccio is Cataloging and Authorities Manager at Marcive, Inc. She received her MLS from Syracuse University, and her work experience in libraries has had a strong emphasis on effective management of technical services.

Charles Pennell is Head of Cataloging at North Carolina State University Libraries.

Andrea Rabbia is Technical Services Librarian at the H. Douglas Barclay Law Library of the Syracuse University College of Law. She received her MLS from Syracuse University and her bachelor's degree from LeMoyne College in Syracuse, New York. She has written several articles on technical services issues in law libraries.

Karen M. Ramsay is Acquisitions Librarian and Head of the Monographic Acquisitions/Copy Cataloging (MACC) Unit at the University Libraries at the University of Rhode Island. She holds a bachelor's degree in secondary education and an MLS from the University of Rhode Island. She has been an adjunct faculty member in the Graduate School of Library and Information Studies since 1994.

Patricia Ratkovich is Monographic Cataloger in the Technical Services Department of the University of Alabama Libraries. She obtained her MLIS from the University of Southern Mississippi.

Deborah Rose-Lefmann is Monographic Cataloger at Northwestern University Library. She has an MLS from the University of Illinois and a Ph.D. in German languages and literatures.

Vicki Toy Smith is Catalog Librarian at the University of Nevada, Reno. She has previously worked at the University of California, Berkeley, the University of Michigan, and University Microfilms International. She has written several articles on technical services and library fundraising/public relations issues.

Elaine L. Westbrooks is Metadata Librarian at Cornell University, where she is responsible for analyzing developments concerning metadata standards and access to electronic publications as well as creating and maintaining repositories of non-MARC metadata. Most of her projects have involved the implementation and maintenance of Dublin Core, MODS, and MARC metadata for the Open Archives Initiative as well as geospatial metadata for Cornell Library's Geospatial information repository.